HAPPINESS
#2

oshimi shuzo

HAPPINESS #2 CONTENTS

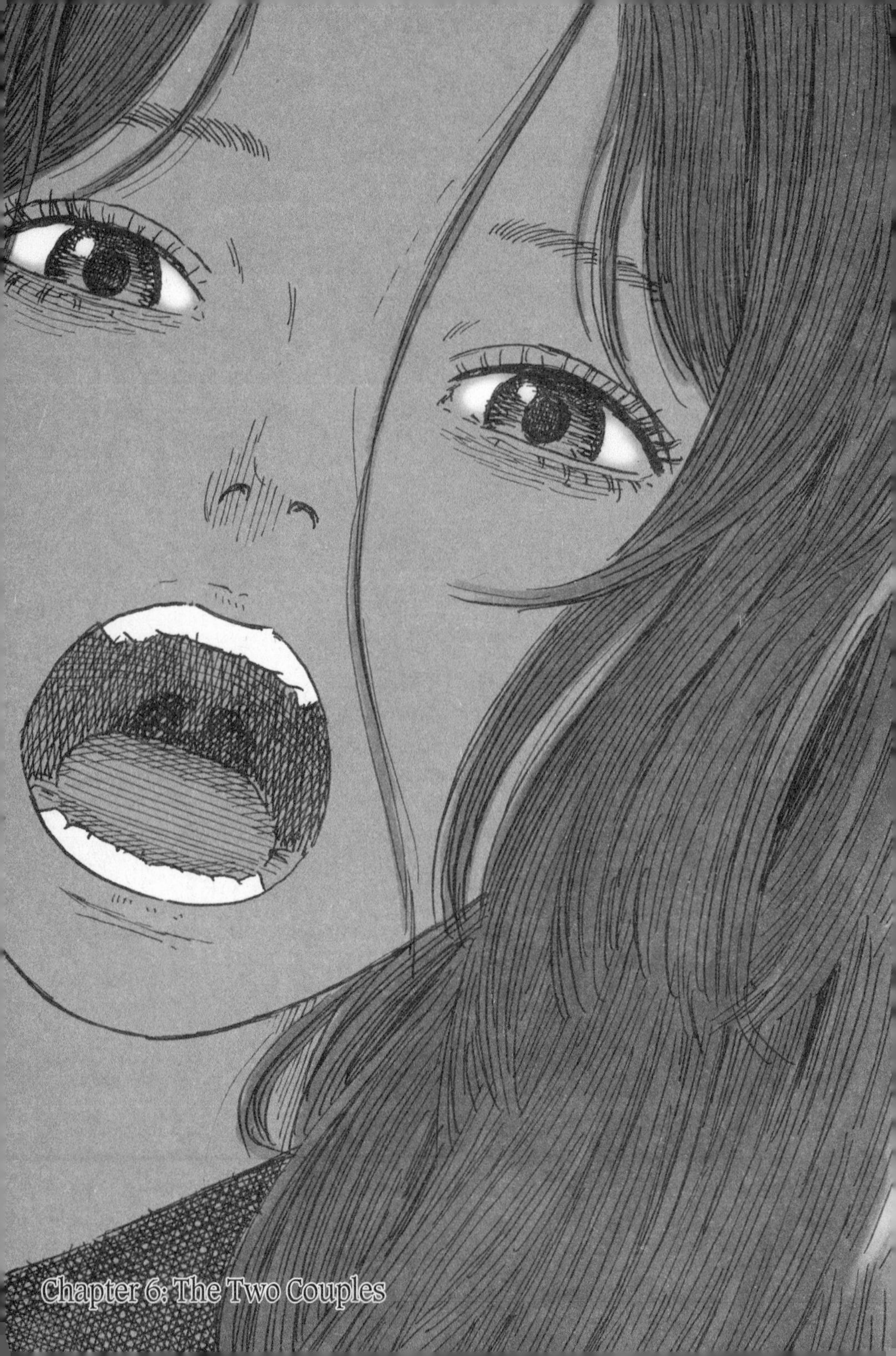
Chapter 6: The Two Couples

HAPPINESS

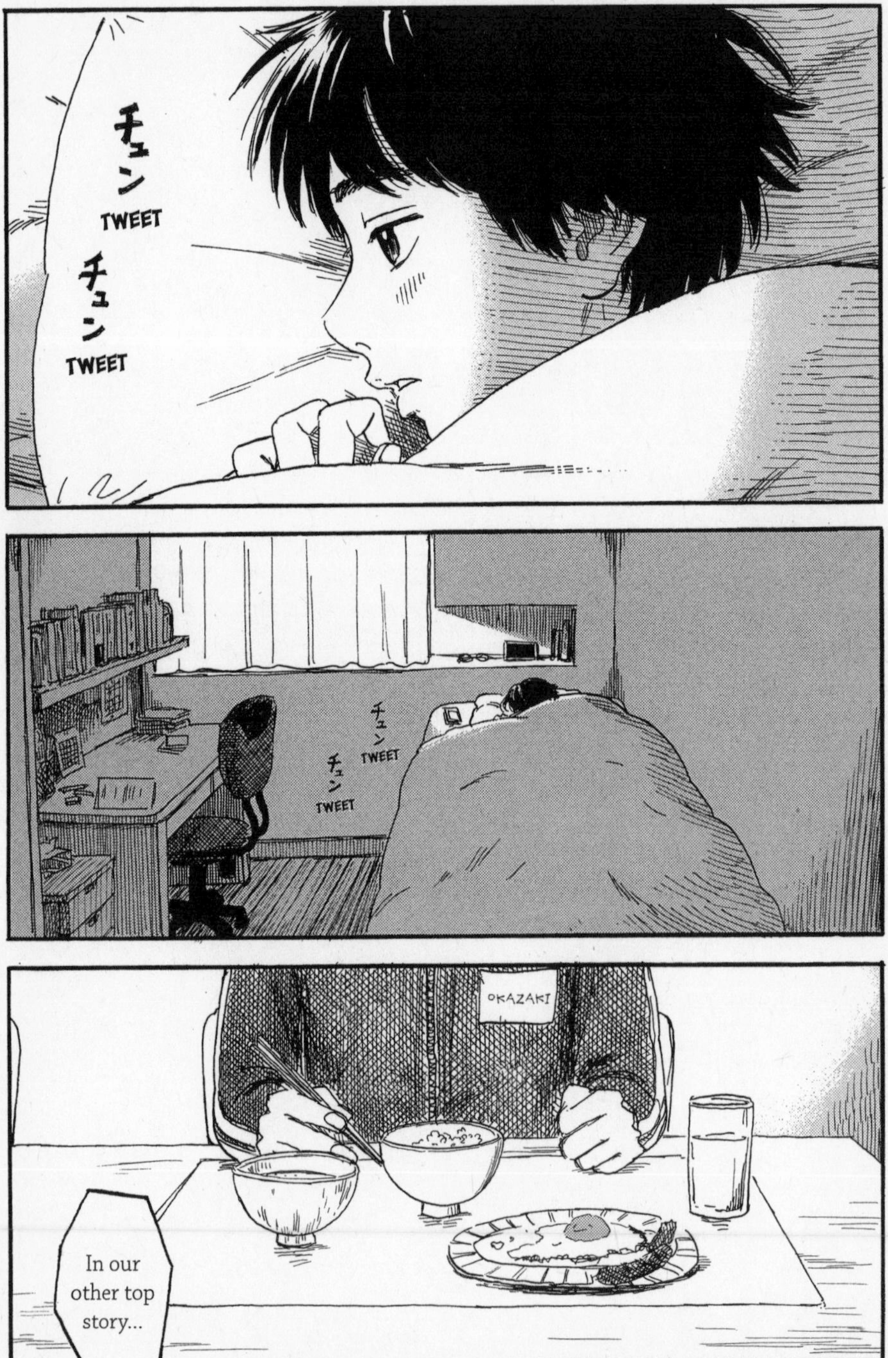
チュン
TWEET
チュン
TWEET
チュン
TWEET
チュン
TWEET
OKAZAKI
In our other top story...

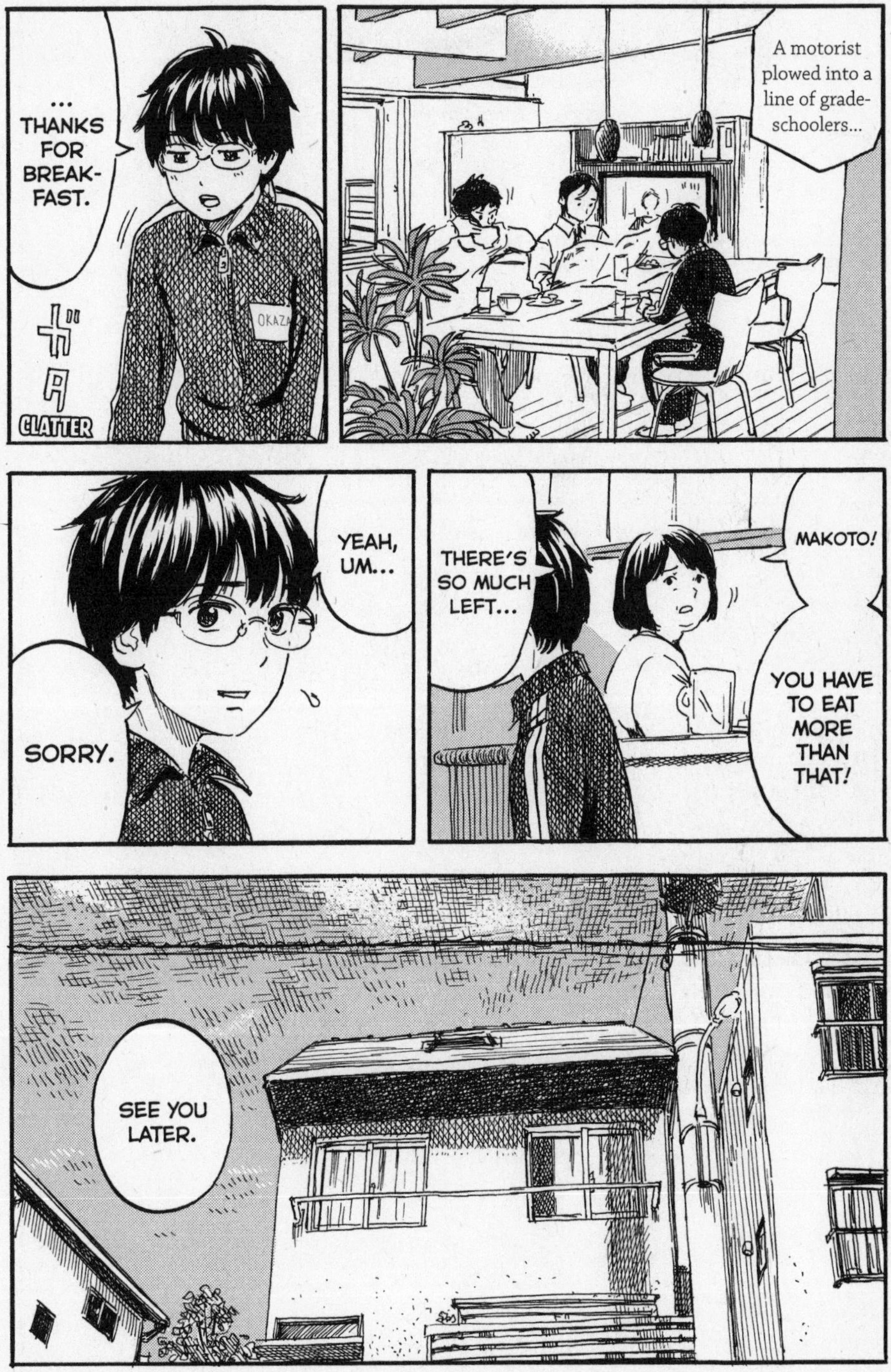
A motorist plowed into a line of grade-schoolers...
... THANKS FOR BREAKFAST.
ガタ
CLATTER
MAKOTO!
YOU HAVE TO EAT MORE THAN THAT!
THERE'S SO MUCH LEFT...
YEAH, UM...
SORRY.
SEE YOU LATER.

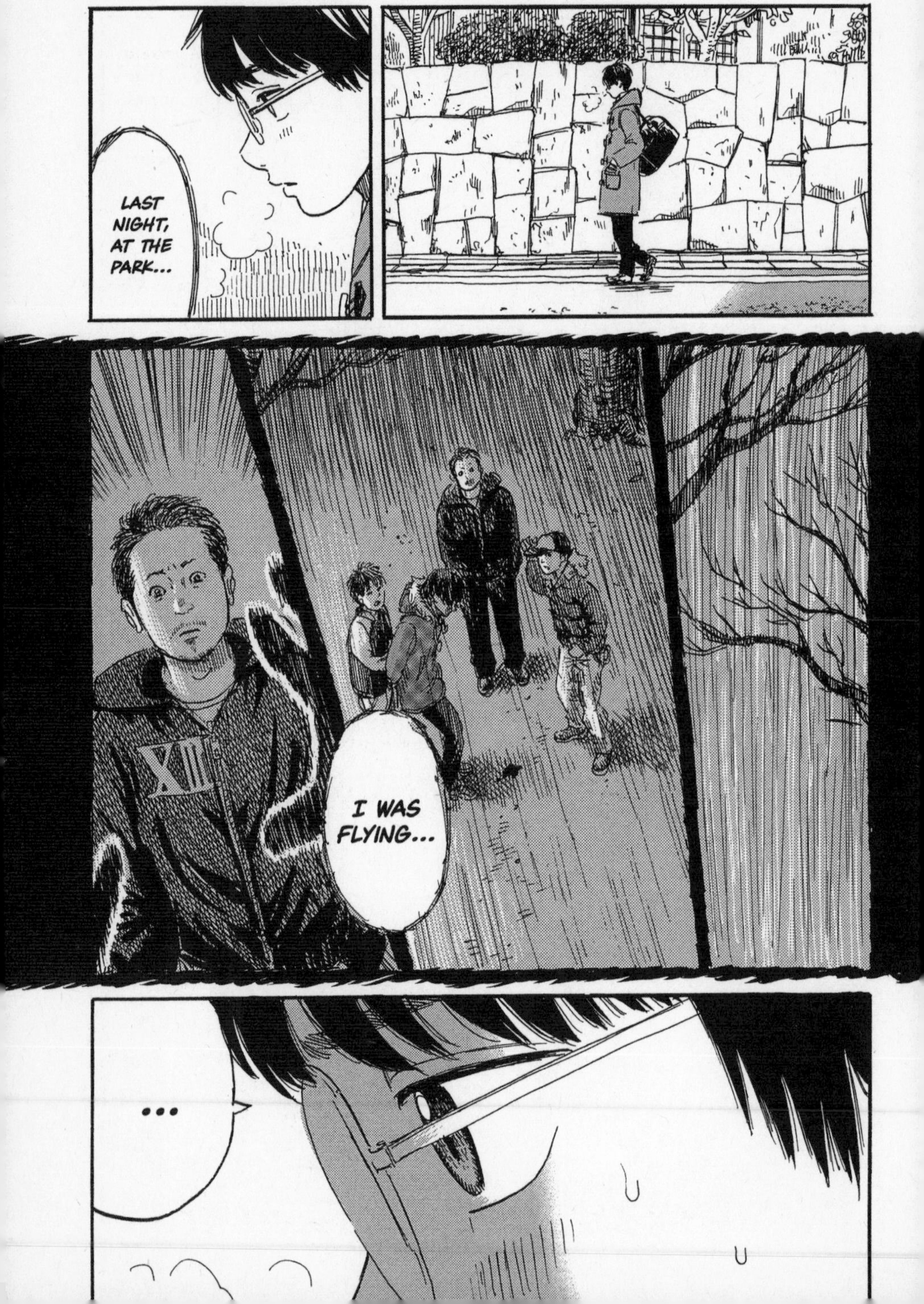
LAST NIGHT, AT THE PARK...
I WAS FLYING...
...

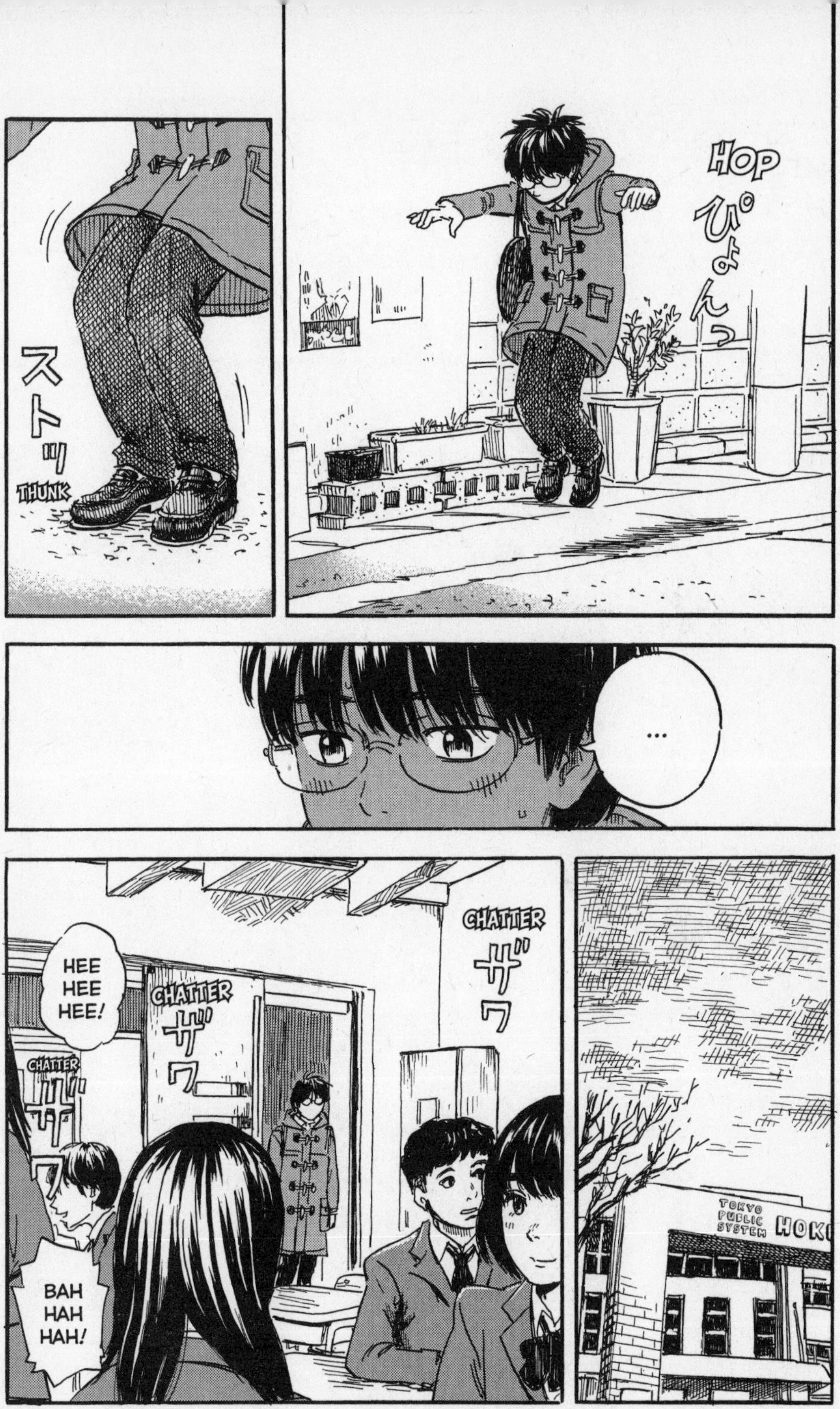
HOP
ぴょんっ
ストッ
THUNK
...
TOKYO PUBLIC SYSTEM
HOK
CHATTER
ザワ
CHATTER
ザワ
HEE HEE HEE!
CHATTER
ザワザワ
BAH HAH HAH!

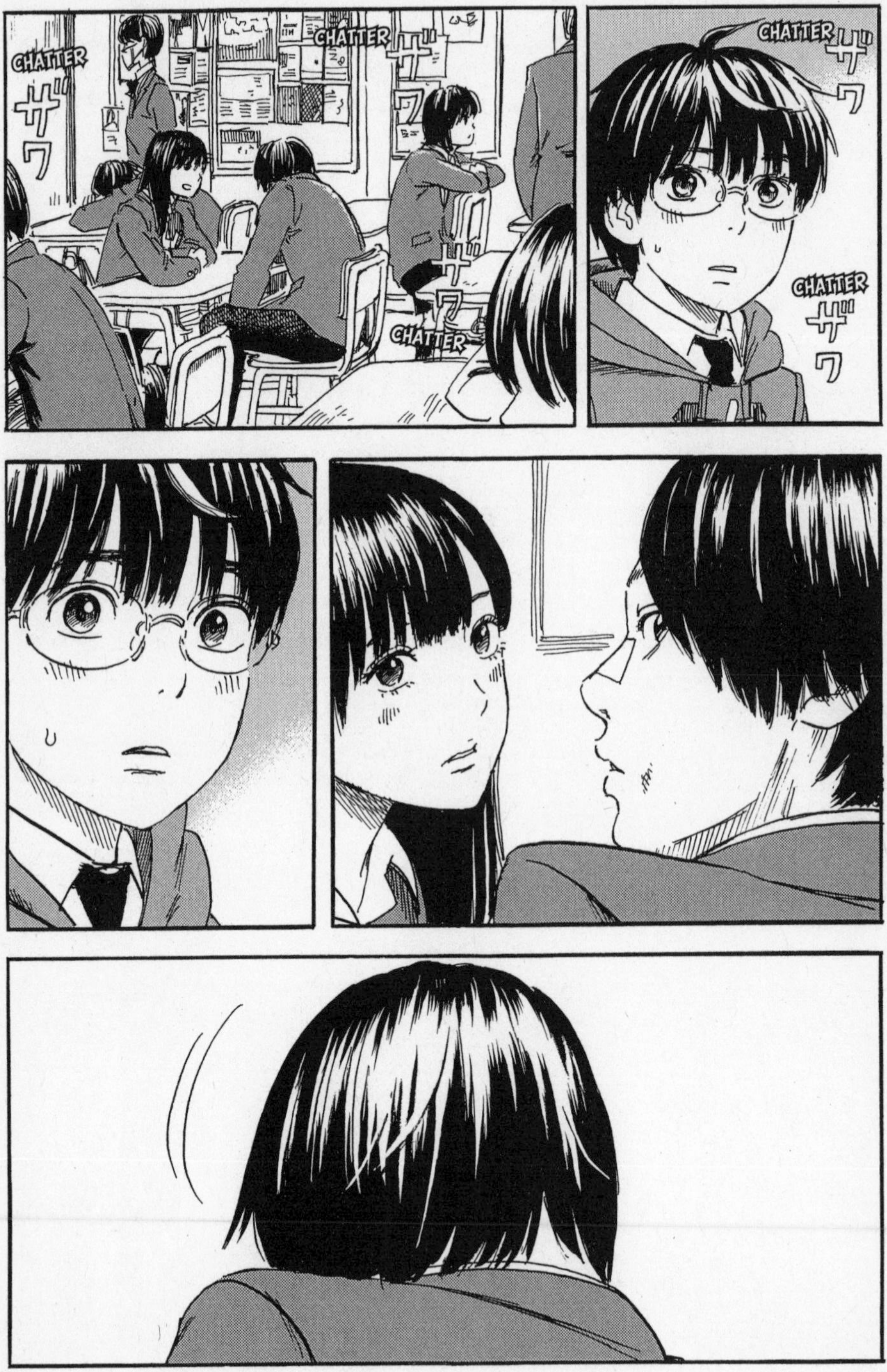
CHATTER ザワ
CHATTER ザワ
CHATTER ザワ
CHATTER ザワ
ザワ CHATTER

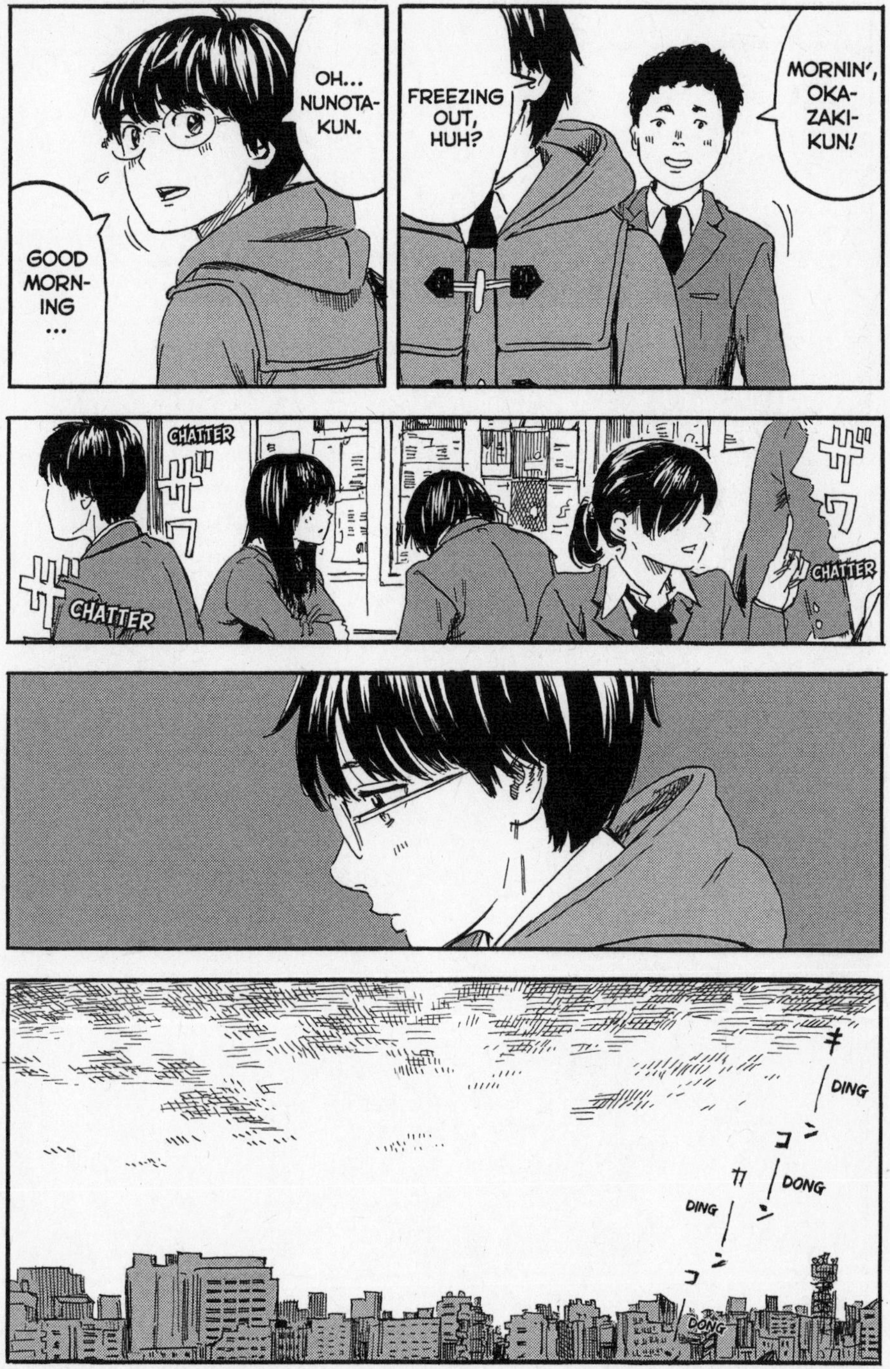
MORNIN', OKA-ZAKI-KUN!
FREEZING OUT, HUH?
OH... NUNOTA-KUN.
GOOD MORN-ING ...
ザワ
CHATTER
CHATTER
ザワ
ザワ
CHATTER
キーンコーン
DING
DONG
カーンコーン
DING
DONG

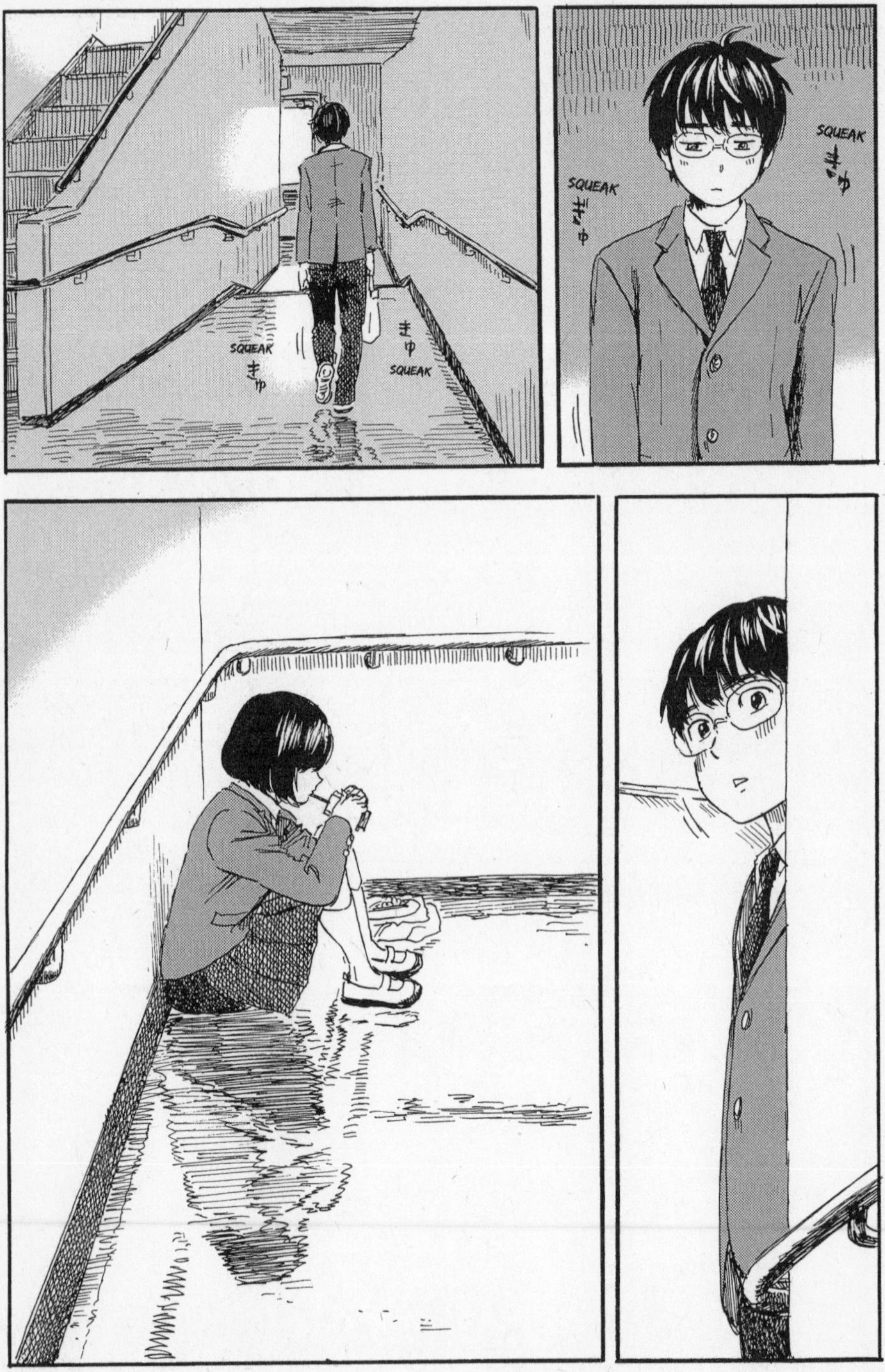
SQUEAK
きゅ
SQUEAK
ぎゅ
きゅ
SQUEAK
SQUEAK
きゅ

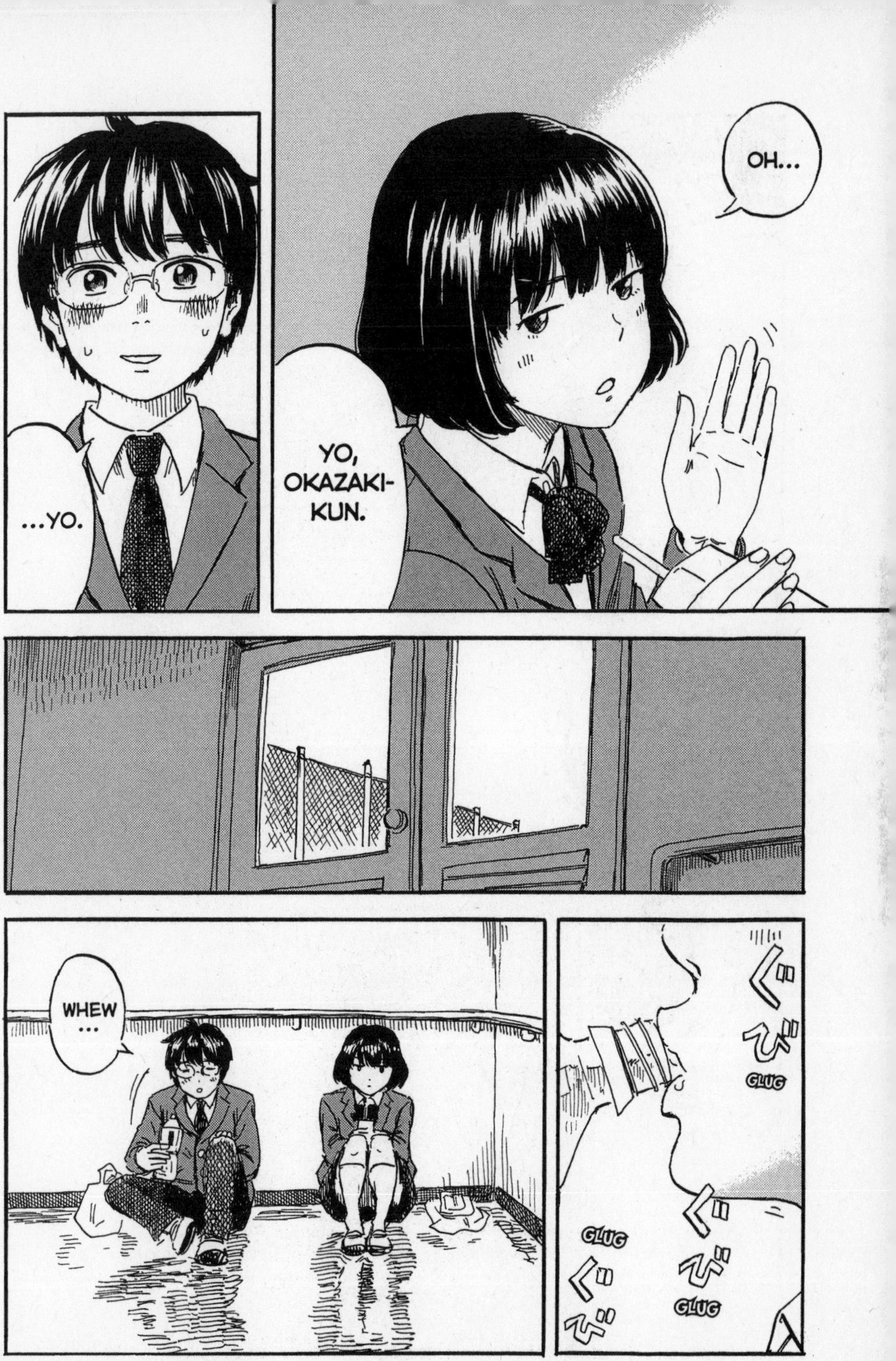
OH...
YO, OKAZAKI-KUN.
...YO.
GLUG
GLUG
GLUG
WHEW ...

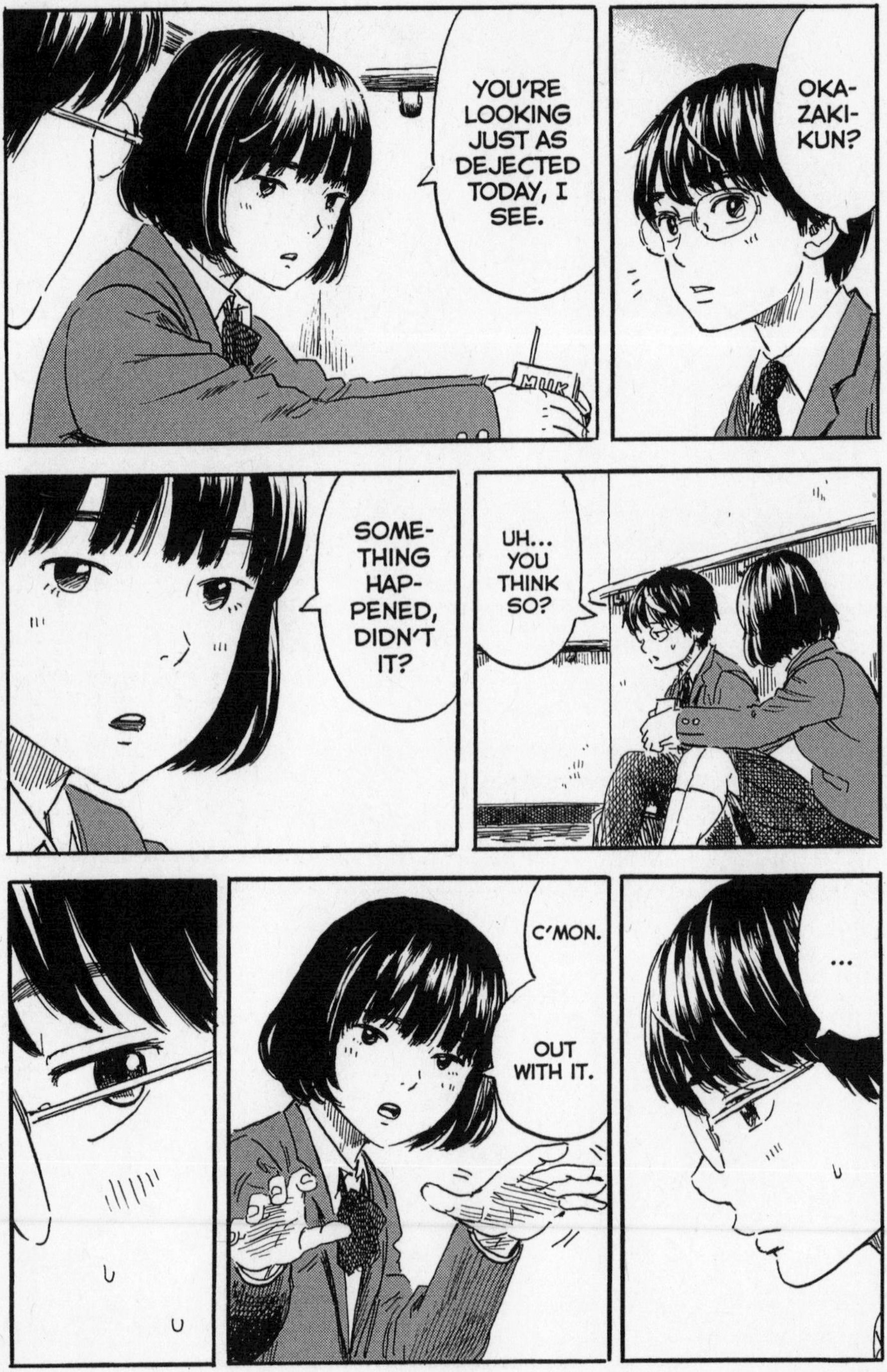
OKA-ZAKI-KUN?
YOU'RE LOOKING JUST AS DEJECTED TODAY, I SEE.
UH... YOU THINK SO?
SOME-THING HAP-PENED, DIDN'T IT?
...
C'MON.
OUT WITH IT.

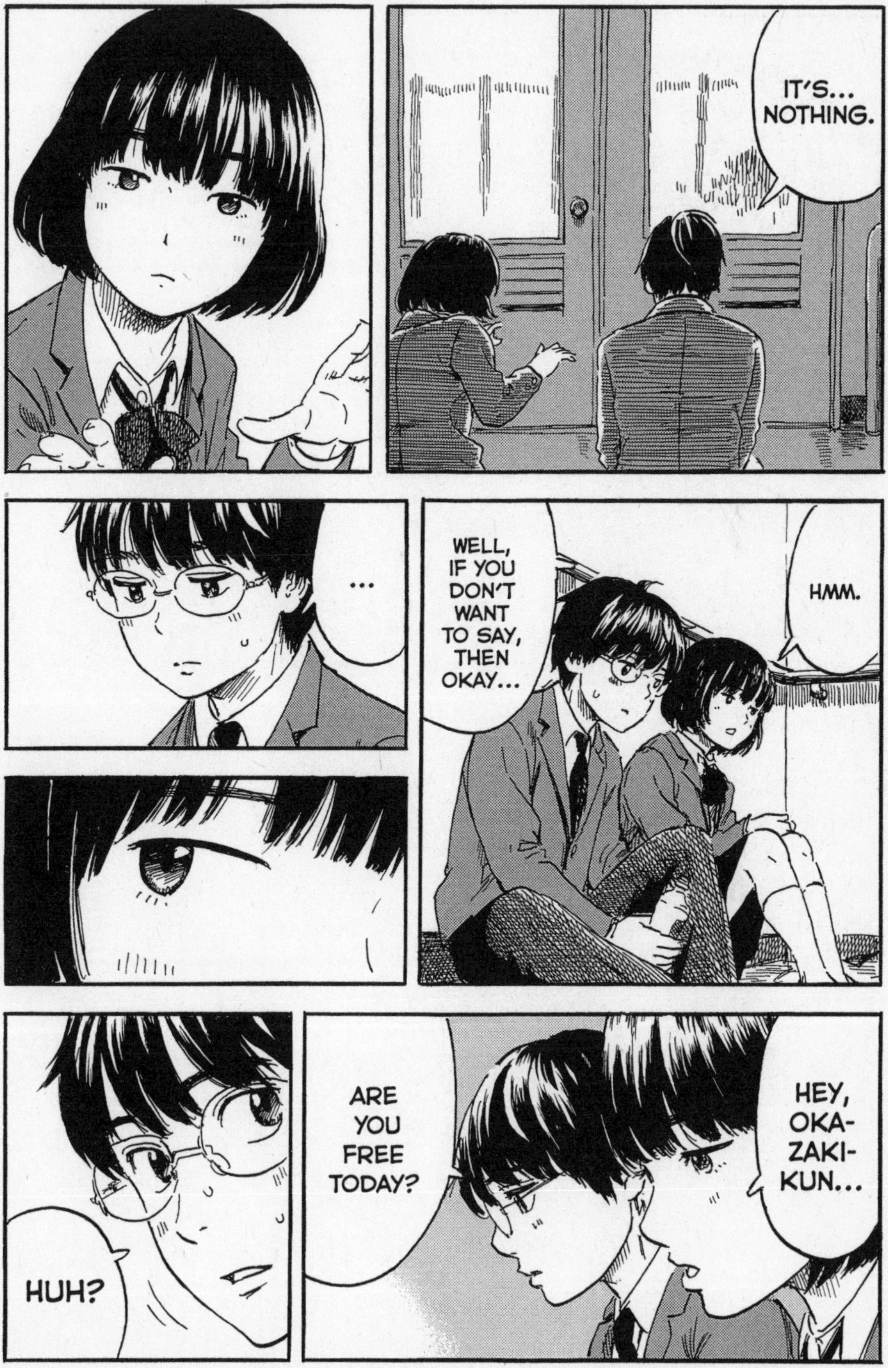
IT'S... NOTHING.
HMM.
WELL, IF YOU DON'T WANT TO SAY, THEN OKAY...
...
HEY, OKA-ZAKI-KUN...
ARE YOU FREE TODAY?
HUH?

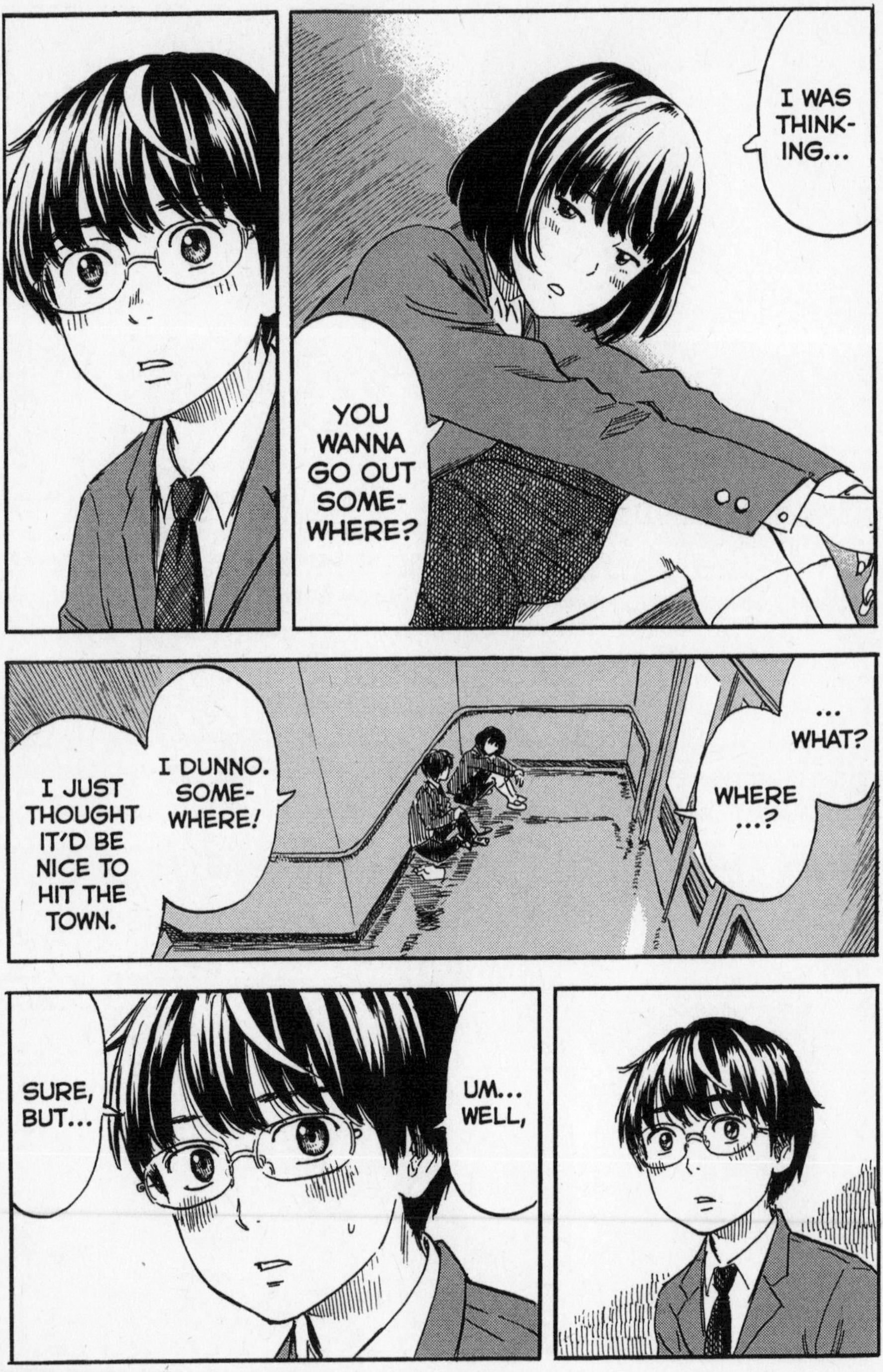
I WAS THINKING...
YOU WANNA GO OUT SOMEWHERE?
... WHAT?
WHERE ...?
I DUNNO. SOMEWHERE!
I JUST THOUGHT IT'D BE NICE TO HIT THE TOWN.
UM... WELL,
SURE, BUT...

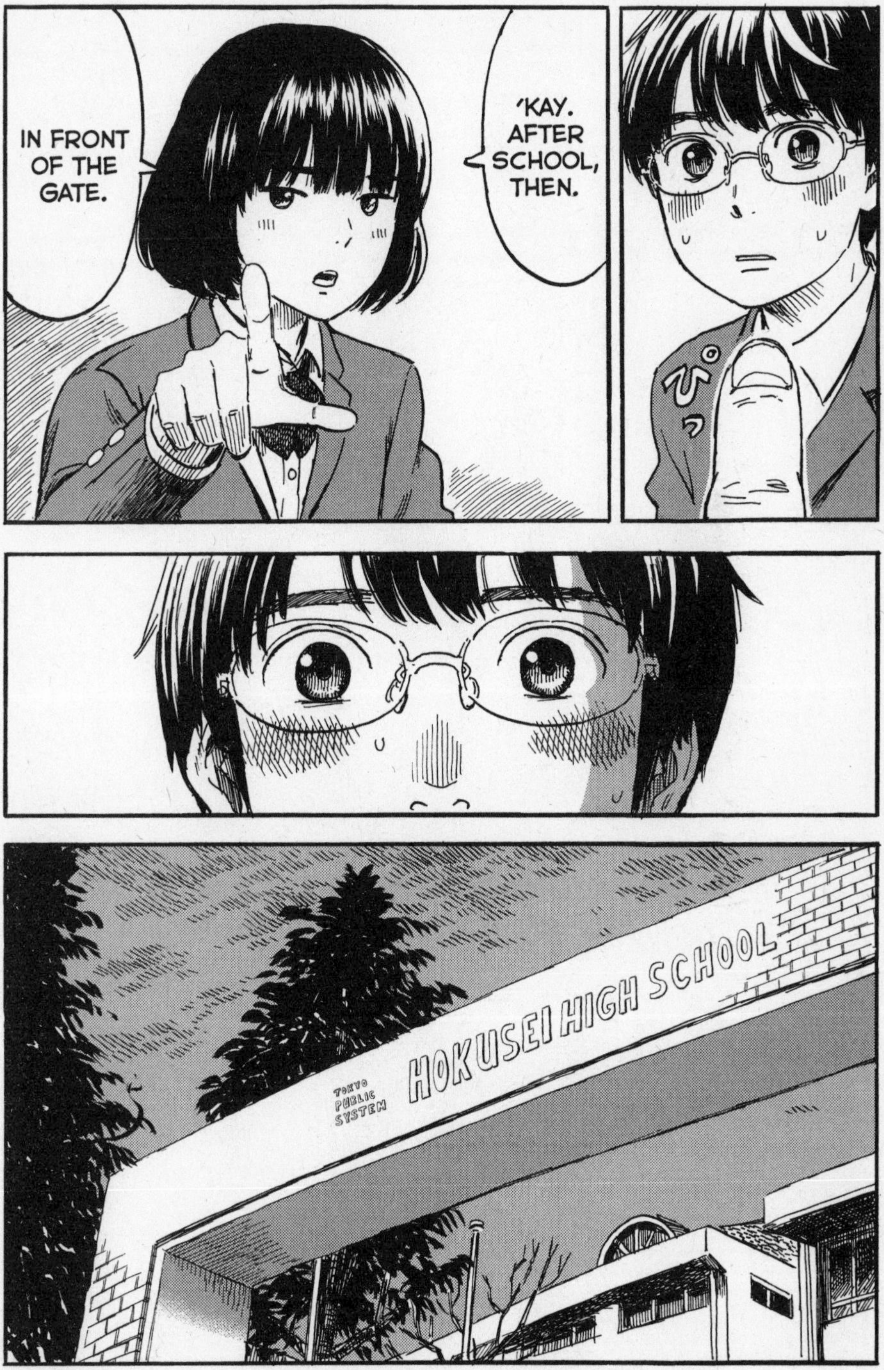
ぴっ
'KAY. AFTER SCHOOL, THEN.
IN FRONT OF THE GATE.
HOKUSEI HIGH SCHOOL
TOKYO PUBLIC SYSTEM

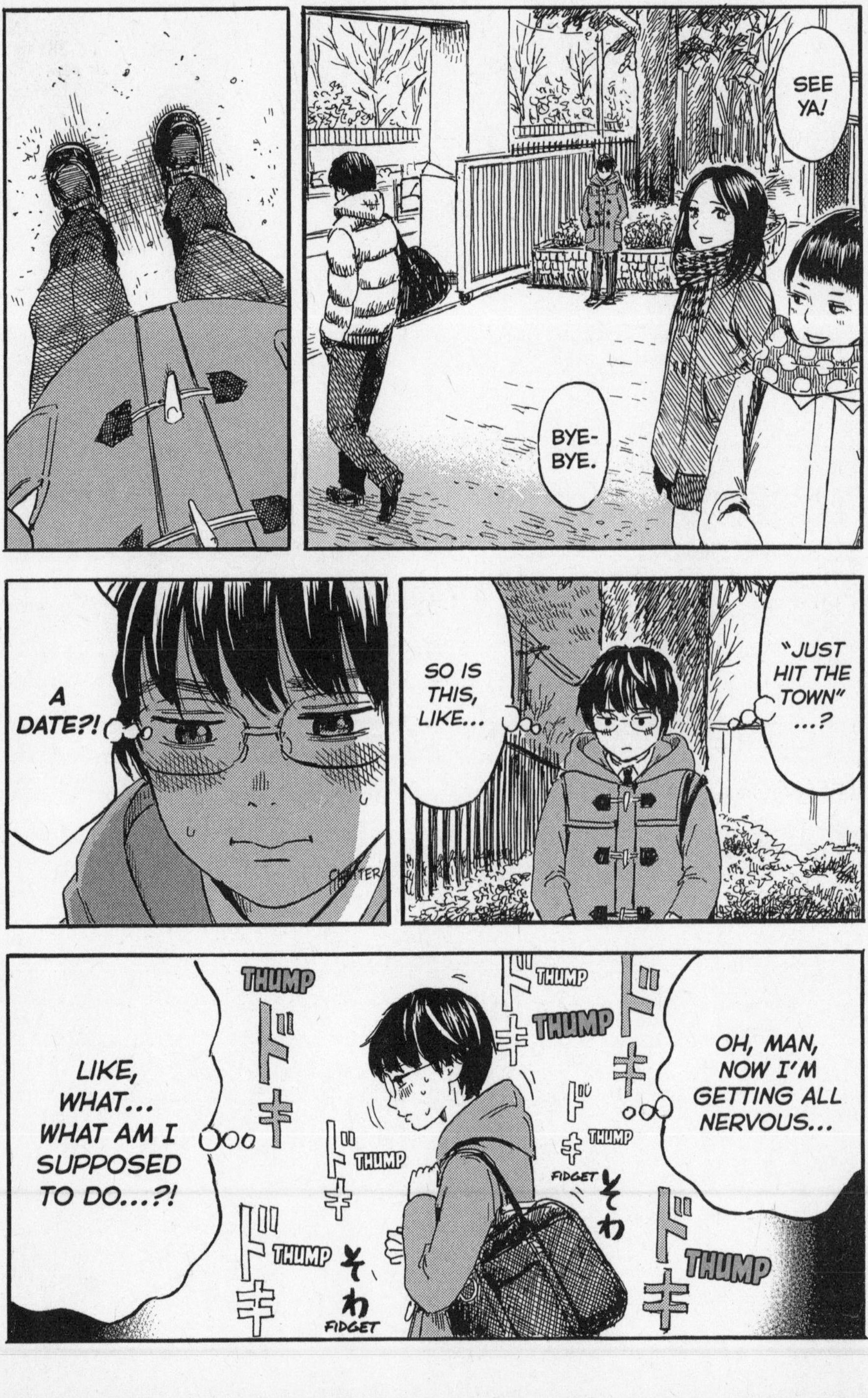
SEE YA!
BYE-BYE.
"JUST HIT THE TOWN" ...?
SO IS THIS, LIKE...
A DATE?!
CHATTER
OH, MAN, NOW I'M GETTING ALL NERVOUS...
ドキ THUMP
ドキ THUMP
ドキ THUMP
ドキ THUMP
そわ FIDGET
ドキ THUMP
ドキ THUMP
ドキ THUMP
そわ FIDGET
LIKE, WHAT... WHAT AM I SUPPOSED TO DO...?!

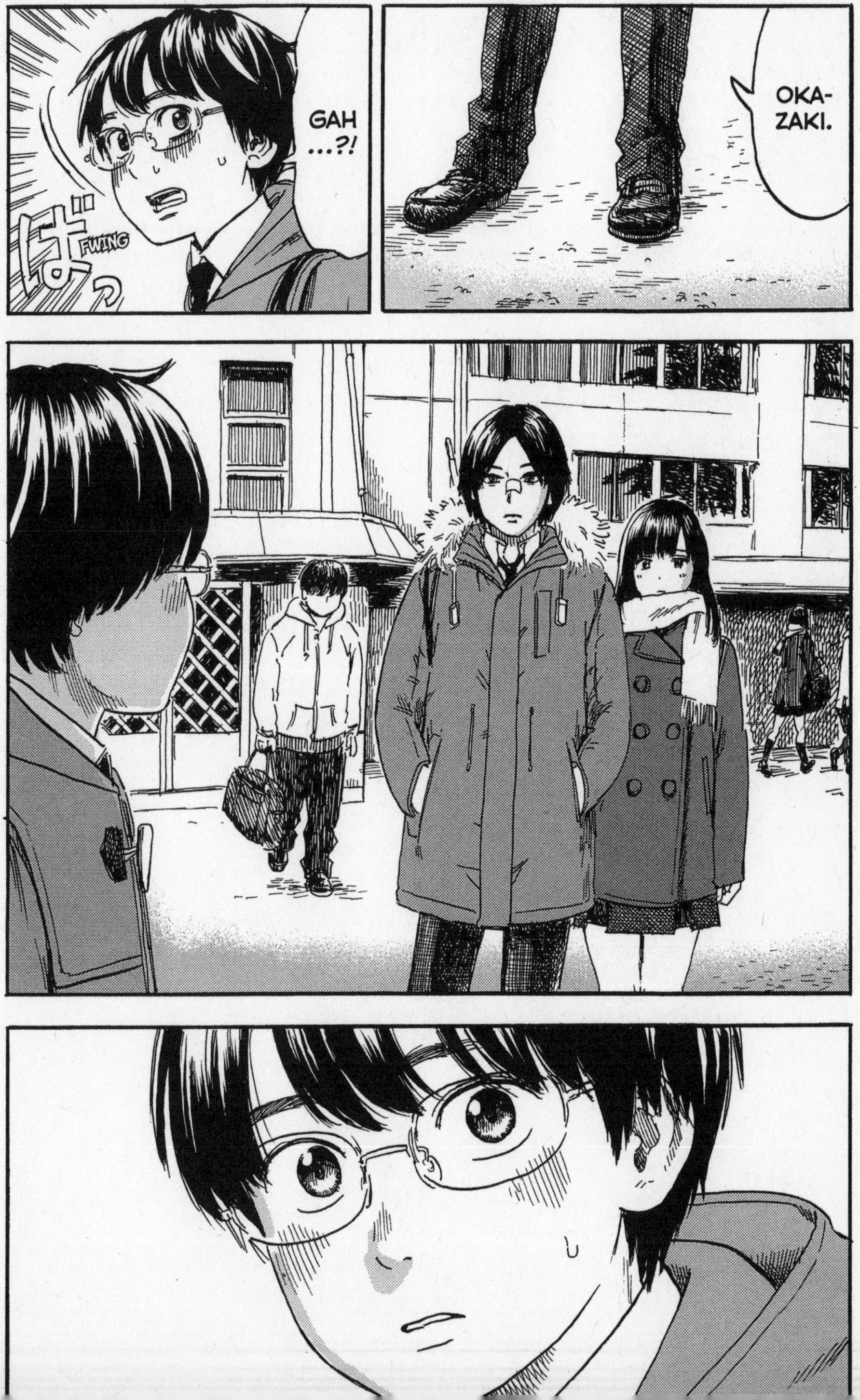
OKA-
ZAKI.
GAH
...?!
ばっ
FWING

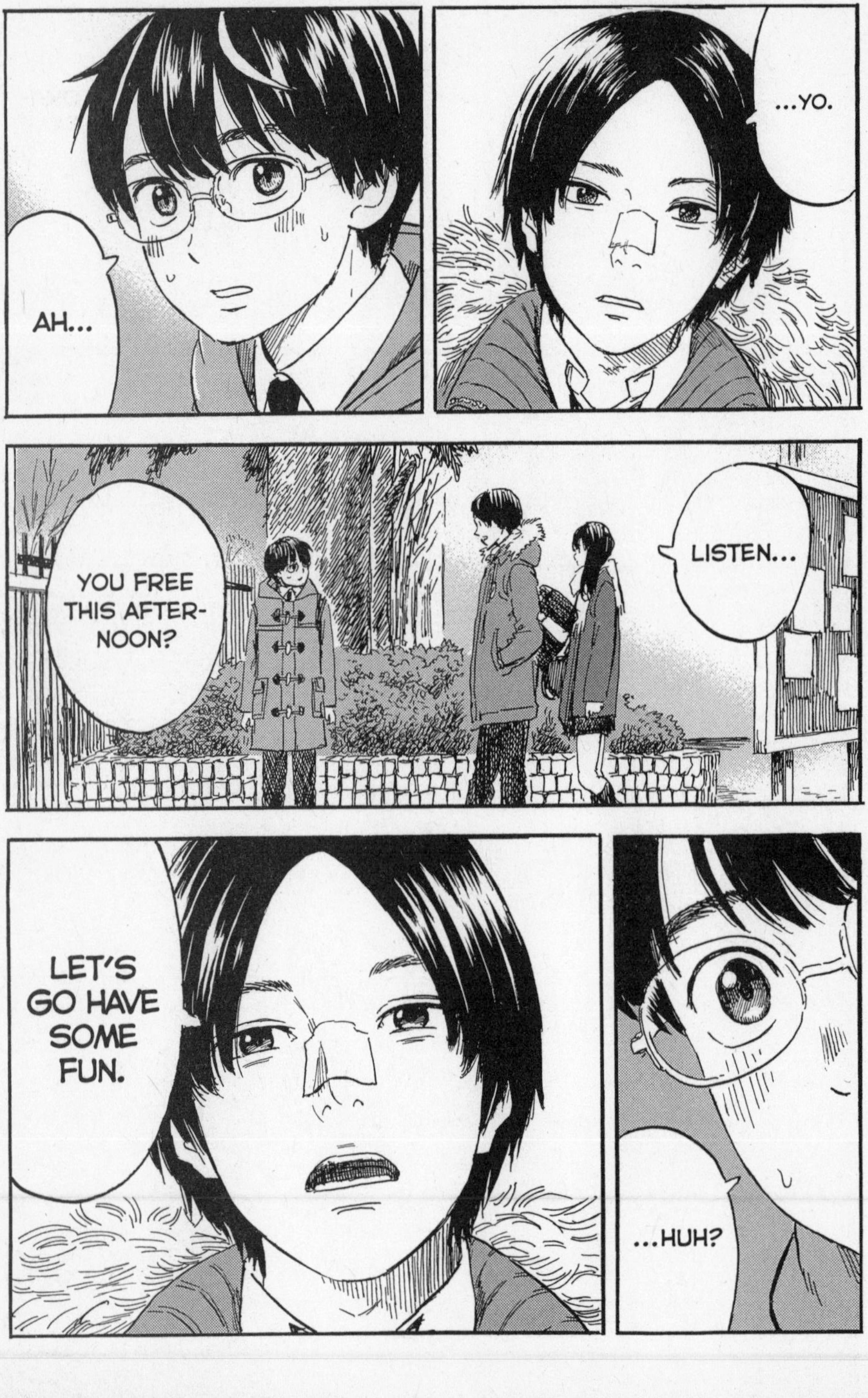
...YO.
AH...
LISTEN...
YOU FREE THIS AFTER-NOON?
...HUH?
LET'S GO HAVE SOME FUN.

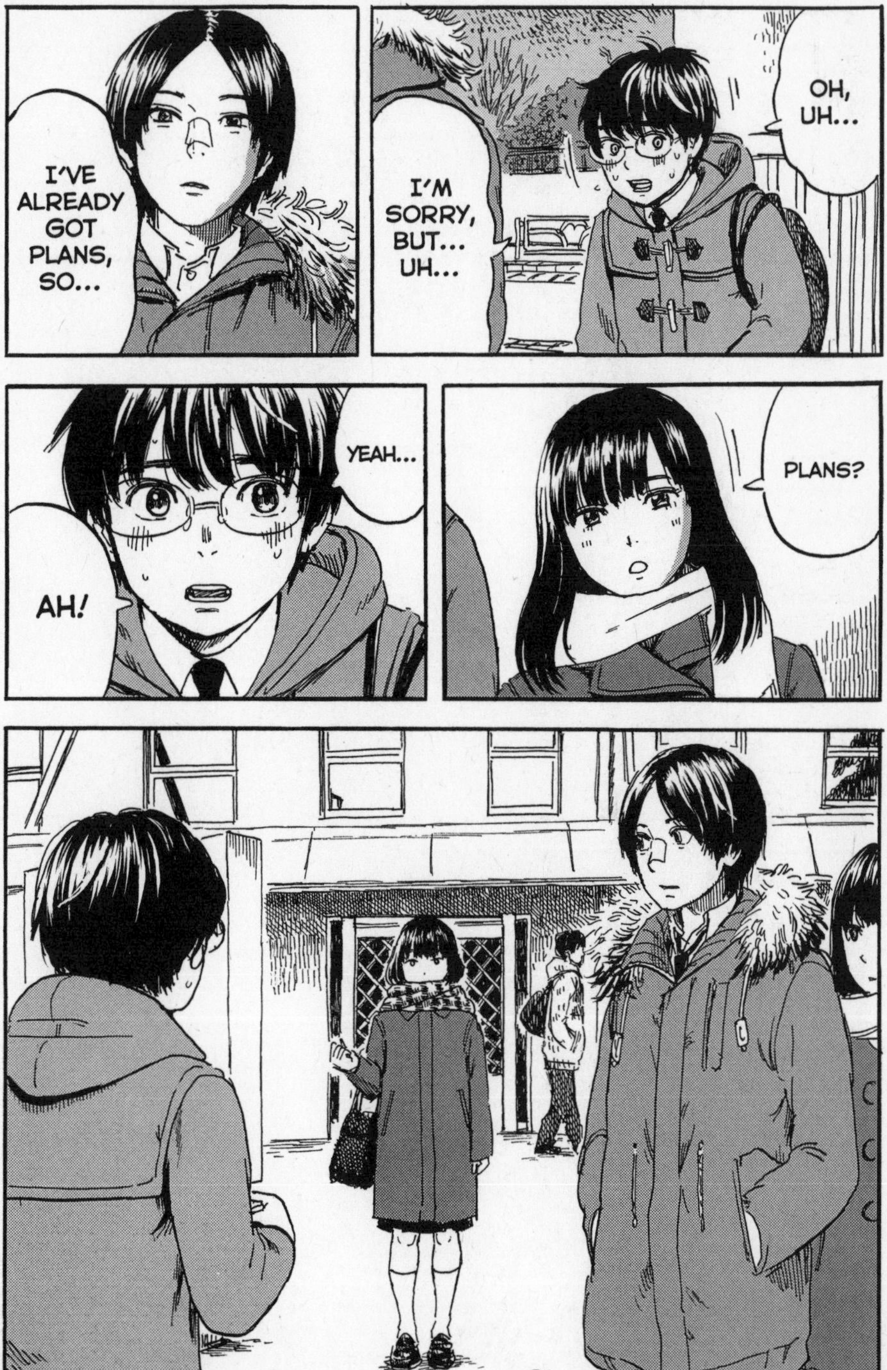
OH, UH...
I'M SORRY, BUT... UH...
I'VE ALREADY GOT PLANS, SO...
PLANS?
YEAH...
AH!

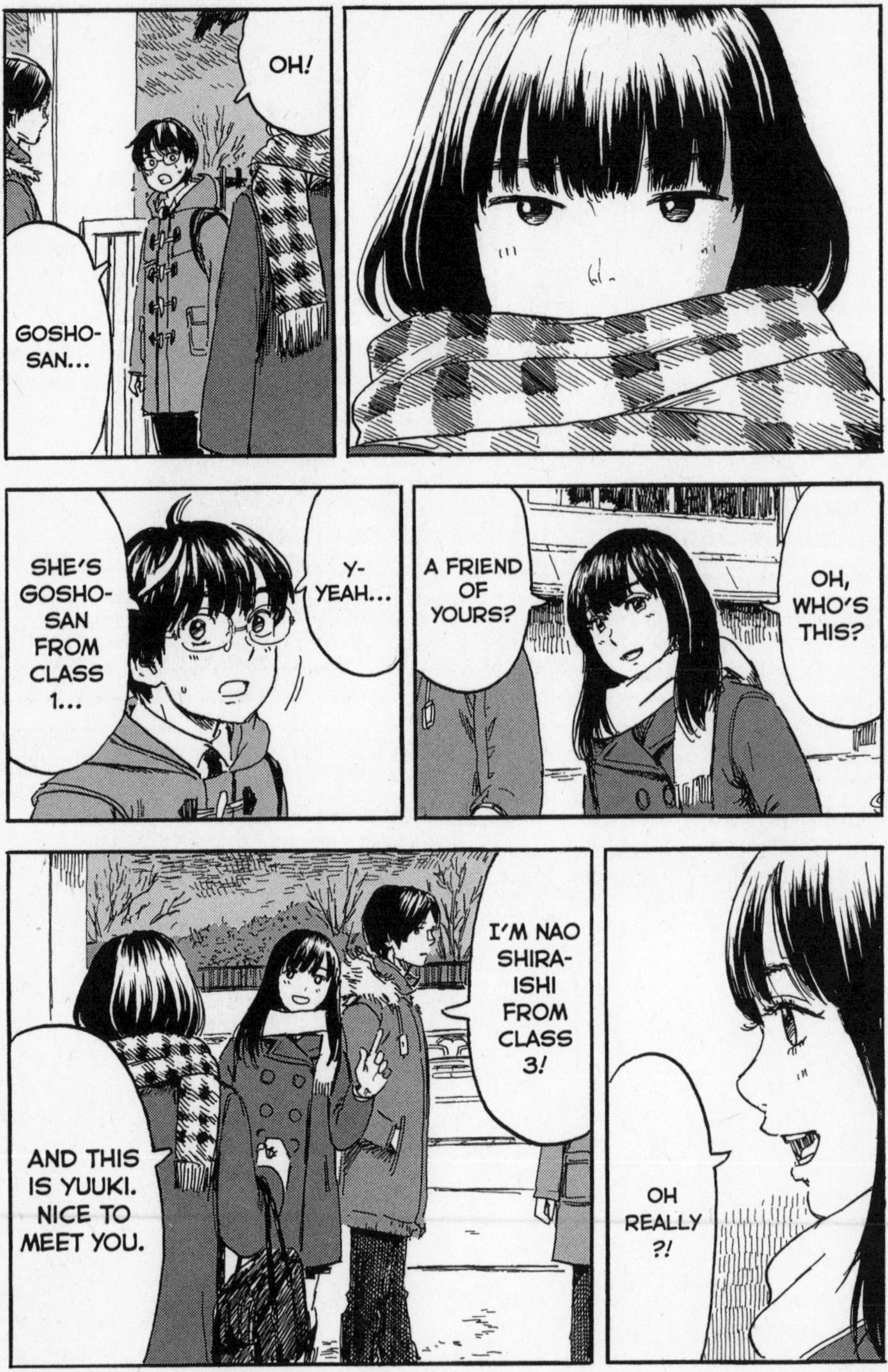
OH!
GOSHO-SAN...
OH, WHO'S THIS?
A FRIEND OF YOURS?
Y-YEAH...
SHE'S GOSHO-SAN FROM CLASS 1...
OH REALLY?!
I'M NAO SHIRAISHI FROM CLASS 3!
AND THIS IS YUUKI. NICE TO MEET YOU.

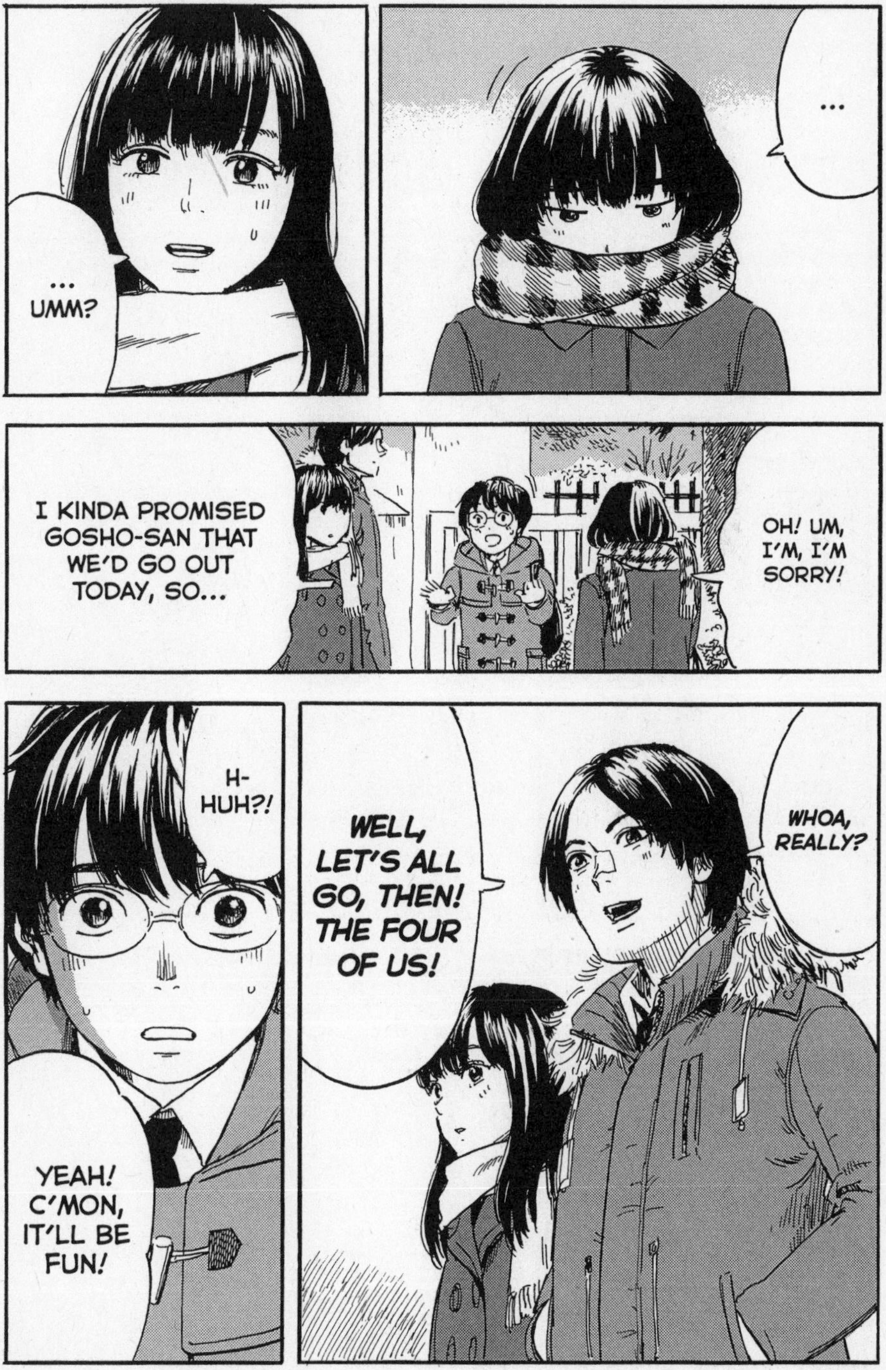
...
... UMM?
OH! UM, I'M, I'M SORRY!
I KINDA PROMISED GOSHO-SAN THAT WE'D GO OUT TODAY, SO...
WHOA, REALLY?
WELL, LET'S ALL GO, THEN! THE FOUR OF US!
H-HUH?!
YEAH! C'MON, IT'LL BE FUN!

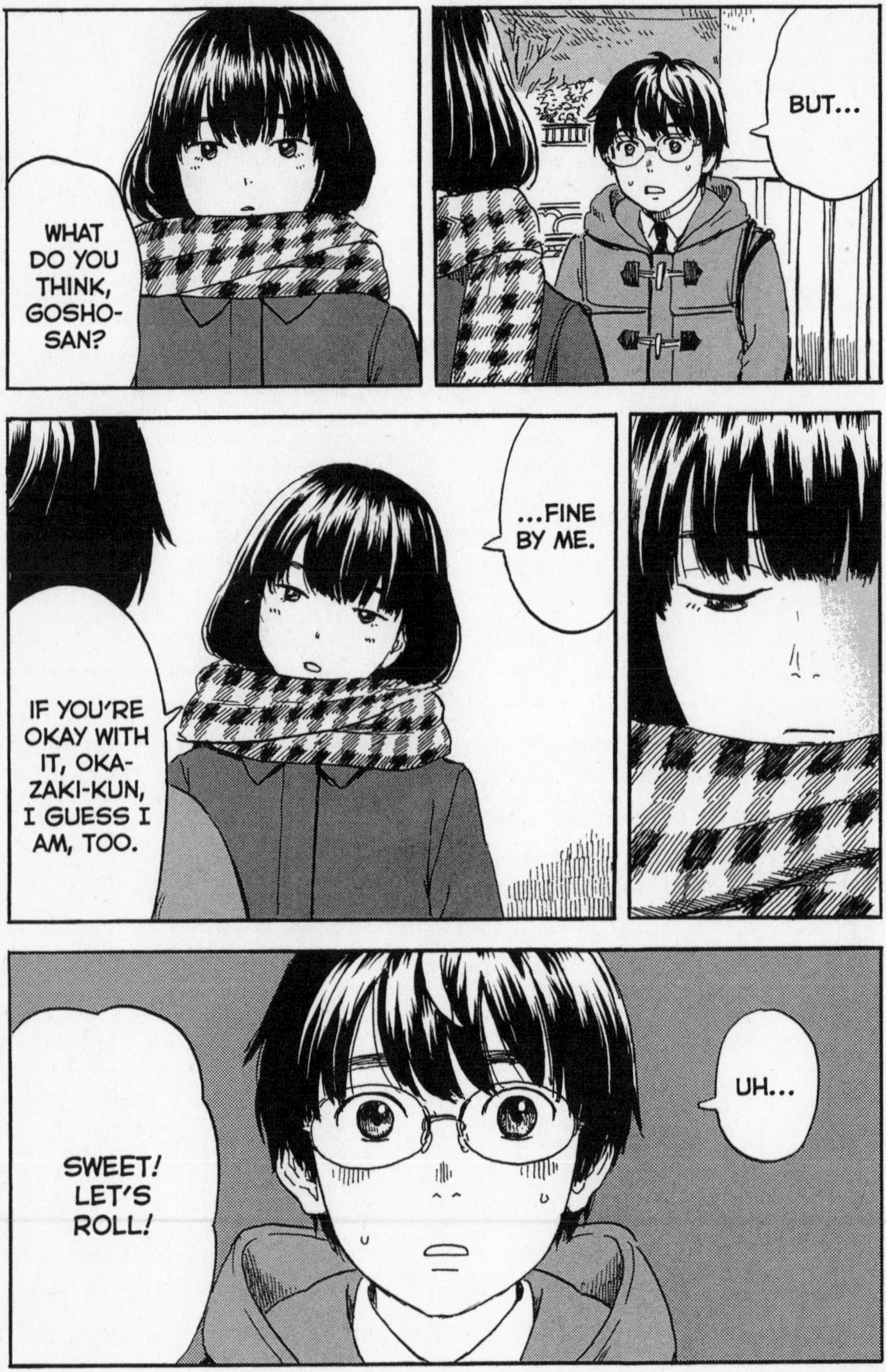
BUT...
WHAT DO YOU THINK, GOSHO-SAN?
...FINE BY ME.
IF YOU'RE OKAY WITH IT, OKA-ZAKI-KUN, I GUESS I AM, TOO.
UH...
SWEET! LET'S ROLL!

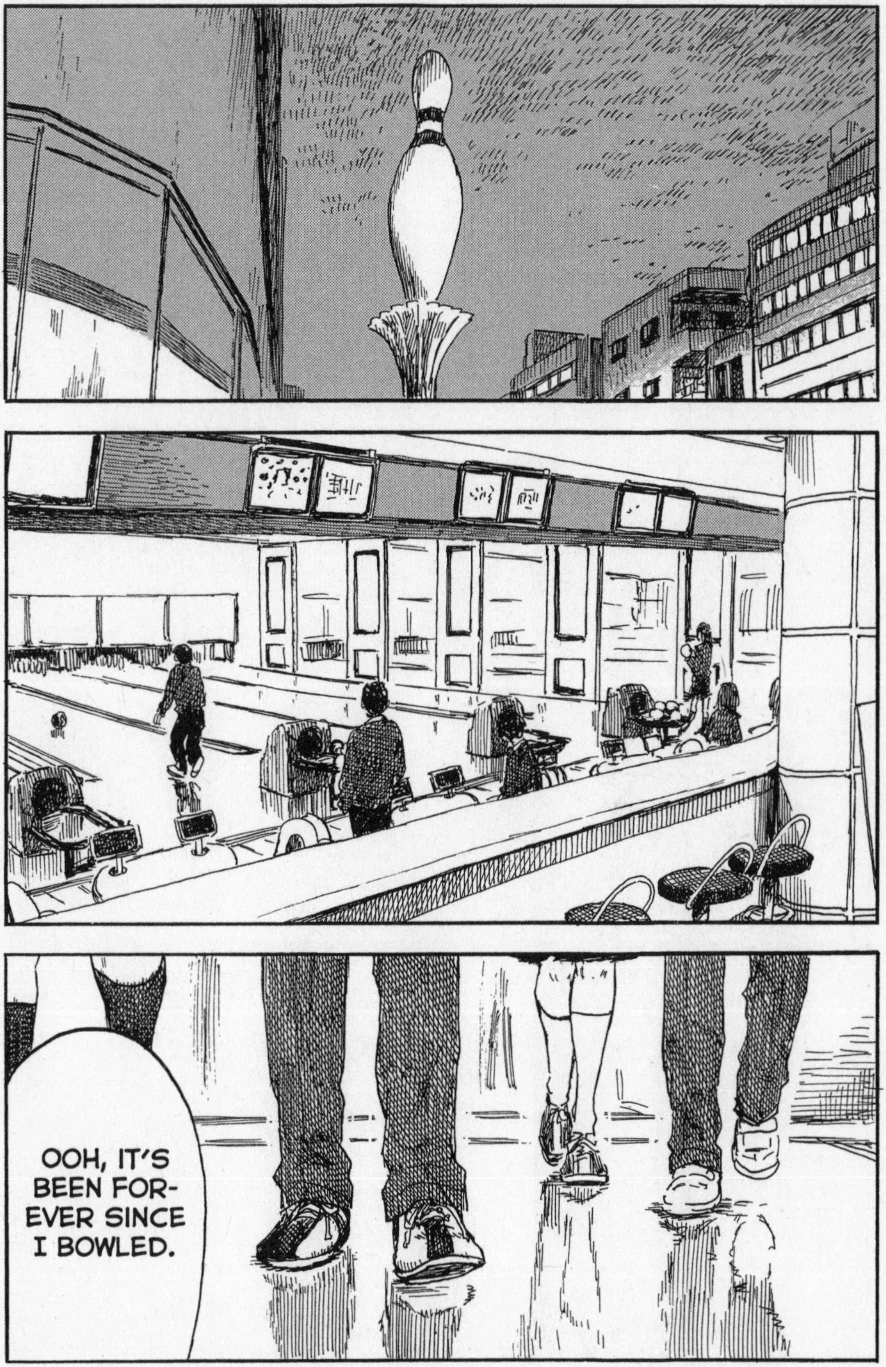
OOH, IT'S BEEN FOR-EVER SINCE I BOWLED.

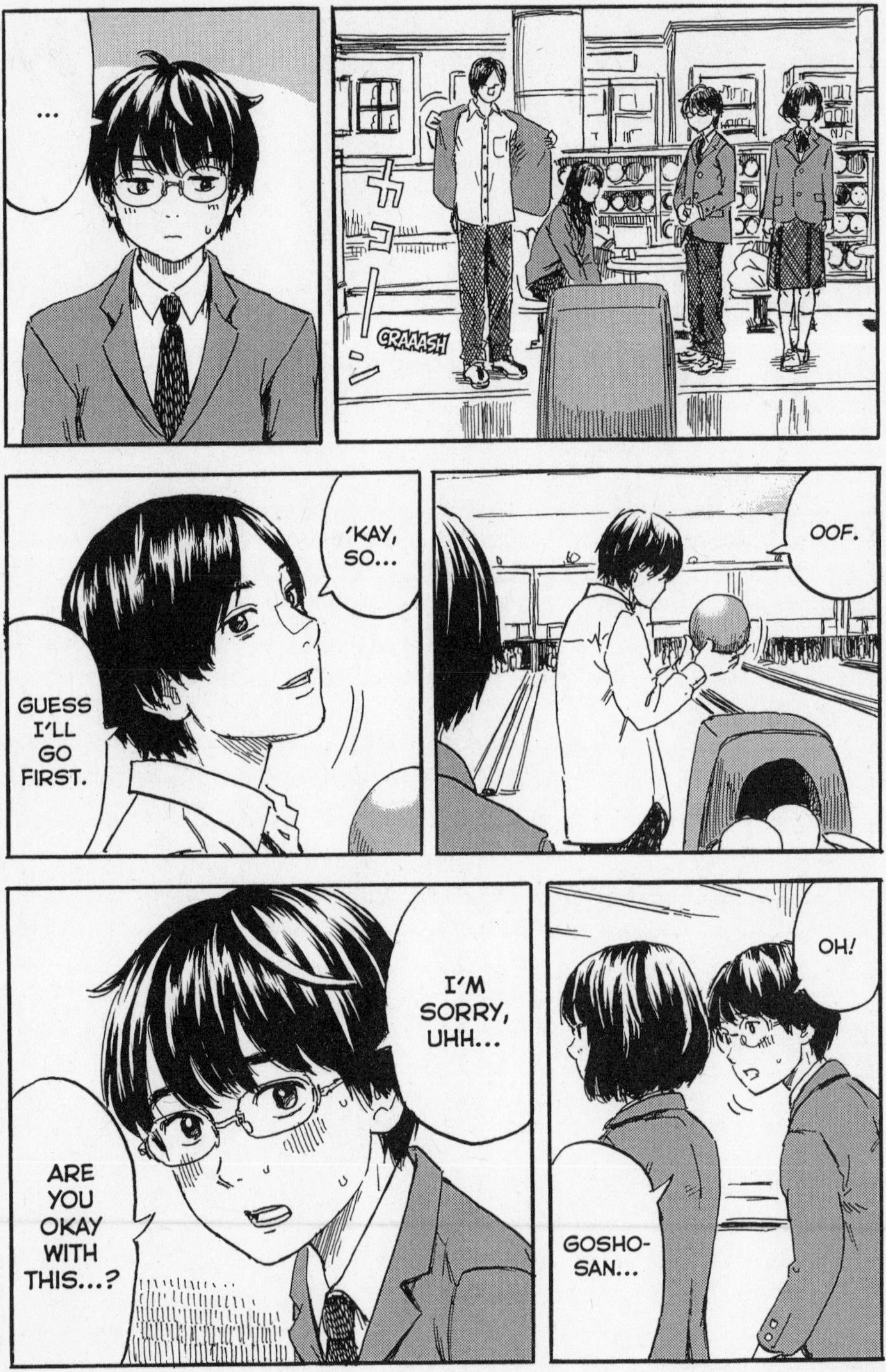
CRAAASH
...
OOF.
'KAY, SO...
GUESS I'LL GO FIRST.
OH!
GOSHO-SAN...
I'M SORRY, UHH...
ARE YOU OKAY WITH THIS...?

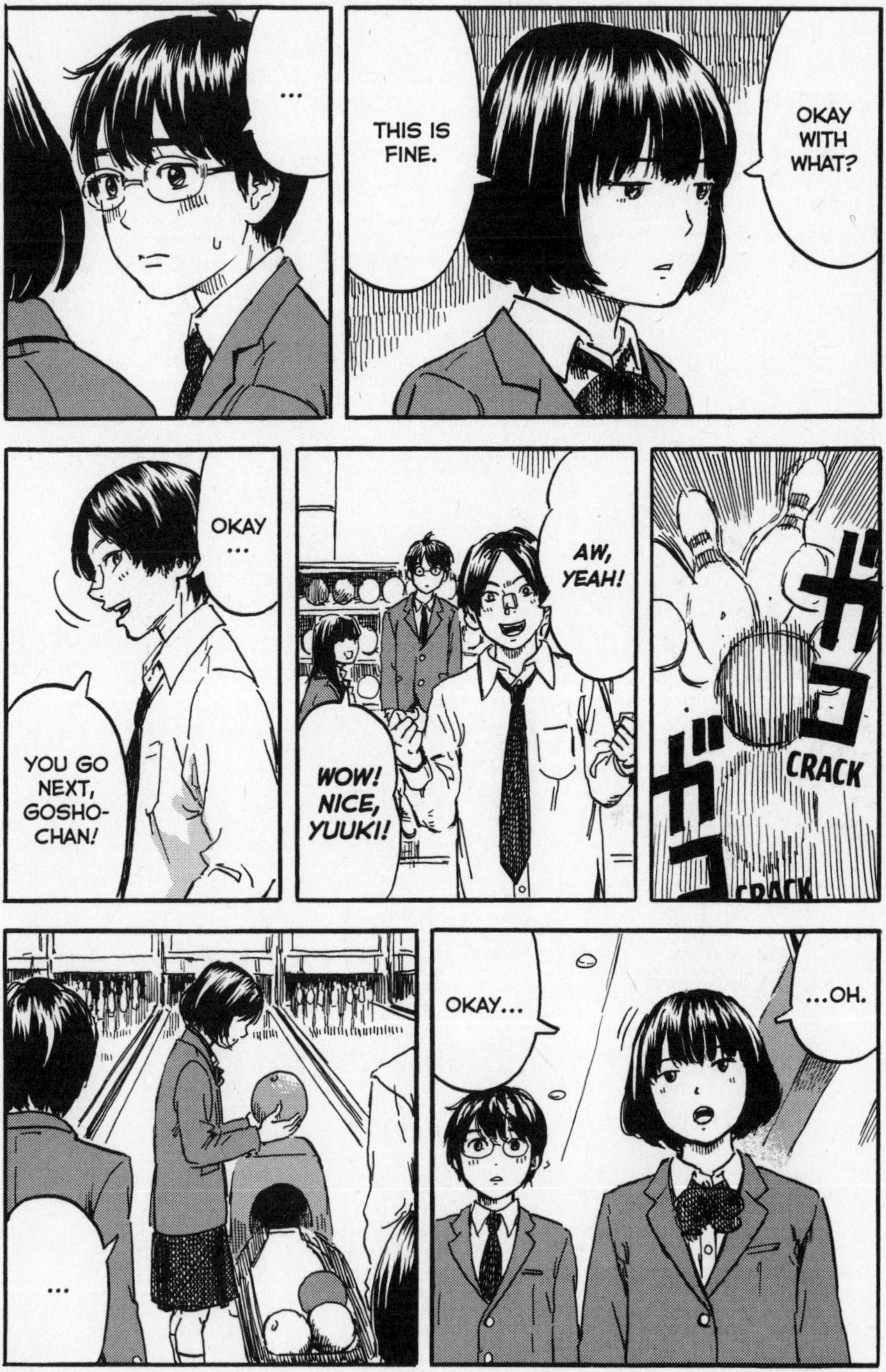
OKAY WITH WHAT?
THIS IS FINE.
...
ガコ
CRACK
ガコ
CRACK
AW, YEAH!
WOW! NICE, YUUKI!
OKAY ...
YOU GO NEXT, GOSHO-CHAN!
...OH.
OKAY...
...

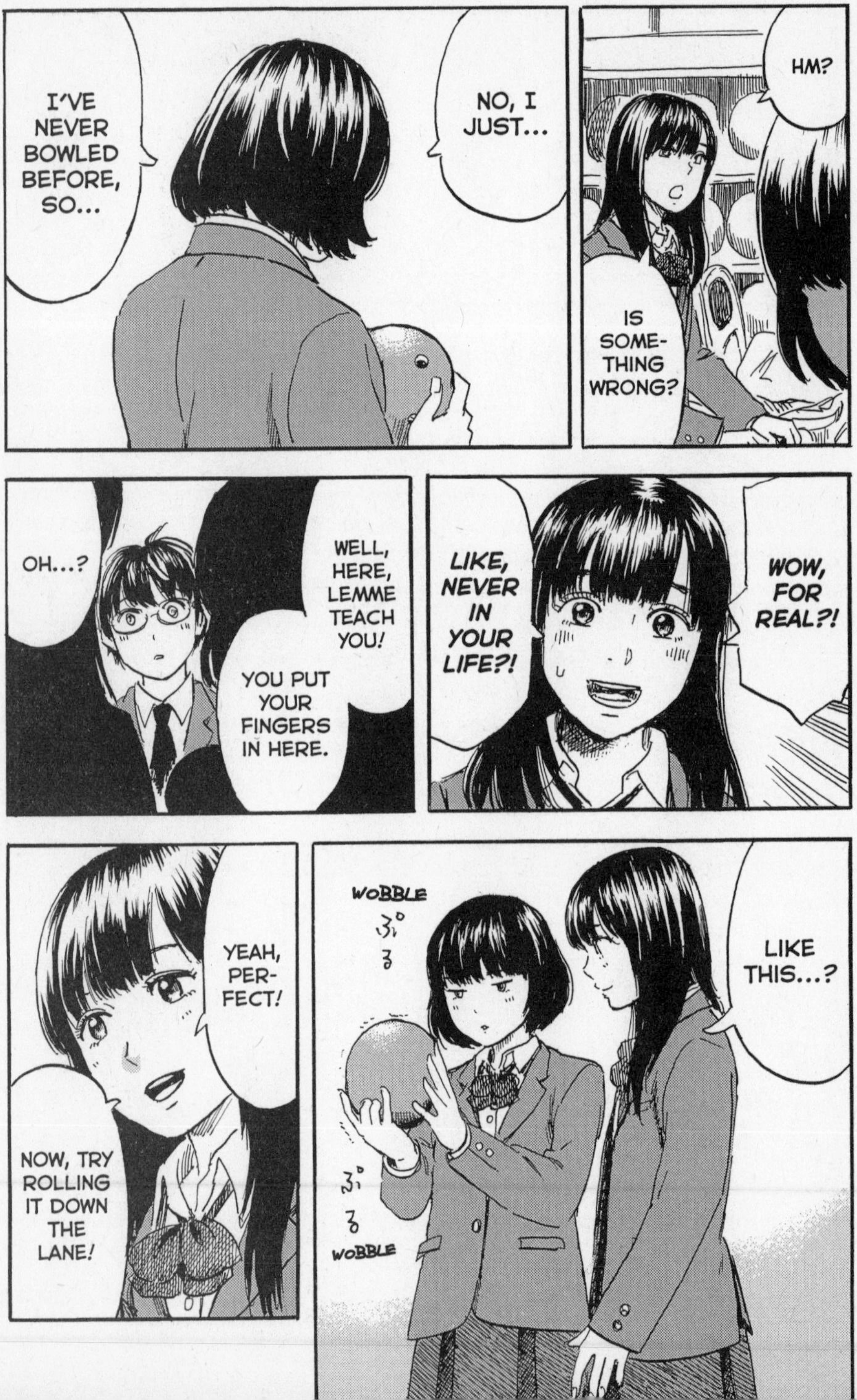
HM?
IS SOMETHING WRONG?
NO, I JUST...
I'VE NEVER BOWLED BEFORE, SO...
WOW, FOR REAL?!
LIKE, NEVER IN YOUR LIFE?!
WELL, HERE, LEMME TEACH YOU!
OH...?
YOU PUT YOUR FINGERS IN HERE.
LIKE THIS...?
WOBBLE
ぷる
ぷる
WOBBLE
YEAH, PERFECT!
NOW, TRY ROLLING IT DOWN THE LANE!

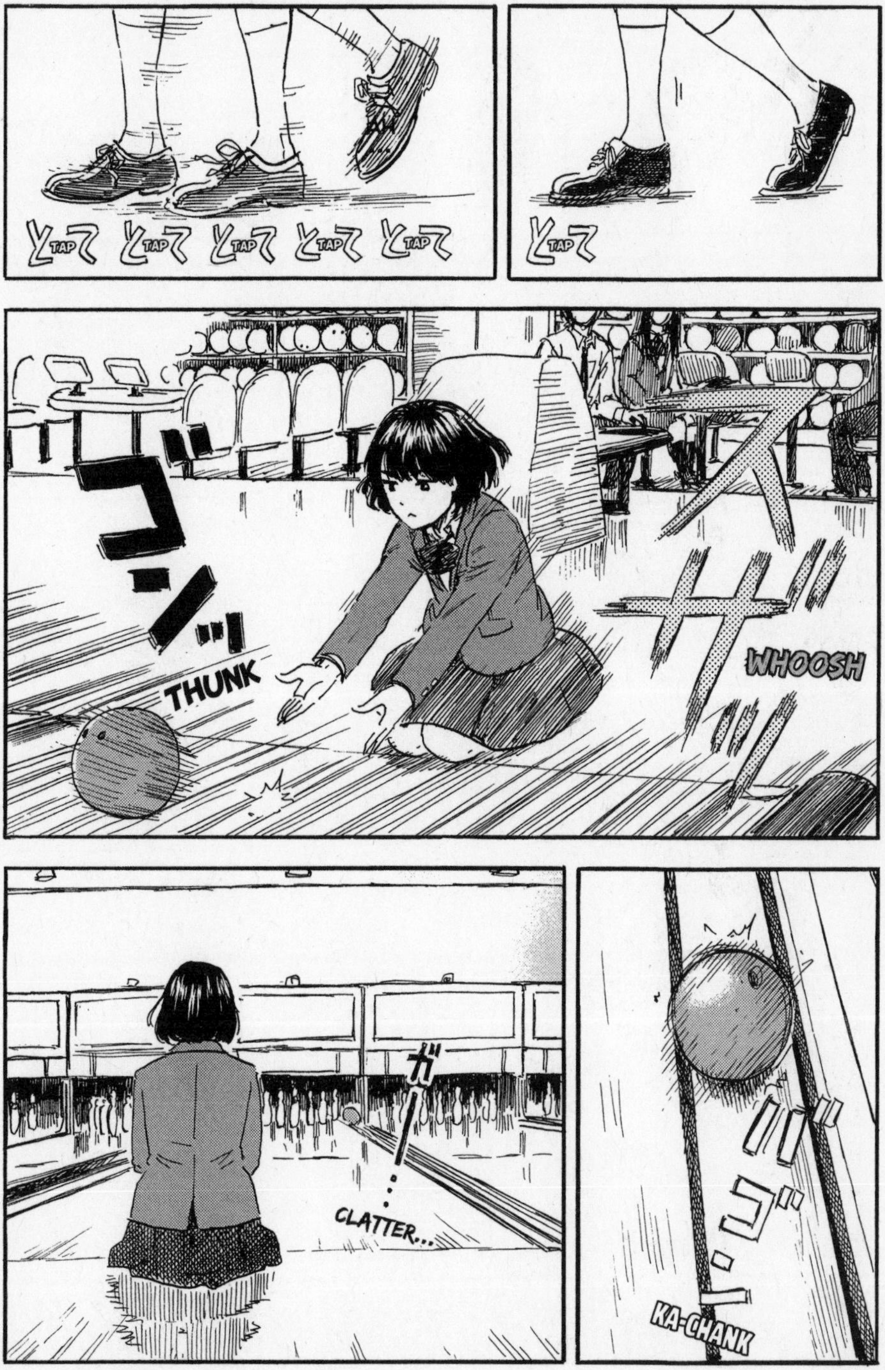
TAP
TAP
TAP
TAP
TAP
TAP
WHOOSH
THUNK
KA-CHANK
CLATTER...

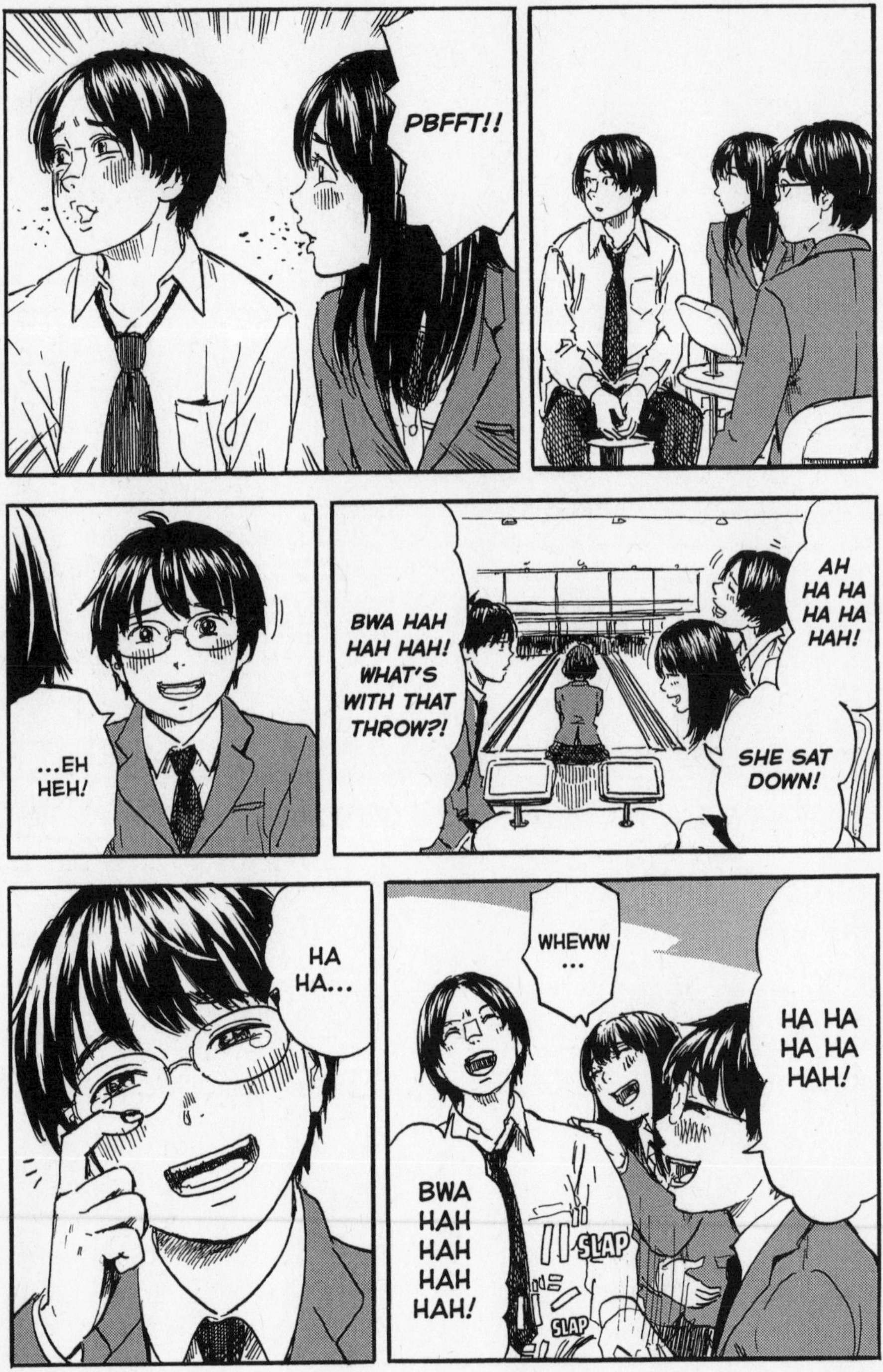
PBFFT!!
AH HA HA HA HA HAH!
SHE SAT DOWN!
BWA HAH HAH HAH! WHAT'S WITH THAT THROW?!
...EH HEH!
HA HA HA HA HAH!
WHEWW ...
SLAP
SLAP
BWA HAH HAH HAH HAH!
HA HA...

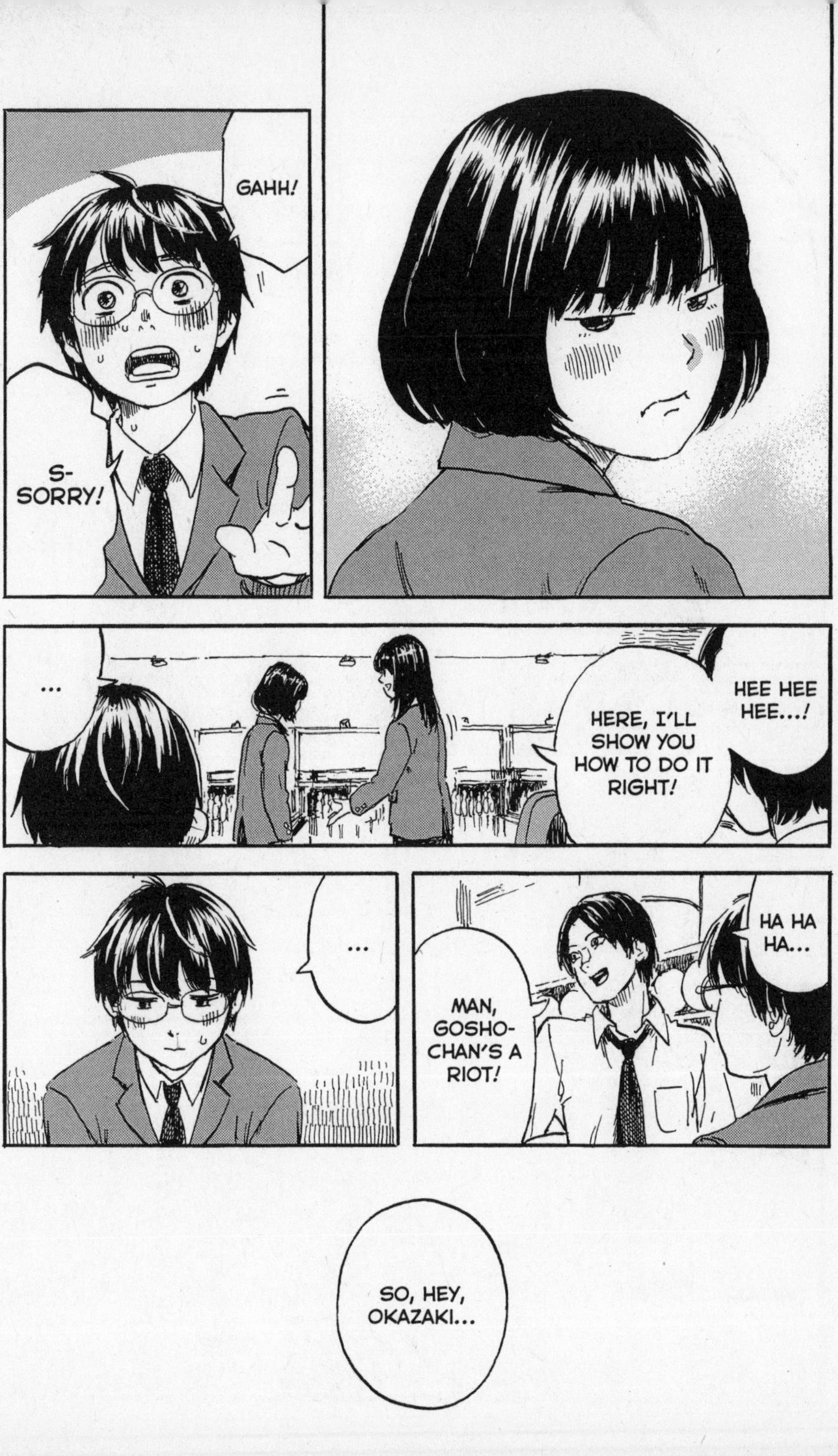
GAHH!
S-SORRY!
HEE HEE HEE...!
HERE, I'LL SHOW YOU HOW TO DO IT RIGHT!
...
HA HA HA...
MAN, GOSHO-CHAN'S A RIOT!
...
SO, HEY, OKAZAKI...

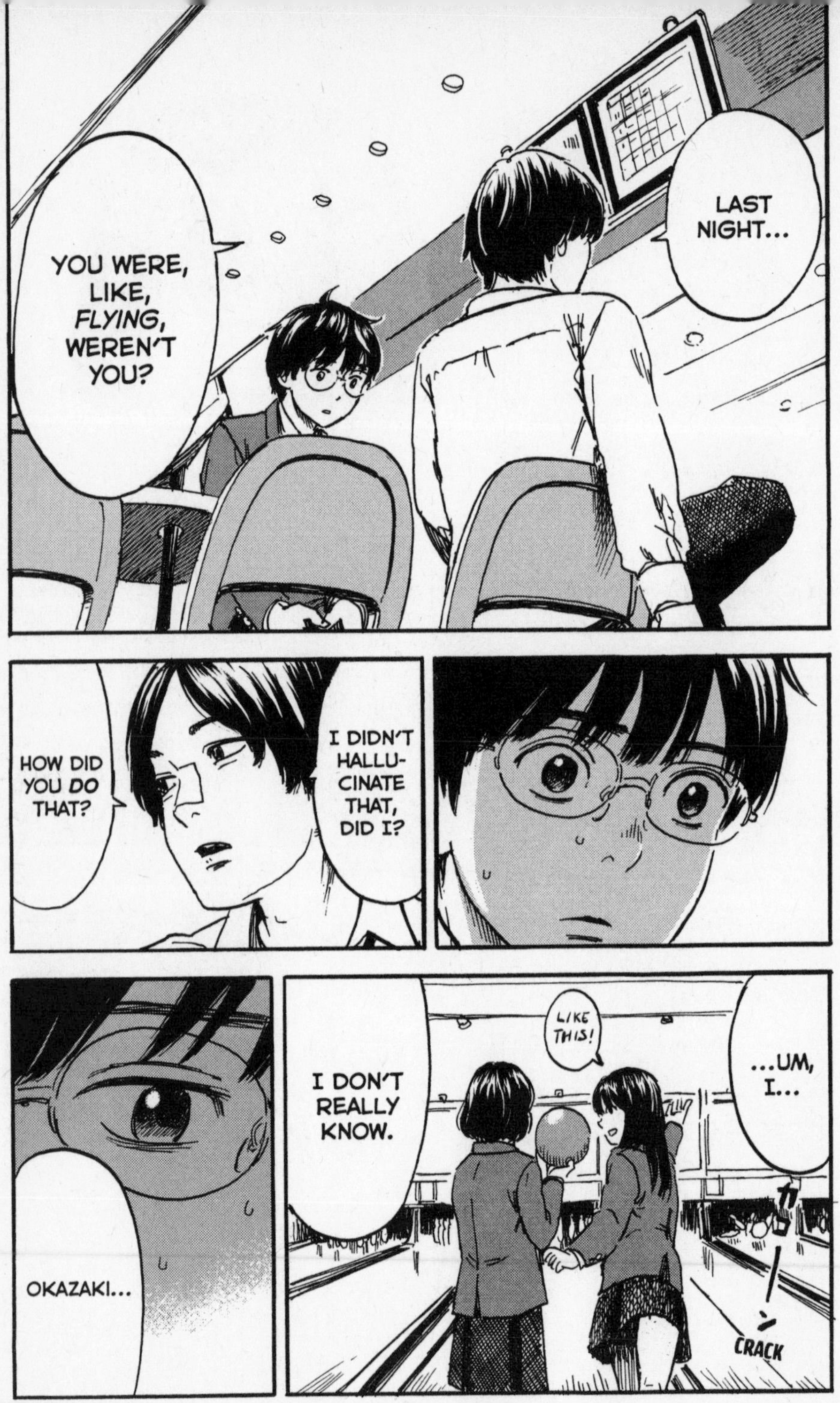

LAST NIGHT...
YOU WERE, LIKE, *FLYING*, WEREN'T YOU?
I DIDN'T HALLU-CINATE THAT, DID I?
HOW DID YOU *DO* THAT?
...UM, I...
LIKE THIS!
I DON'T REALLY KNOW.
CRACK
OKAZAKI...

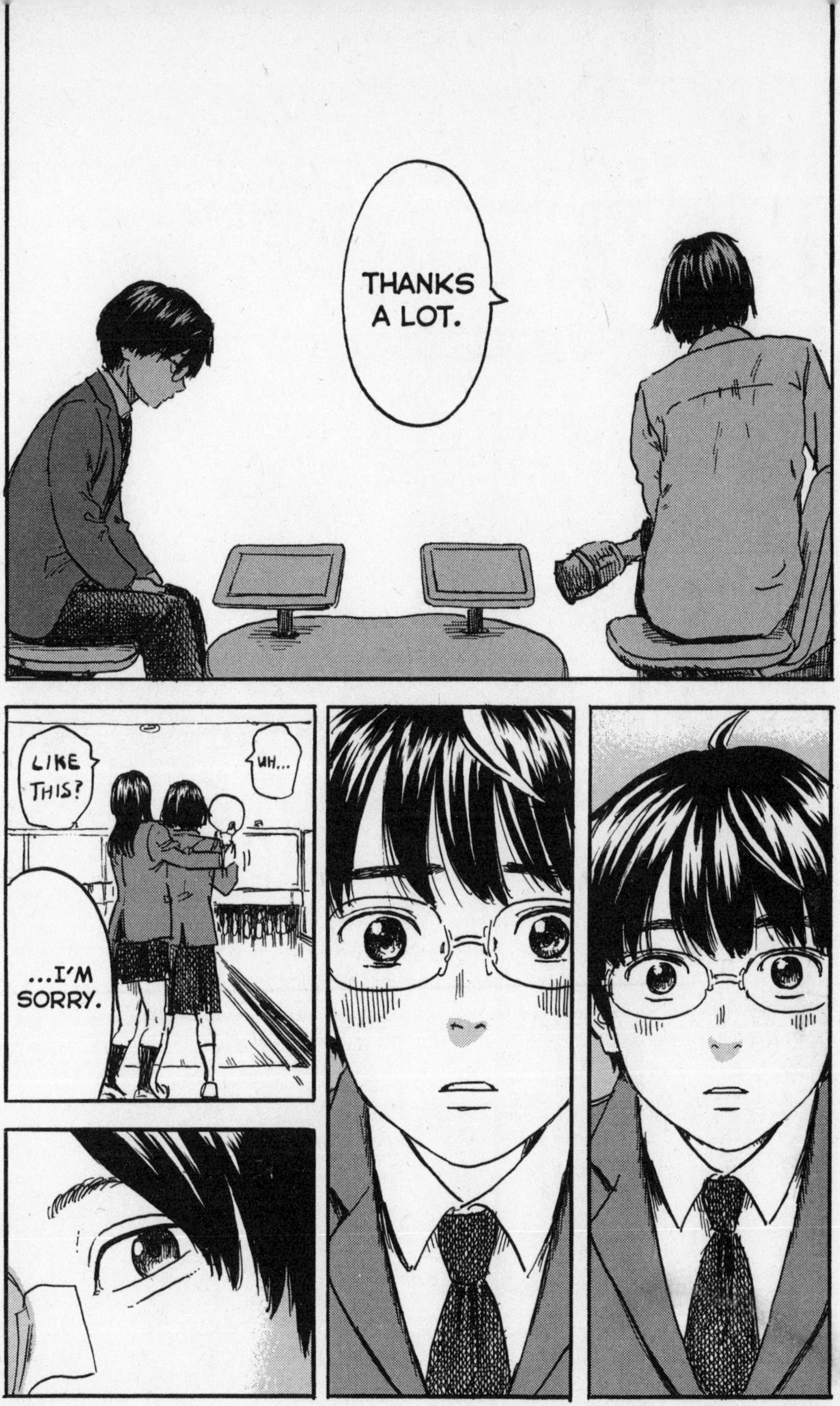
THANKS A LOT.
UH...
LIKE THIS?
...I'M SORRY.

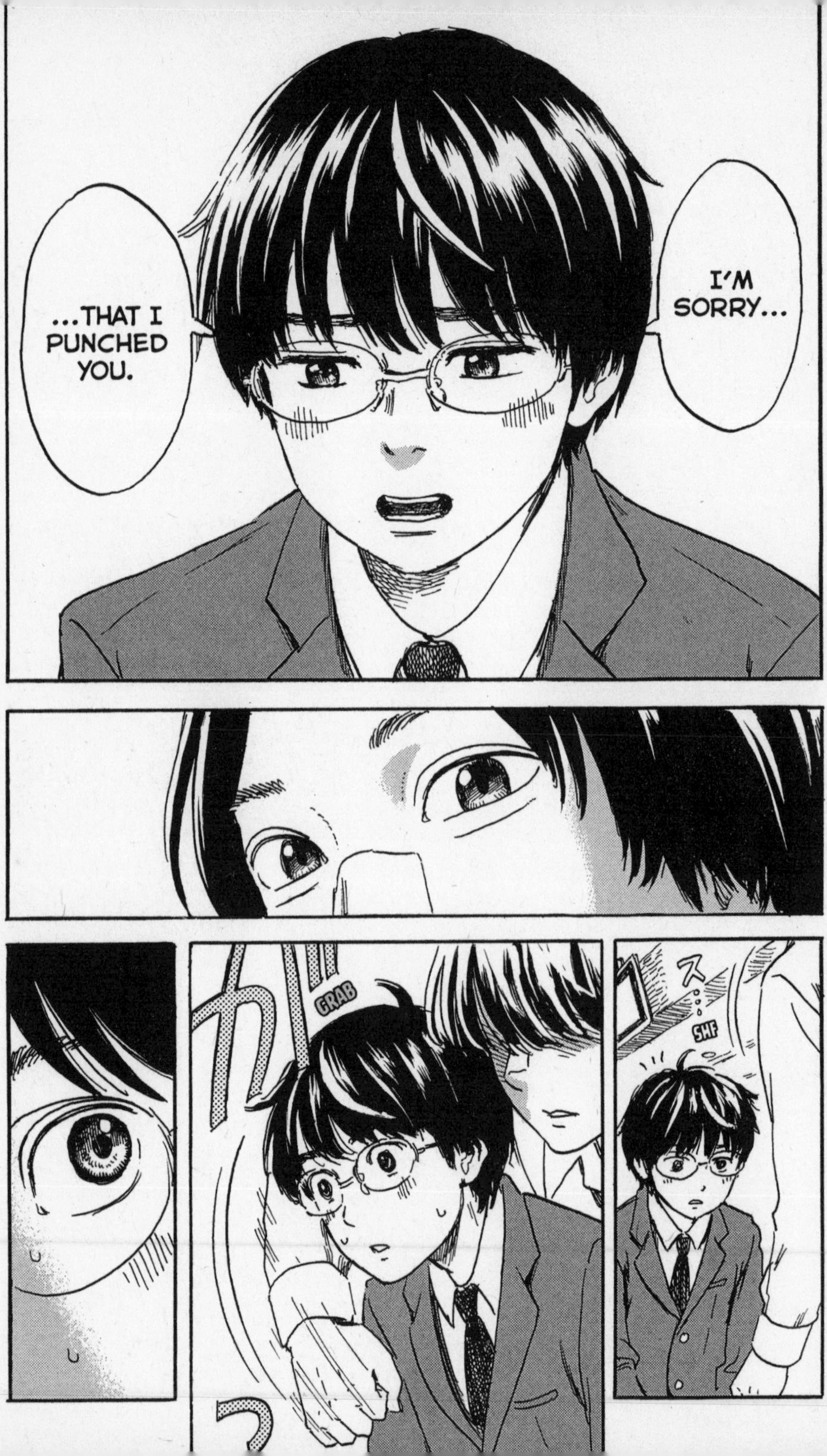
I'M SORRY...
...THAT I PUNCHED YOU.
ス
SHF
GRAB

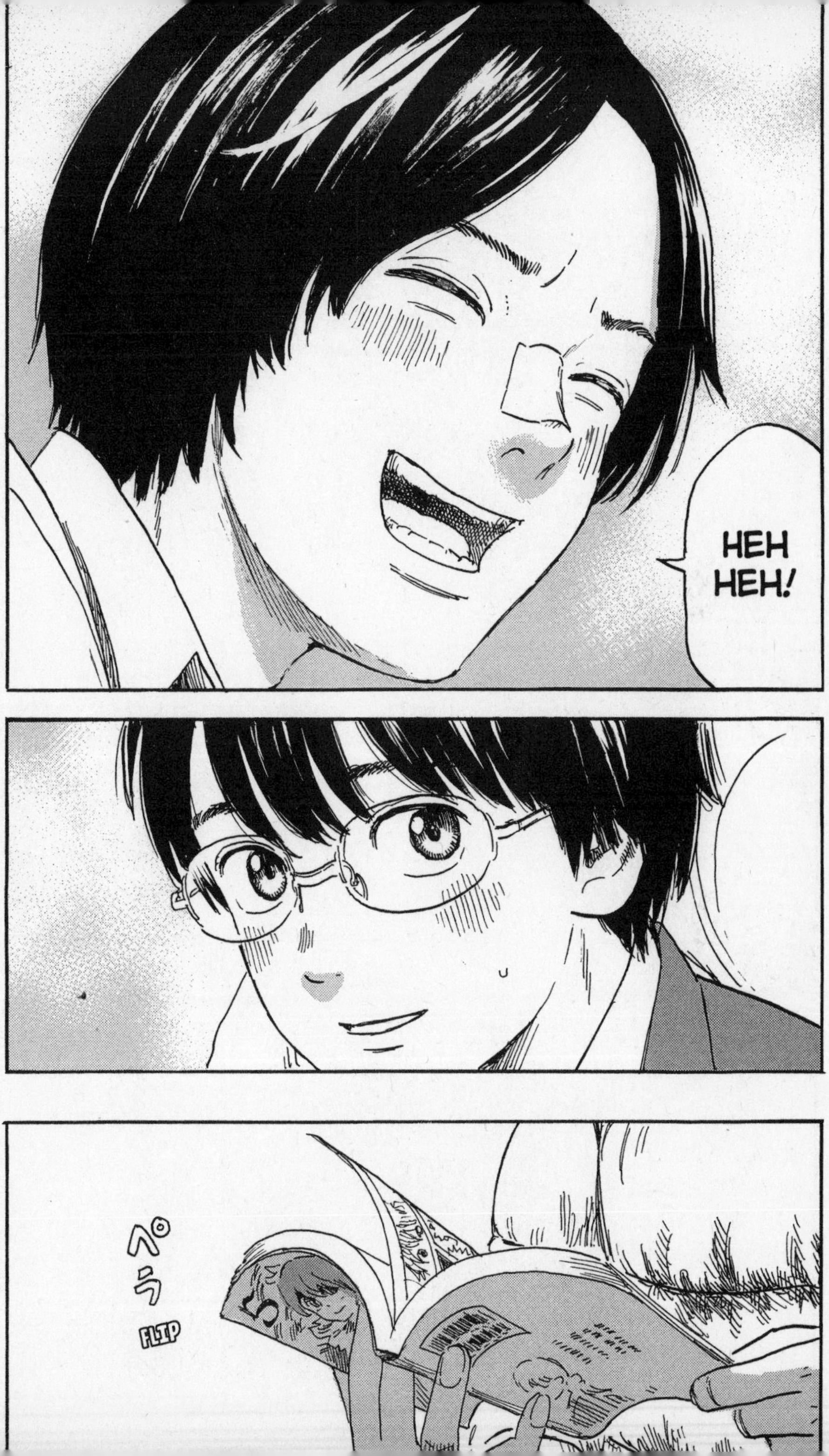
HEH HEH!
ぺら
FLIP

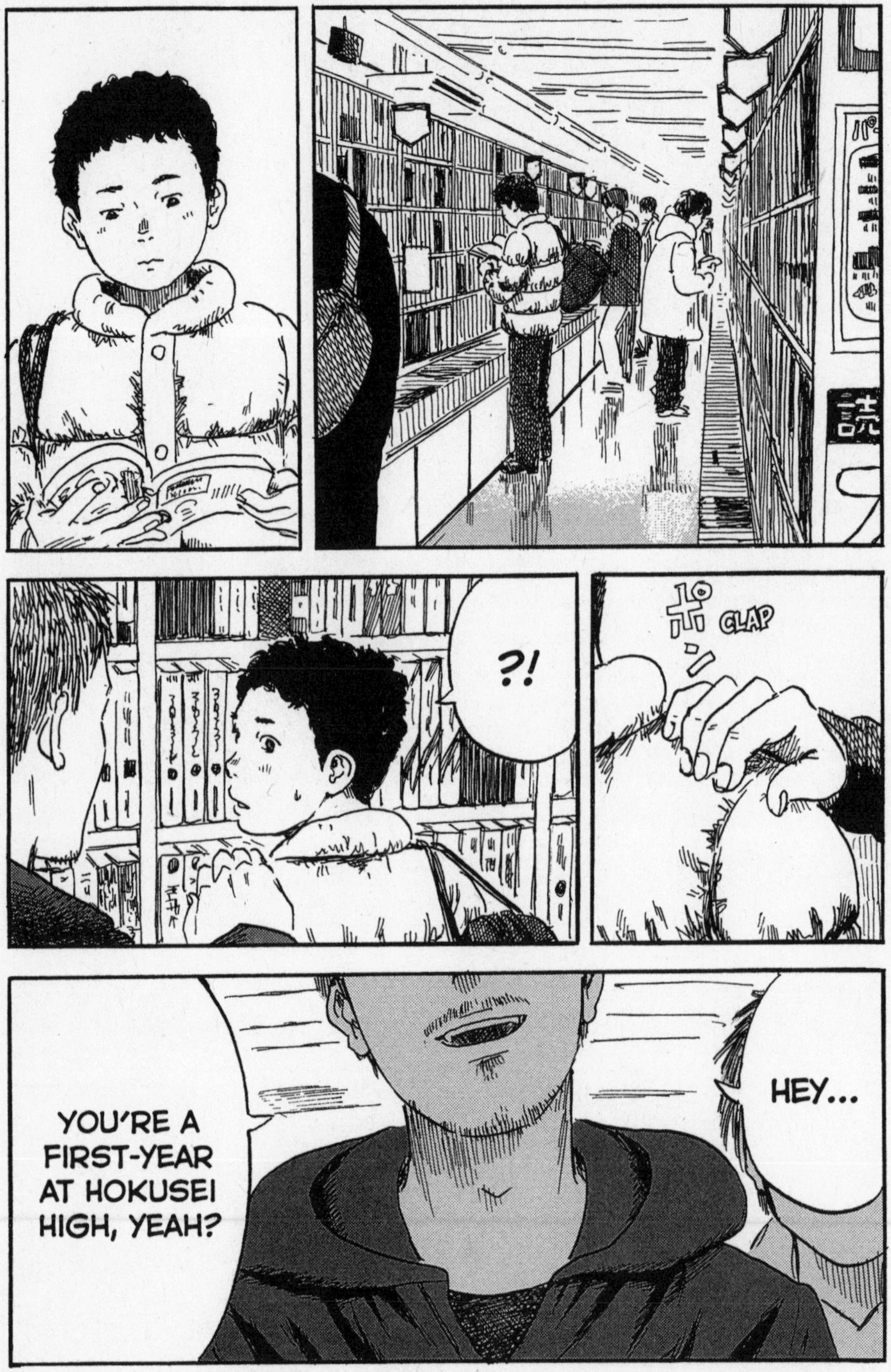
パ
読
ポン
CLAP
?!
HEY...
YOU'RE A FIRST-YEAR AT HOKUSEI HIGH, YEAH?

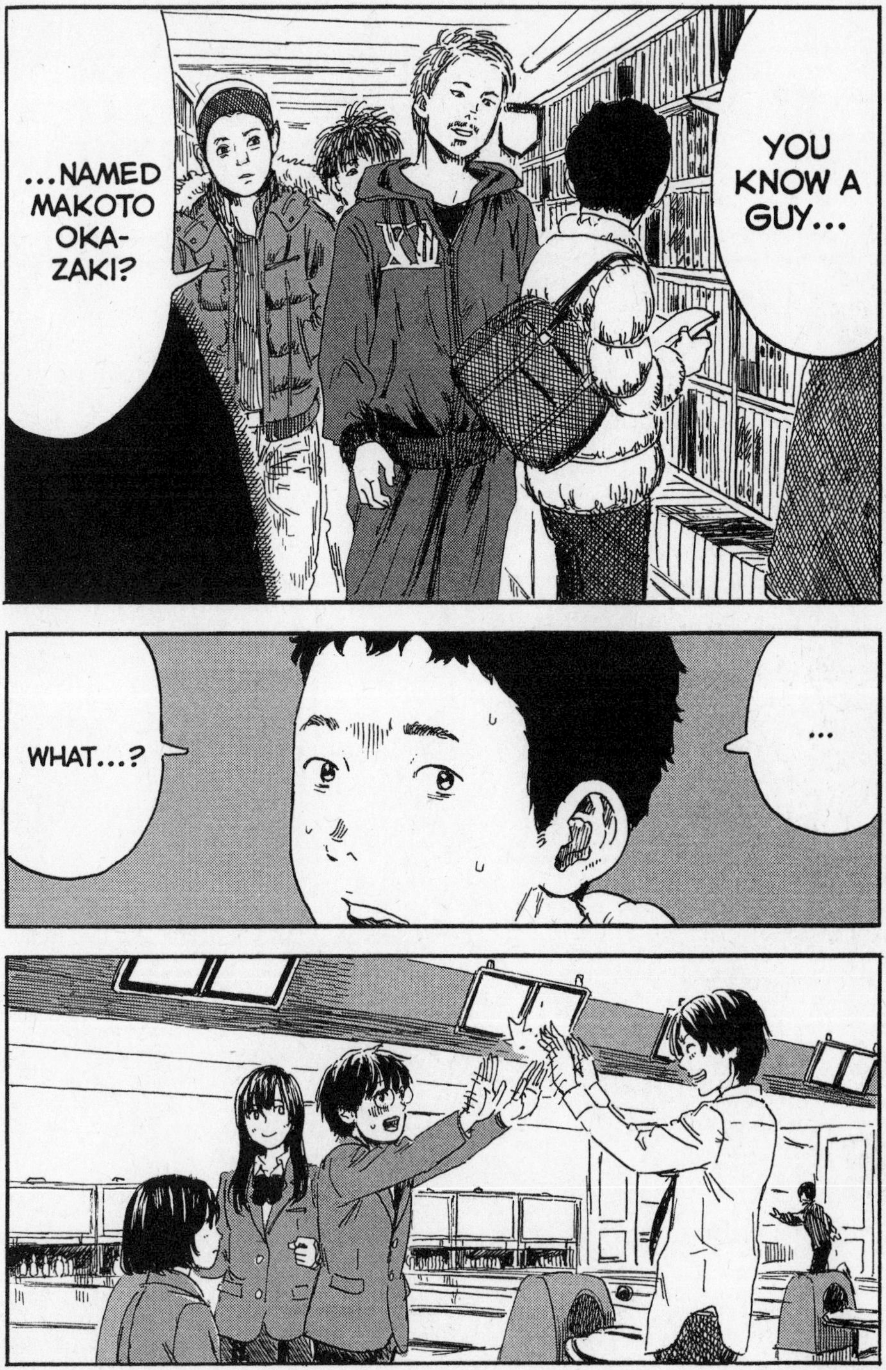
YOU KNOW A GUY...
...NAMED MAKOTO OKA-ZAKI?
...
WHAT...?

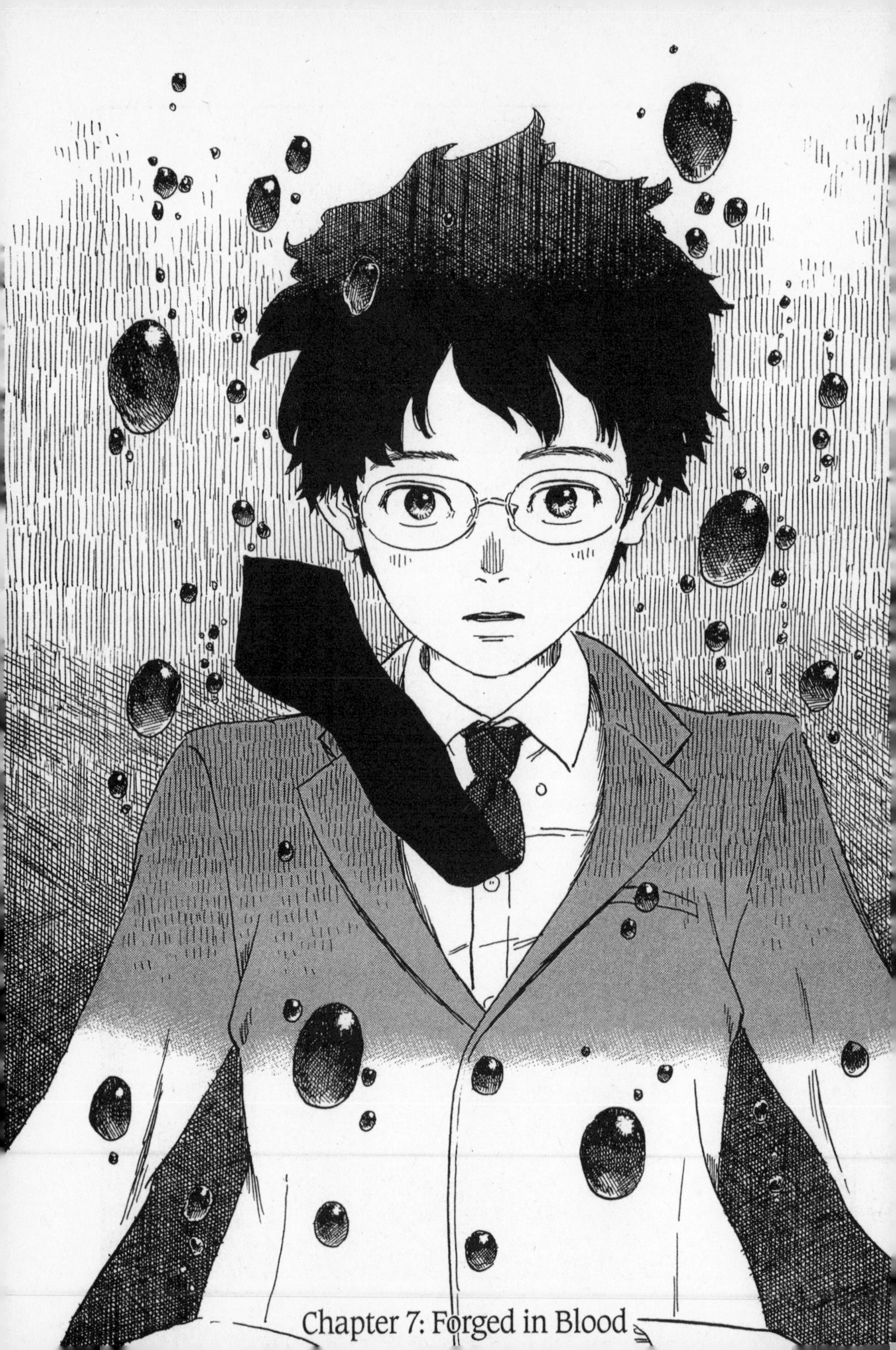

Chapter 7: Forged in Blood

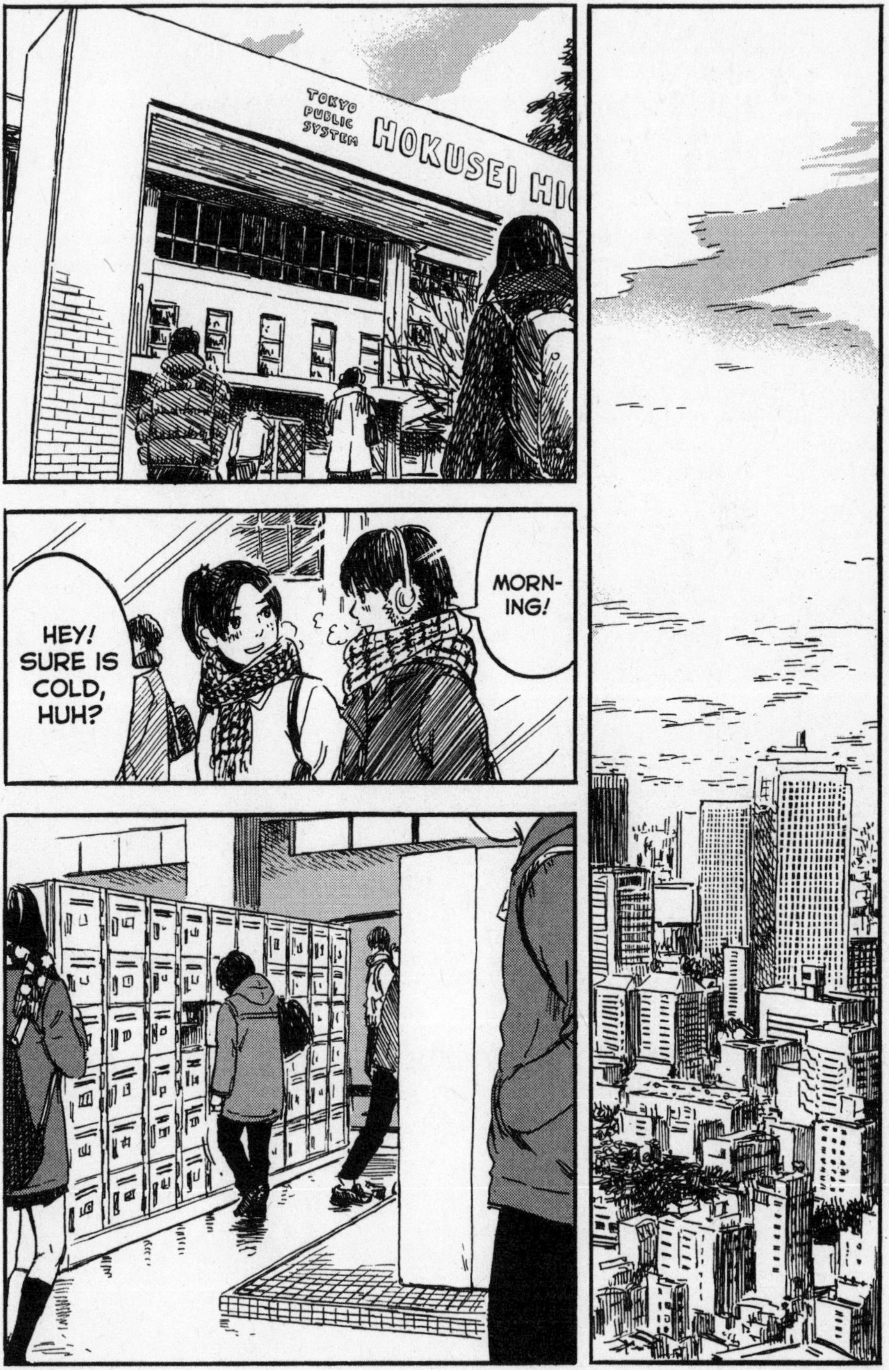
TOKYO PUBLIC SYSTEM
HOKUSEI HI
MORN-ING!
HEY! SURE IS COLD, HUH?

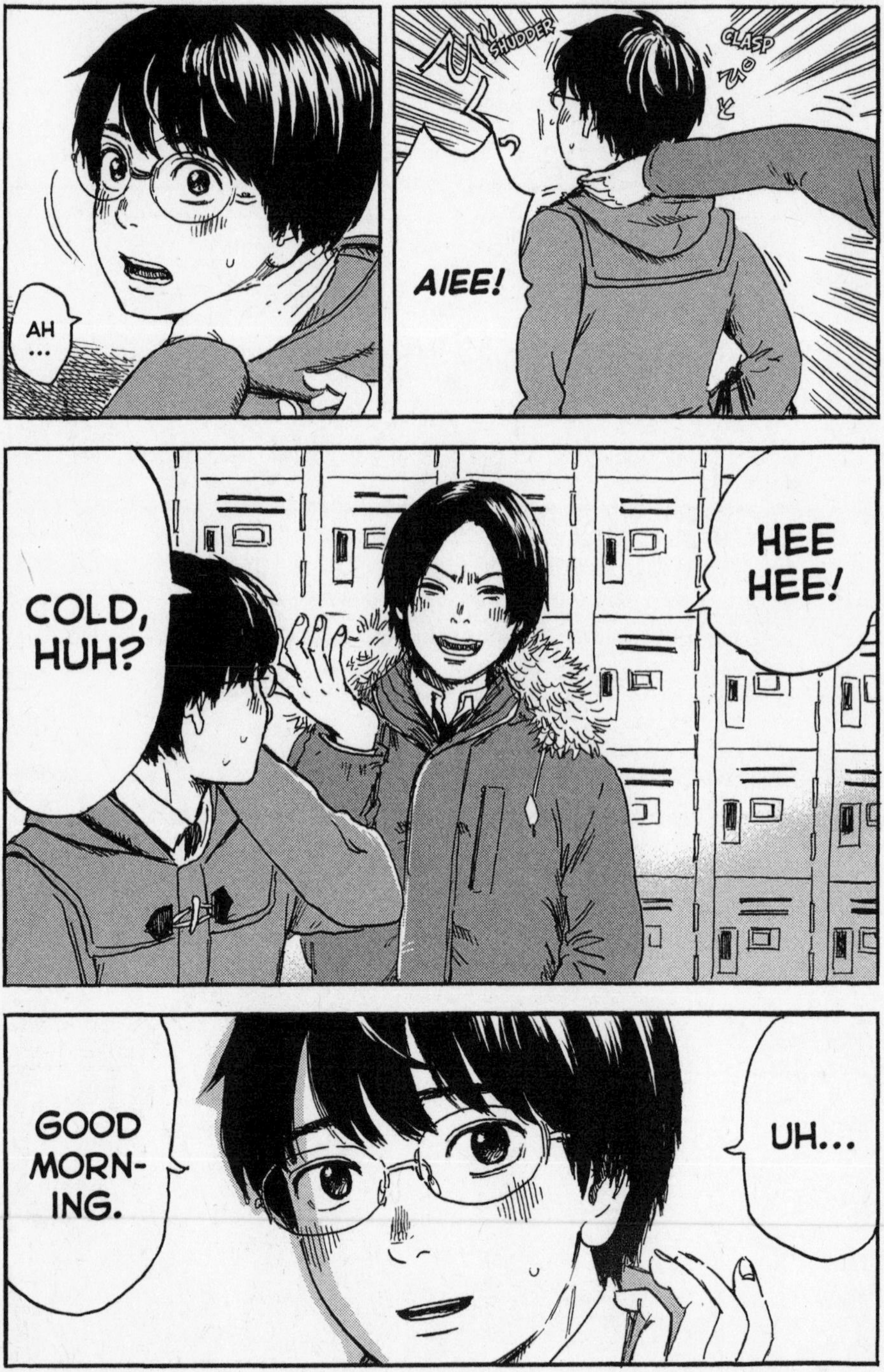
SHUDDER
CLASP
AIEE!
AH ...
HEE HEE!
COLD, HUH?
UH...
GOOD MORNING.

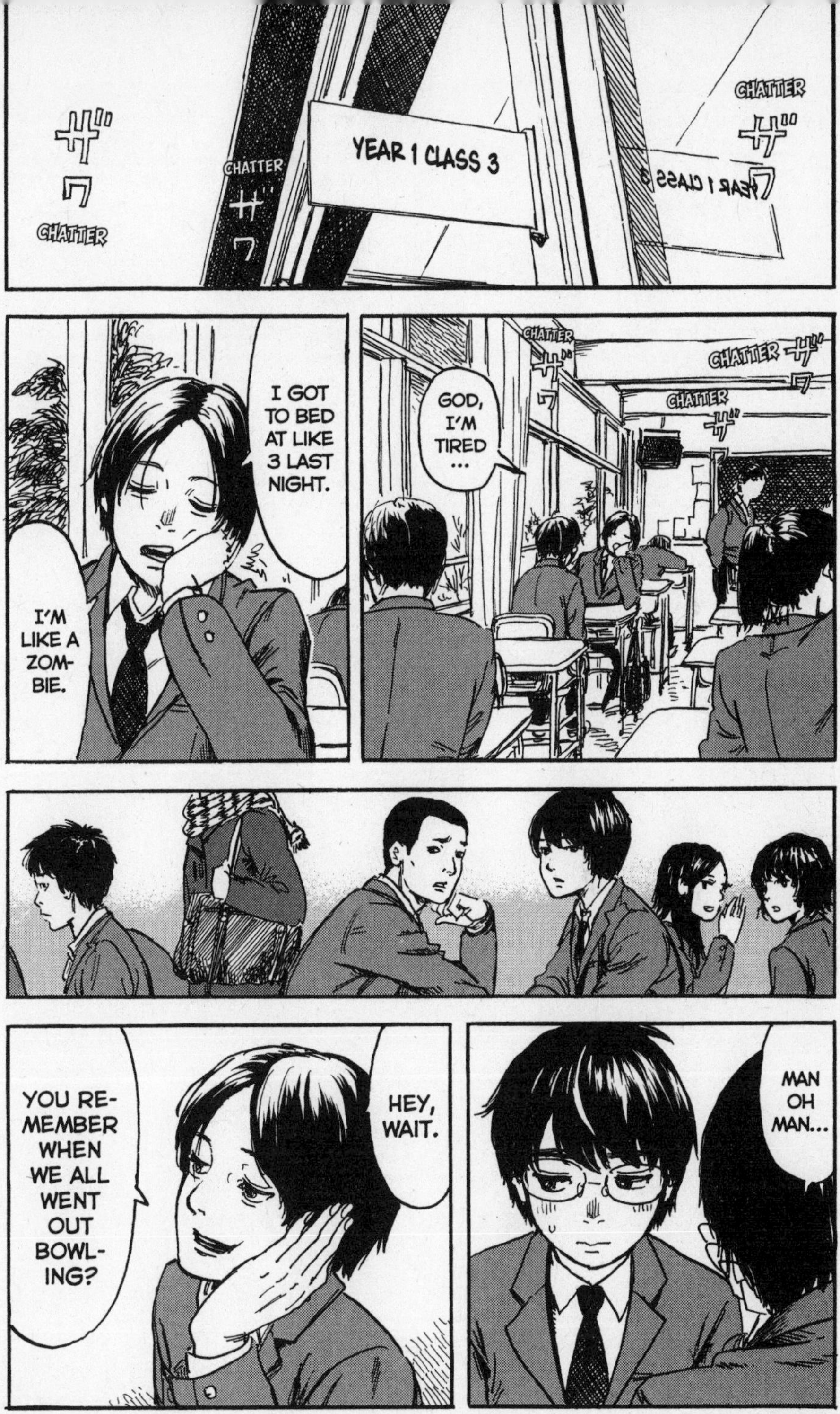
CHATTER
ザワ
YEAR 1 CLASS 3
CHATTER
ザワ
ザワ
CHATTER
CHATTER
ザワ
CHATTER
ザワ
CHATTER
ザワ
GOD, I'M TIRED...
I GOT TO BED AT LIKE 3 LAST NIGHT.
I'M LIKE A ZOM-BIE.
MAN OH MAN...
HEY, WAIT.
YOU RE-MEMBER WHEN WE ALL WENT OUT BOWL-ING?

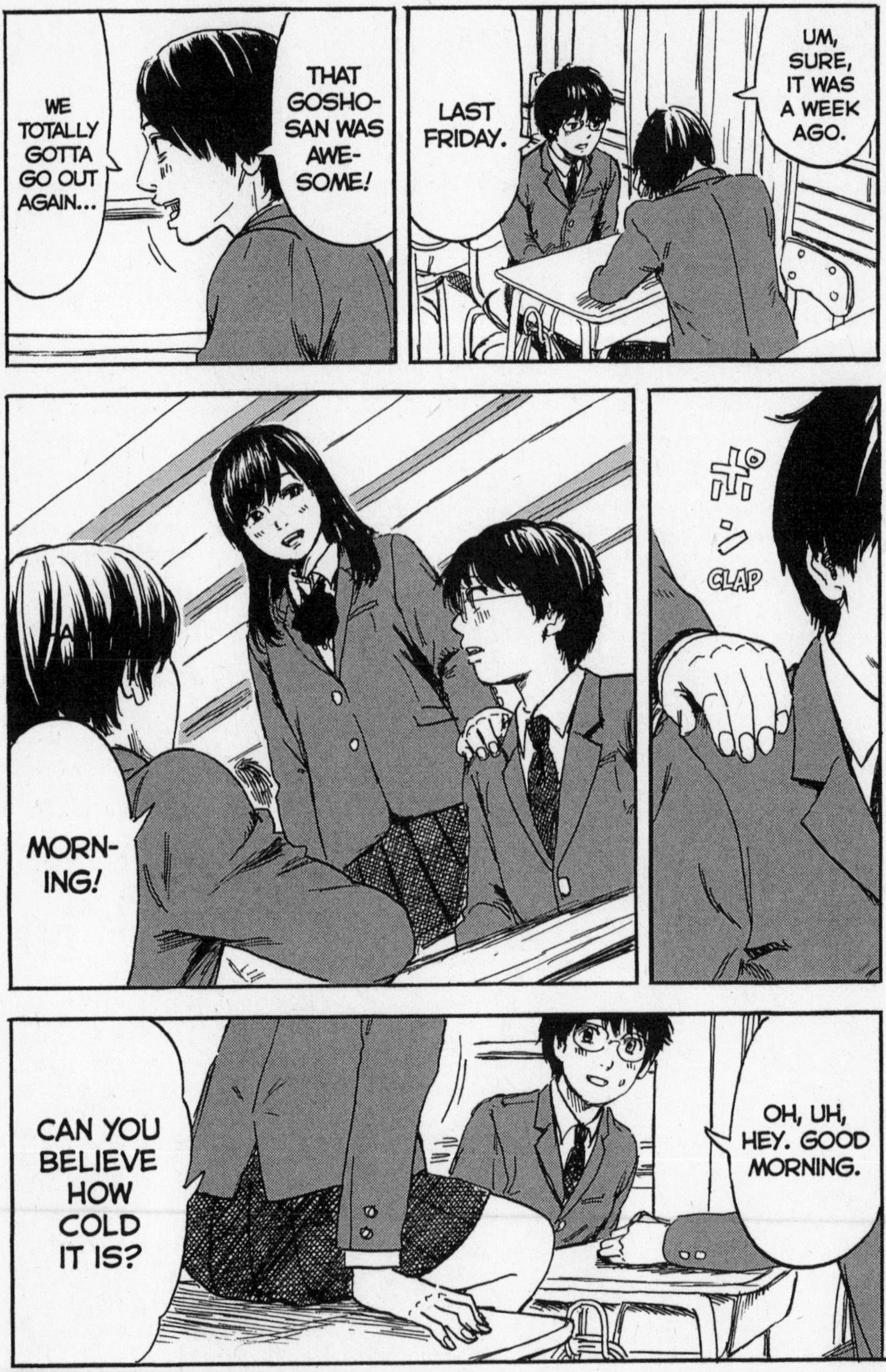
UM, SURE, IT WAS A WEEK AGO.
LAST FRIDAY.
THAT GOSHO-SAN WAS AWESOME!
WE TOTALLY GOTTA GO OUT AGAIN...
ポン
CLAP
MORNING!
OH, UH, HEY. GOOD MORNING.
CAN YOU BELIEVE HOW COLD IT IS?

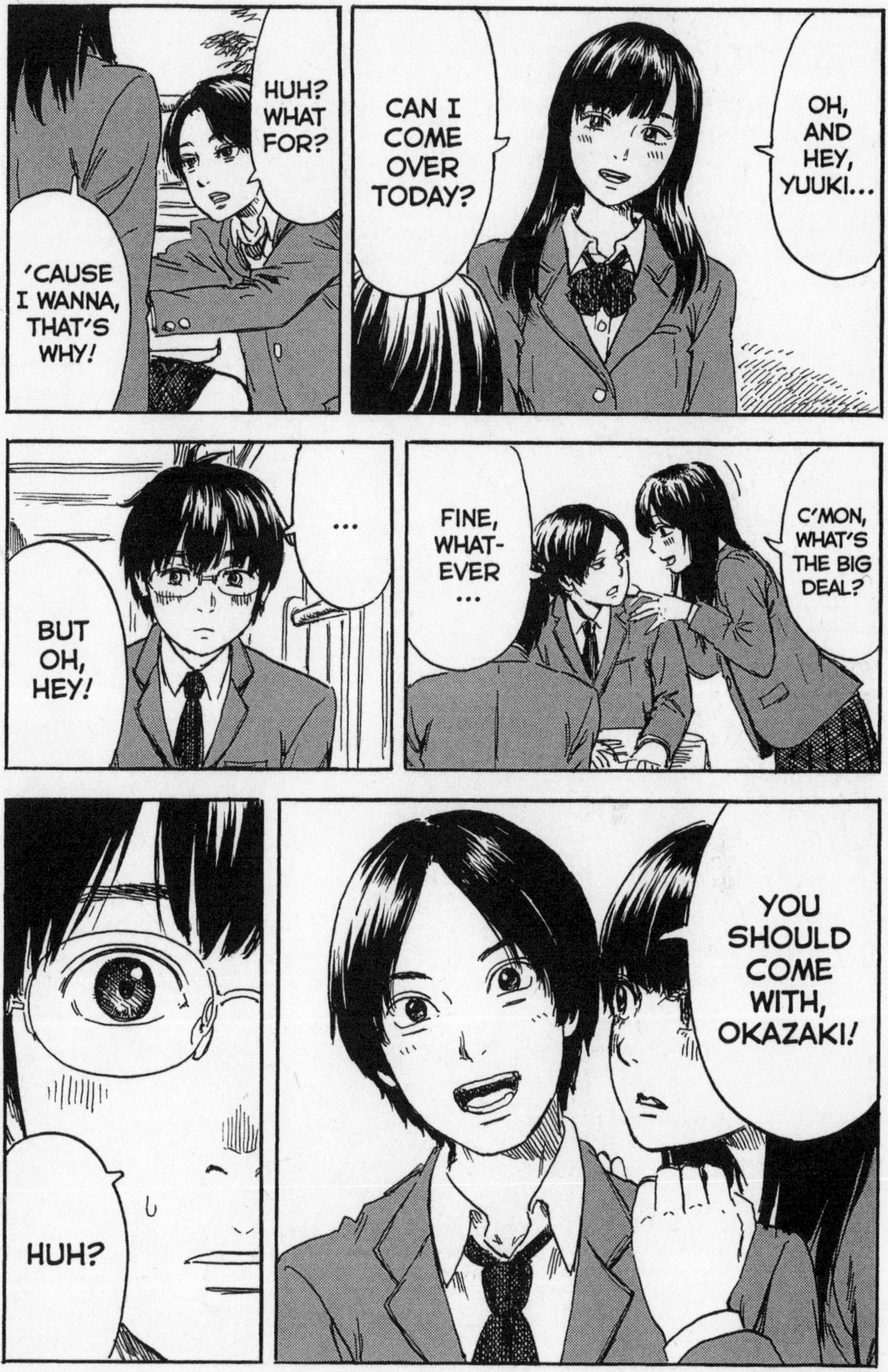
OH, AND HEY, YUUKI...
CAN I COME OVER TODAY?
HUH? WHAT FOR?
'CAUSE I WANNA, THAT'S WHY!
C'MON, WHAT'S THE BIG DEAL?
FINE, WHAT-EVER ...
...
BUT OH, HEY!
YOU SHOULD COME WITH, OKAZAKI!
HUH?

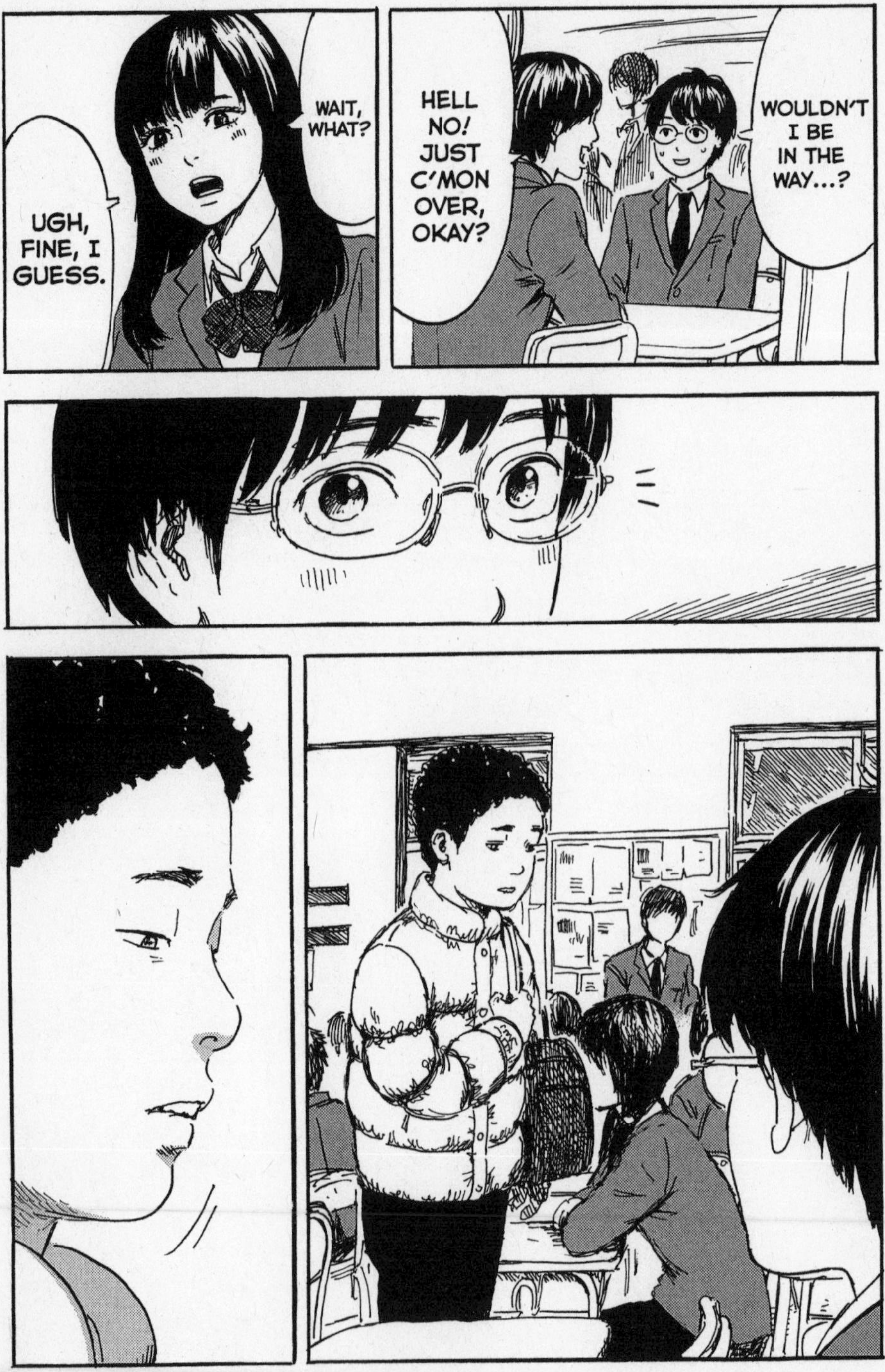
WOULDN'T I BE IN THE WAY...?
HELL NO! JUST C'MON OVER, OKAY?
WAIT, WHAT?
UGH, FINE, I GUESS.

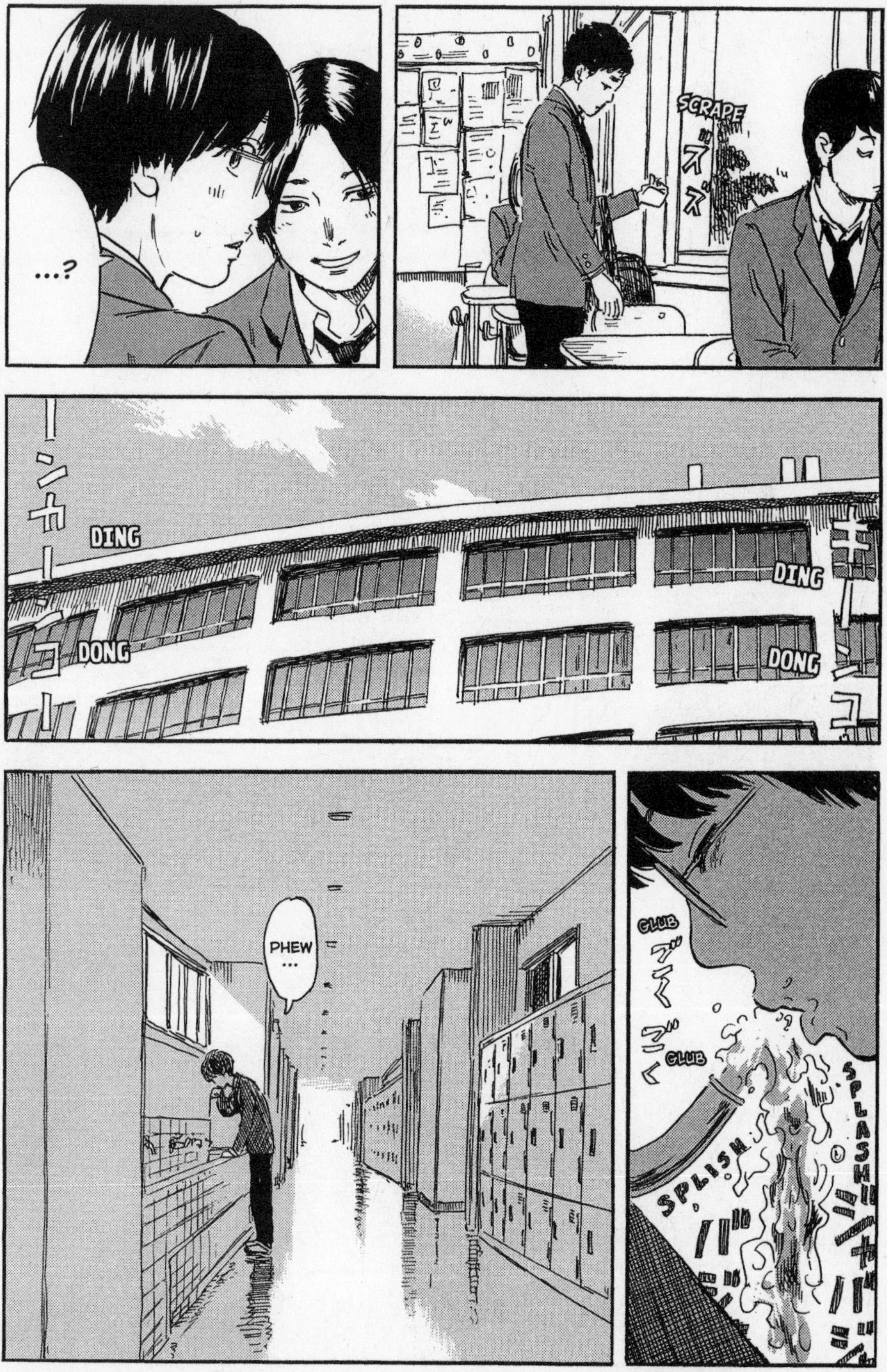
SCRAPE
ズズ
...?
DING
DONG
DING
DONG
GLUB
GLUB
SPLISH
SPLASH
PHEW...

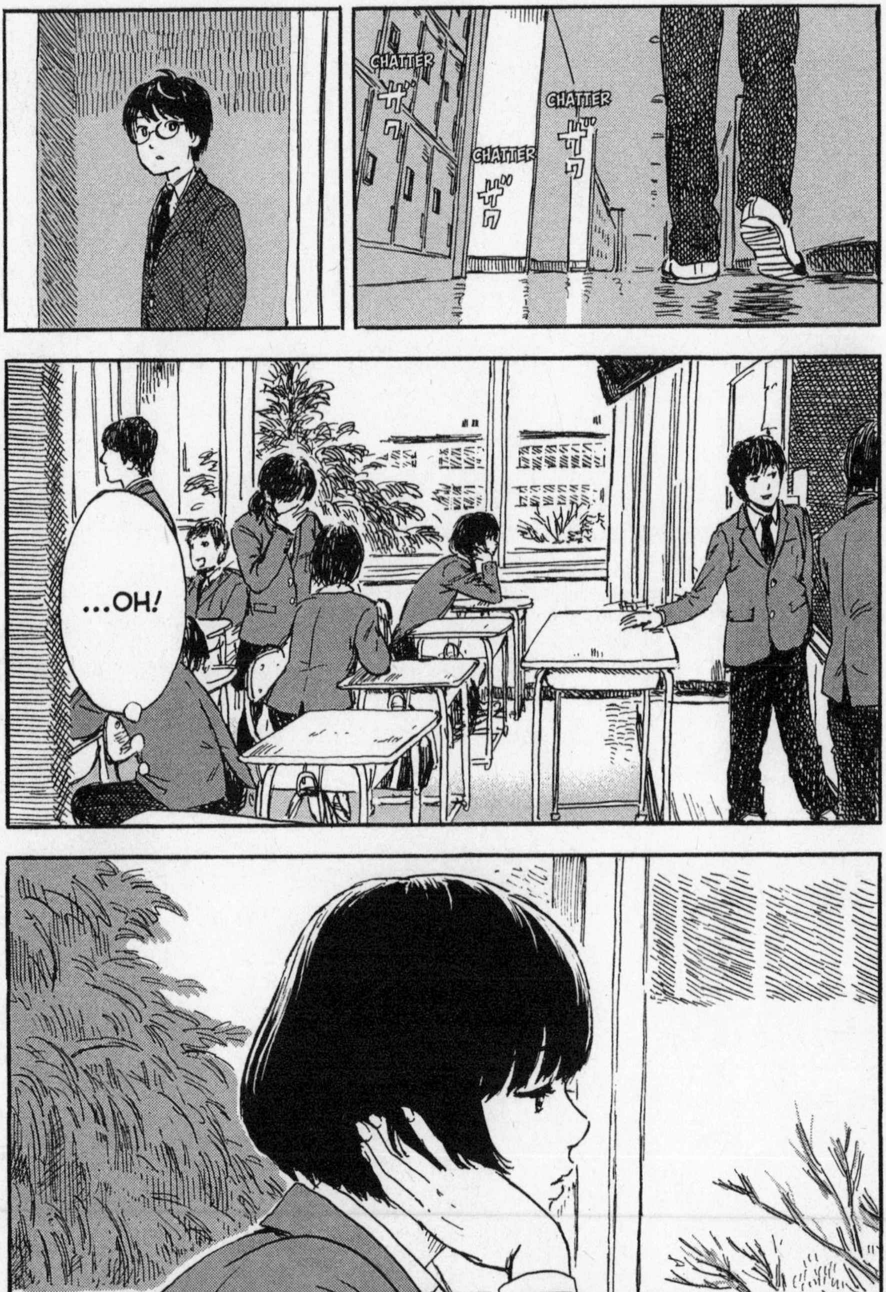
CHATTER
ザワ
CHATTER
ザワ
CHATTER
ザワ
...OH!

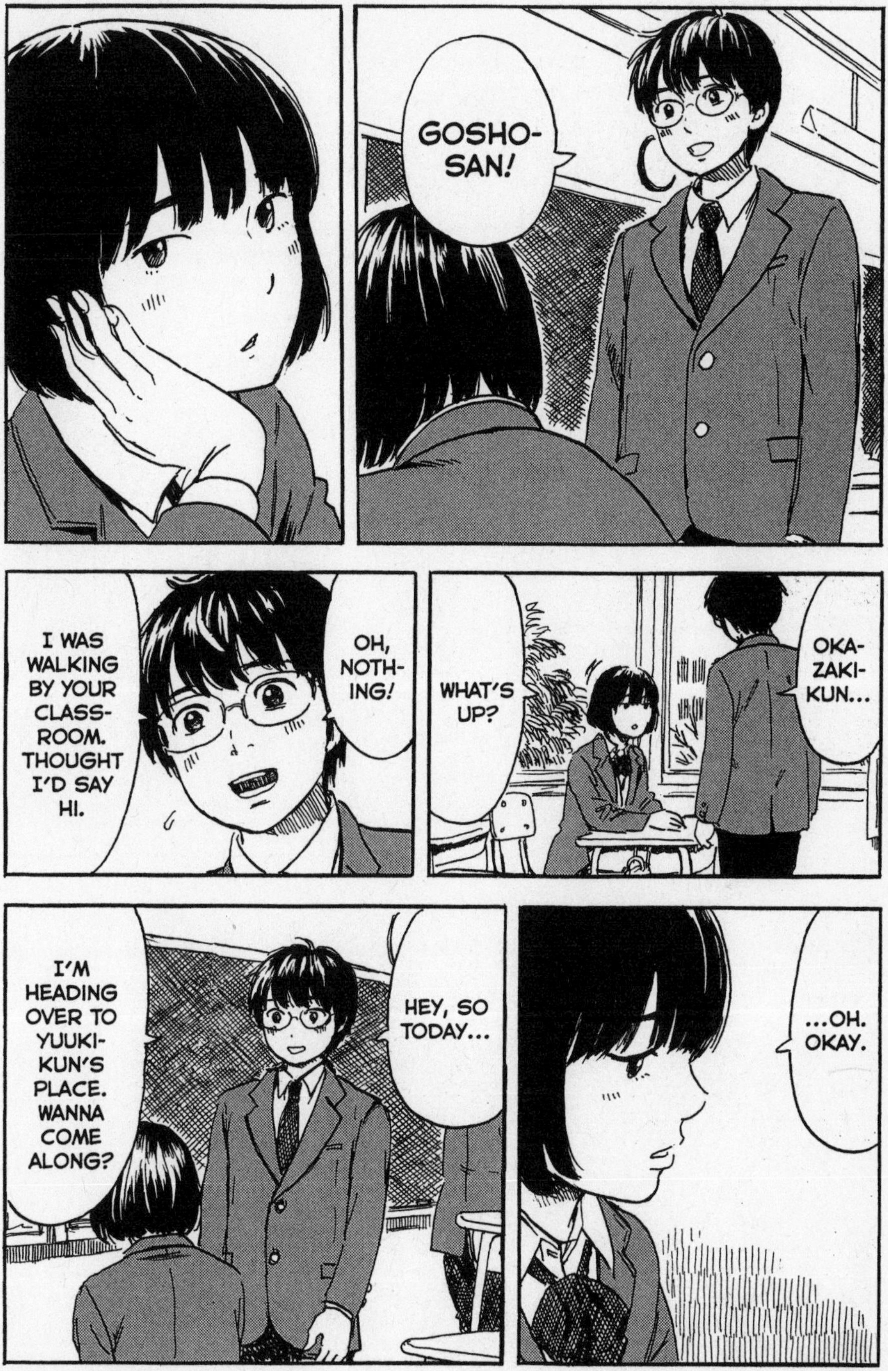
GOSHO-SAN!
OKAZAKI-KUN...
WHAT'S UP?
OH, NOTHING!
I WAS WALKING BY YOUR CLASSROOM. THOUGHT I'D SAY HI.
...OH. OKAY.
HEY, SO TODAY...
I'M HEADING OVER TO YUUKI-KUN'S PLACE. WANNA COME ALONG?

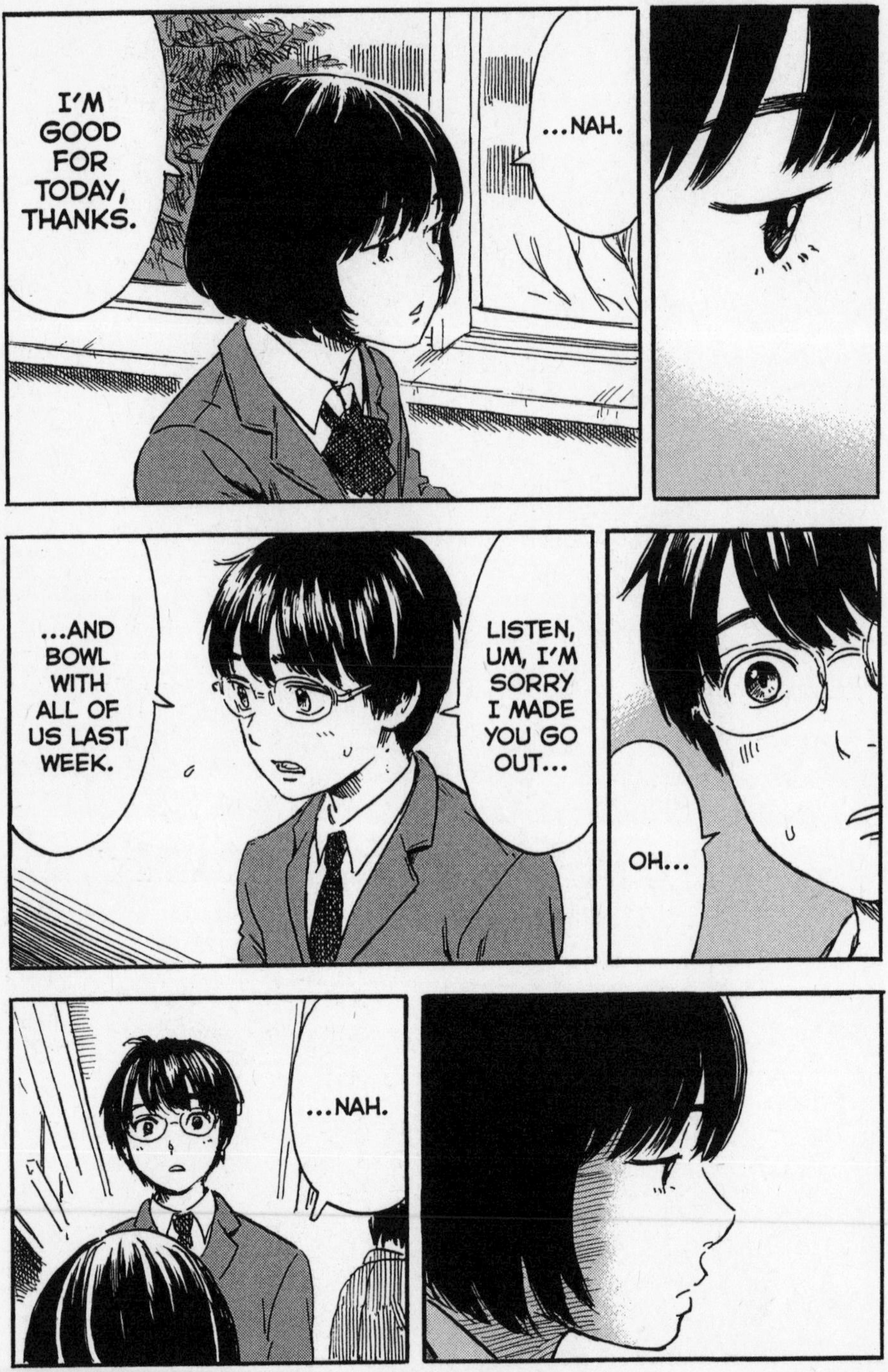
...NAH.
I'M GOOD FOR TODAY, THANKS.
OH...
LISTEN, UM, I'M SORRY I MADE YOU GO OUT...
...AND BOWL WITH ALL OF US LAST WEEK.
...NAH.

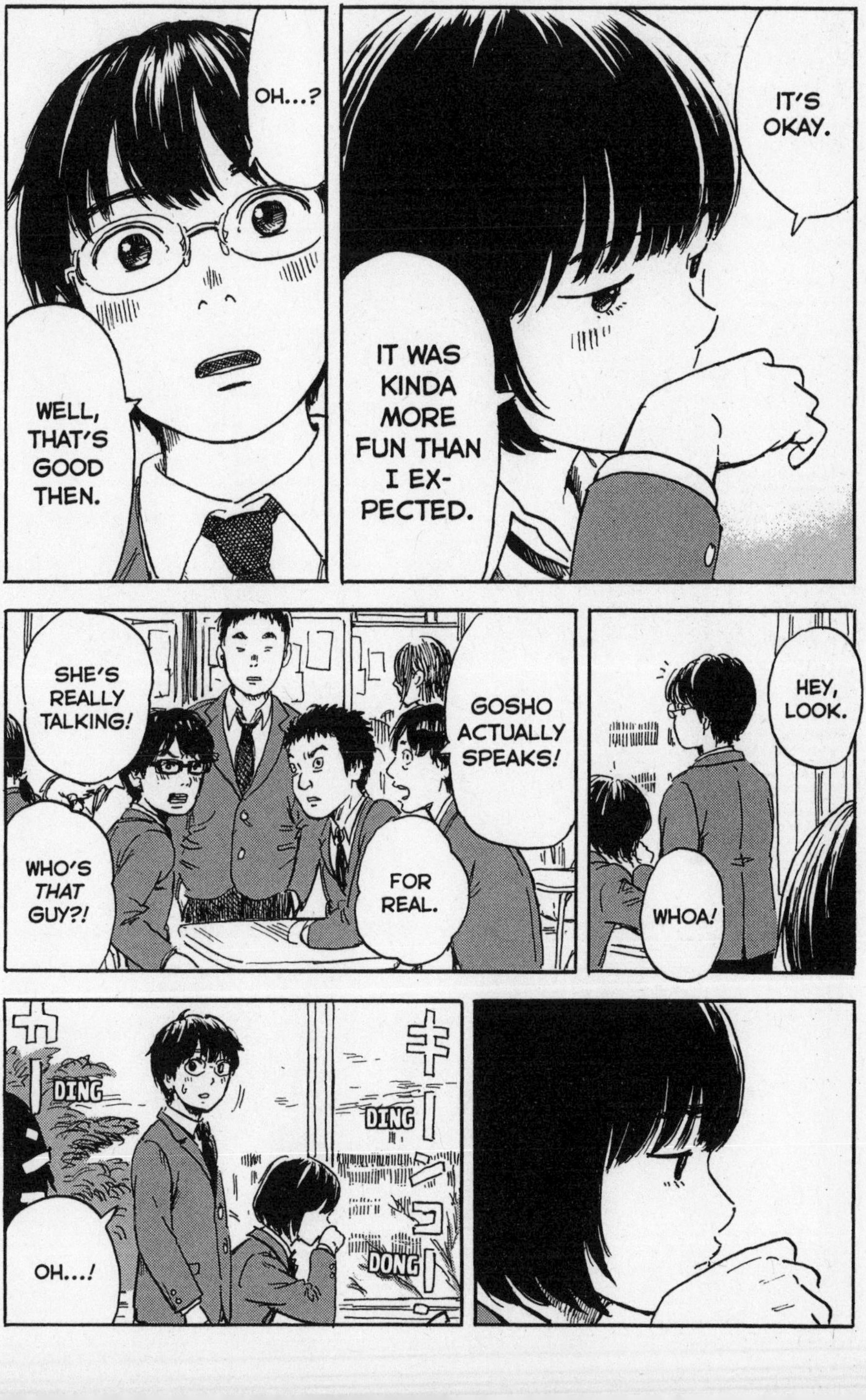
IT'S OKAY.
IT WAS KINDA MORE FUN THAN I EX- PECTED.
OH...?
WELL, THAT'S GOOD THEN.
HEY, LOOK.
WHOA!
GOSHO ACTUALLY SPEAKS!
SHE'S REALLY TALKING!
FOR REAL.
WHO'S THAT GUY?!
キーンコーン
DING
DING
DONG
カー
DING
OH...!

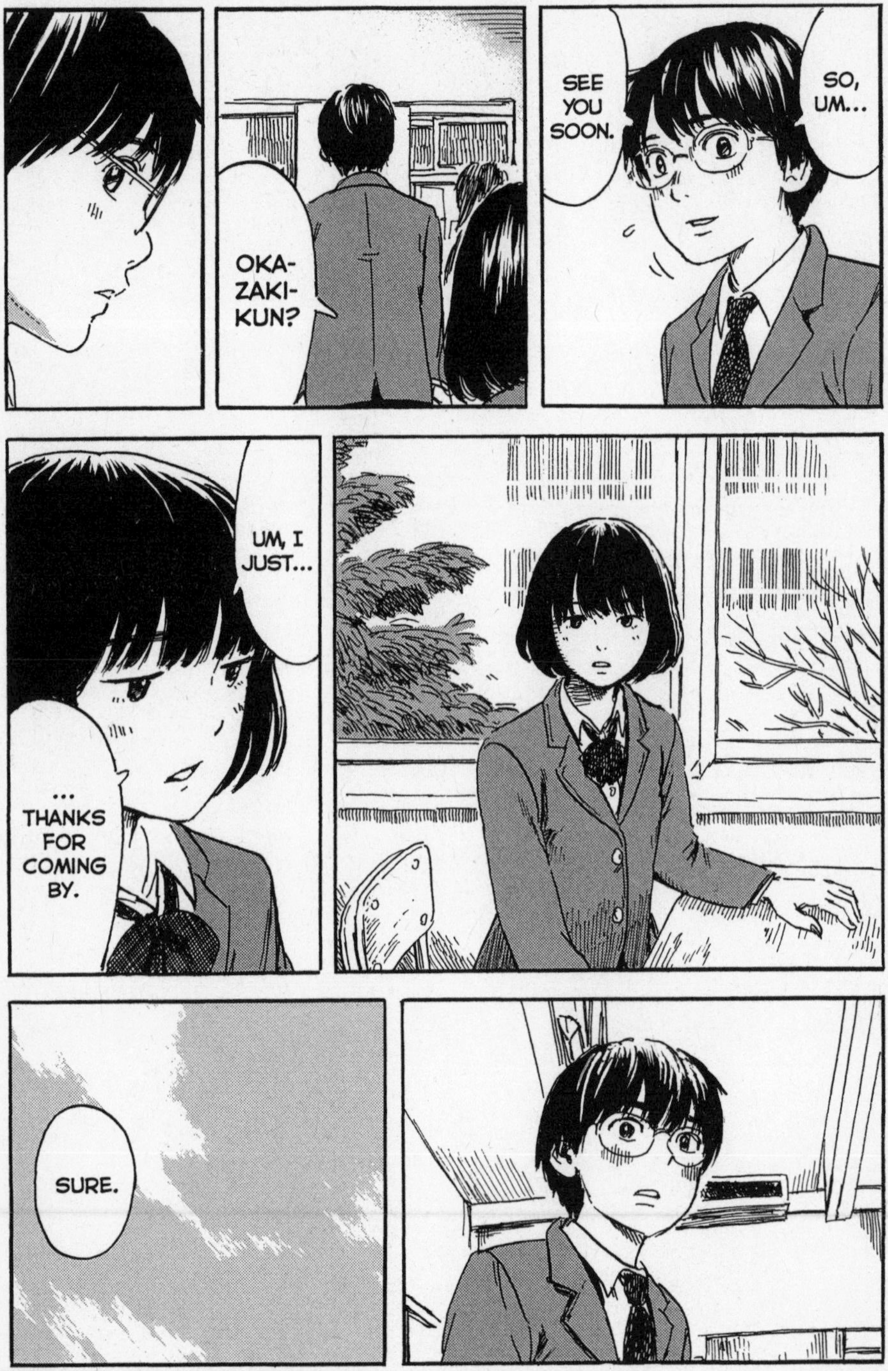
SO, UM...
SEE YOU SOON.
OKA-ZAKI-KUN?
UM, I JUST...
... THANKS FOR COMING BY.
SURE.

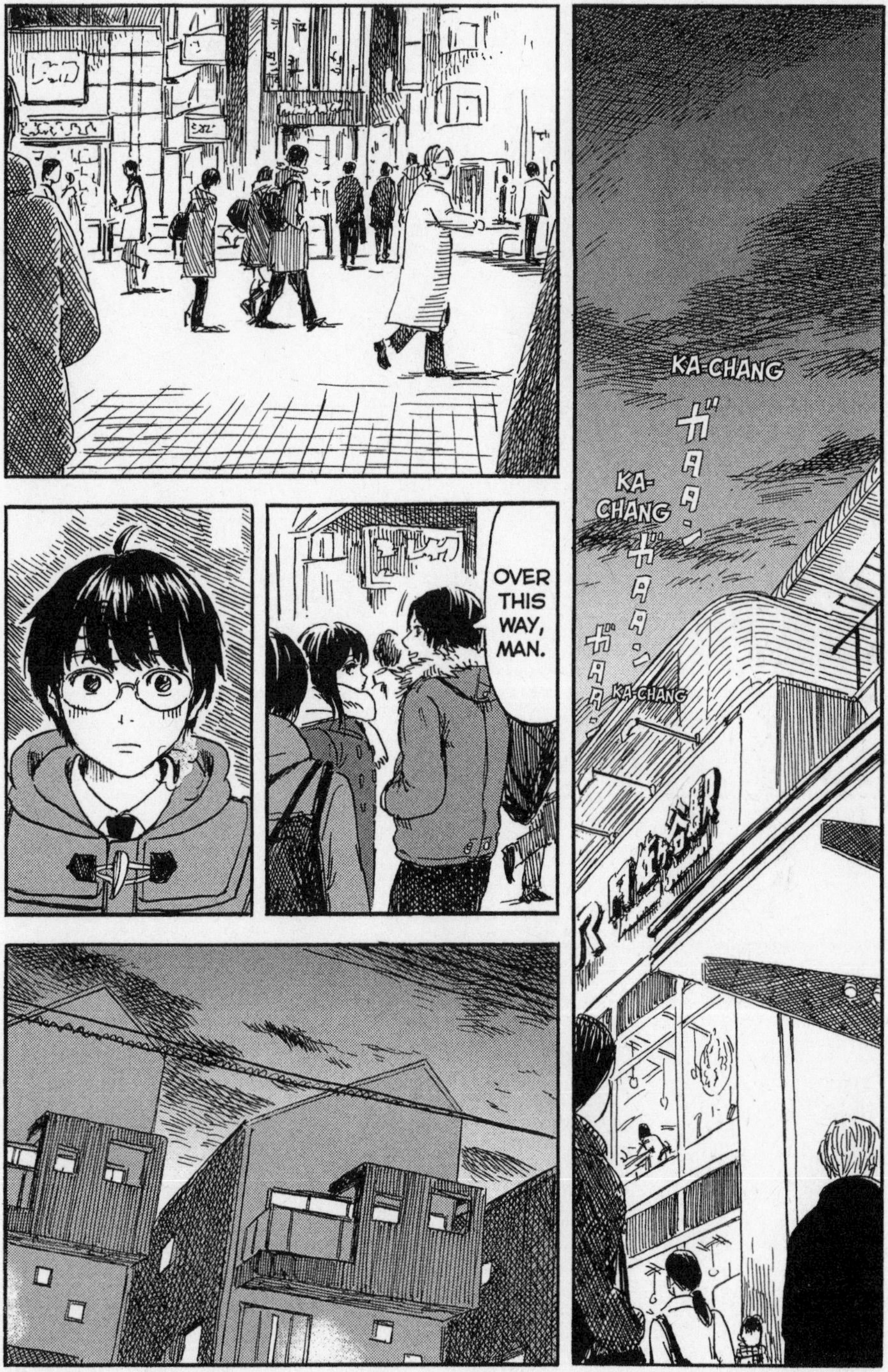
KA-CHANG
ガタタン
KA-CHANG
ガタタン
ガタタン
KA-CHANG
OVER THIS WAY, MAN.

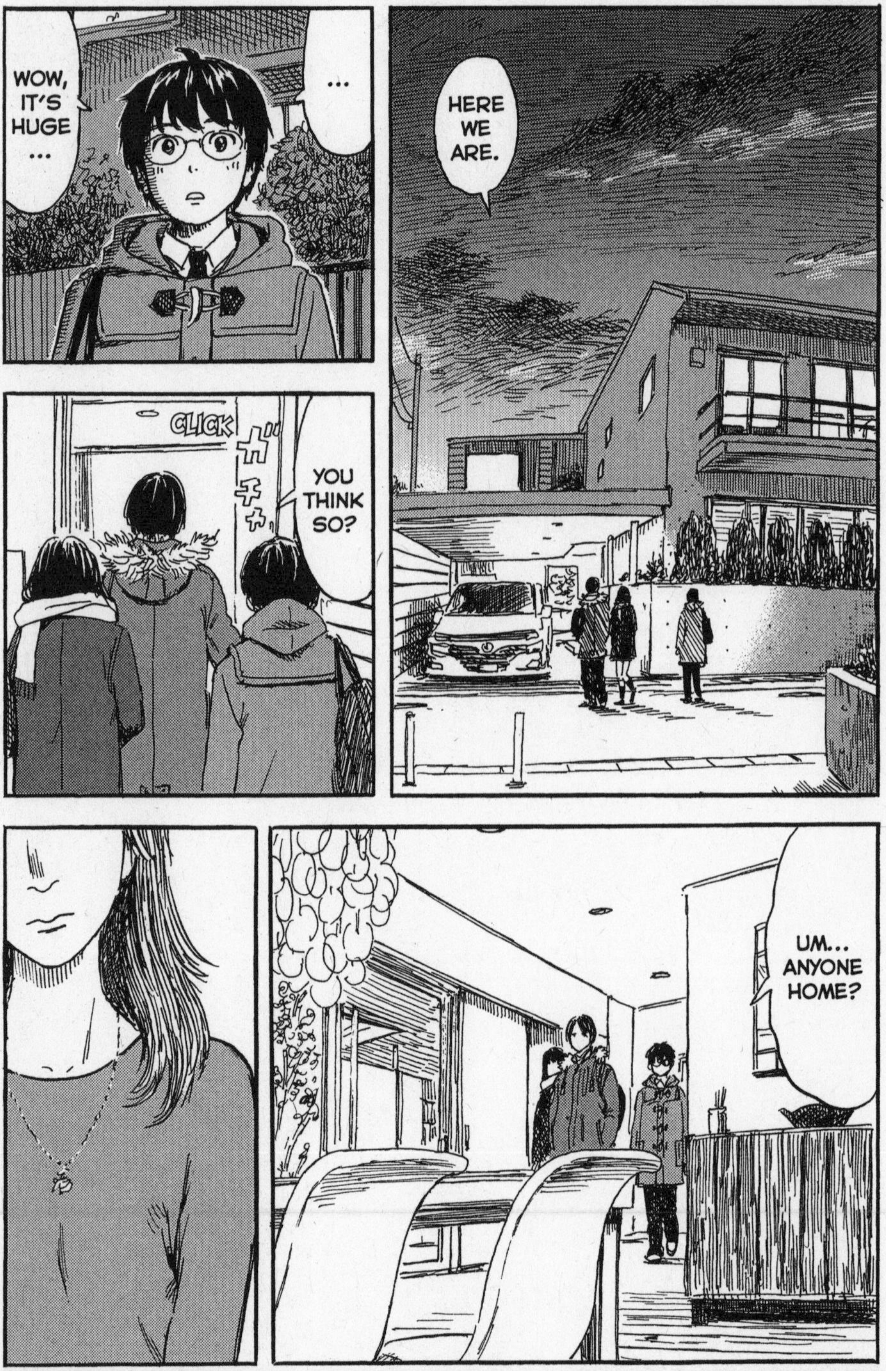
HERE WE ARE.
...
WOW, IT'S HUGE ...
CLICK
ガチャ
YOU THINK SO?
UM... ANYONE HOME?

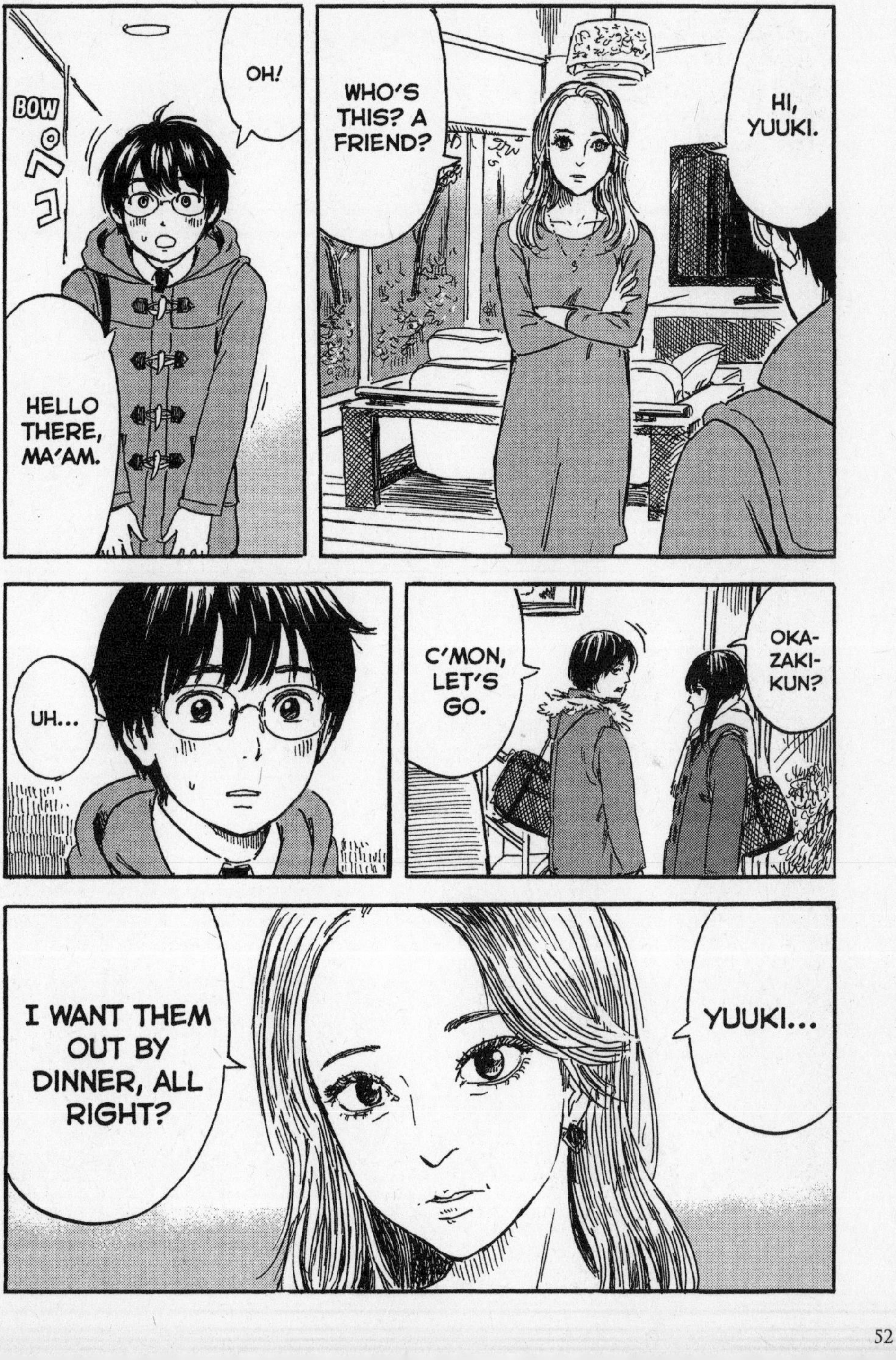
HI, YUUKI.
WHO'S THIS? A FRIEND?
OH!
BOW
HELLO THERE, MA'AM.
OKA-ZAKI-KUN?
C'MON, LET'S GO.
UH...
YUUKI...
I WANT THEM OUT BY DINNER, ALL RIGHT?

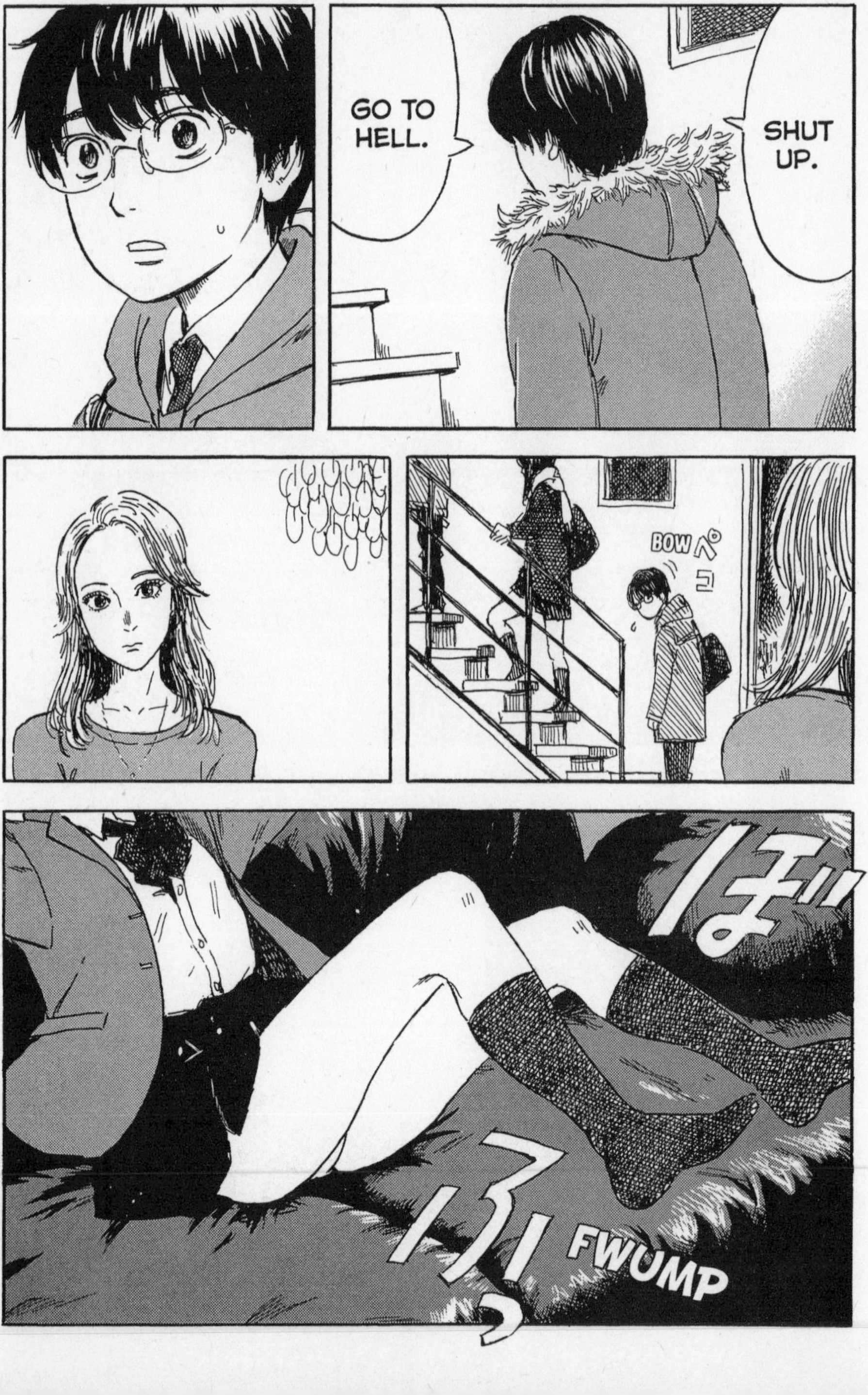
SHUT UP.
GO TO HELL.
BOW
ペコ
FWUMP

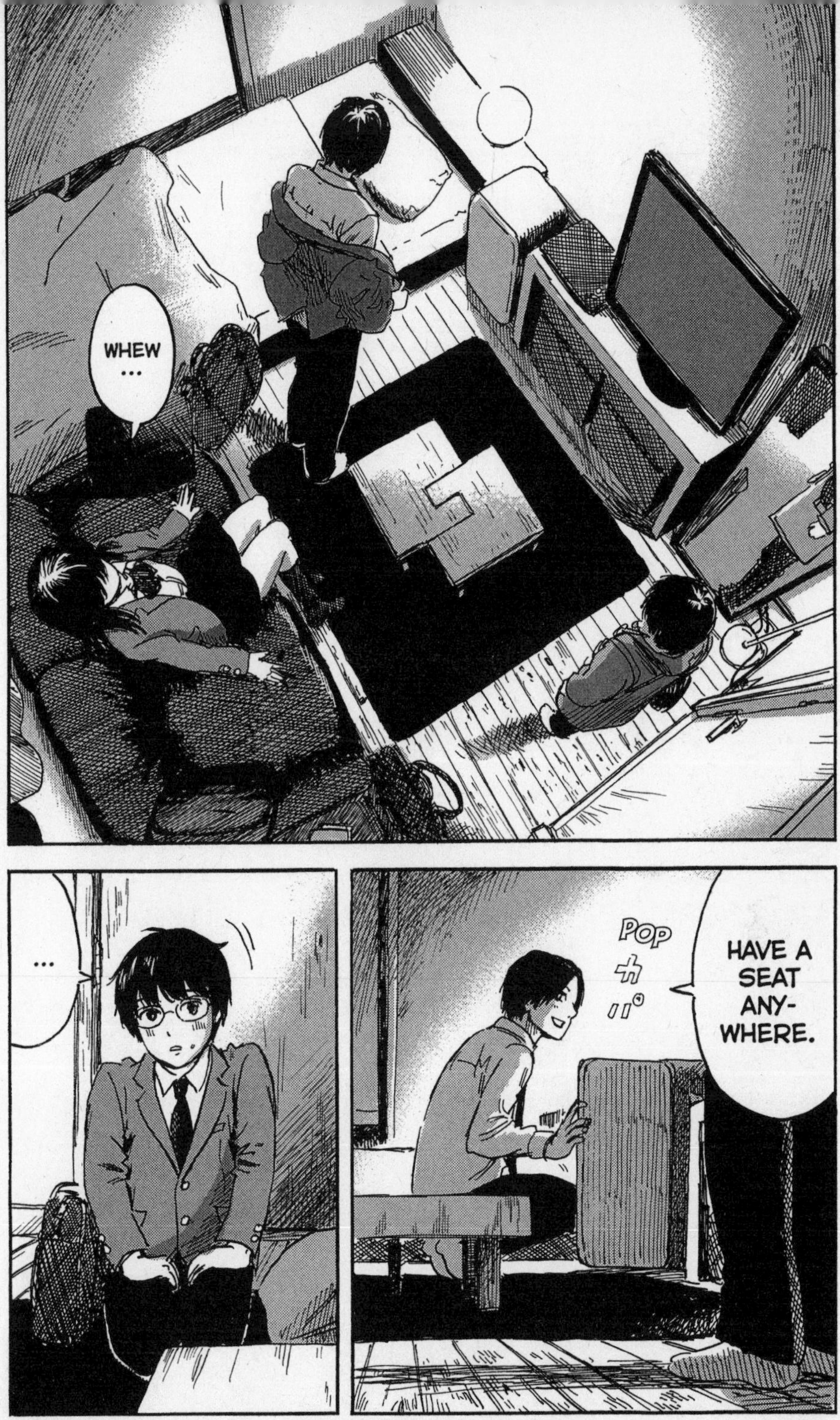
WHEW ...
HAVE A SEAT ANY-WHERE.
POP
カパ
...

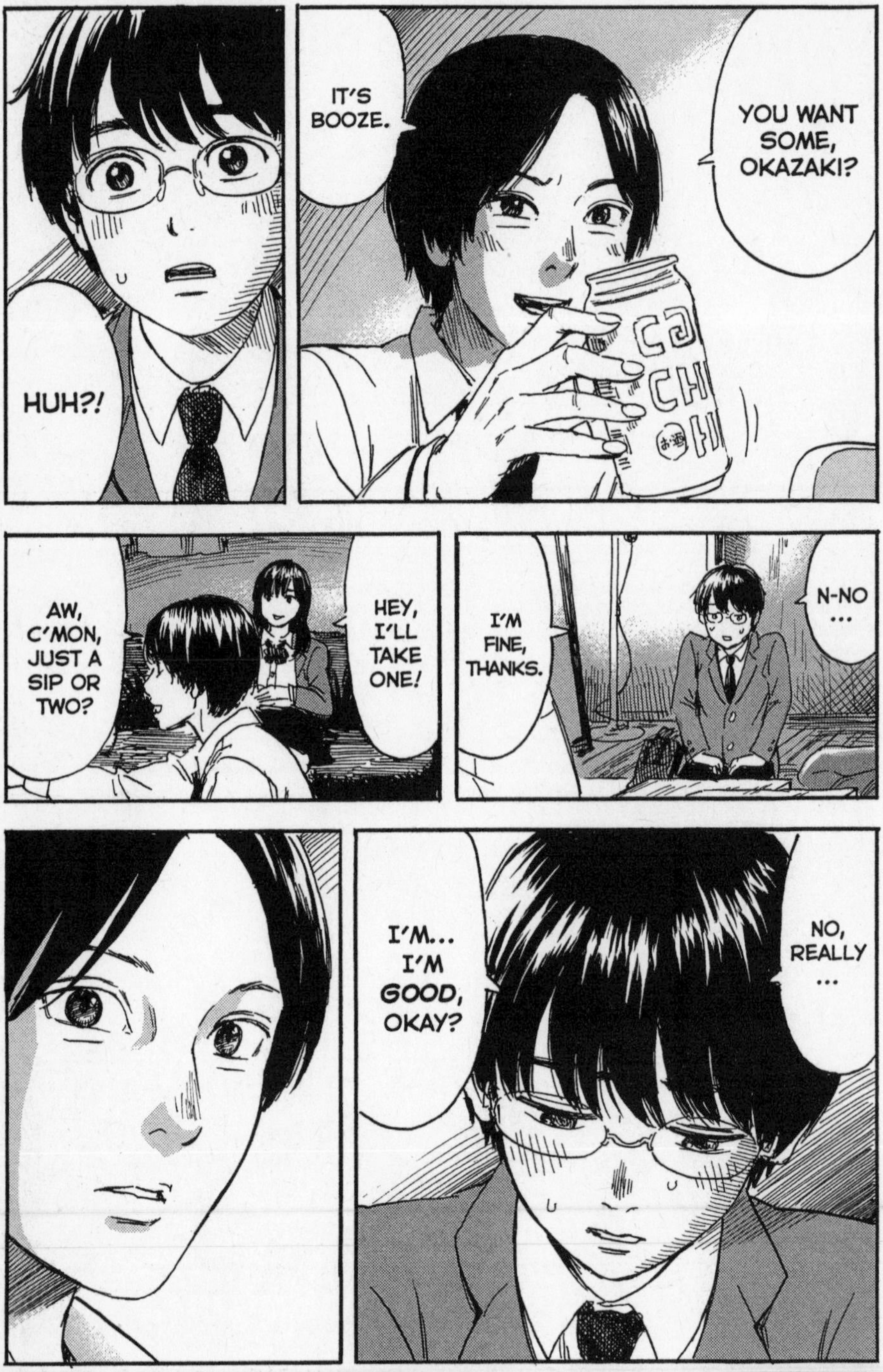
IT'S BOOZE.
YOU WANT SOME, OKAZAKI?
HUH?!
N-NO ...
I'M FINE, THANKS.
HEY, I'LL TAKE ONE!
AW, C'MON, JUST A SIP OR TWO?
NO, REALLY ...
I'M... I'M *GOOD*, OKAY?

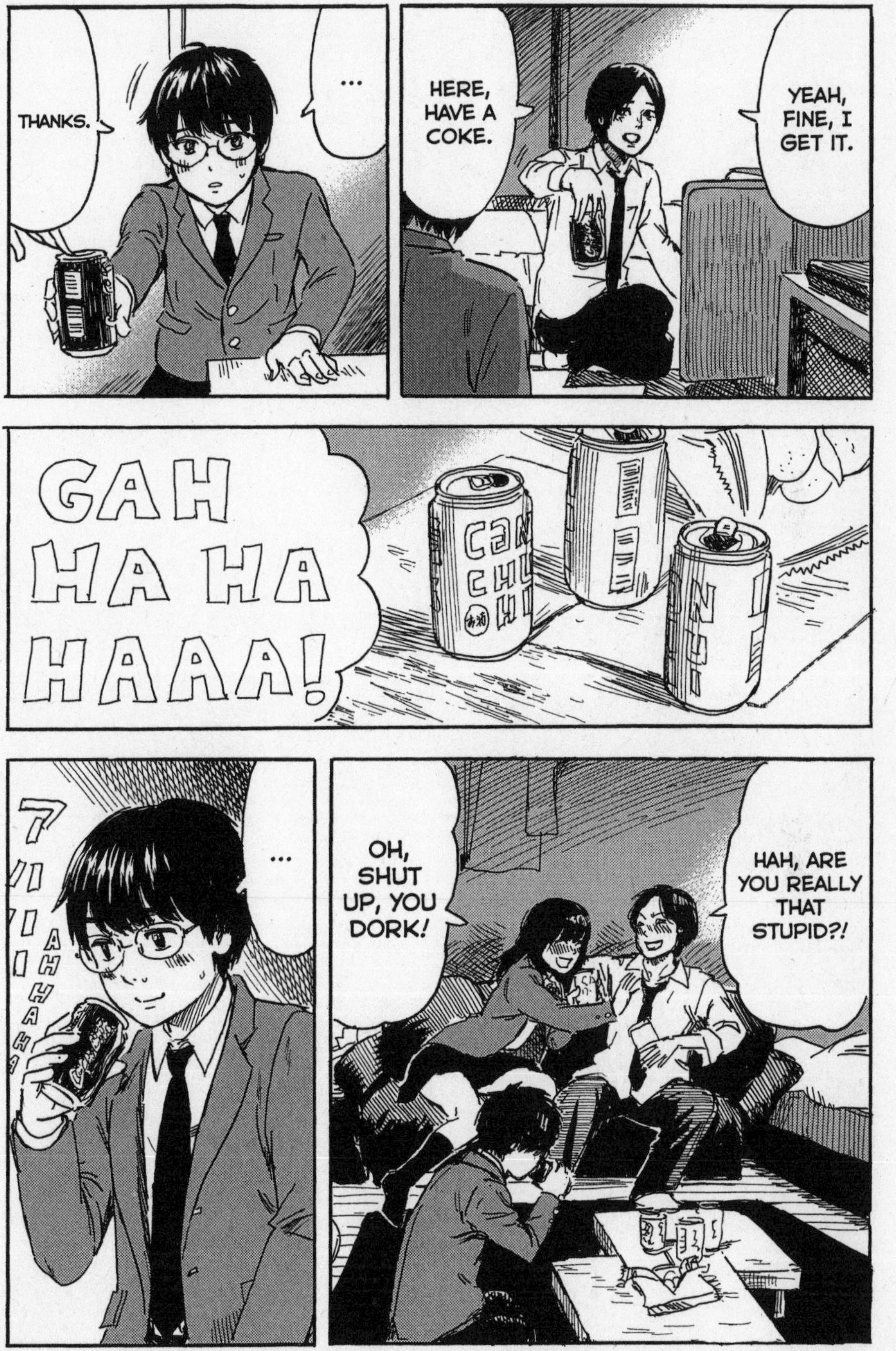
YEAH, FINE, I GET IT.
HERE, HAVE A COKE.
...
THANKS.
GAH HA HA HAAA!
HAH, ARE YOU REALLY THAT STUPID?!
OH, SHUT UP, YOU DORK!
...
AHHAHAHA

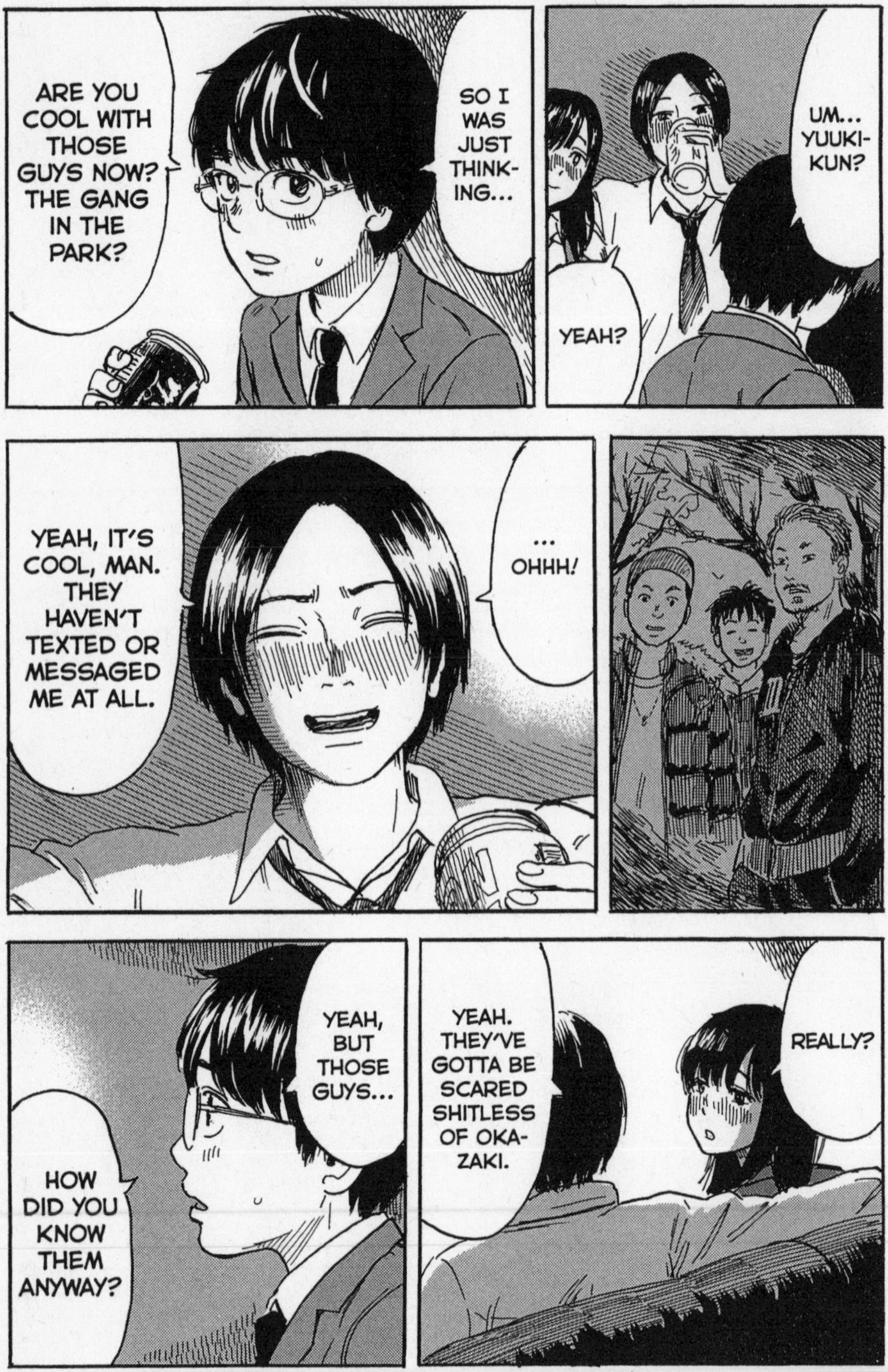
UM... YUUKI-KUN?
YEAH?
SO I WAS JUST THINKING...
ARE YOU COOL WITH THOSE GUYS NOW? THE GANG IN THE PARK?
... OHHH!
YEAH, IT'S COOL, MAN. THEY HAVEN'T TEXTED OR MESSAGED ME AT ALL.
REALLY?
YEAH. THEY'VE GOTTA BE SCARED SHITLESS OF OKA-ZAKI.
YEAH, BUT THOSE GUYS...
HOW DID YOU KNOW THEM ANYWAY?

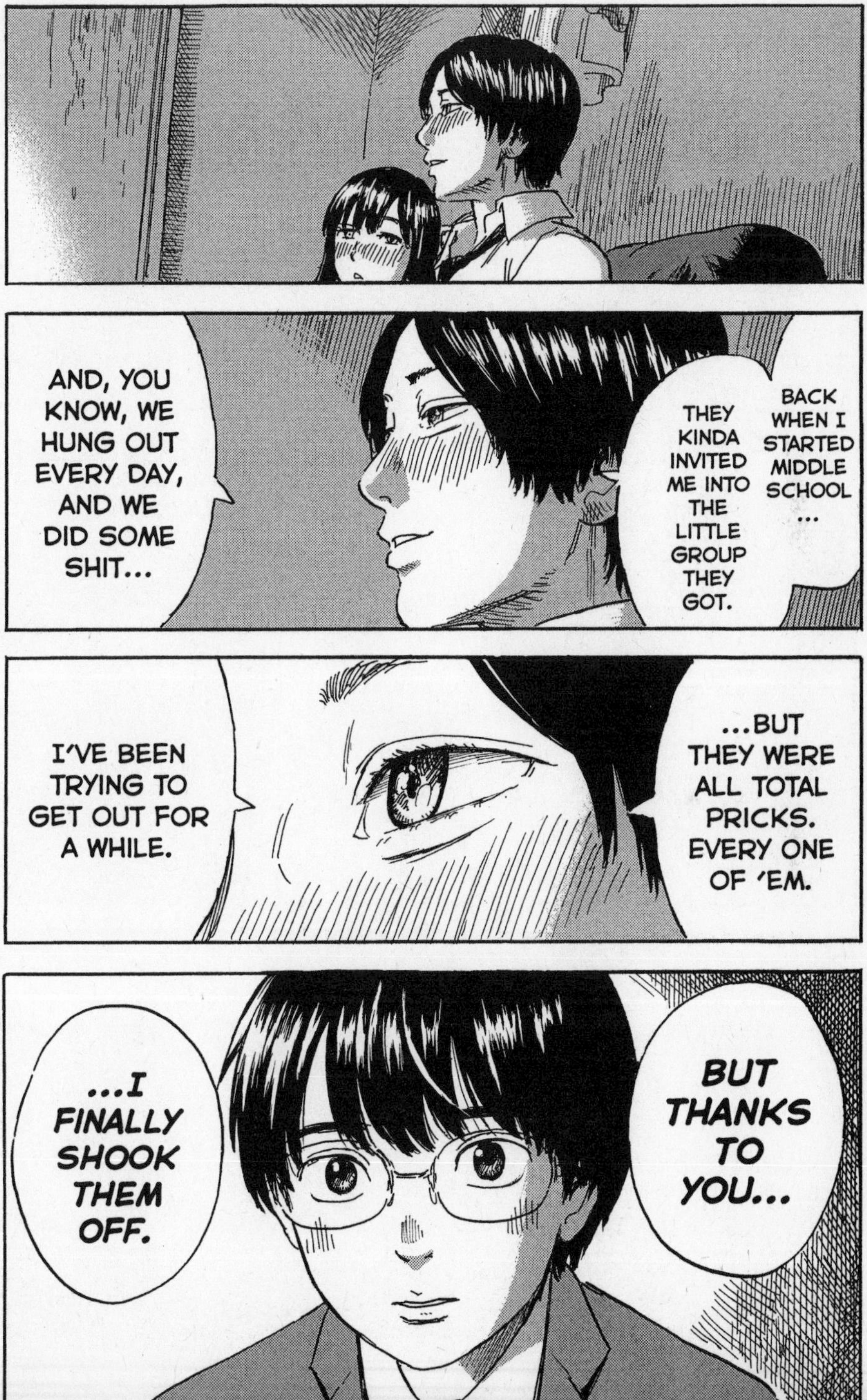
BACK WHEN I STARTED MIDDLE SCHOOL...
THEY KINDA INVITED ME INTO THE LITTLE GROUP THEY GOT.
AND, YOU KNOW, WE HUNG OUT EVERY DAY, AND WE DID SOME SHIT...
...BUT THEY WERE ALL TOTAL PRICKS. EVERY ONE OF 'EM.
I'VE BEEN TRYING TO GET OUT FOR A WHILE.
BUT THANKS TO YOU...
...I FINALLY SHOOK THEM OFF.

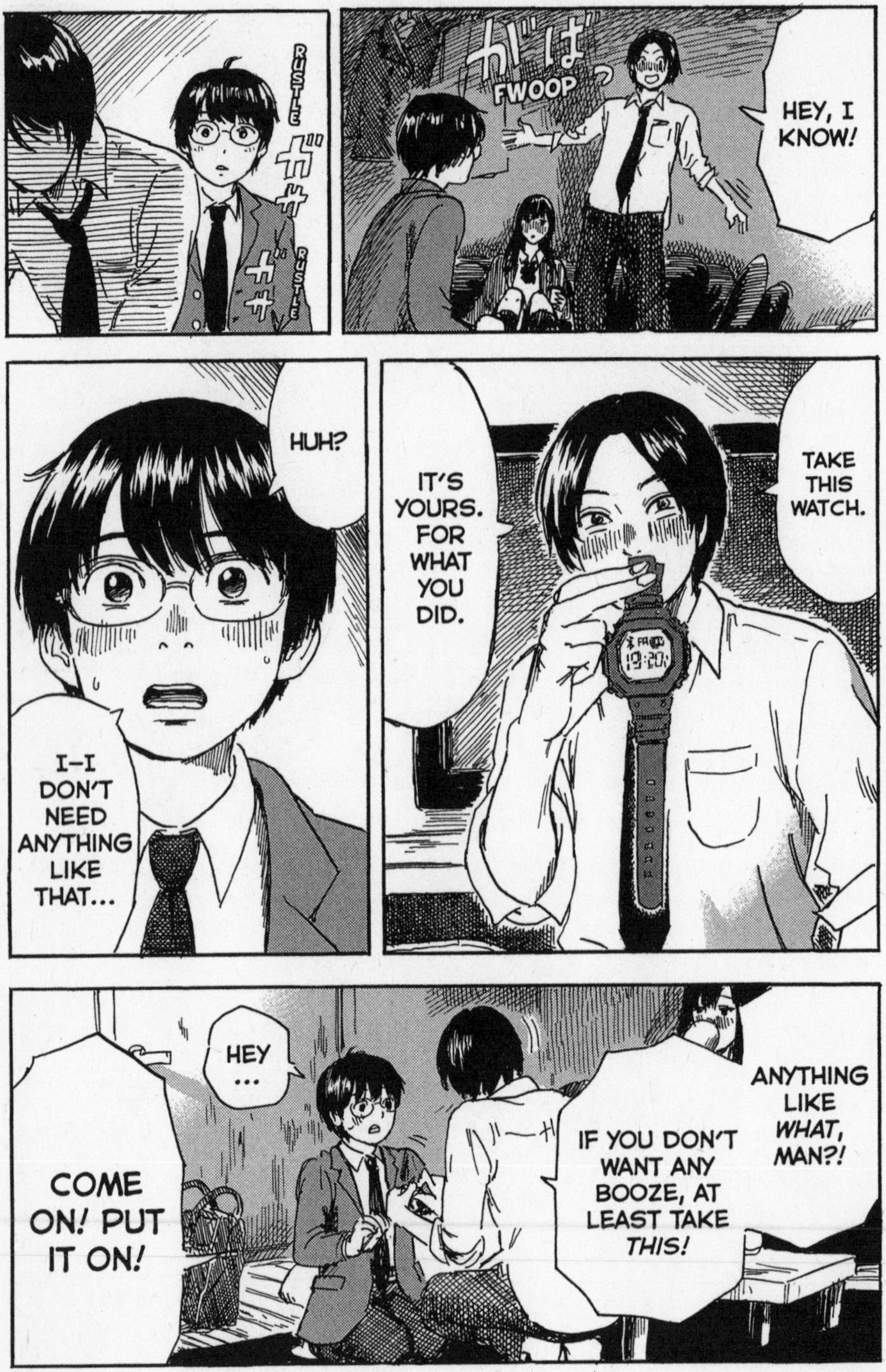
がば
FWOOP
HEY, I KNOW!
RUSTLE
ガサ
ガサ
RUSTLE
TAKE THIS WATCH.
IT'S YOURS. FOR WHAT YOU DID.
HUH?
I-I DON'T NEED ANYTHING LIKE THAT...
ANYTHING LIKE *WHAT,* MAN?!
IF YOU DON'T WANT ANY BOOZE, AT LEAST TAKE *THIS!*
HEY ...
COME ON! PUT IT ON!

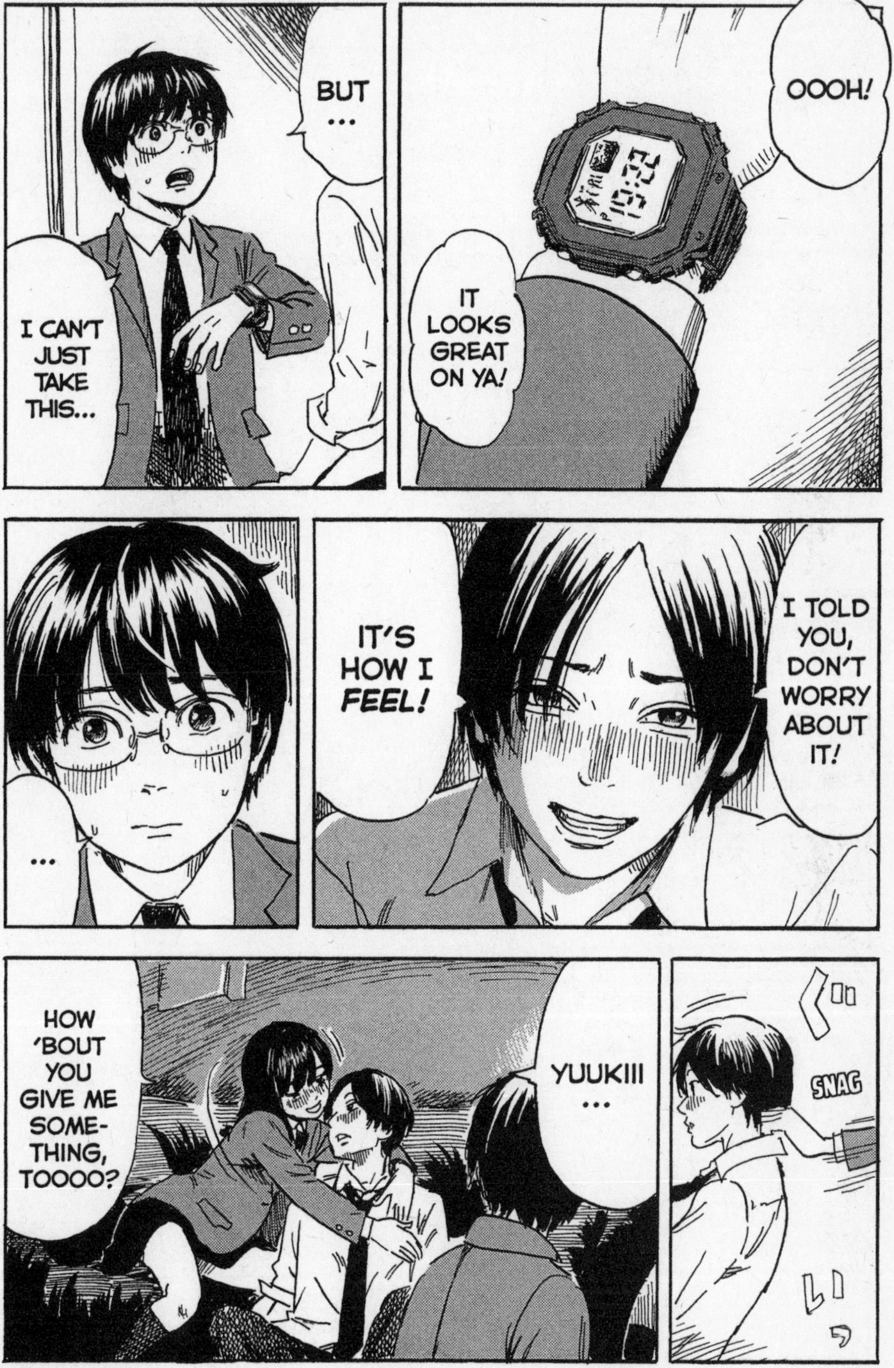
OOOH!
IT LOOKS GREAT ON YA!
BUT ...
I CAN'T JUST TAKE THIS...
I TOLD YOU, DON'T WORRY ABOUT IT!
IT'S HOW I *FEEL*!
...
SNAG
YUUKIII ...
HOW 'BOUT YOU GIVE ME SOME-THING, TOOOO?

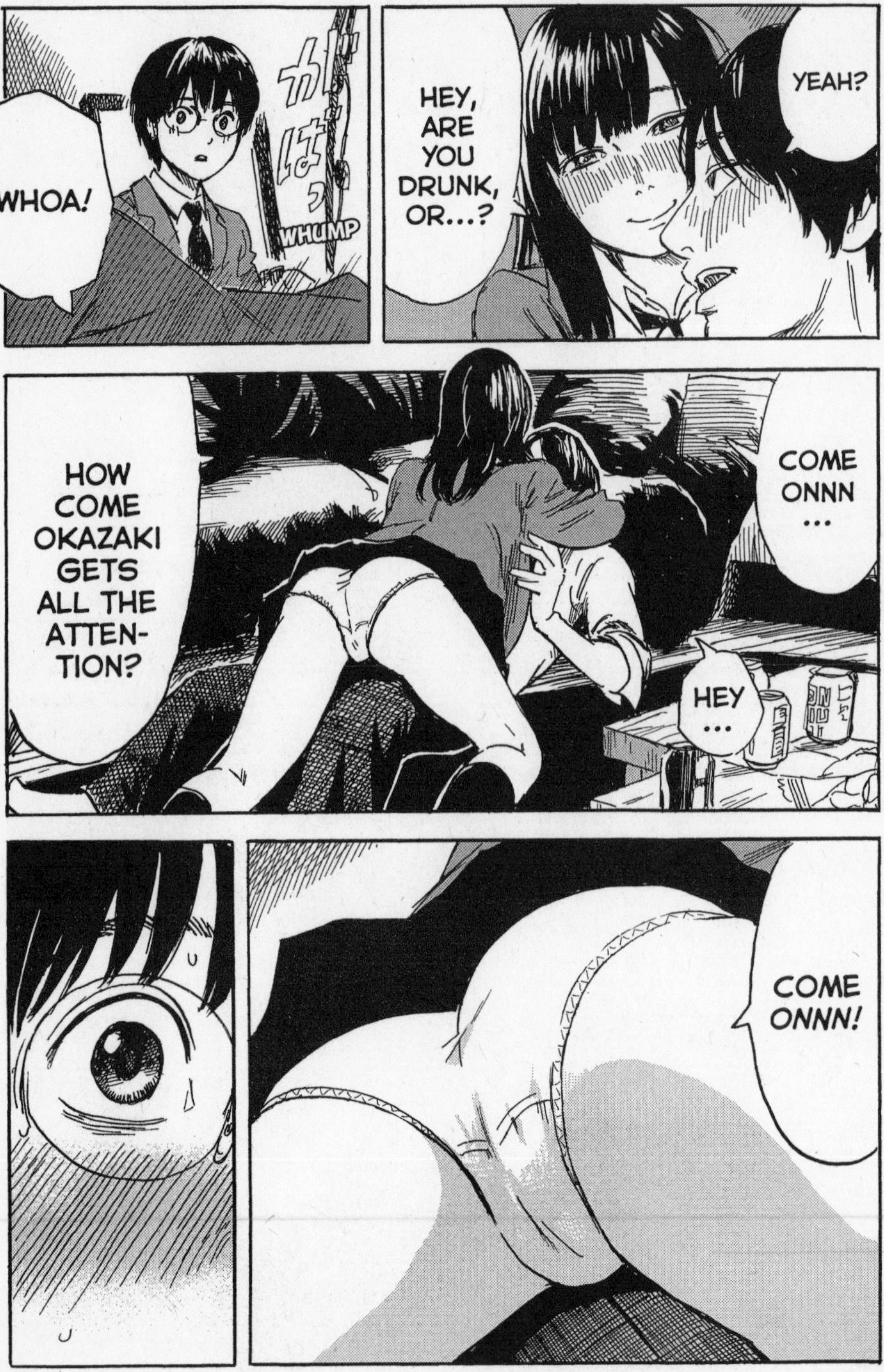
YEAH?
HEY, ARE YOU DRUNK, OR...?
WHUMP
WHOA!
COME ONNN ...
HEY ...
HOW COME OKAZAKI GETS ALL THE ATTENTION?
COME ONNN!

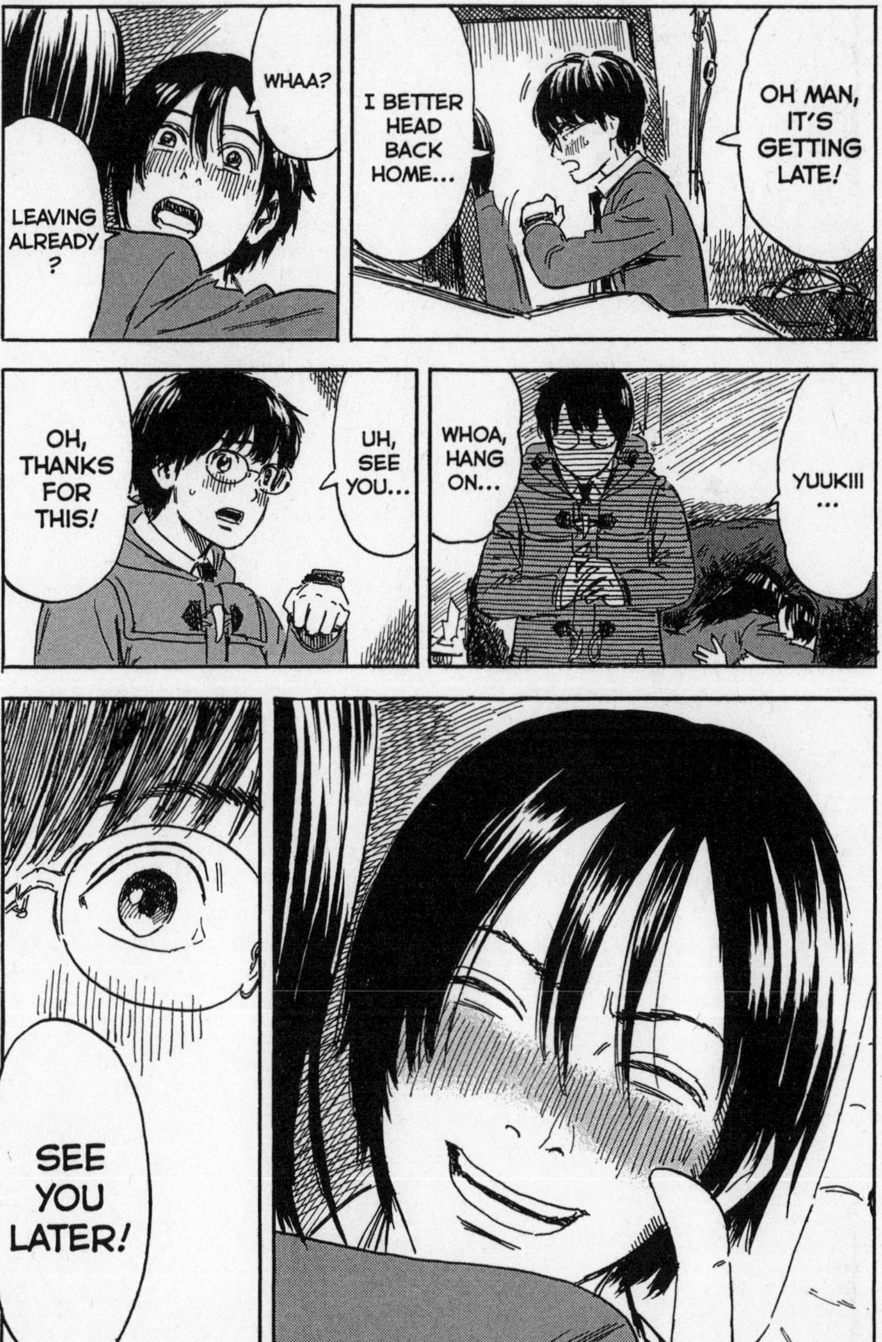
OH MAN, IT'S GETTING LATE!
I BETTER HEAD BACK HOME...
WHAA?
LEAVING ALREADY ?
YUUKIII ...
WHOA, HANG ON...
UH, SEE YOU...
OH, THANKS FOR THIS!
SEE YOU LATER!

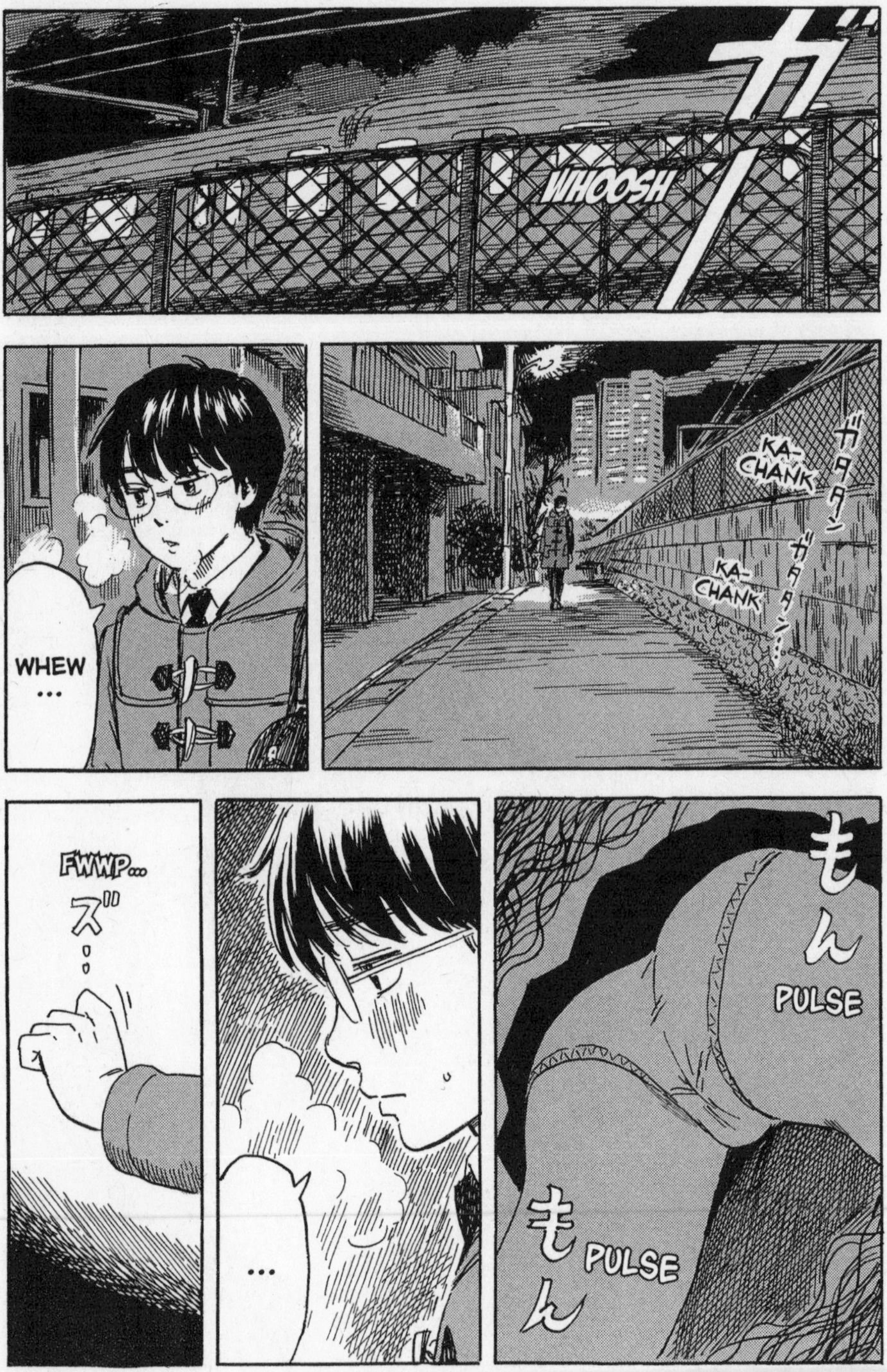
ガ
WHOOSH
ガタタン
KA-CHANK
ガタタン…
KA-CHANK
WHEW …
もん
PULSE
もん
PULSE
…
FWWP…
ズ

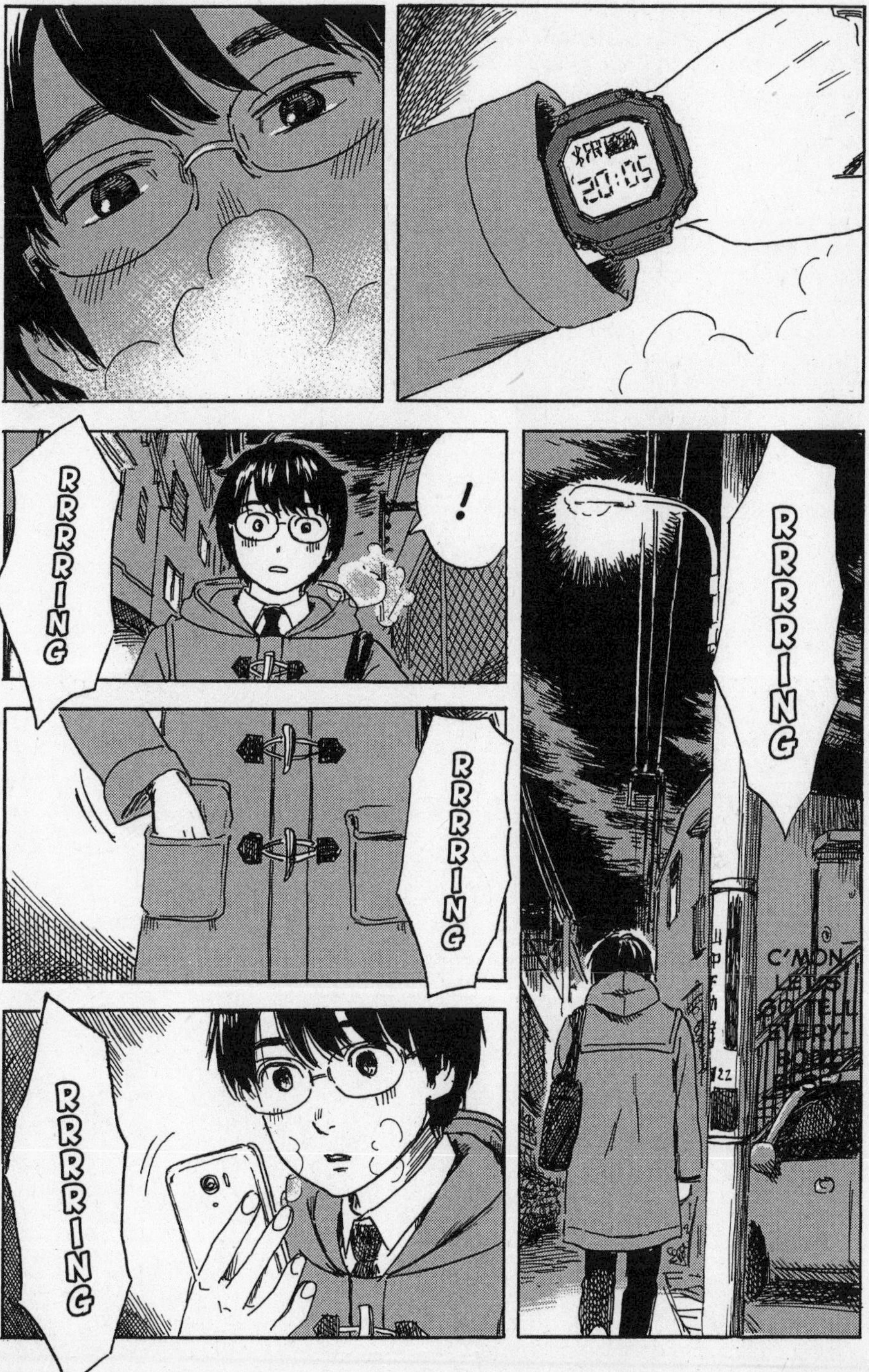

RRRRING
C'MON LET'S GO TELL EVERY-
!
RRRRING
RRRRING
RRRRING

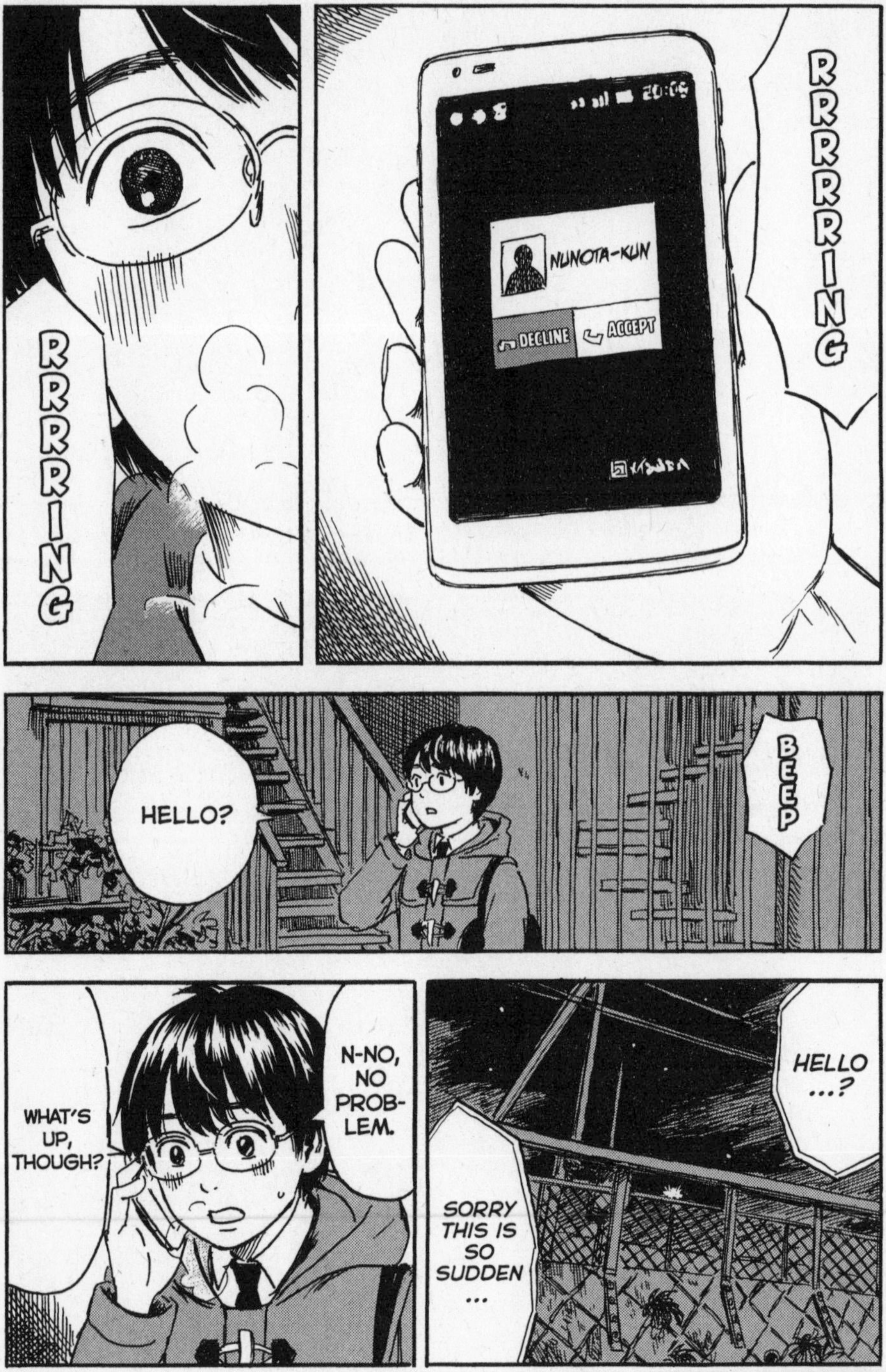
RRRRRING
NUNOTA-KUN
DECLINE
ACCEPT
RRRRING
BEEP
HELLO?
HELLO ...?
SORRY THIS IS SO SUDDEN ...
N-NO, NO PROB-LEM.
WHAT'S UP, THOUGH?

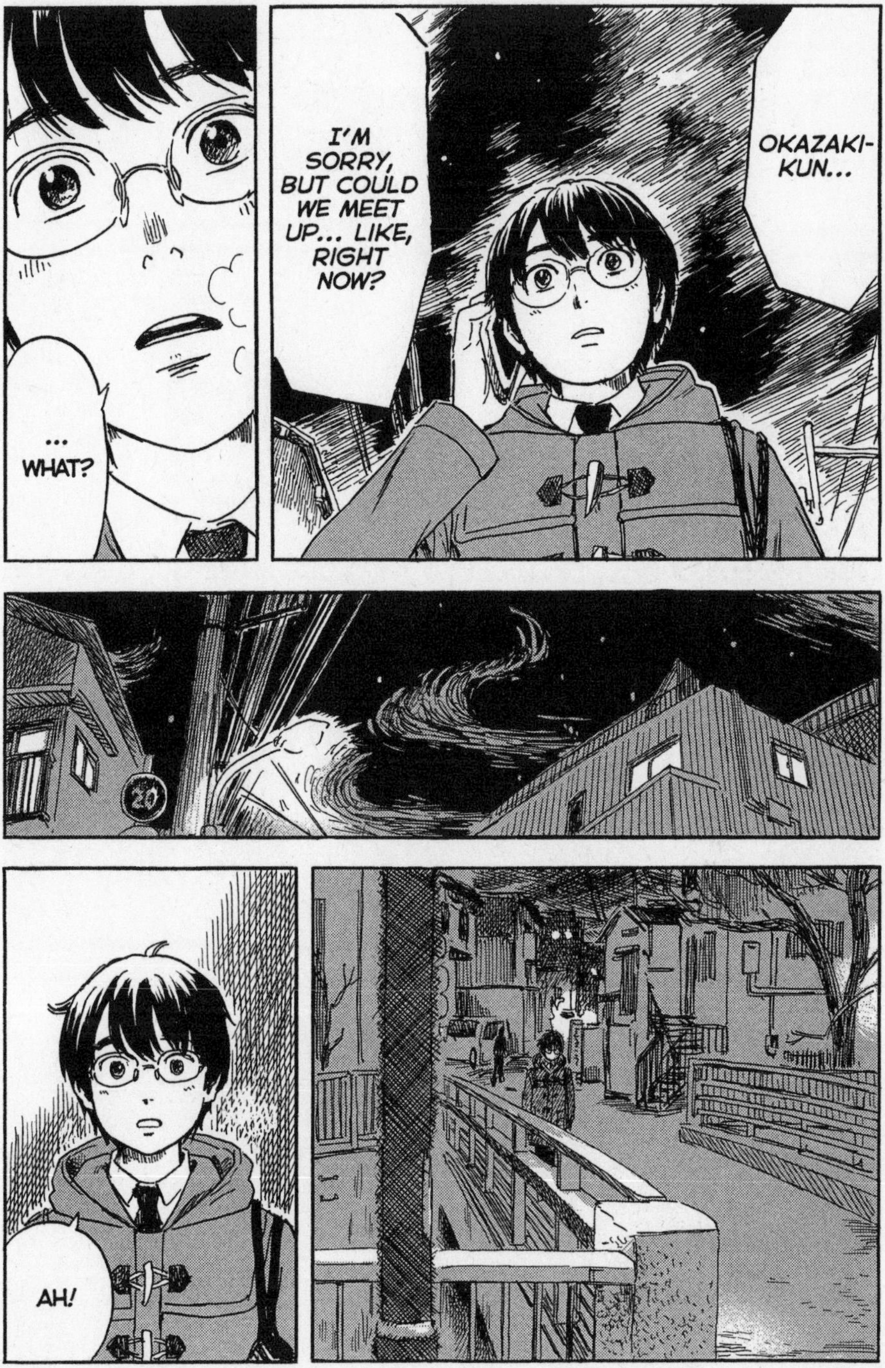
OKAZAKI-KUN...
I'M SORRY, BUT COULD WE MEET UP... LIKE, RIGHT NOW?
... WHAT?
AH!

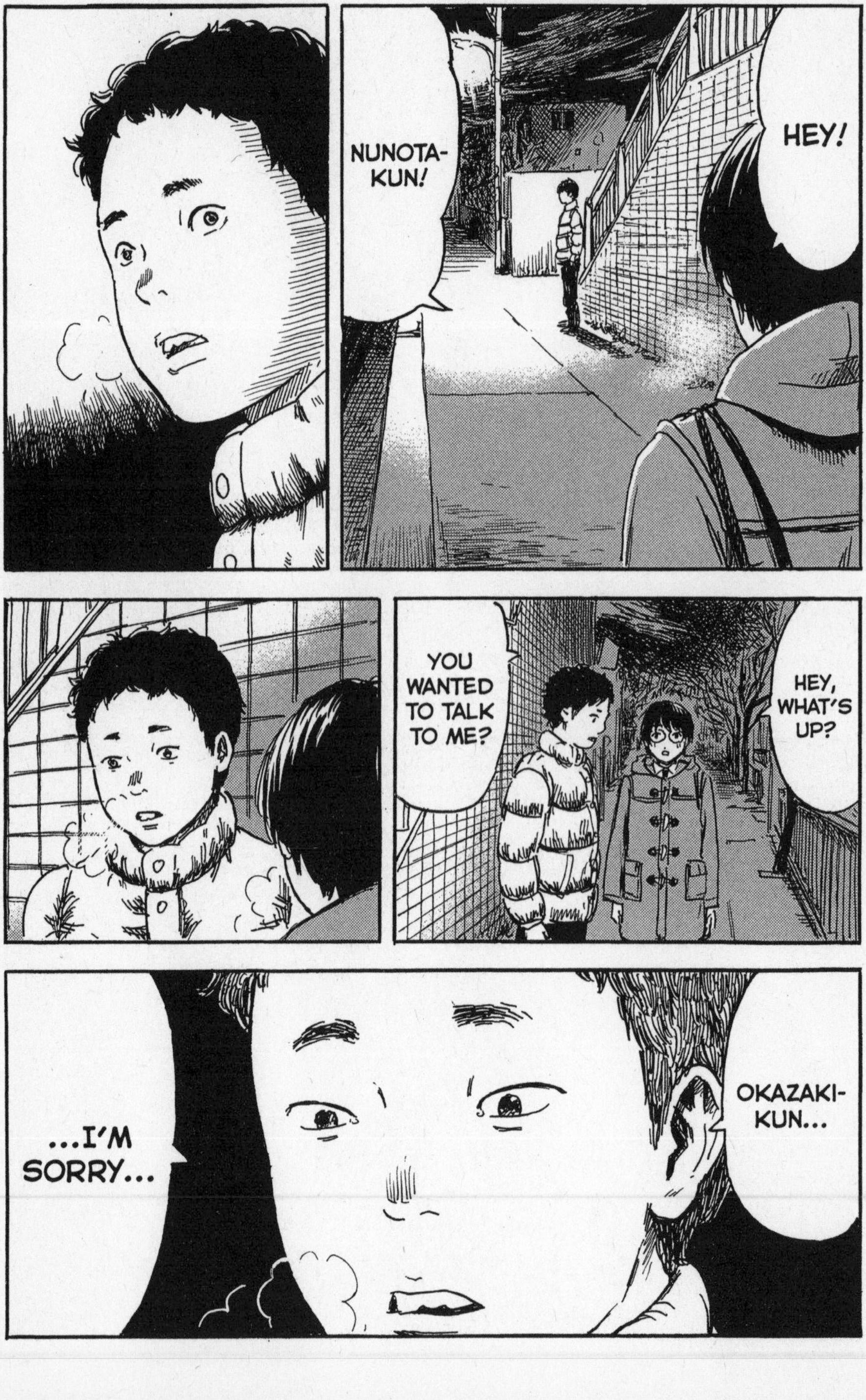
HEY!
NUNOTA-KUN!
HEY, WHAT'S UP?
YOU WANTED TO TALK TO ME?
OKAZAKI-KUN...
...I'M SORRY...

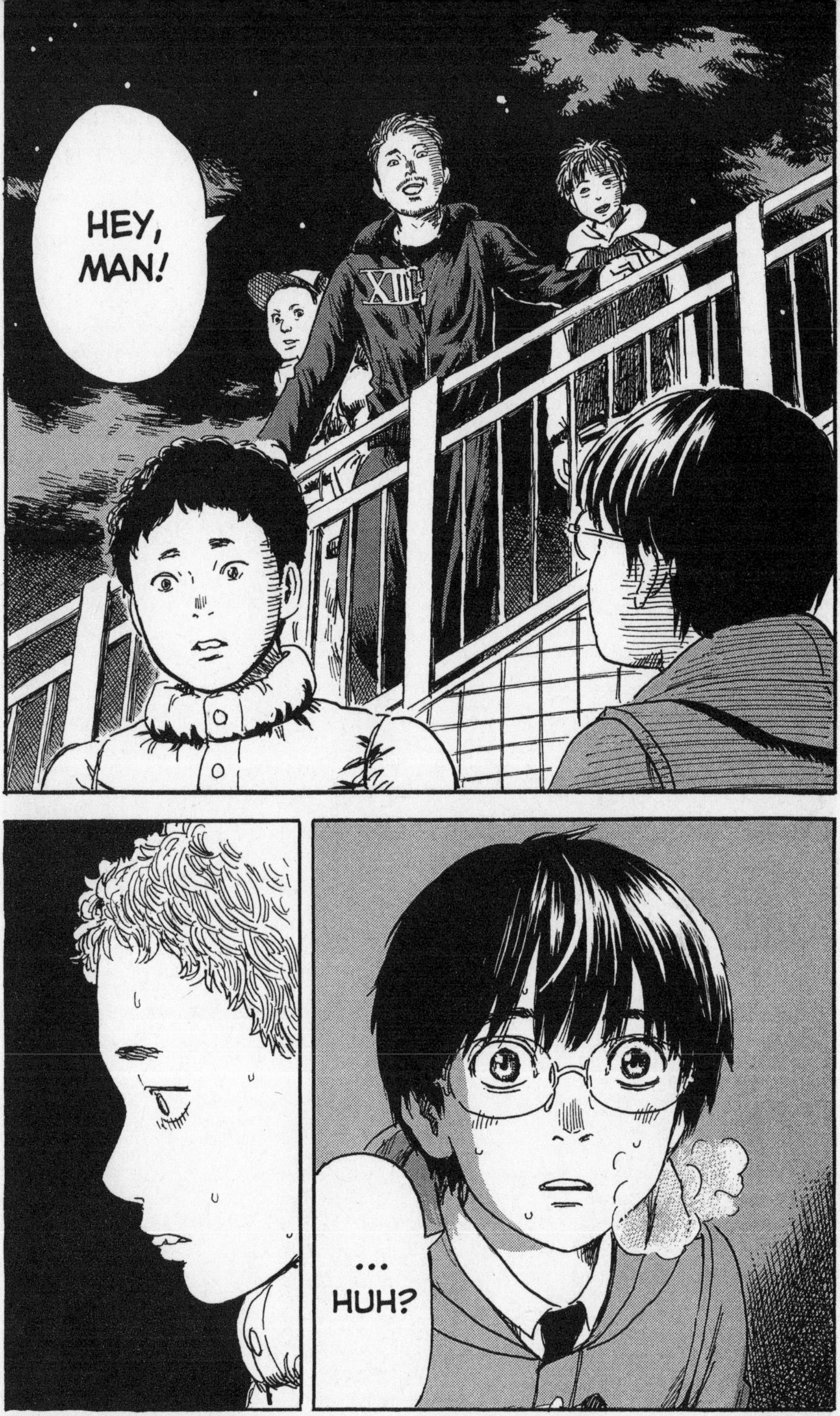
HEY, MAN!
... HUH?

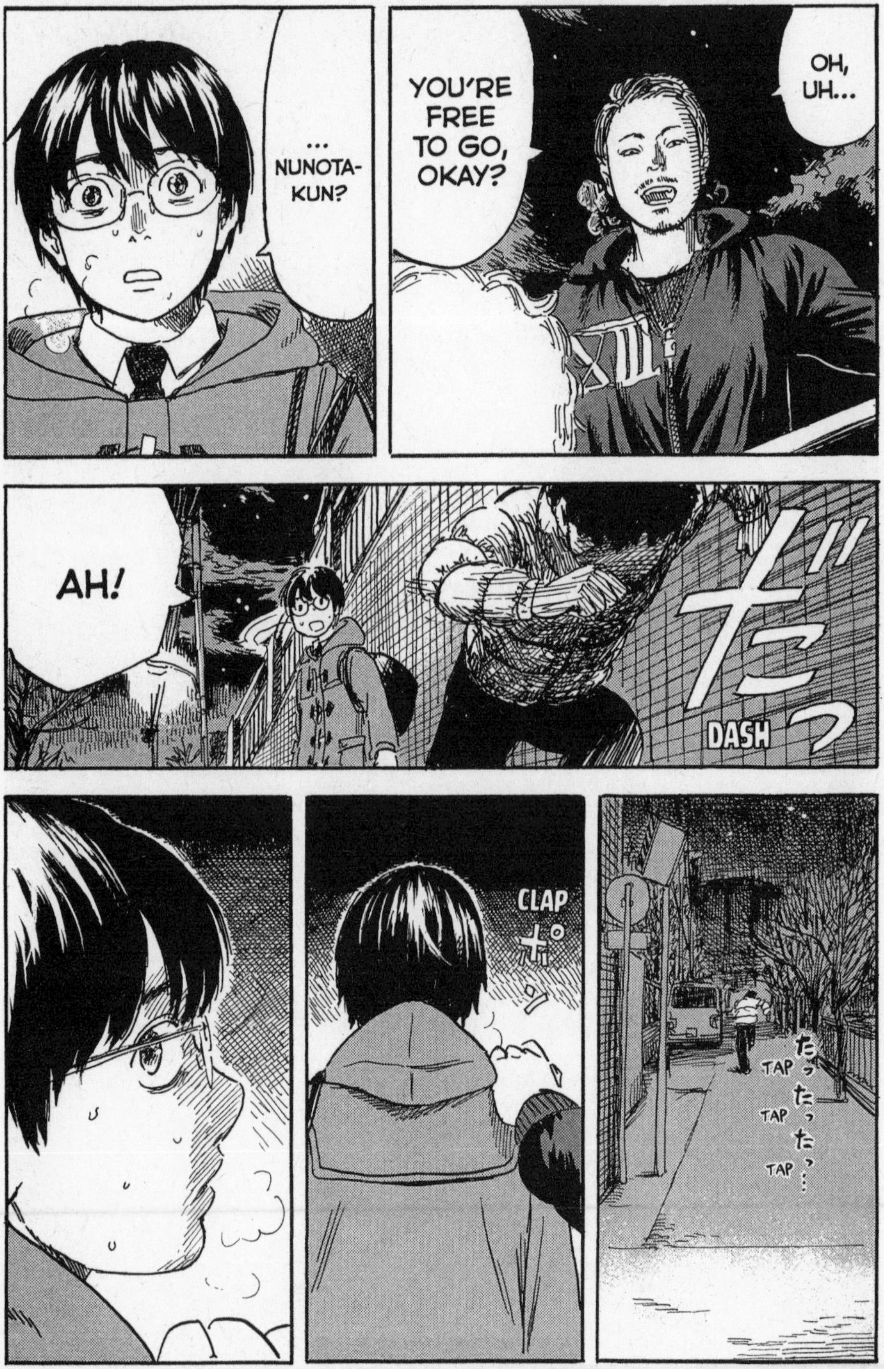
OH, UH...
YOU'RE FREE TO GO, OKAY?
... NUNOTA-KUN?
だっ
DASH
AH!
たったったっ…
TAP
TAP
TAP
ポン
CLAP

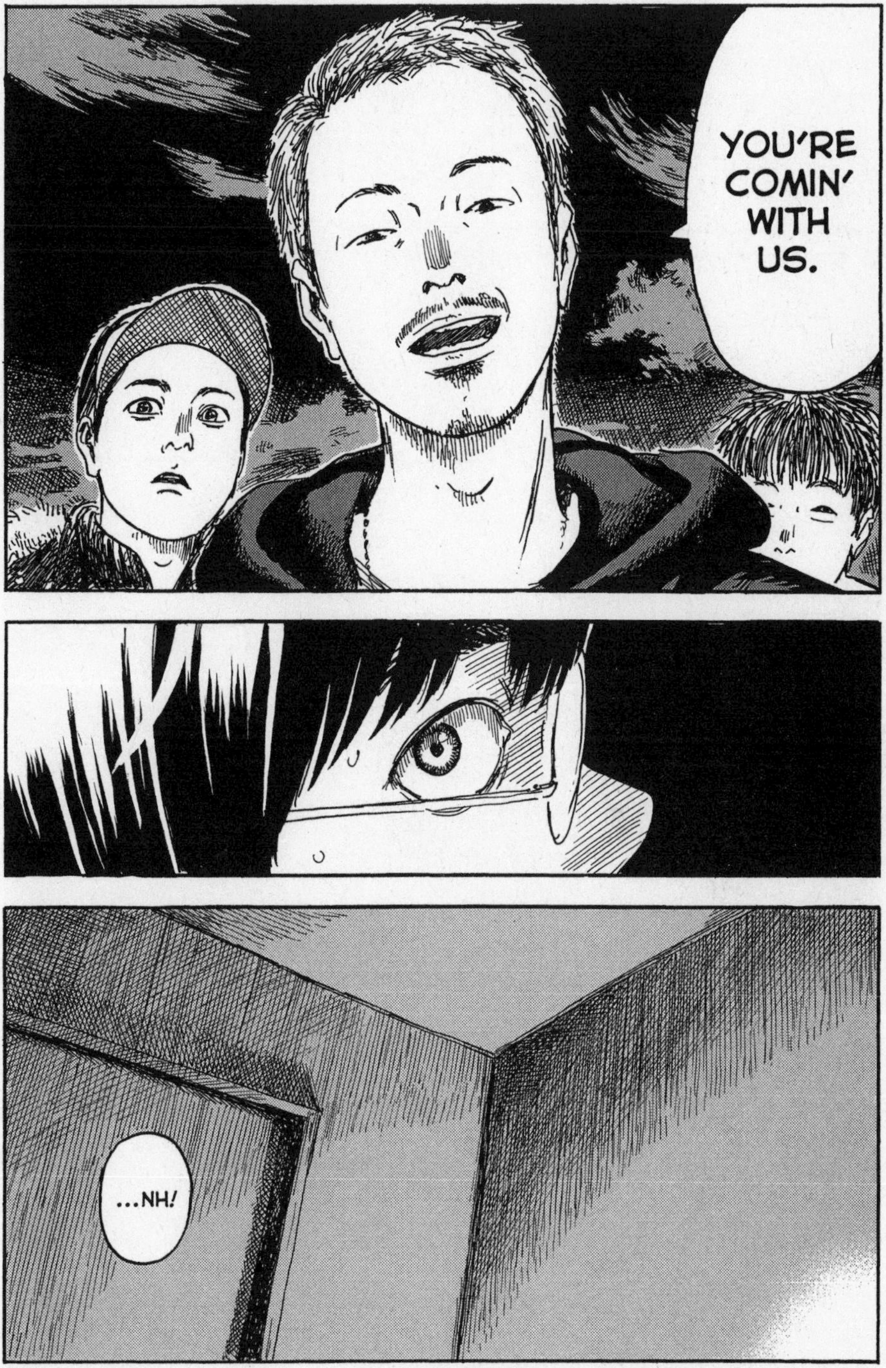
YOU'RE COMIN' WITH US.
...NH!

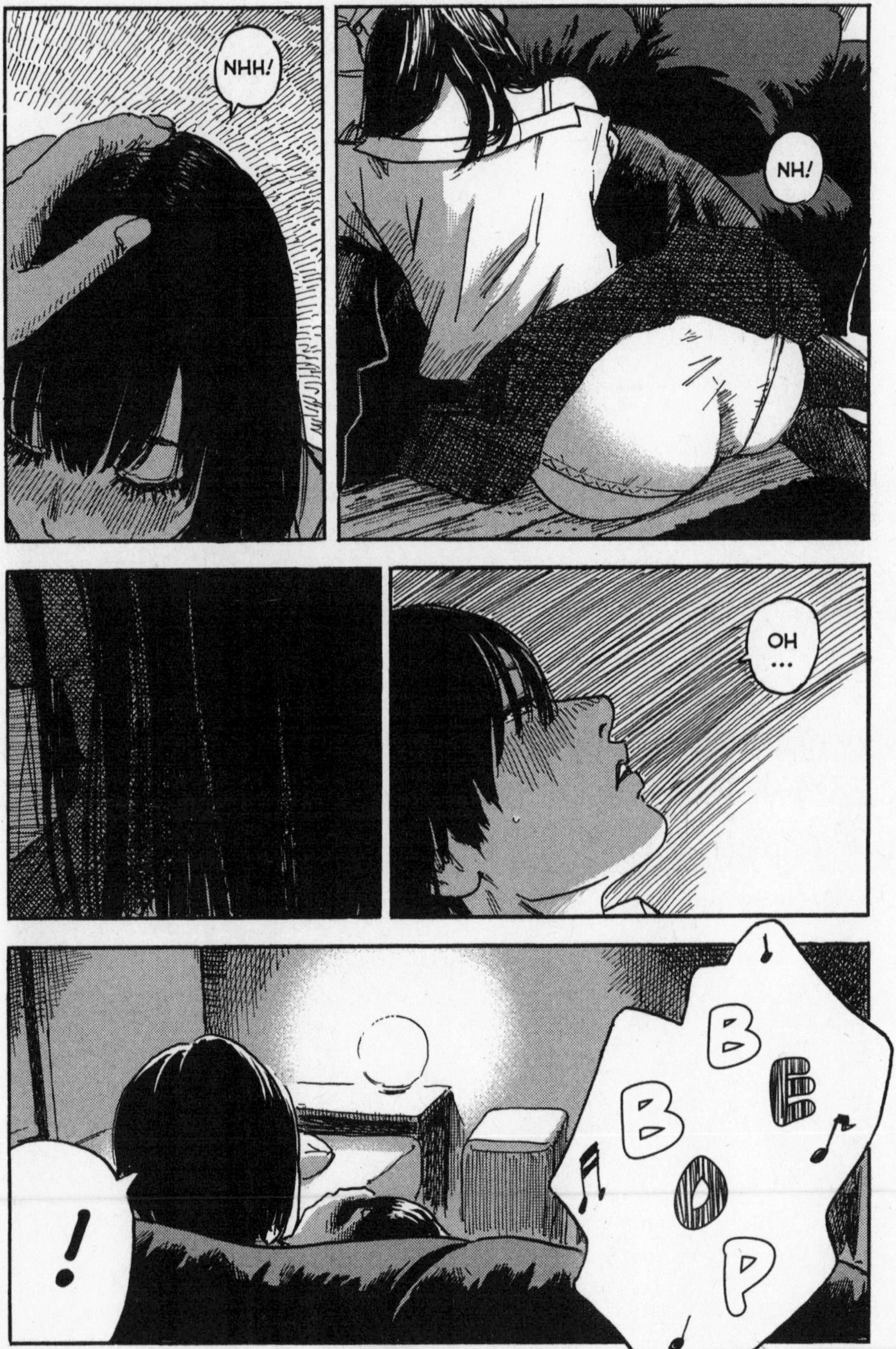
NH!
NHH!
OH ...
BEBOP
!

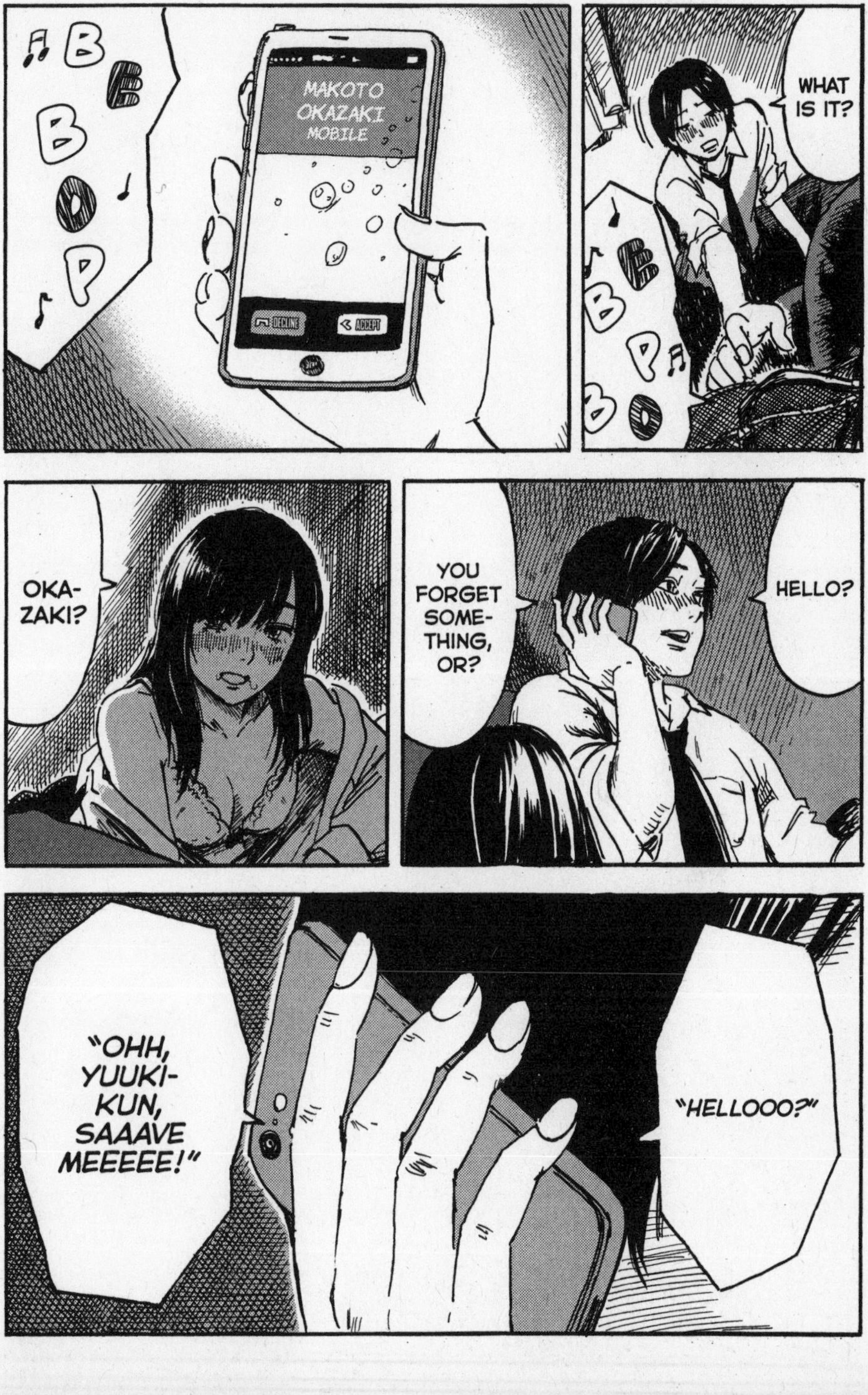
WHAT IS IT?
BEBOP
MAKOTO OKAZAKI MOBILE
DECLINE
ACCEPT
BEBOP
HELLO?
YOU FORGET SOME-THING, OR?
OKA-ZAKI?
"HELLOOO?"
"OHH, YUUKI-KUN, SAAVE MEEEEE!"

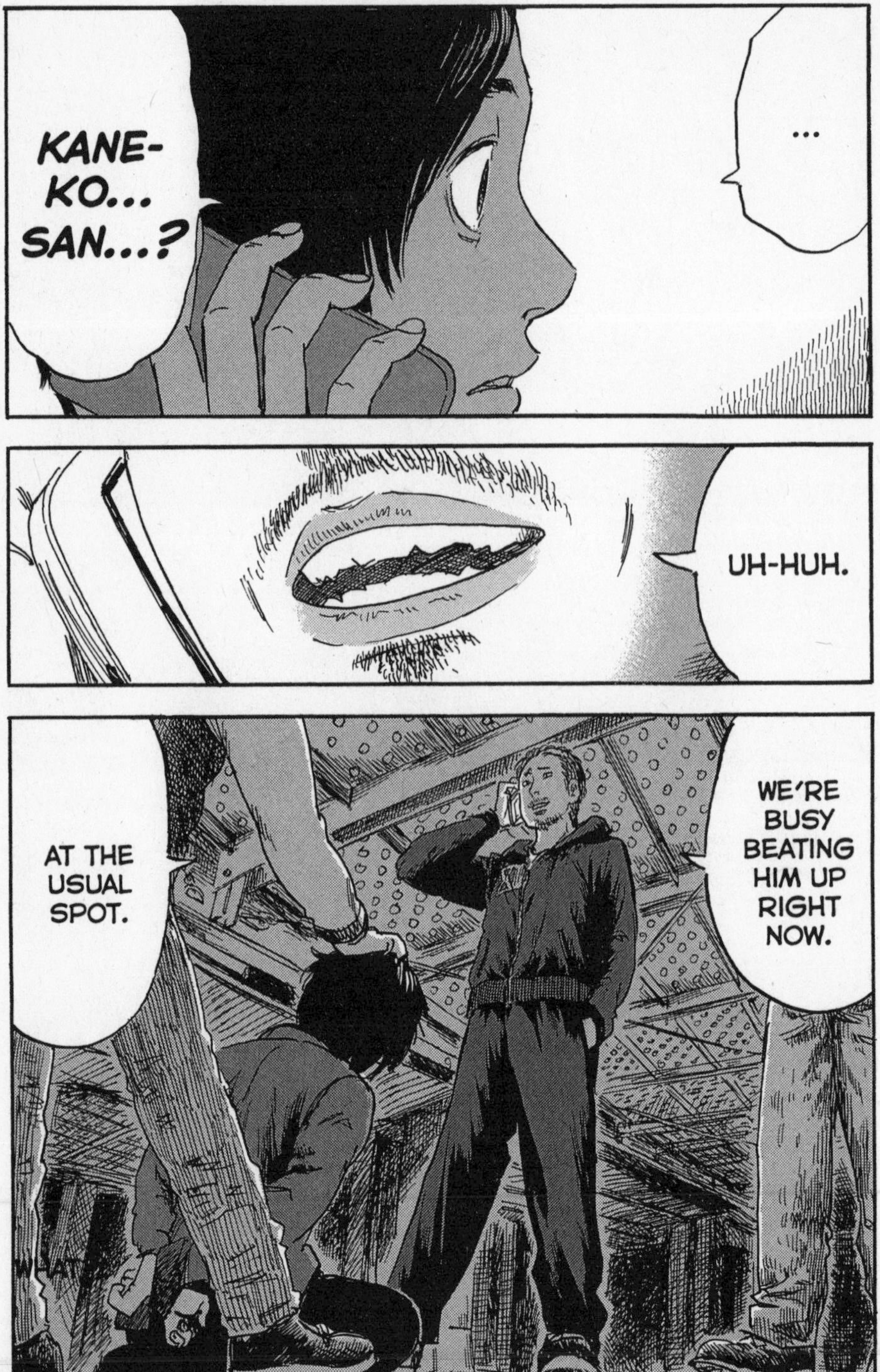
...
KANE-KO... SAN...?
UH-HUH.
WE'RE BUSY BEATING HIM UP RIGHT NOW.
AT THE USUAL SPOT.

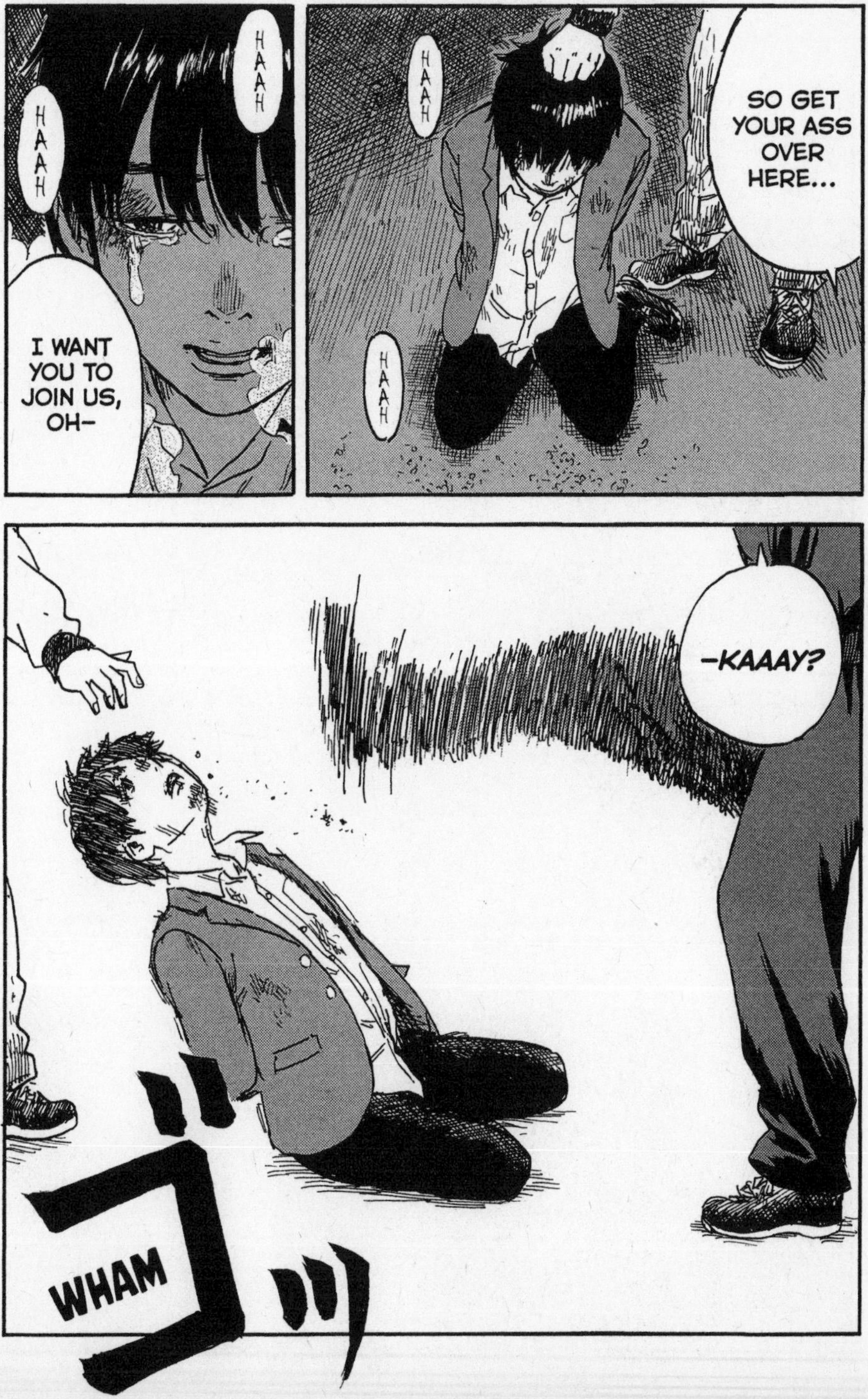
SO GET YOUR ASS OVER HERE...
HAAAH
HAAAH
HAAAH
HAAAH
I WANT YOU TO JOIN US, OH-
-KAAAY?
WHAM

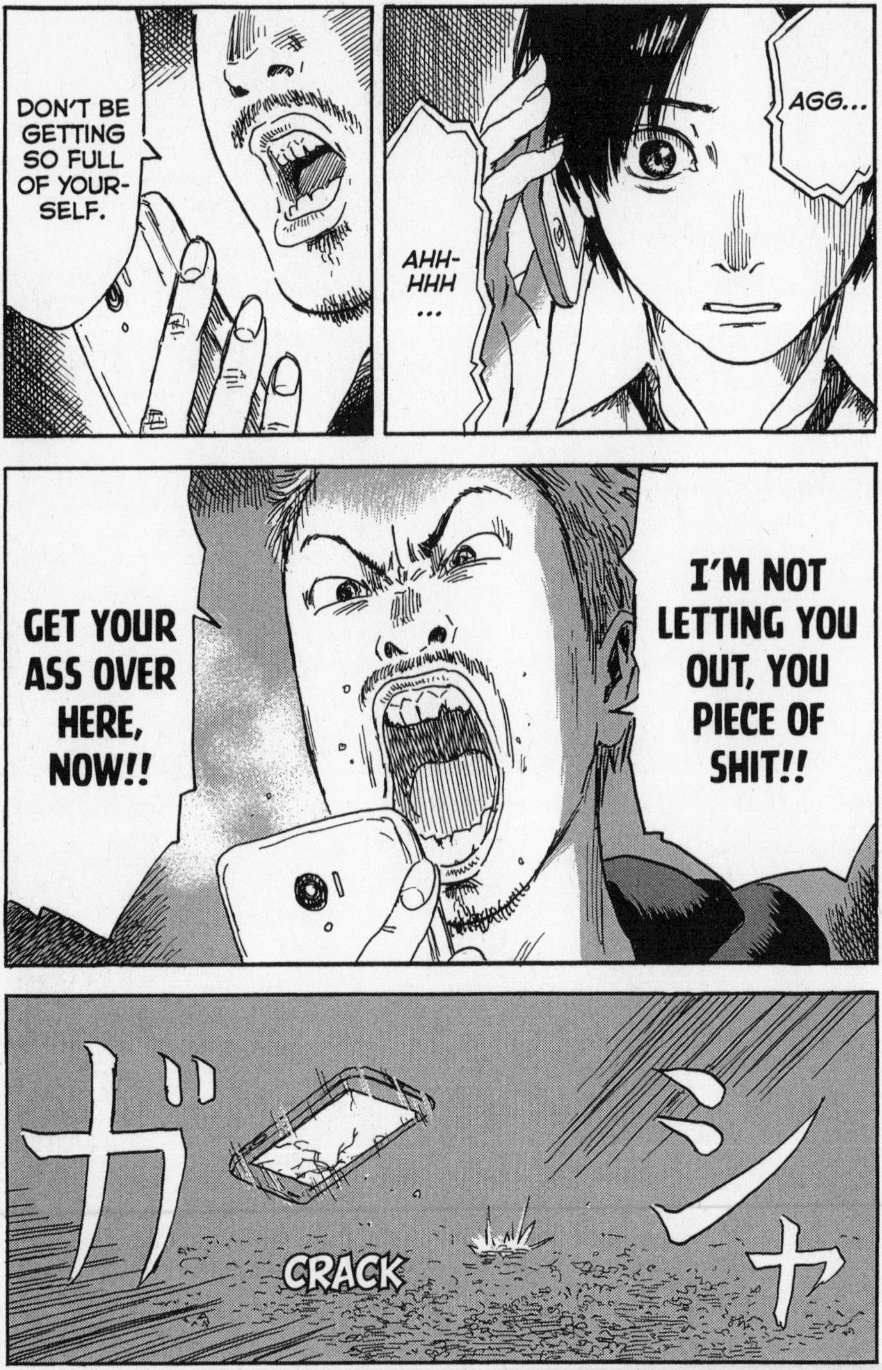
AGG...
AHH-HHH ...
DON'T BE GETTING SO FULL OF YOUR-SELF.
I'M NOT LETTING YOU OUT, YOU PIECE OF SHIT!!
GET YOUR ASS OVER HERE, NOW!!
ガシャ
CRACK

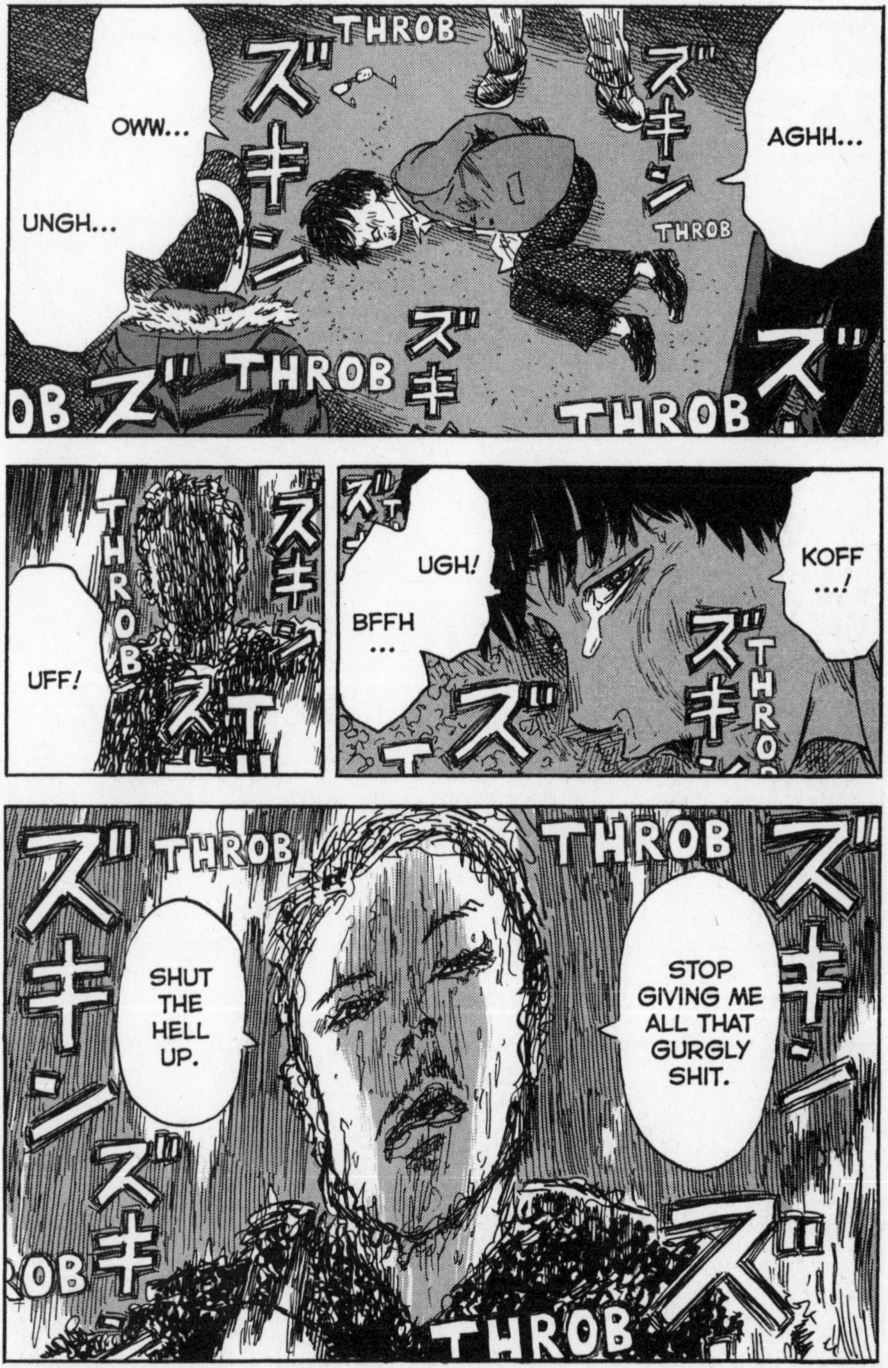
AGHH...
THROB
THROB
THROB
OWW...
UNGH...
THROB
KOFF ...!
THROB
UGH!
BFFH ...
THROB
UFF!
THROB
STOP GIVING ME ALL THAT GURGLY SHIT.
THROB
THROB
SHUT THE HELL UP.
THROB

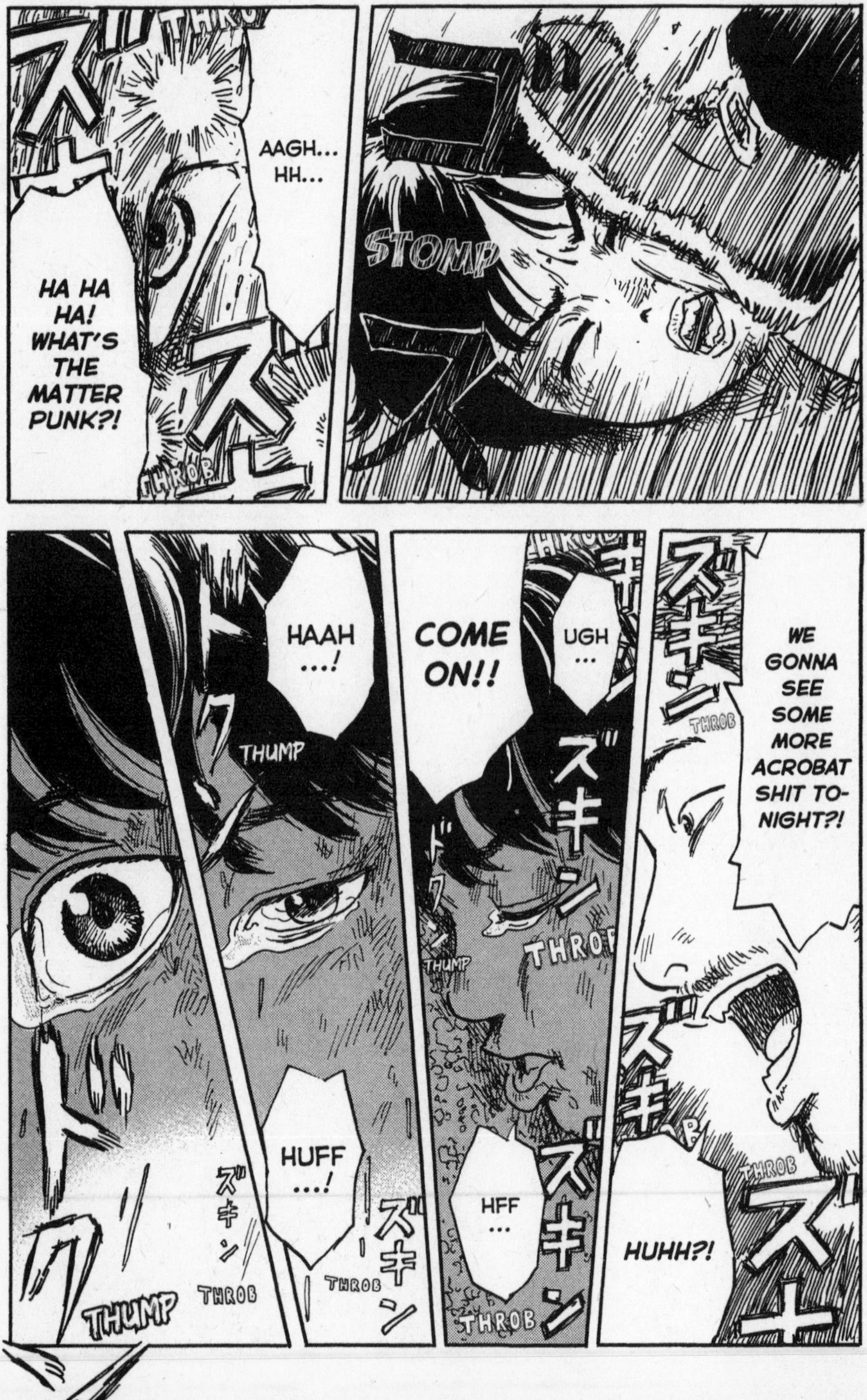

STOMP
AAGH... HH...
THRO
HA HA HA! WHAT'S THE MATTER PUNK?!
THROB
WE GONNA SEE SOME MORE ACROBAT SHIT TO-NIGHT?!
THROB
THROB
HUHH?!
THROB
UGH...
COME ON!!
THROB
THUMP
HFF...
THROB
HAAH...!
THUMP
HUFF...!
THROB
THROB
THUMP

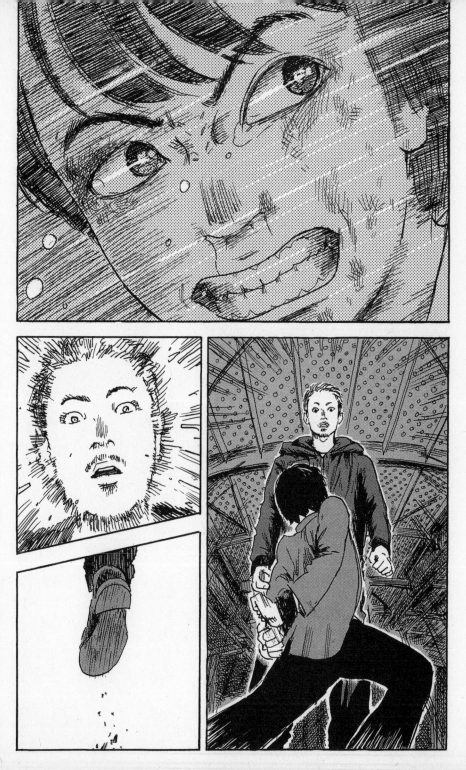

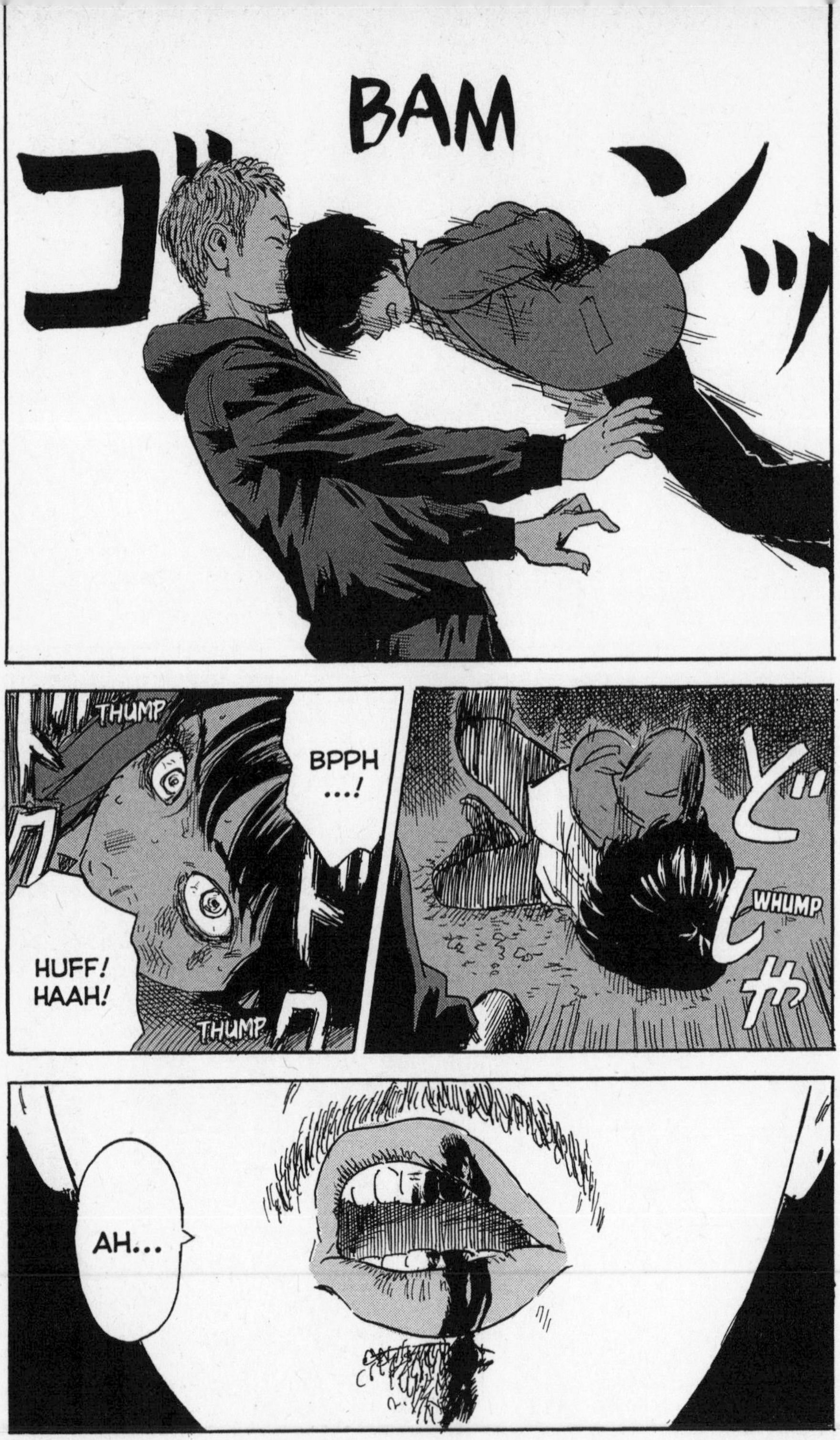
BAM
ゴンッ
どしゃ
WHUMP
THUMP
BPPH ...!
HUFF! HAAH!
THUMP
AH...

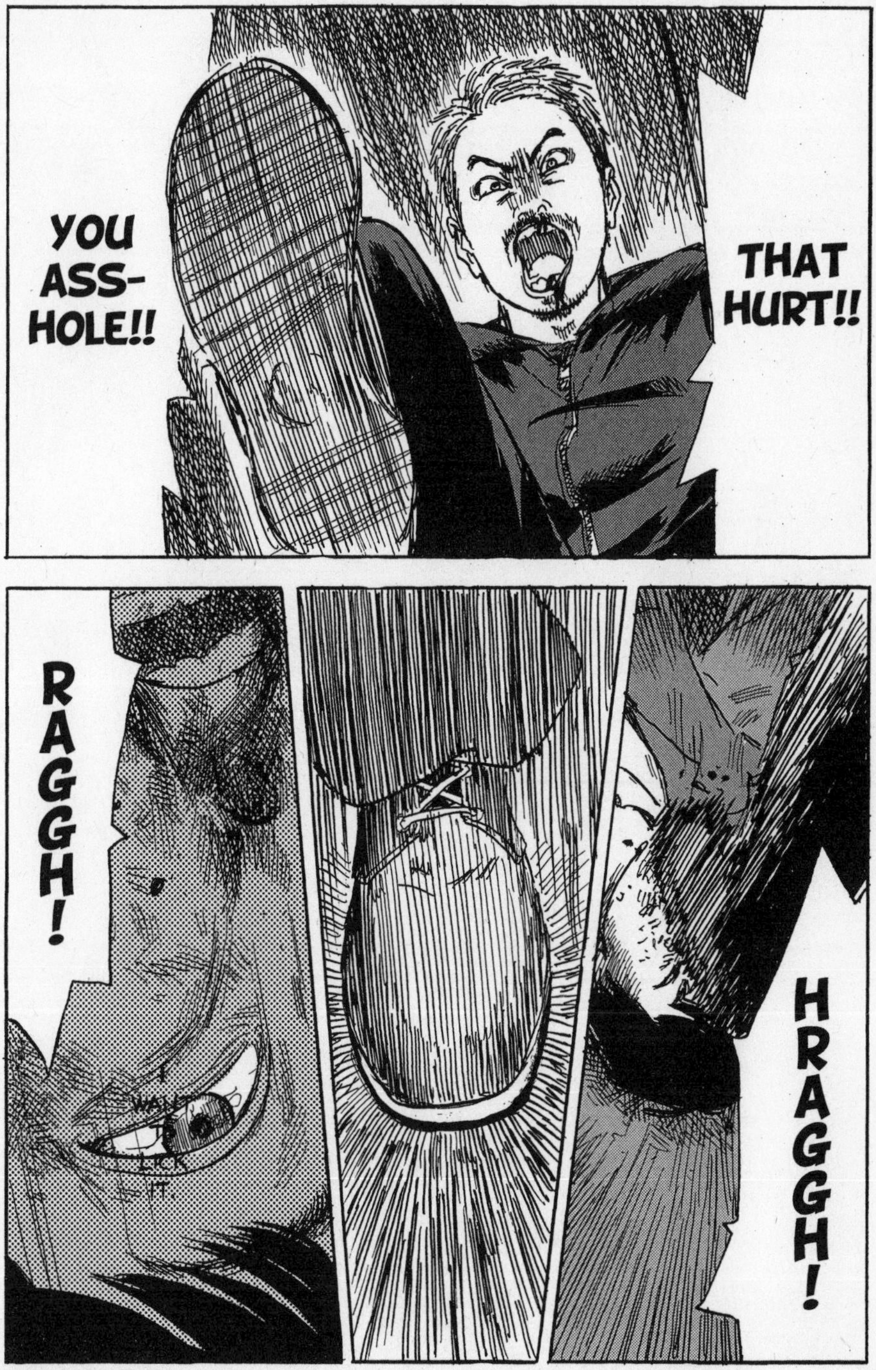
THAT HURT!!
YOU ASS-HOLE!!
HRAGGH!
RAGGGH!

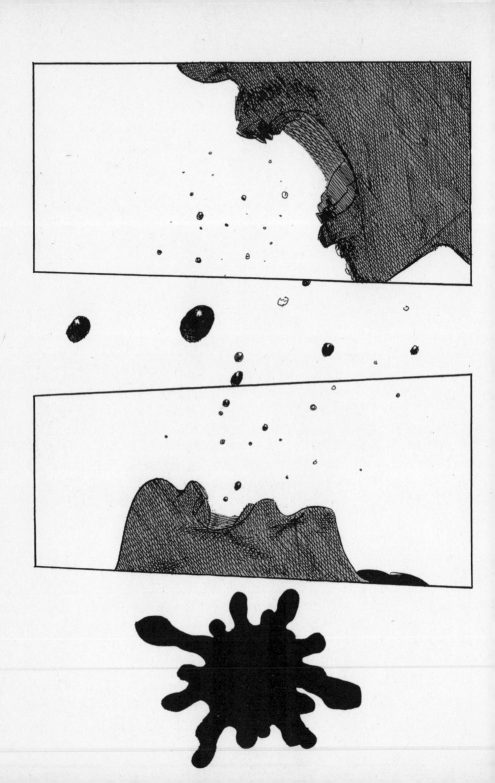

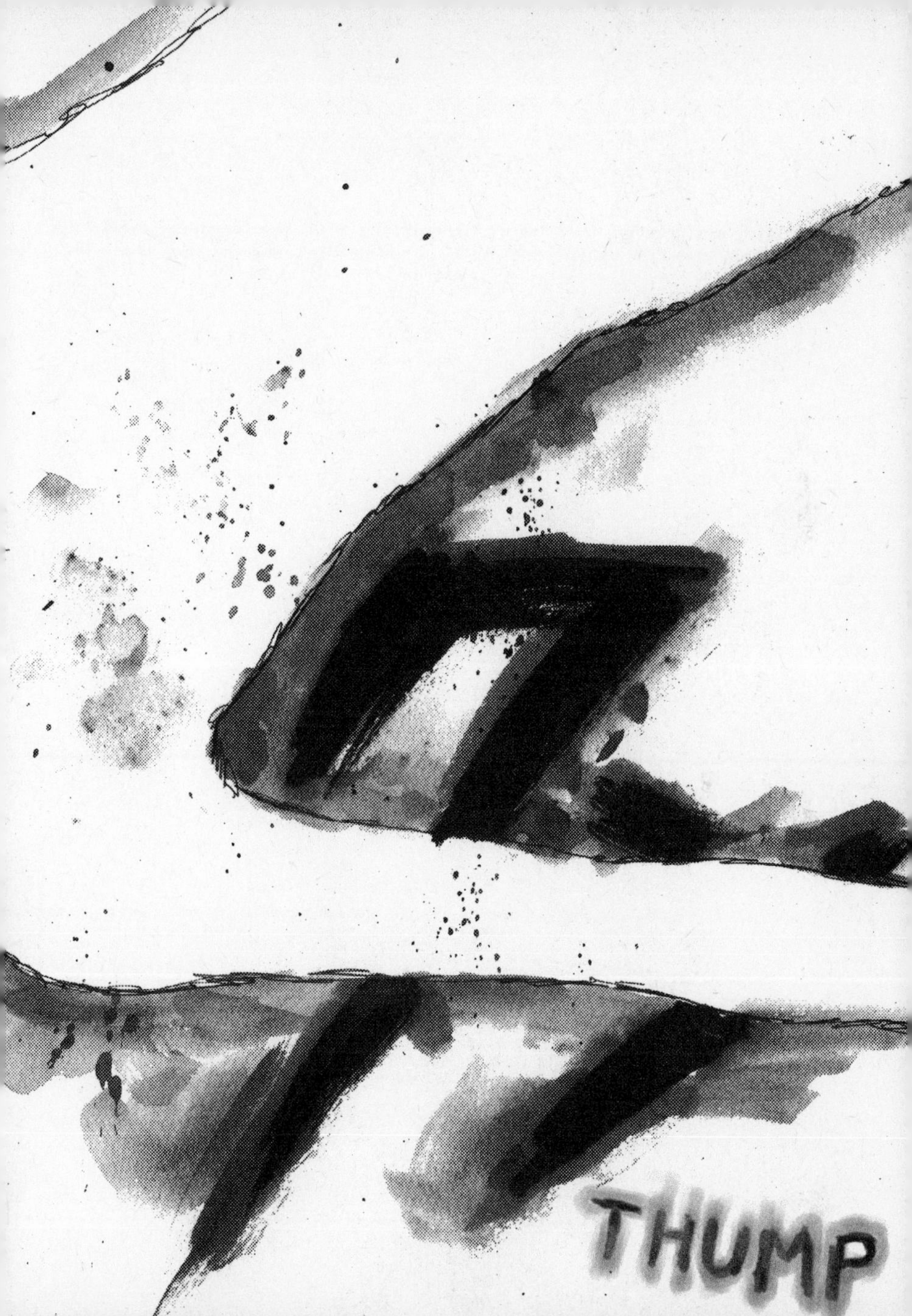
THUMP

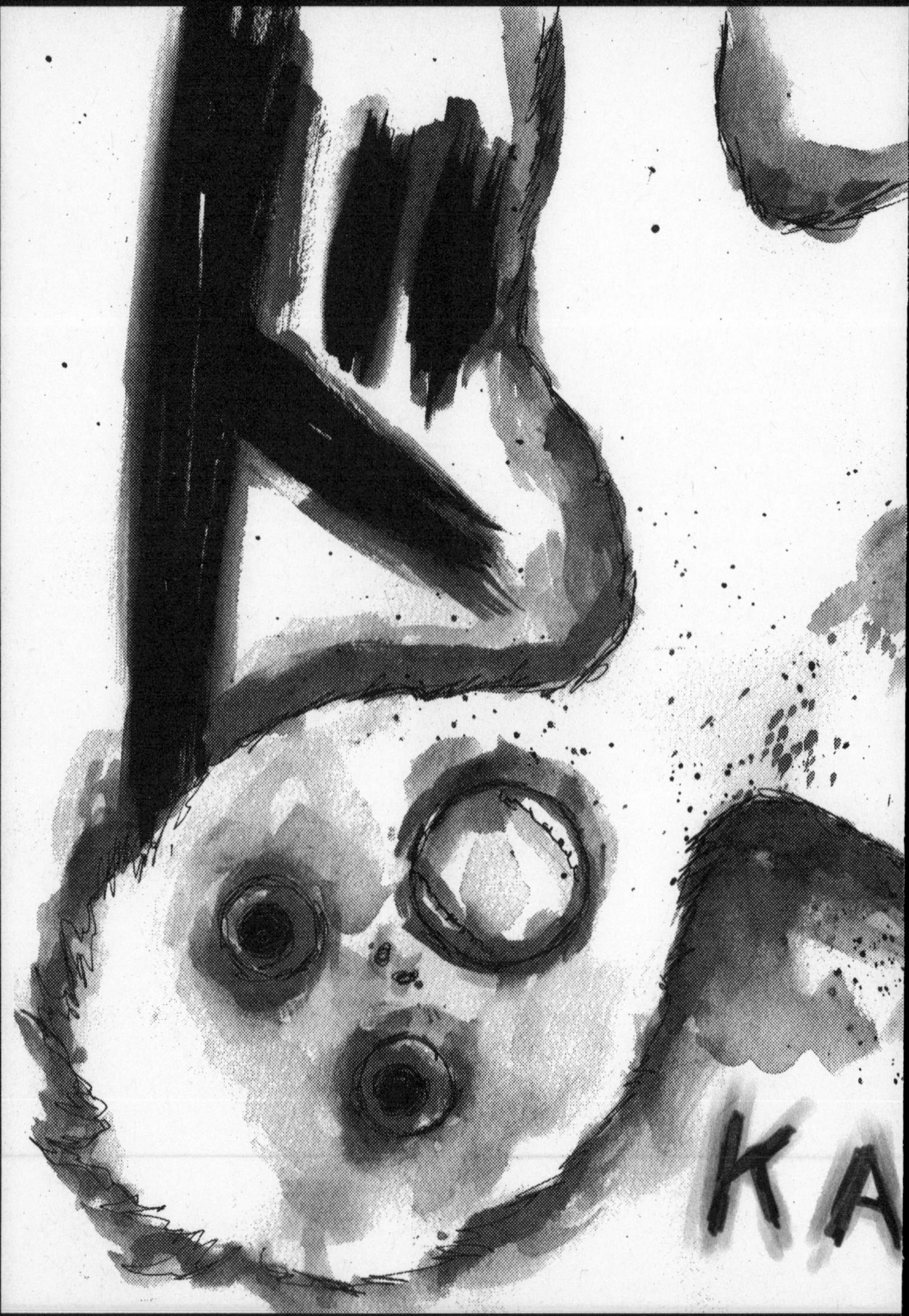
KA

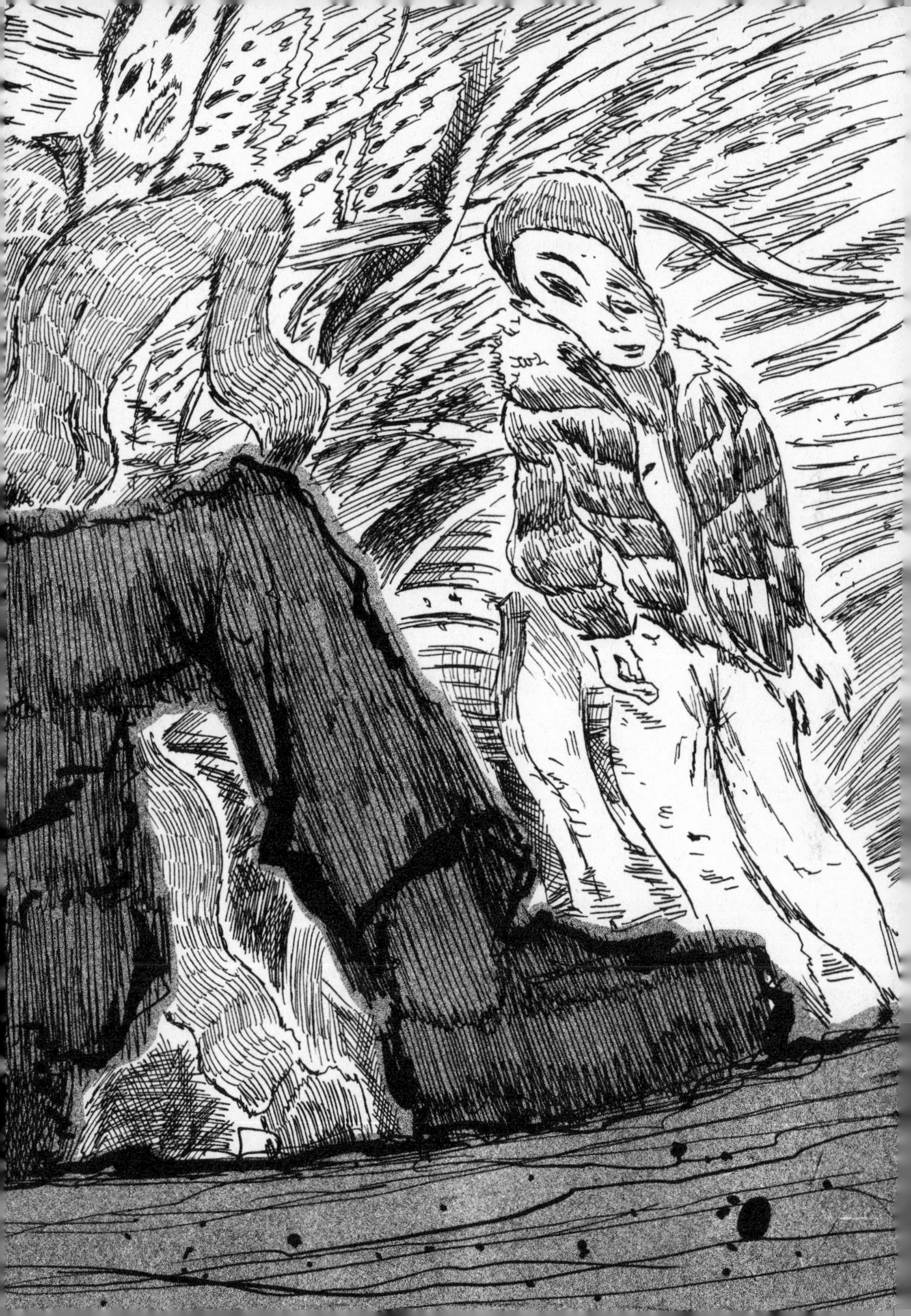

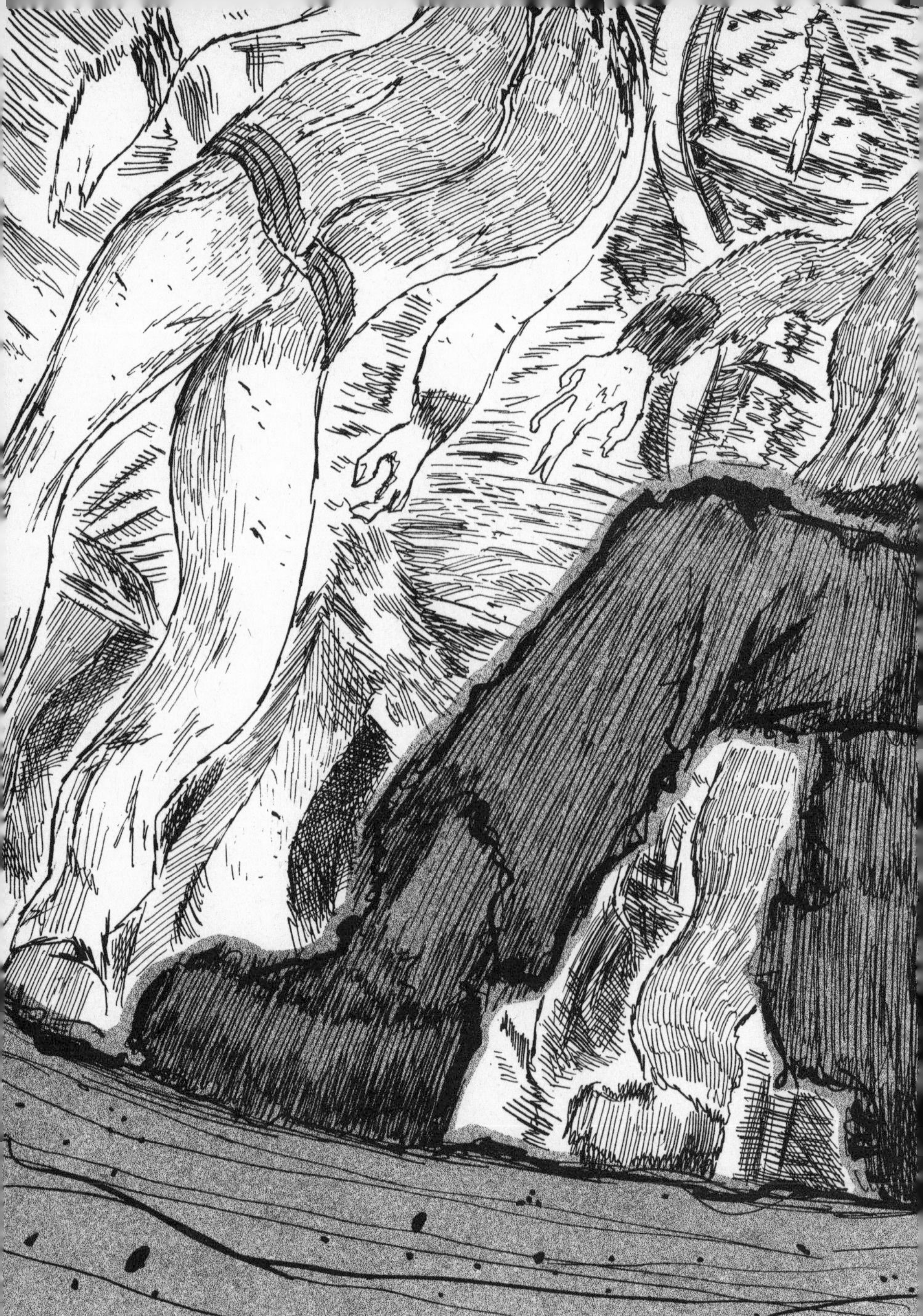

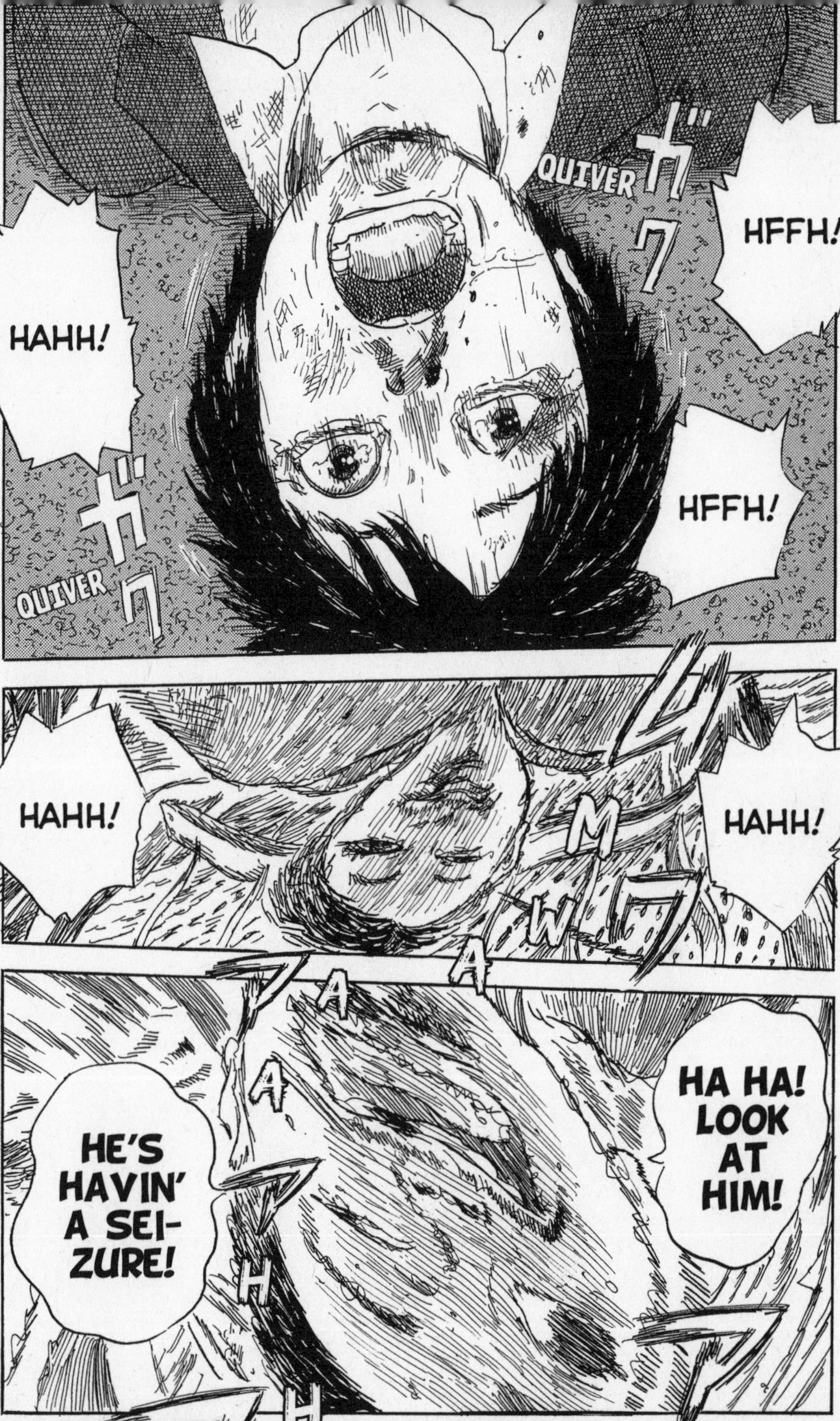
HFFH!
QUIVER
HFFH!
HAHH!
QUIVER
HAHH!
MWAAAHH
HAHH!
HA HA! LOOK AT HIM!
HE'S HAVIN' A SEI-ZURE!

Chapter 8: Cries and Shouts

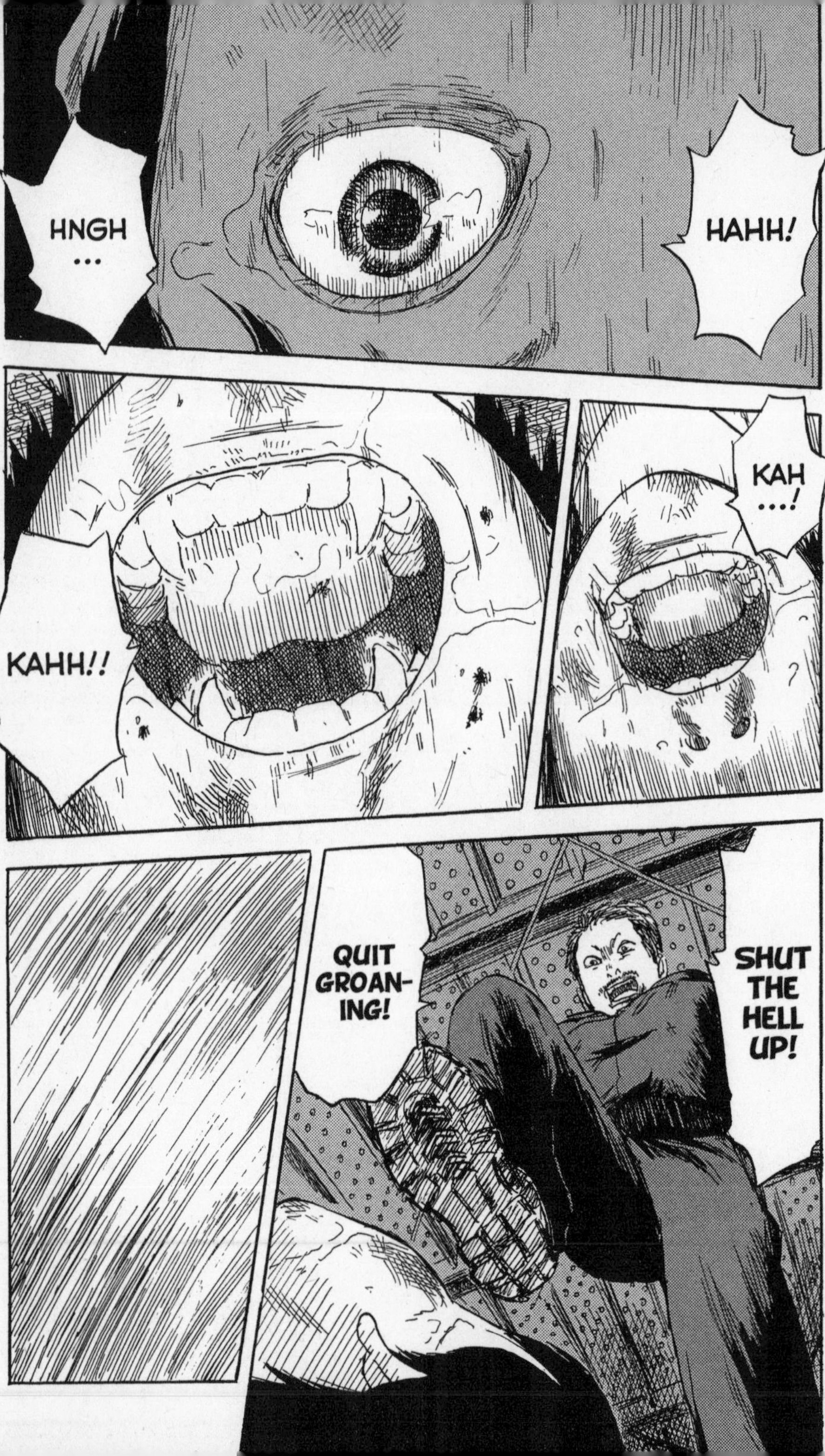
HAHH!
HNGH ...
KAH ...!
KAHH!!
SHUT THE HELL UP!
QUIT GROAN-ING!

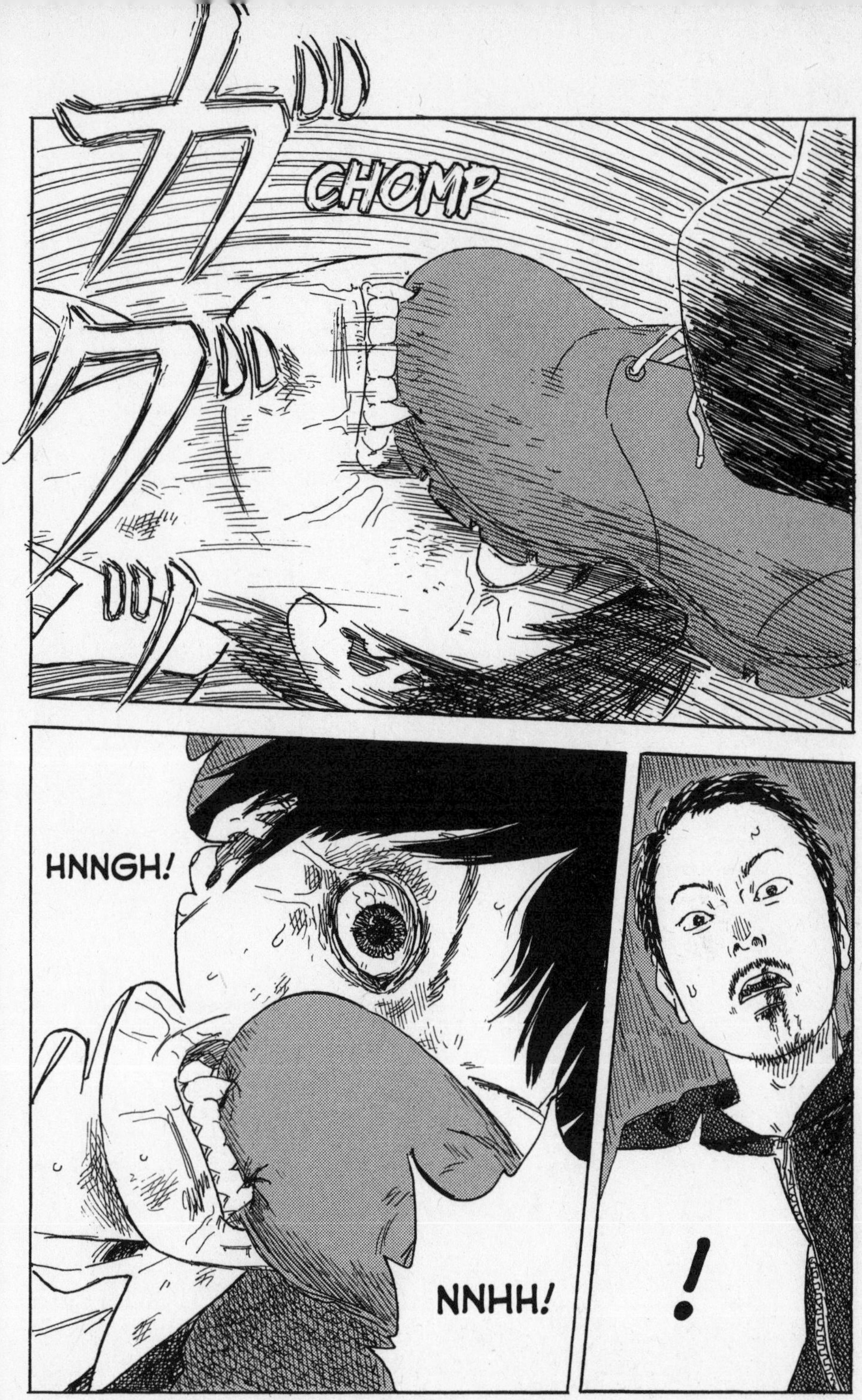
CHOMP
!
HNNGH!
NNHH!

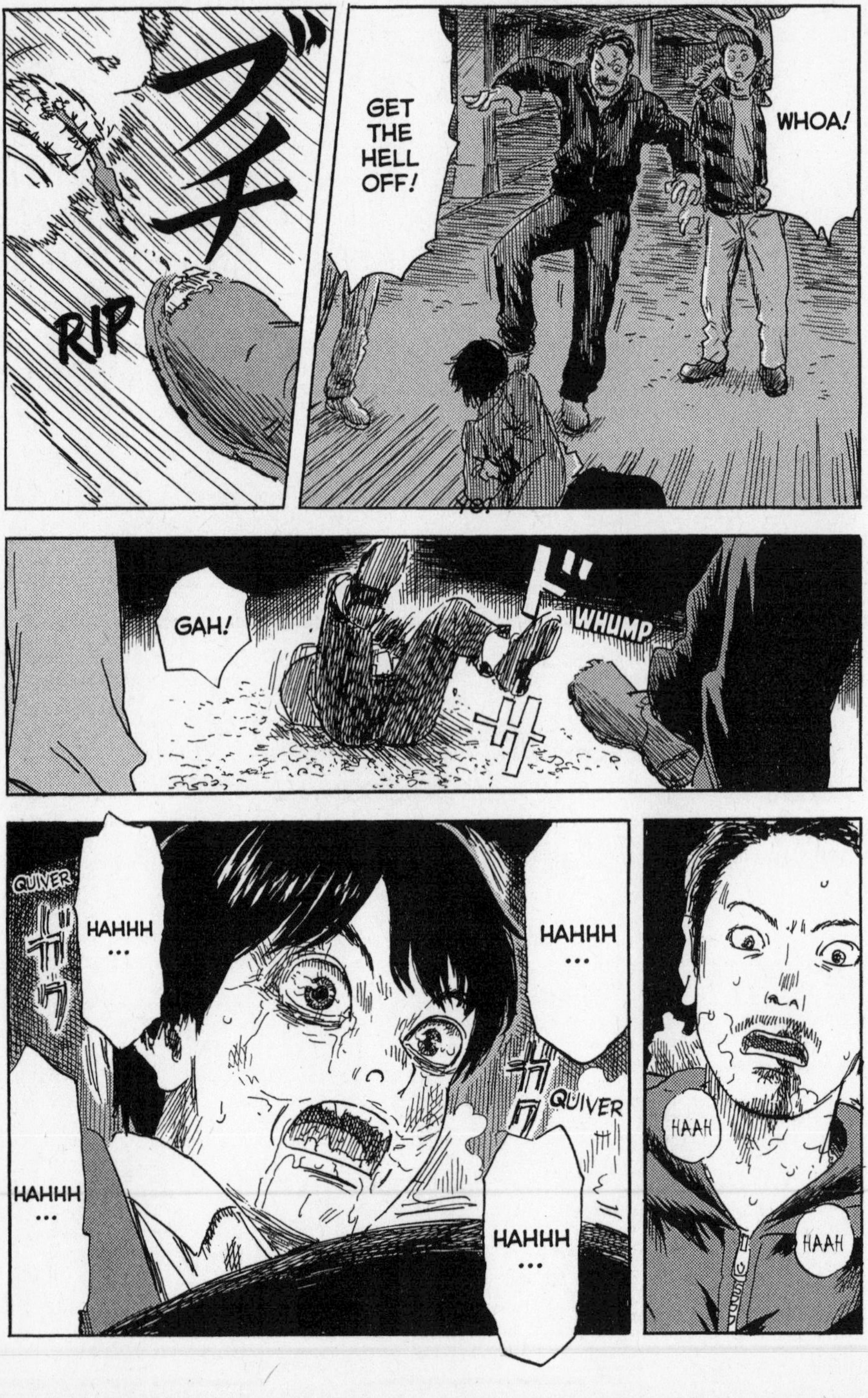
WHOA!
GET THE HELL OFF!
ブチ
RIP
WHUMP
ド
GAH!
HAAH
HAAH
HAHHH ...
QUIVER
HAHHH ...
QUIVER
HAHHH ...
HAHHH ...

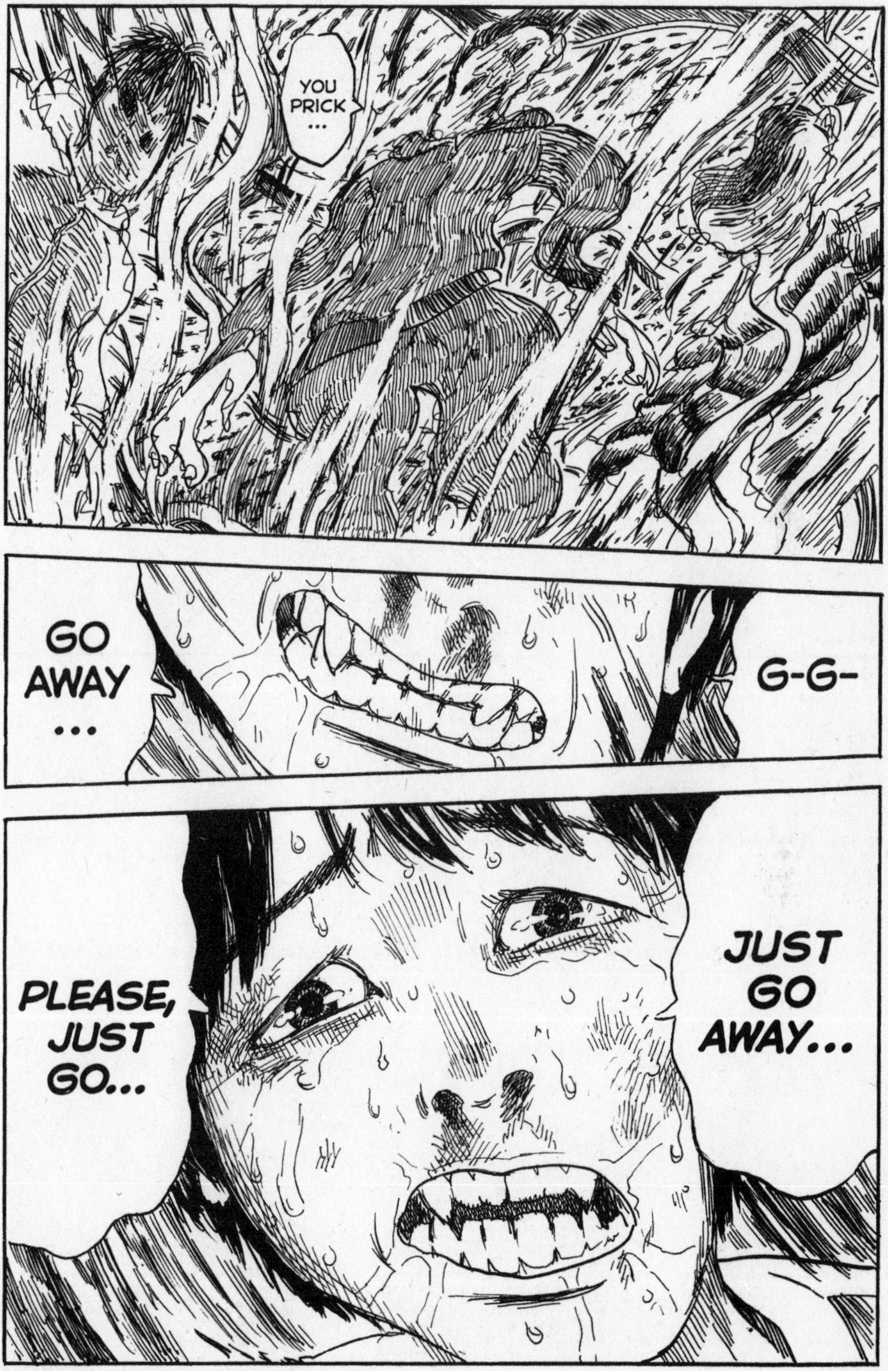
YOU PRICK...
G-G-
GO AWAY...
JUST GO AWAY...
PLEASE, JUST GO...

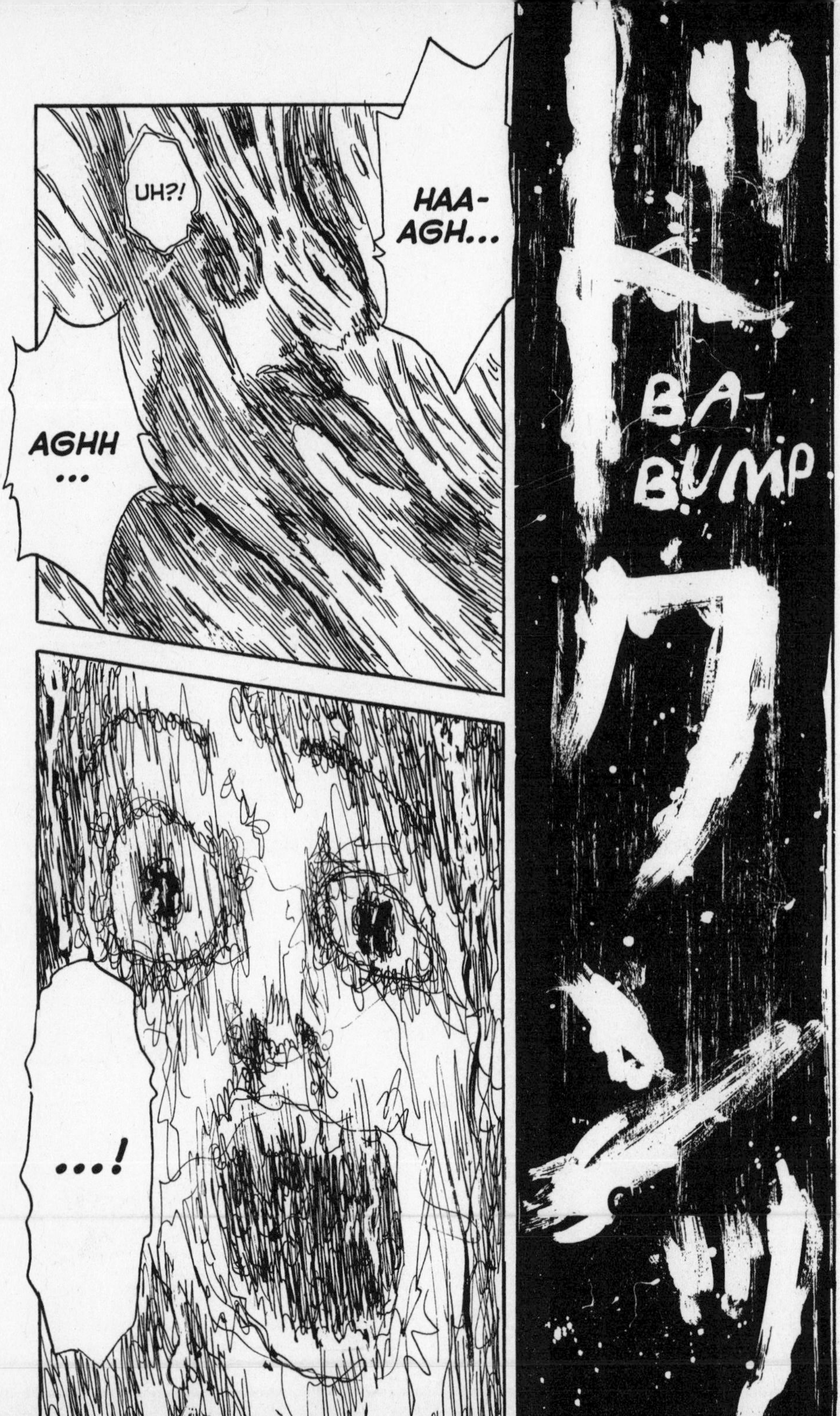
BA-BUMP
HAA-AGH...
UH?!
AGHH...
...!

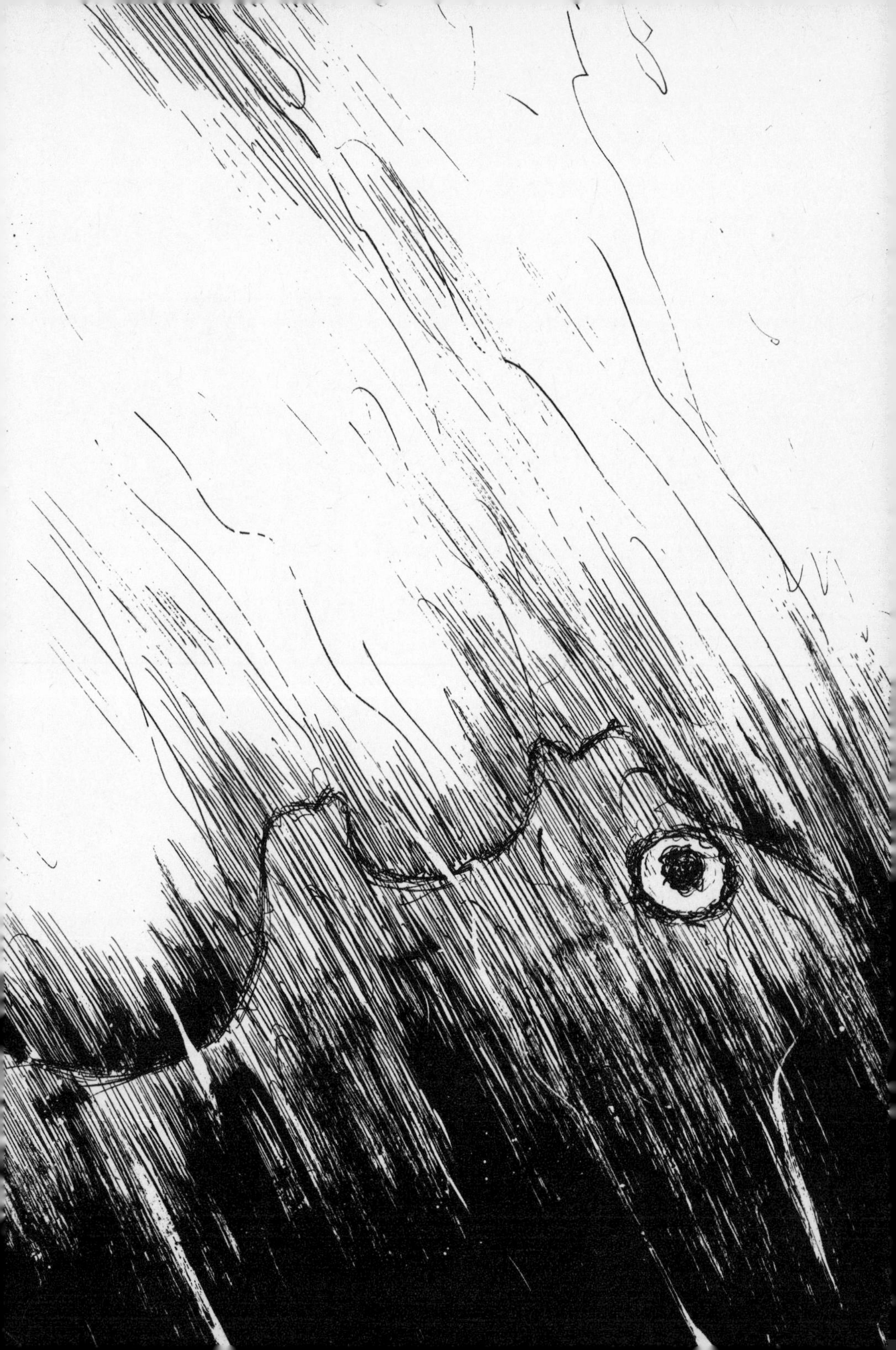

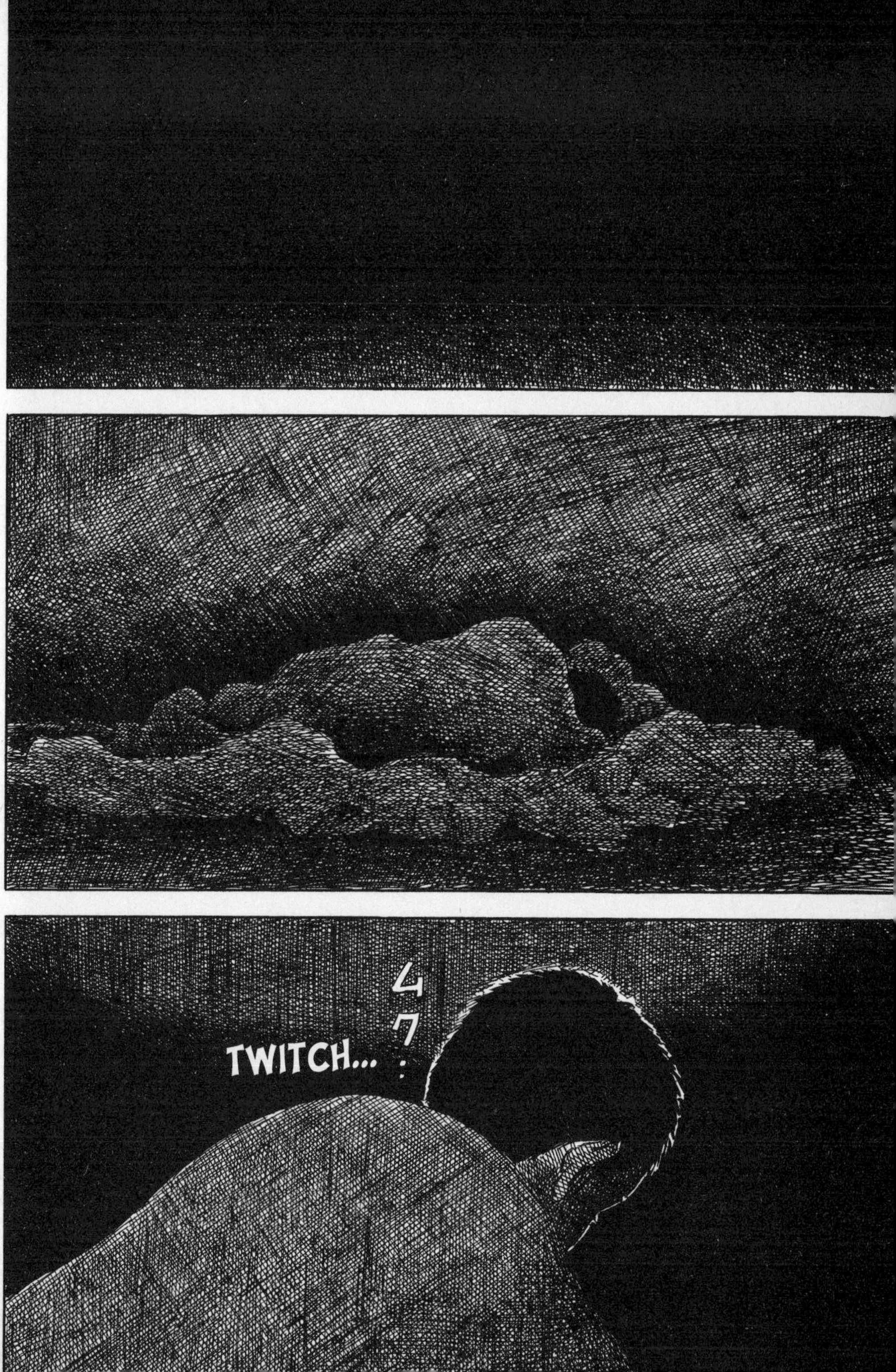
ムク
TWITCH...

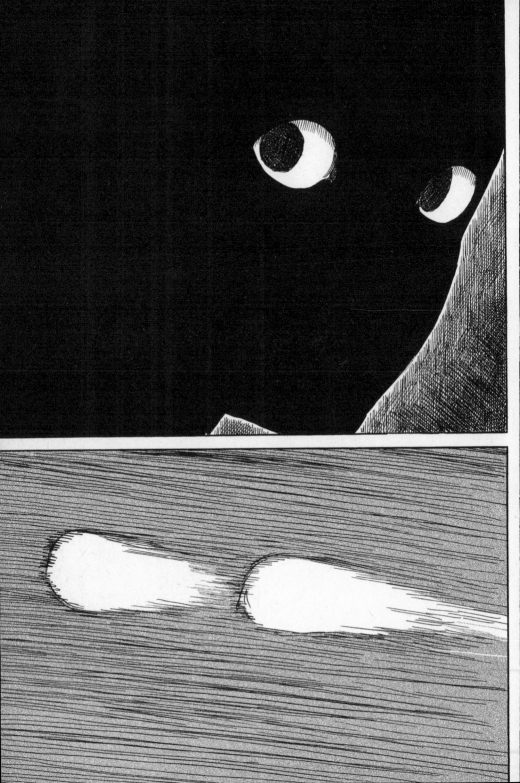

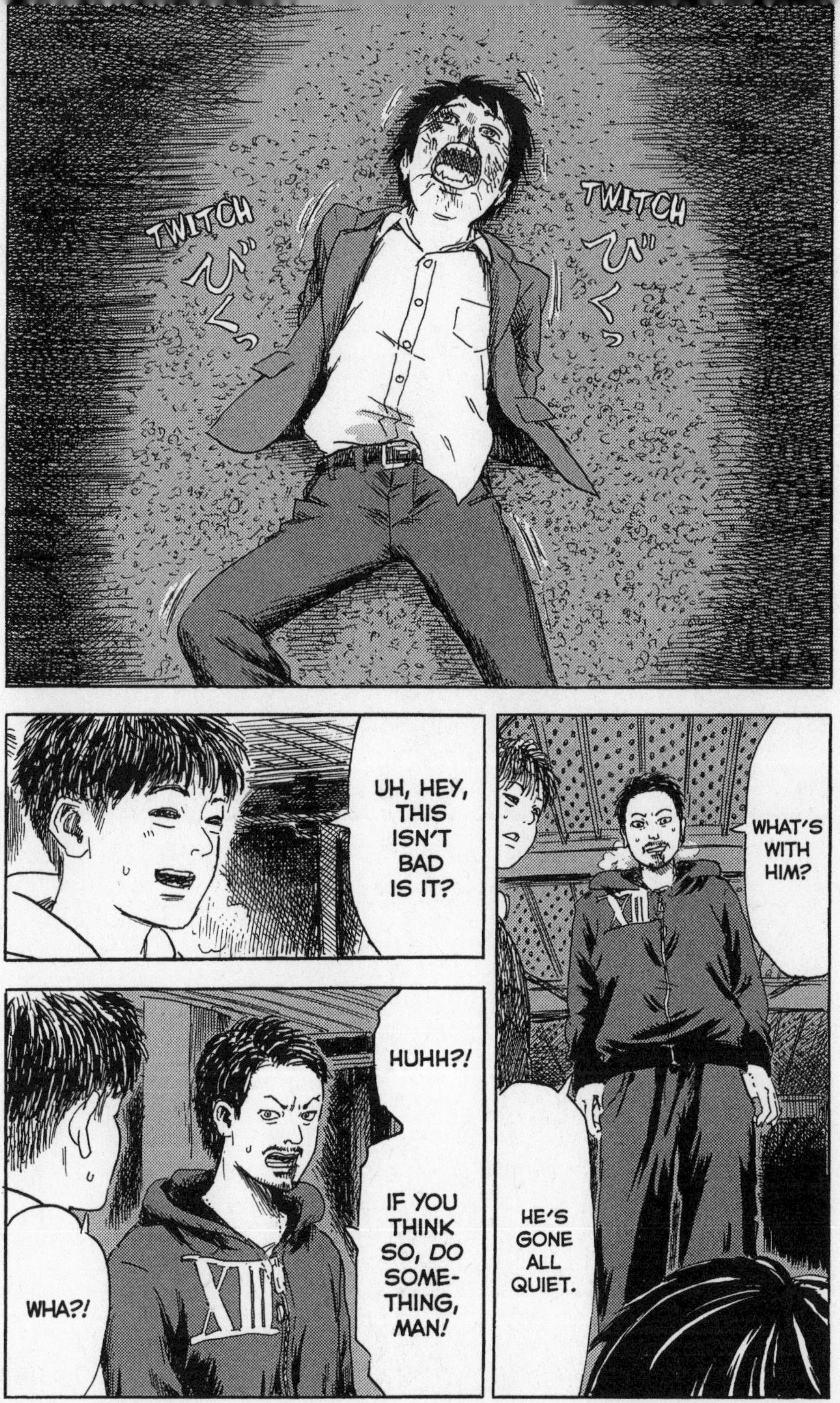

TWITCH
びくっ
TWITCH
びくっ
WHAT'S WITH HIM?
HE'S GONE ALL QUIET.
UH, HEY, THIS ISN'T BAD IS IT?
HUHH?!
IF YOU THINK SO, *DO* SOME-THING, MAN!
WHA?!

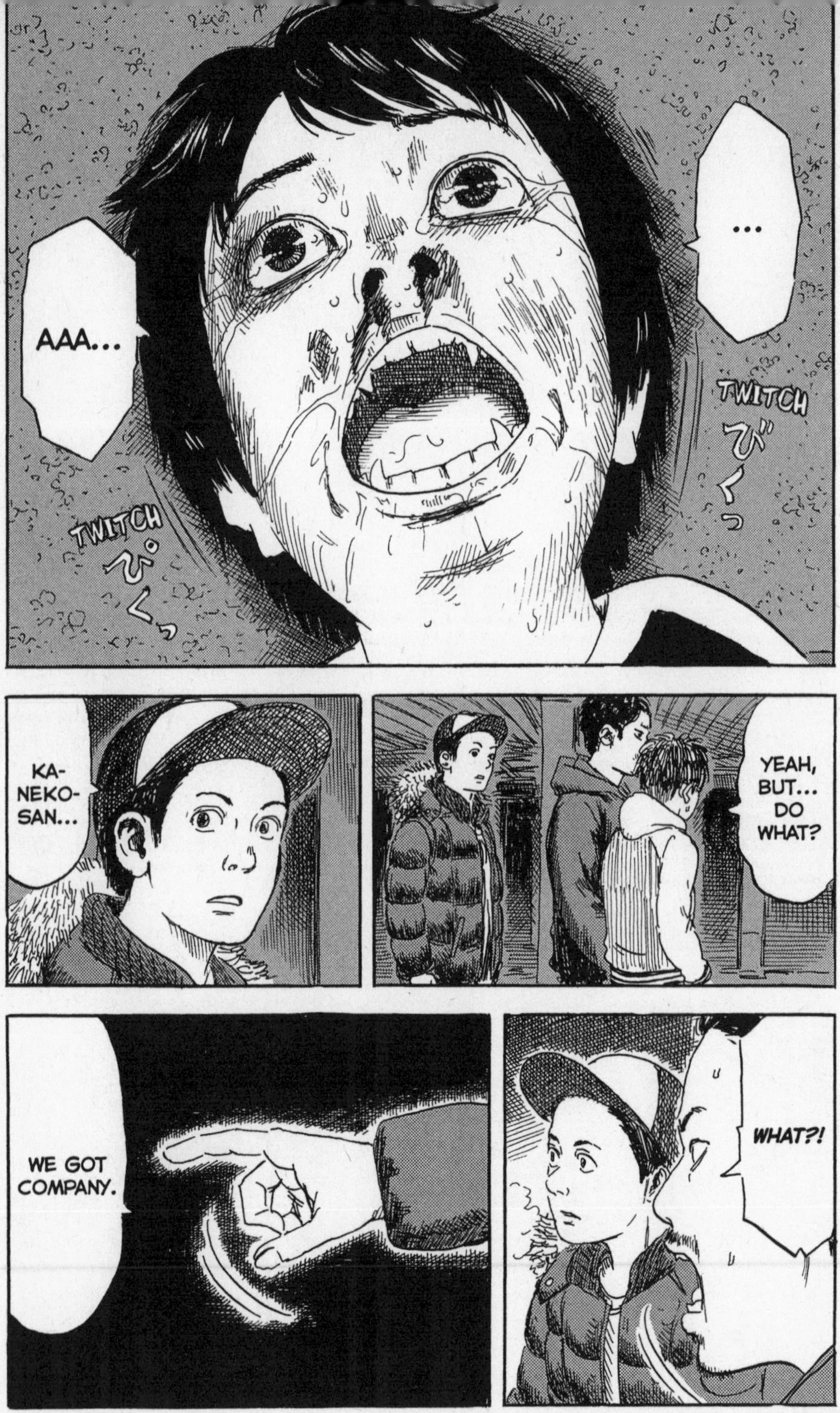
...
TWITCH
びくっ
AAA...
TWITCH
ぴくっ
YEAH, BUT... DO WHAT?
KA-NEKO-SAN...
WHAT?!
WE GOT COMPANY.

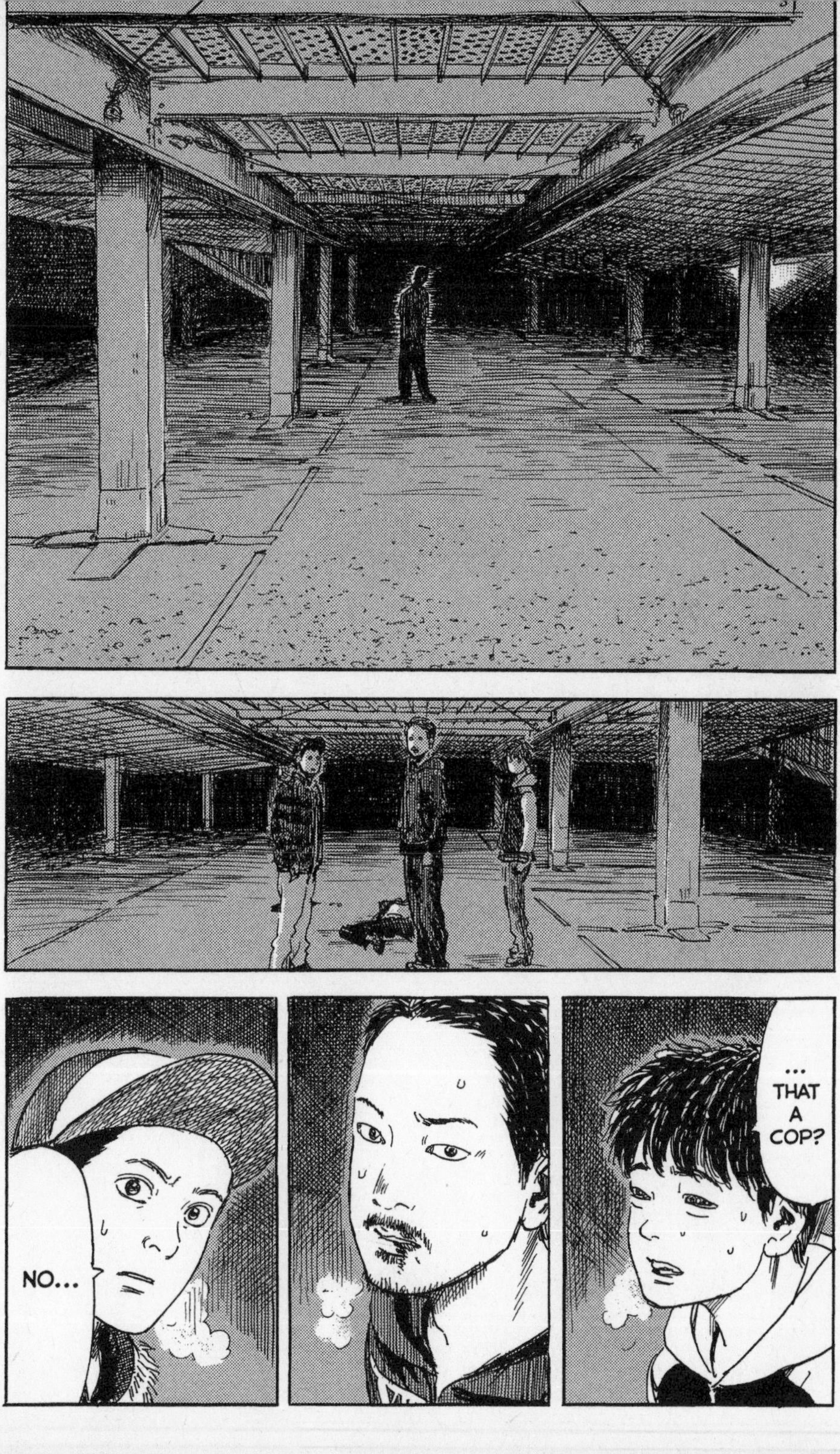
... THAT A COP?
NO...

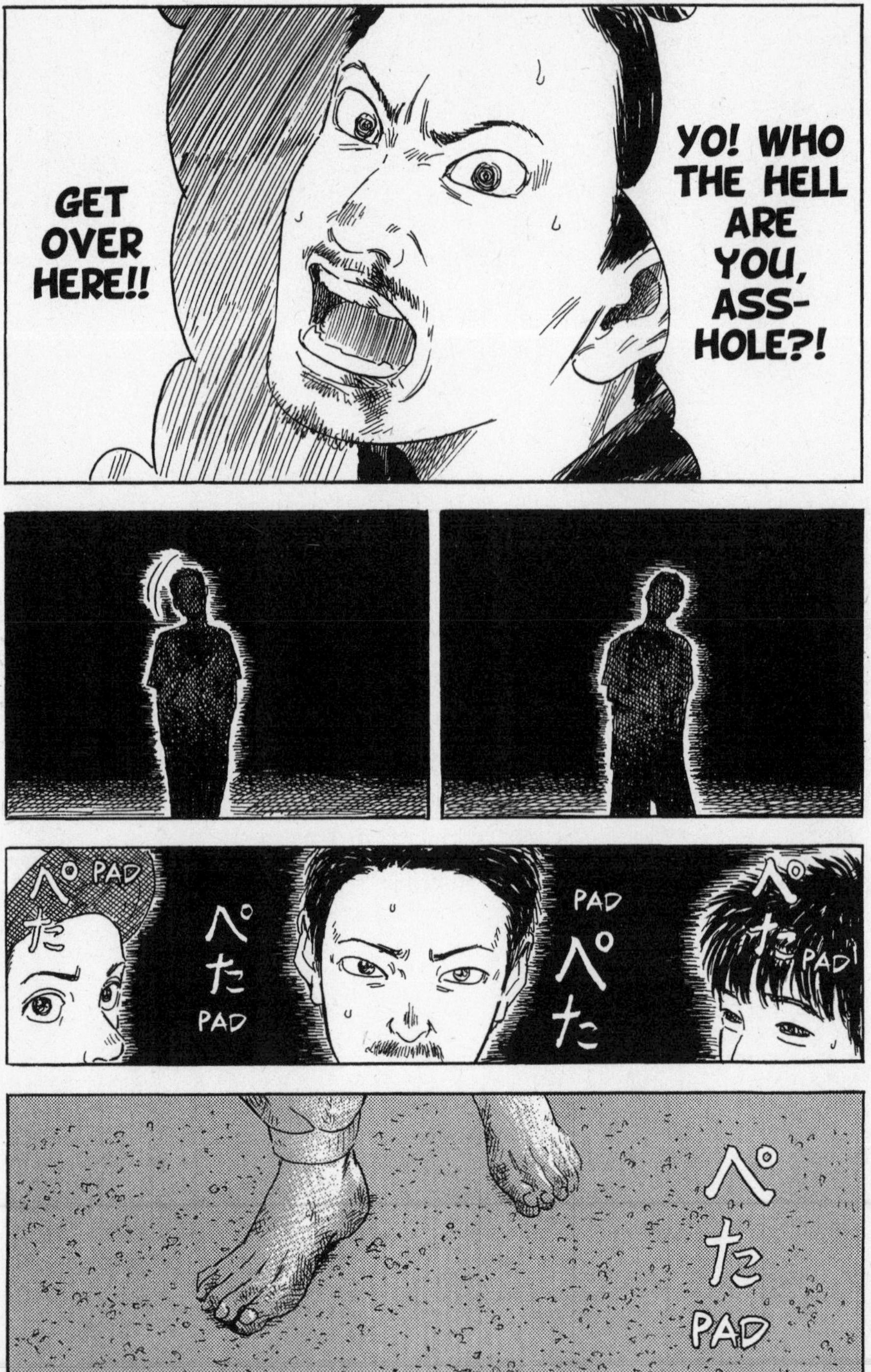
YO! WHO THE HELL ARE YOU, ASS-HOLE?!
GET OVER HERE!!
ぺた PAD
PAD ぺた
ぺた PAD
ぺた PAD
ぺた PAD

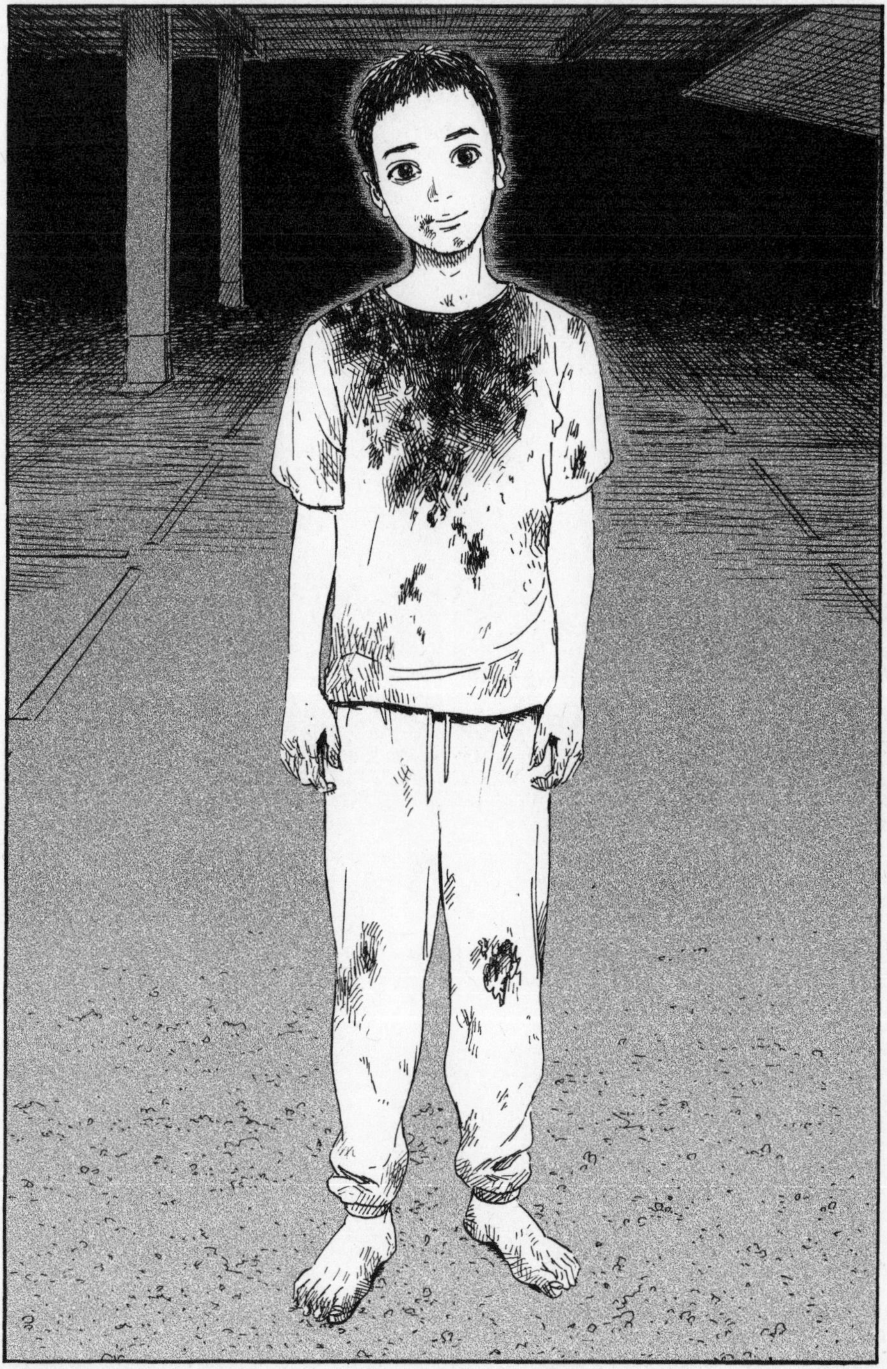

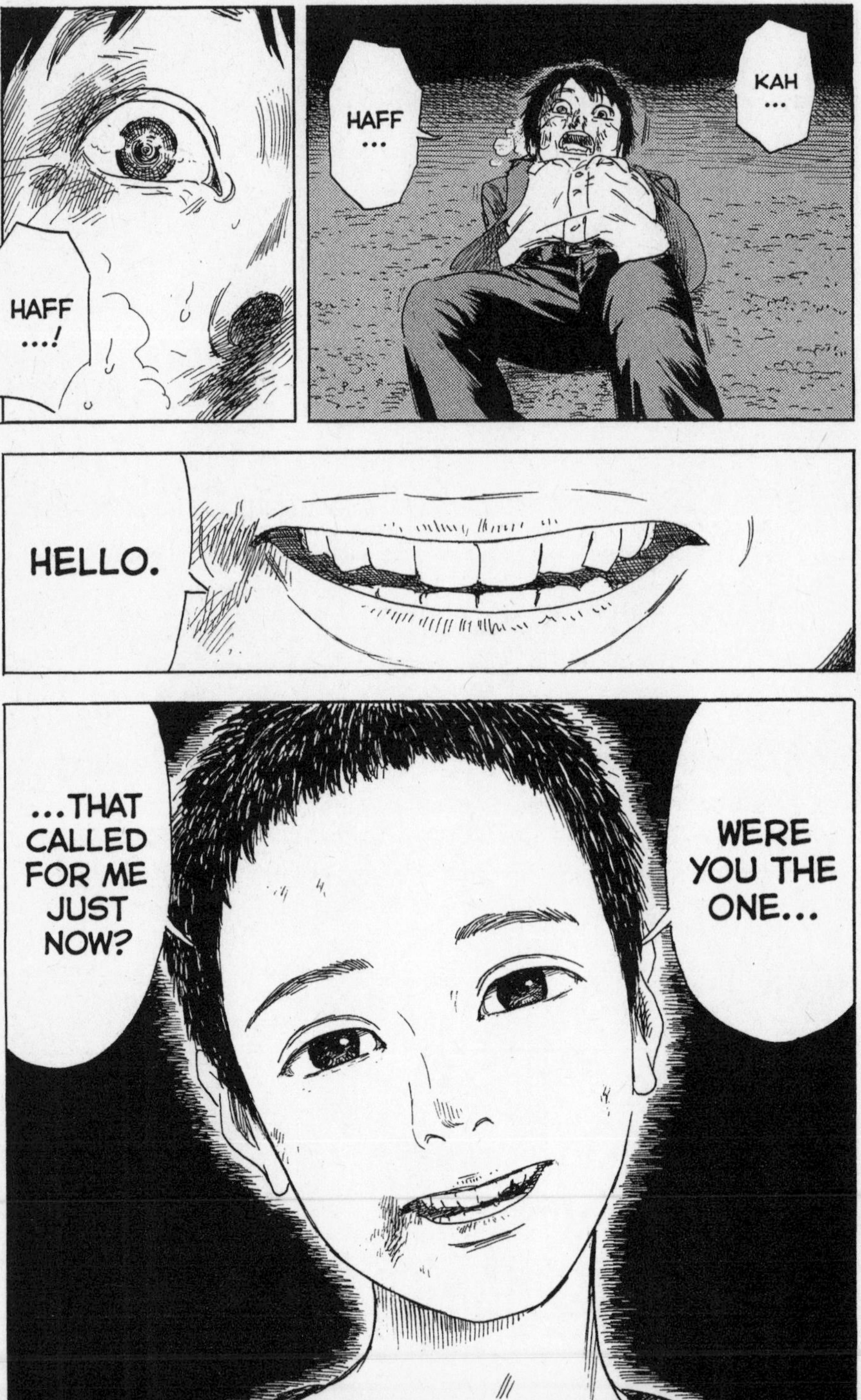
KAH ...
HAFF ...
HAFF ...!
HELLO.
WERE YOU THE ONE...
...THAT CALLED FOR ME JUST NOW?

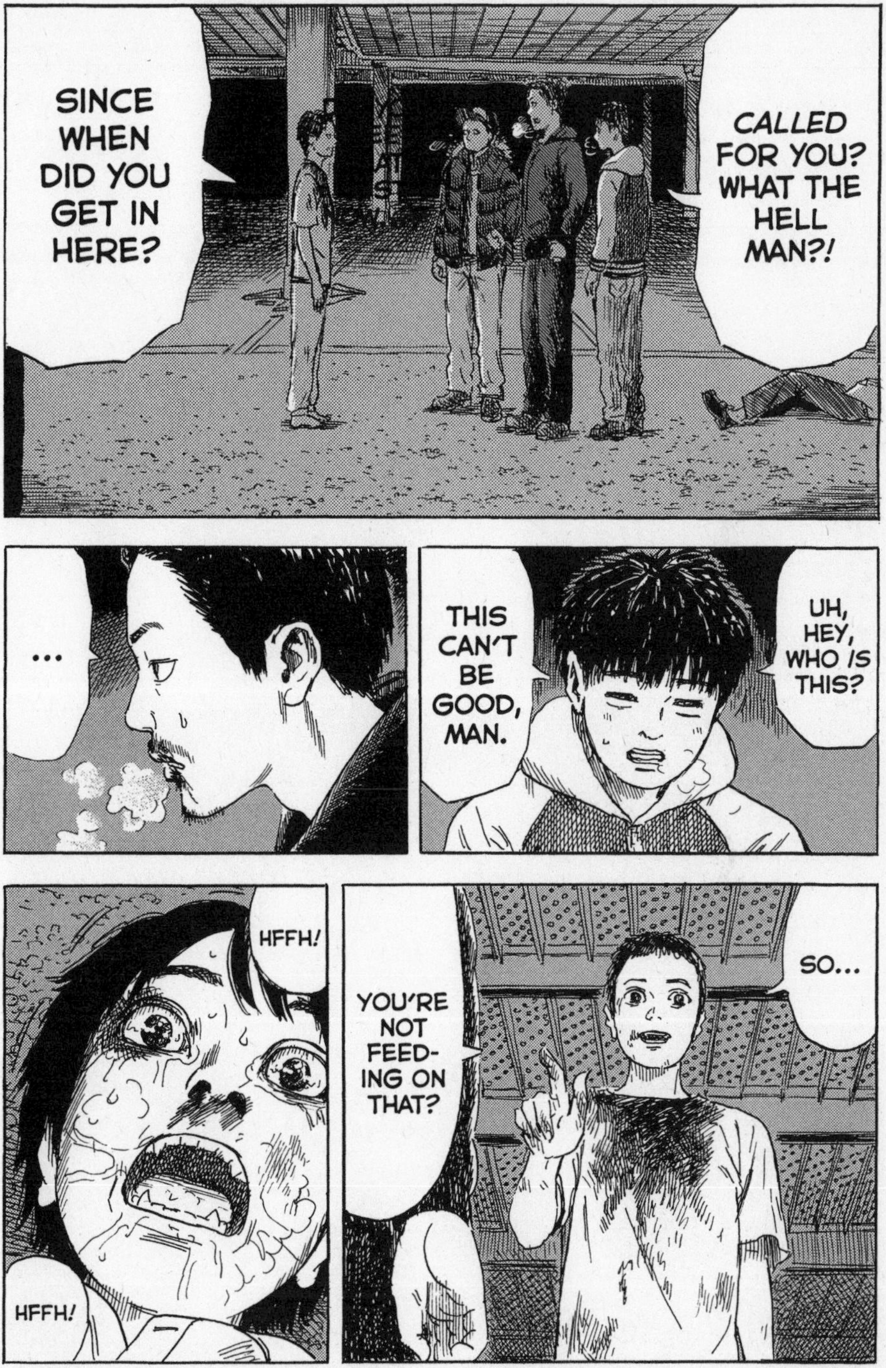
CALLED FOR YOU? WHAT THE HELL MAN?!
SINCE WHEN DID YOU GET IN HERE?
UH, HEY, WHO IS THIS?
THIS CAN'T BE GOOD, MAN.
...
SO...
YOU'RE NOT FEED-ING ON THAT?
HFFH!
HFFH!

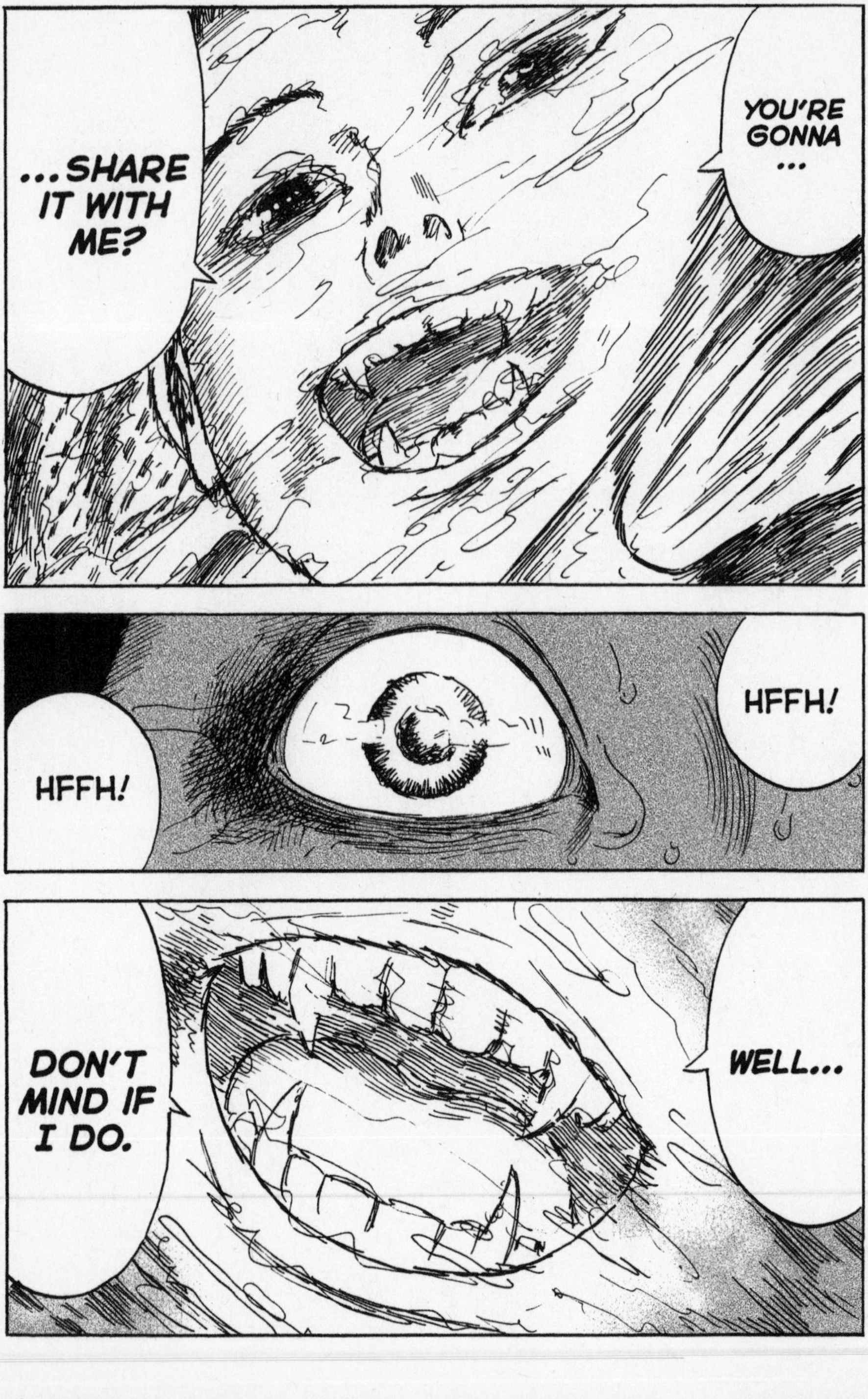
YOU'RE GONNA ...
...SHARE IT WITH ME?
HFFH!
HFFH!
WELL...
DON'T MIND IF I DO.

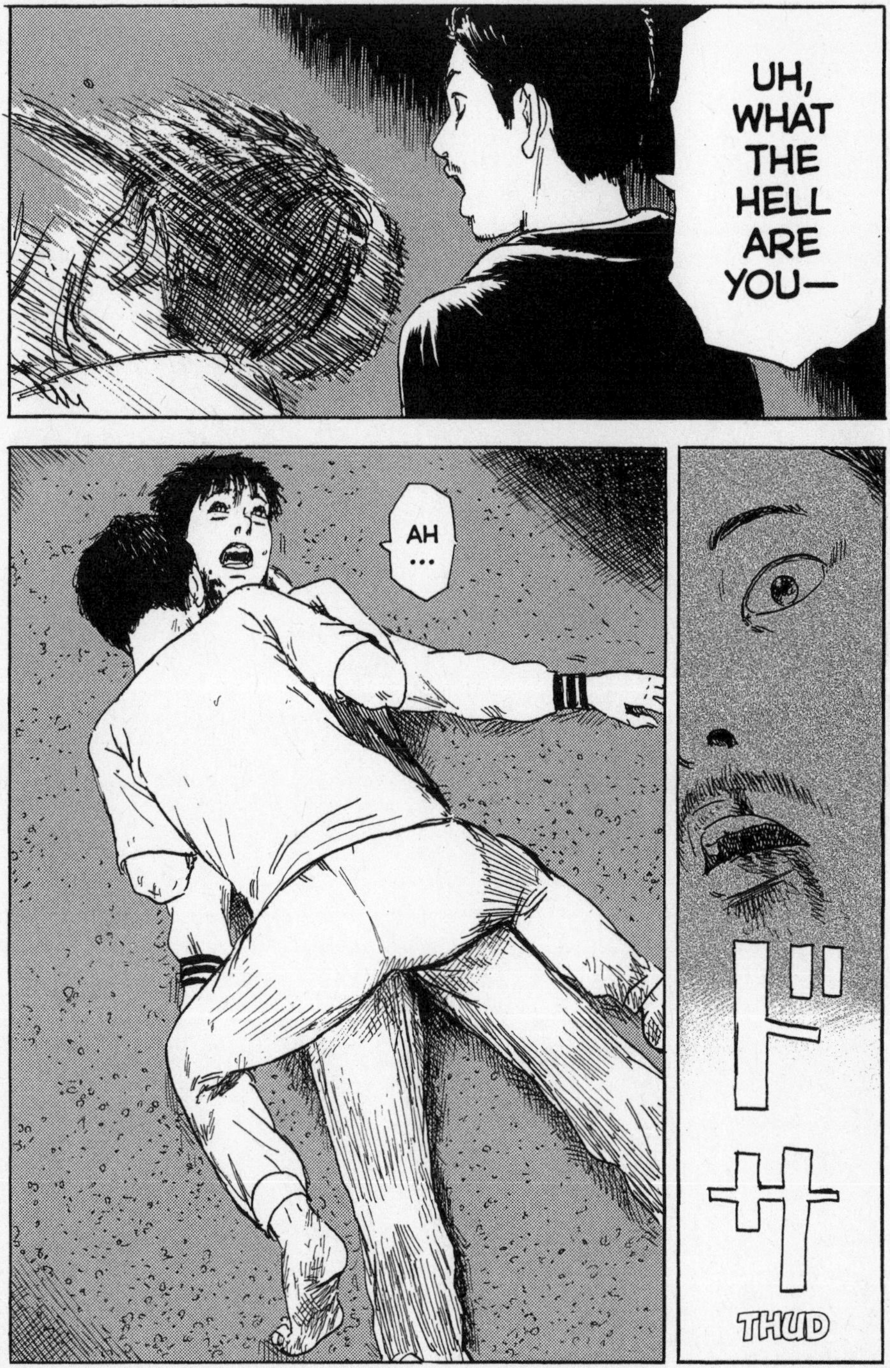
UH, WHAT THE HELL ARE YOU—
ドサッ
THUD
AH ...

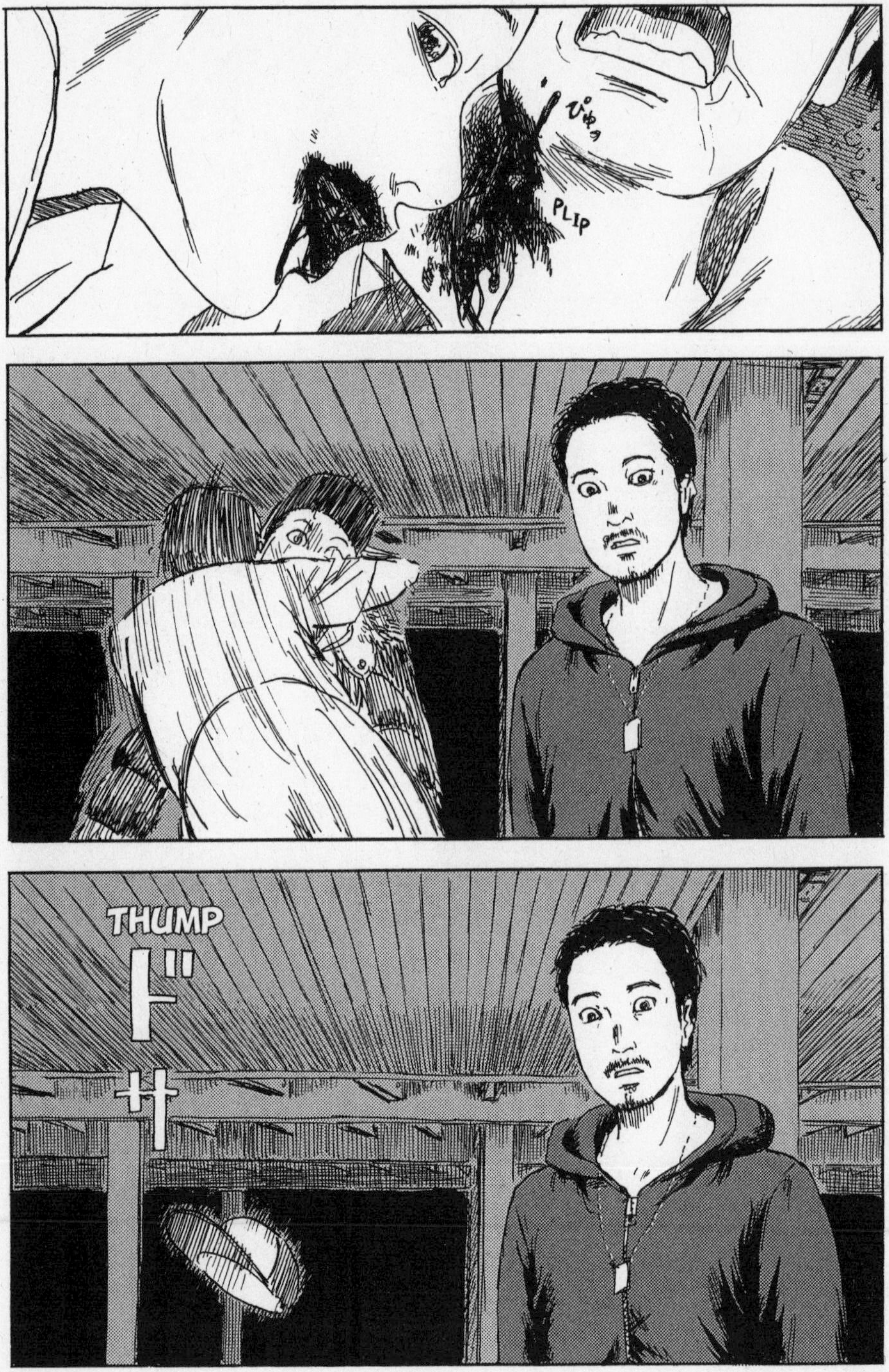
ぴゅっ
PLIP
THUMP
ドサ

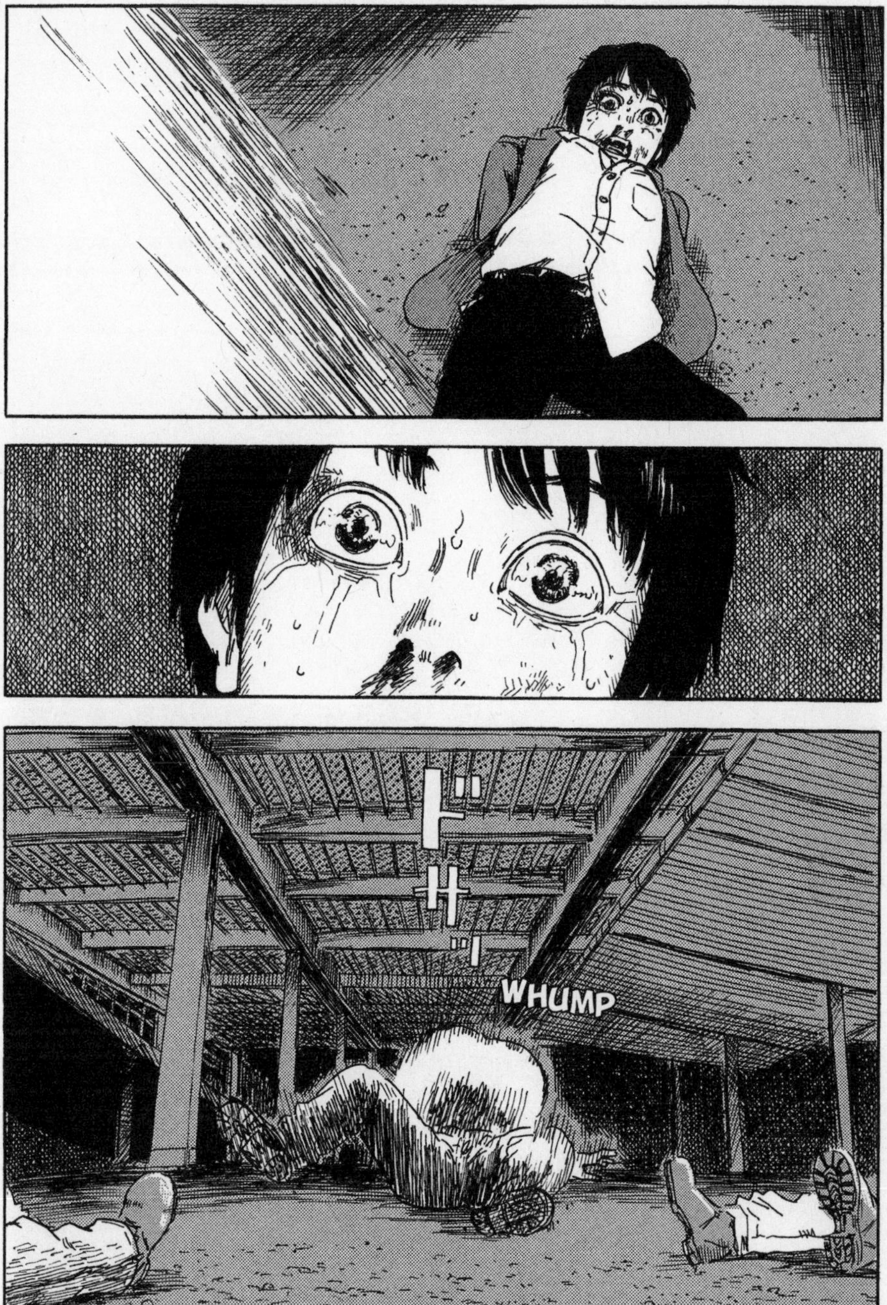
ドサッ
WHUMP

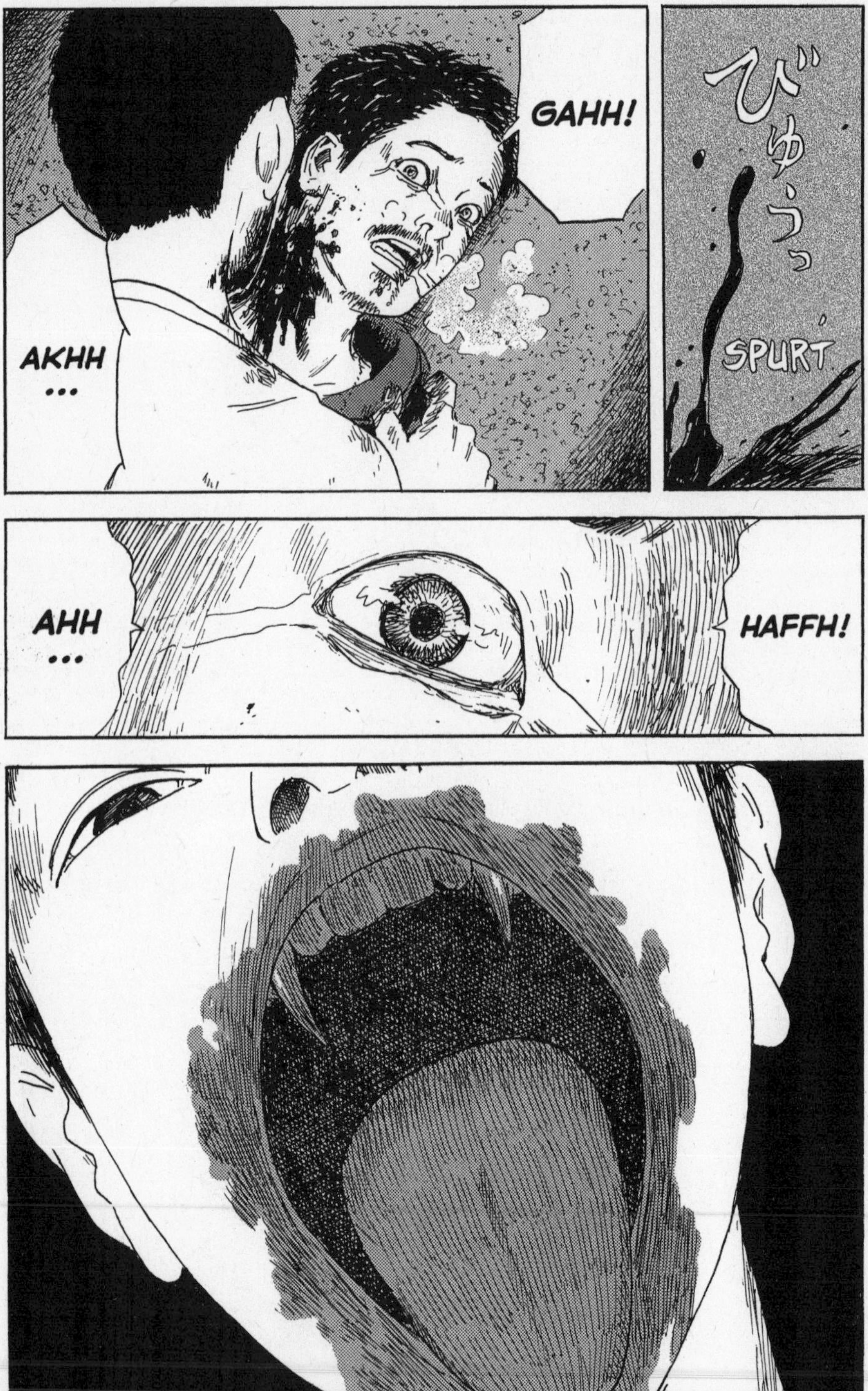
びゅうっ
SPURT
GAHH!
AKHH ...
HAFFH!
AHH ...

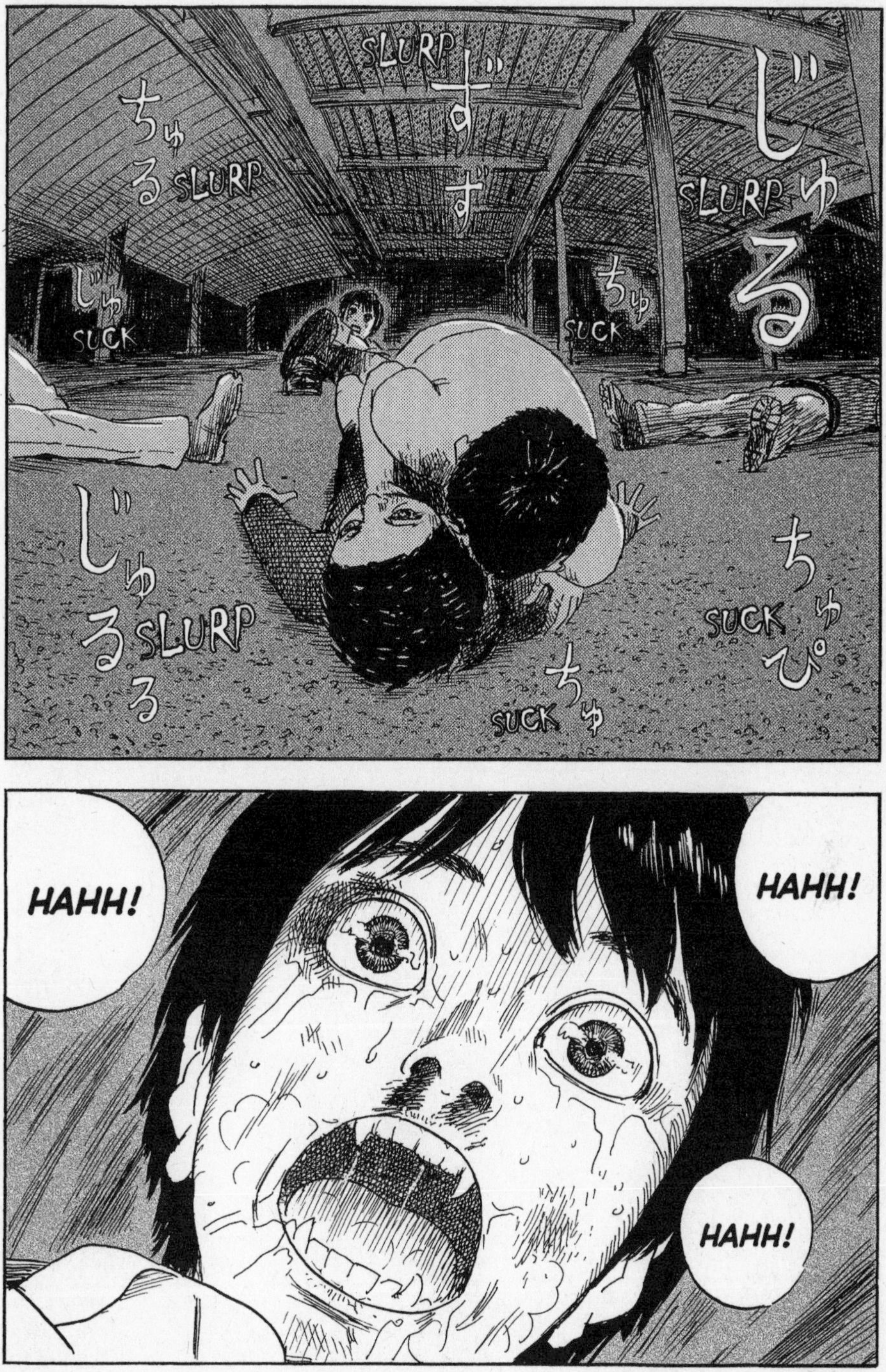
じゅる
SLURP
ずず
SLURP
ちゅる
SLURP
ちゅ
SUCK
じゅ
SUCK
ちゅぴ
SUCK
ちゅ
SUCK
じゅるる
SLURP
HAHH!
HAHH!
HAHH!

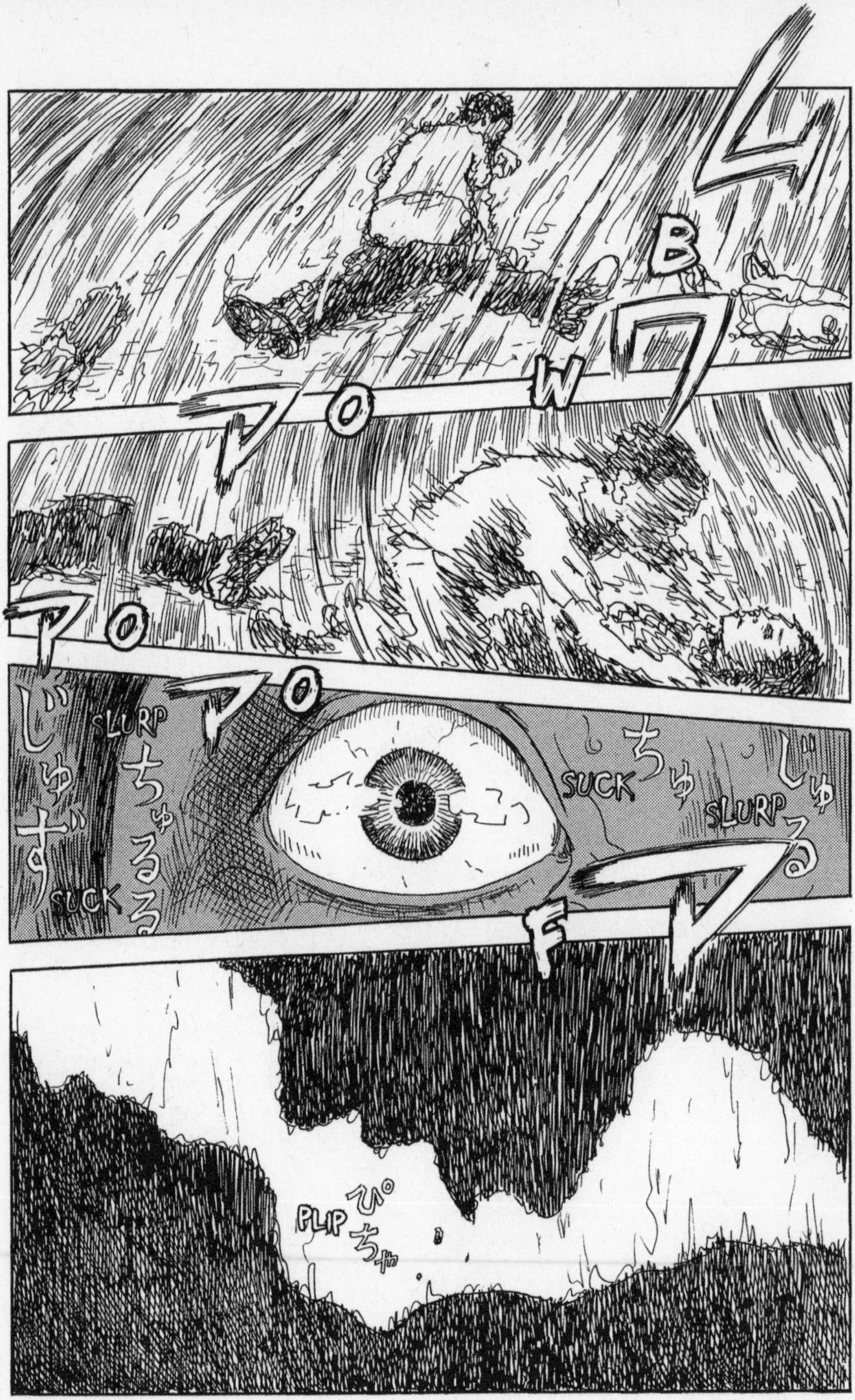
ム
B
ワ
W
フ
O
ア
O
ア
O
ア
F
じゅる
SLURP
ちゅ
SUCK
ちゅるる
SLURP
じゅず
SUCK
ぴちゅ
PLIP

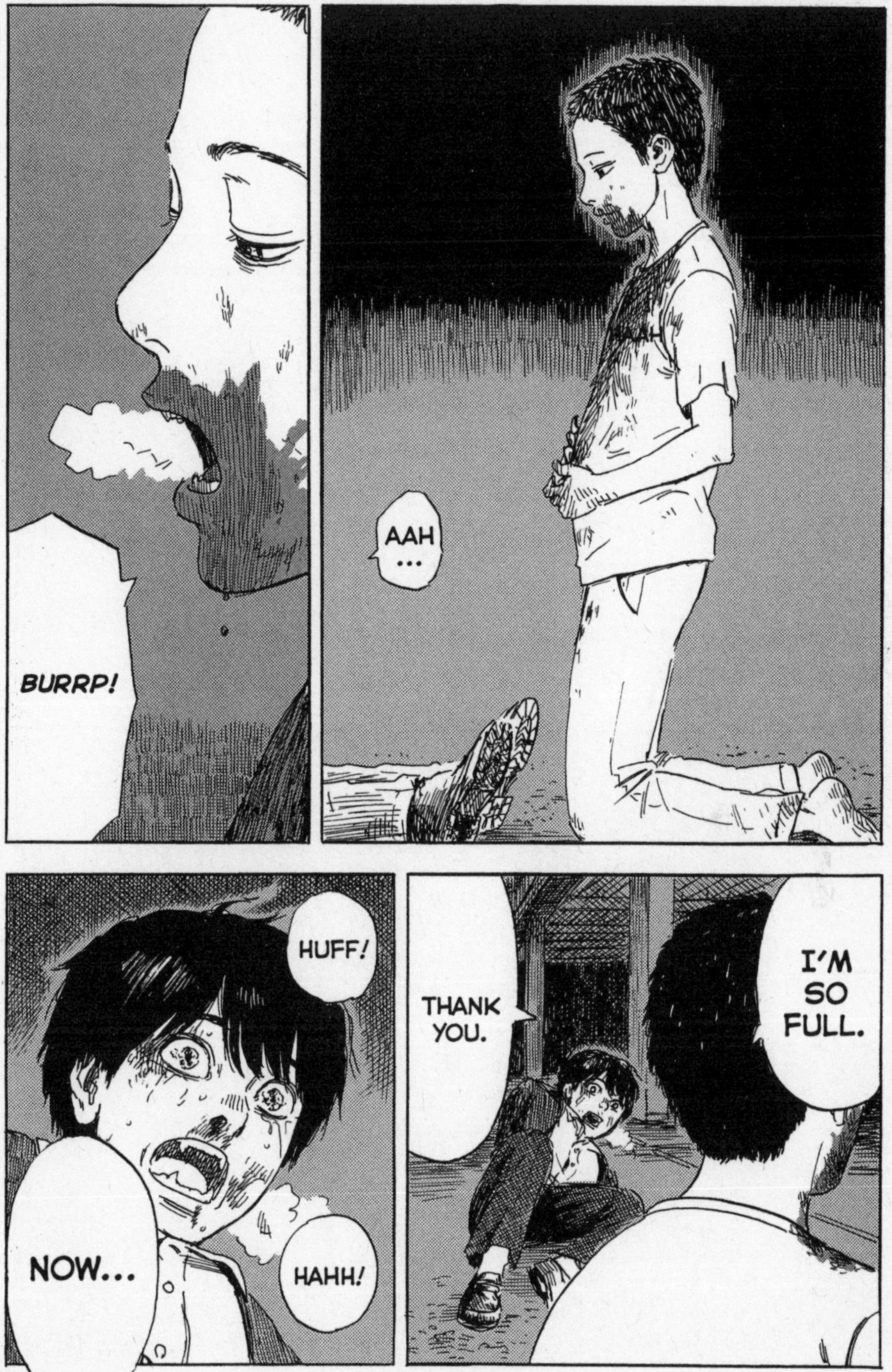
AAH ...
BURRP!
I'M SO FULL.
THANK YOU.
HUFF!
HAHH!
NOW...

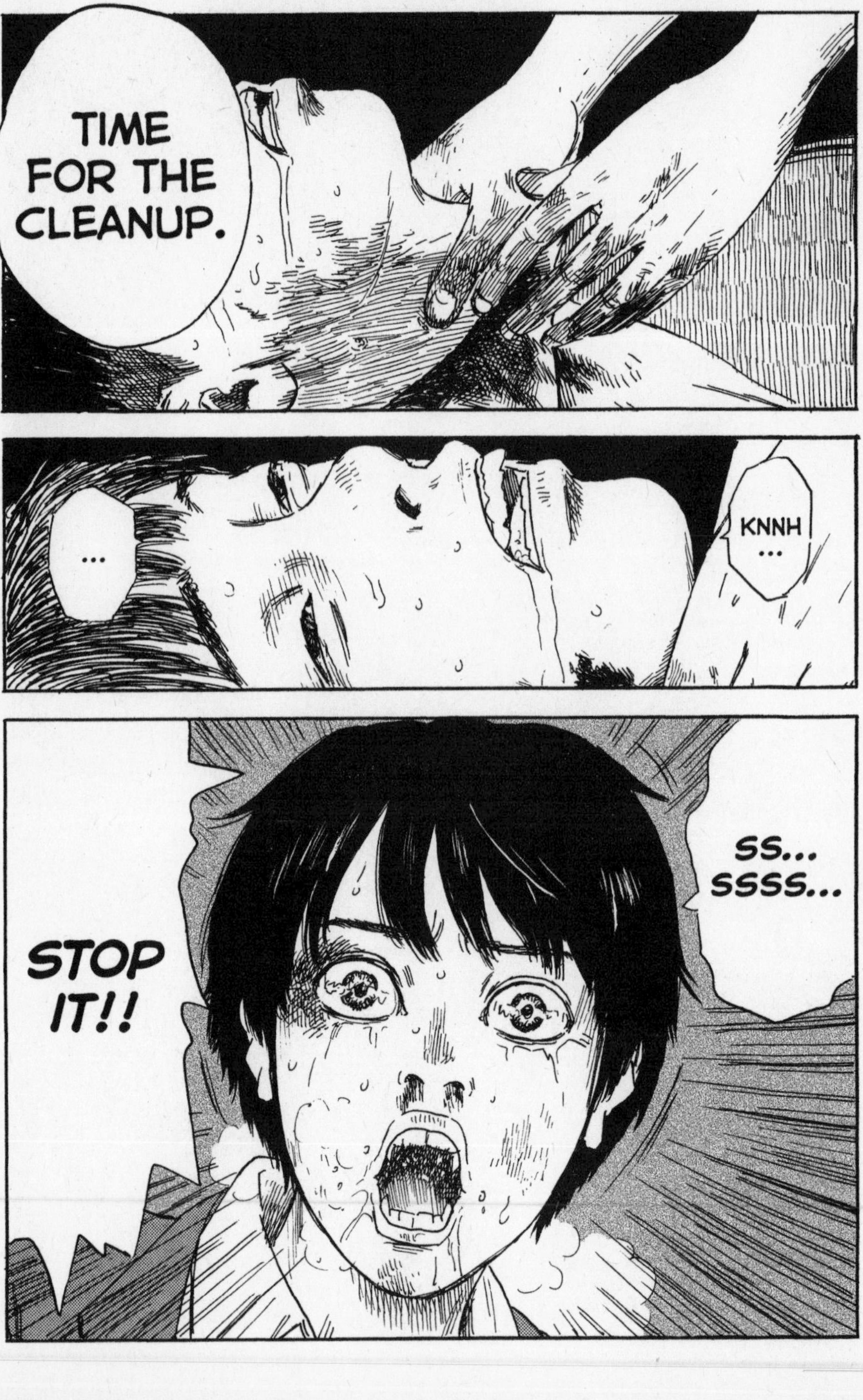
TIME FOR THE CLEANUP.
KNNH ...
...
SS... SSSS...
STOP IT!!

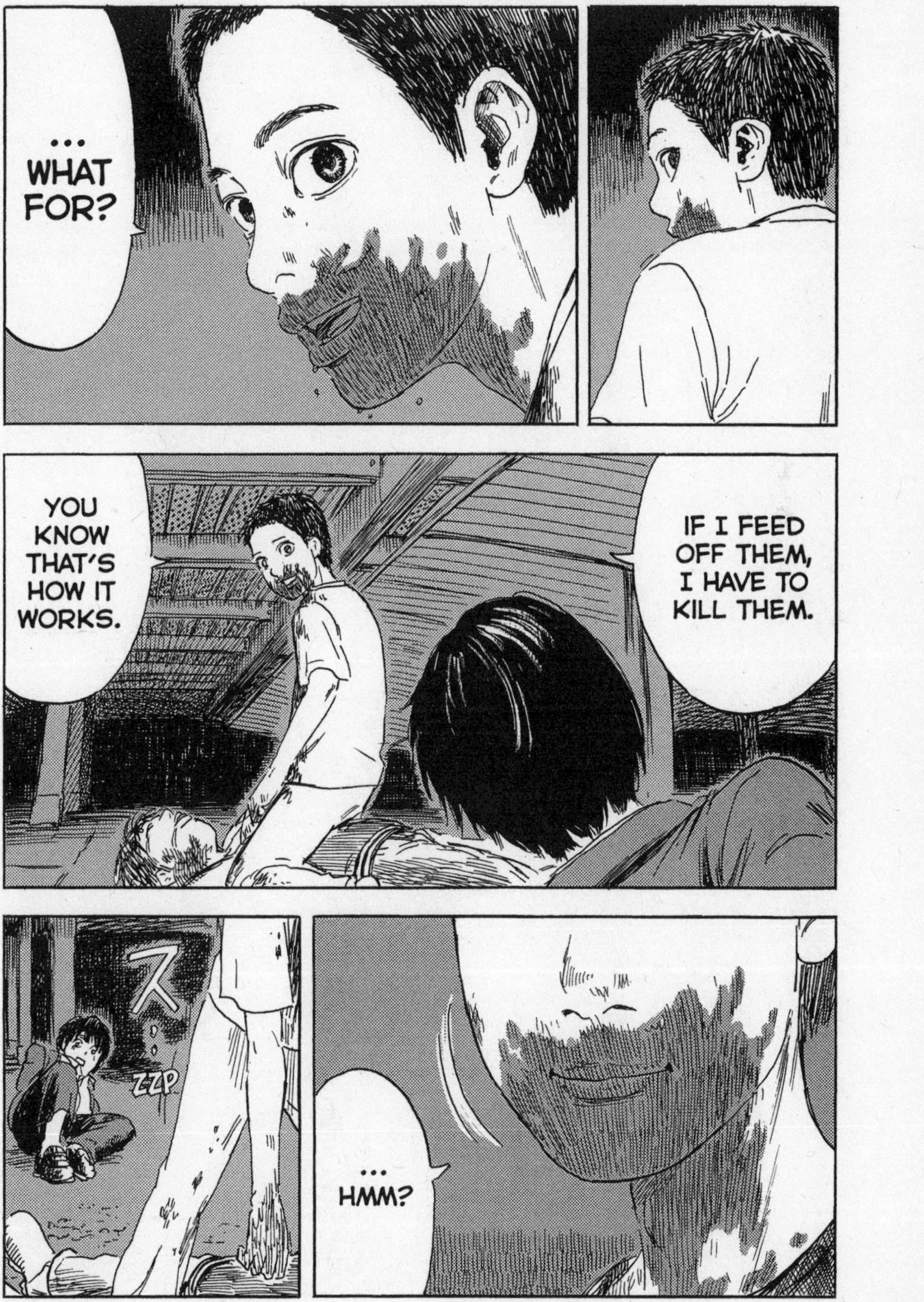
... WHAT FOR?
IF I FEED OFF THEM, I HAVE TO KILL THEM.
YOU KNOW THAT'S HOW IT WORKS.
... HMM?
ス
ZZP

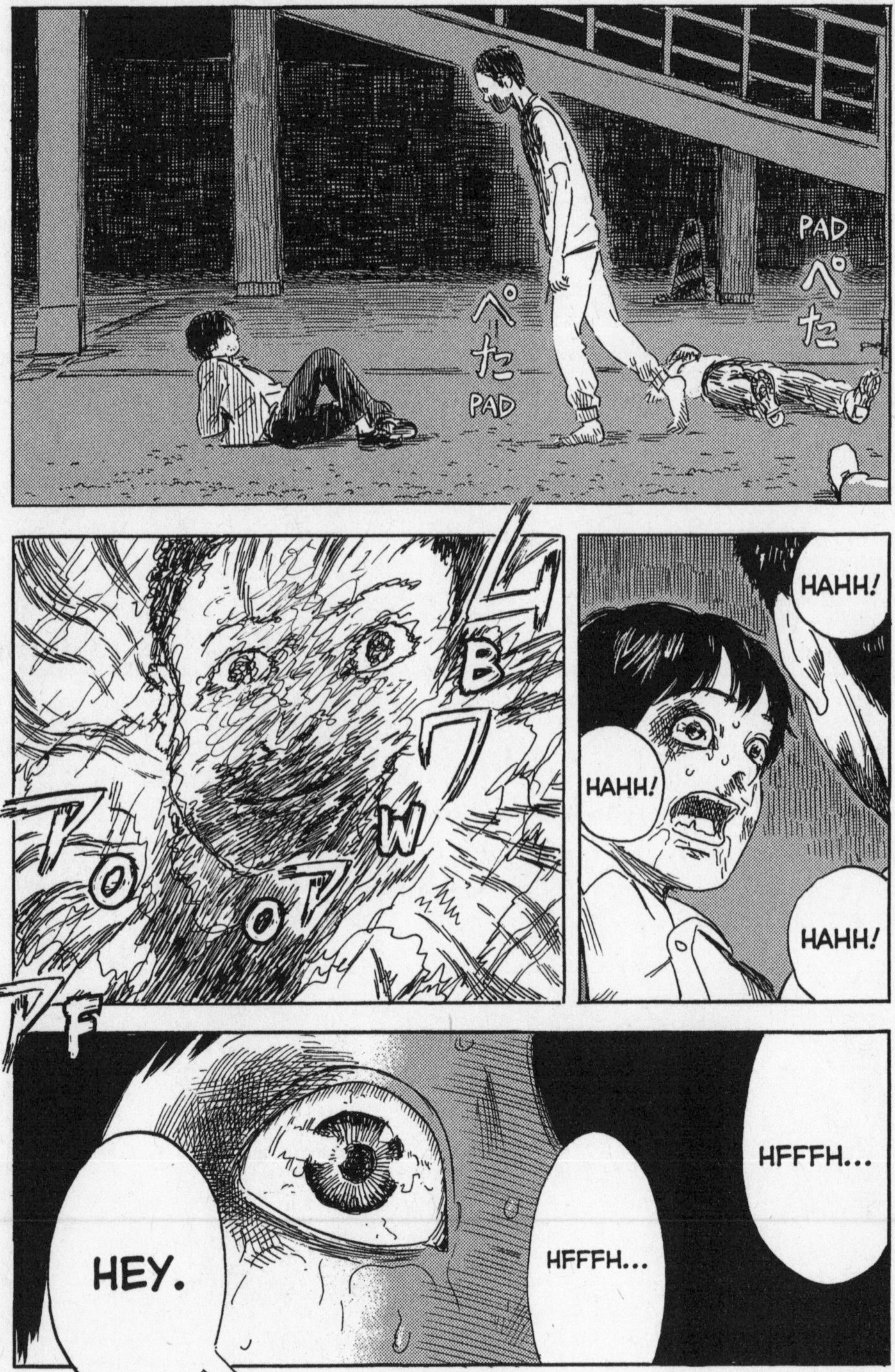
PAD
ぺた
ぺた
PAD
HAHH!
HAHH!
HAHH!
ムB
ワW
アO
アO
アF
HFFFH...
HFFFH...
HEY.

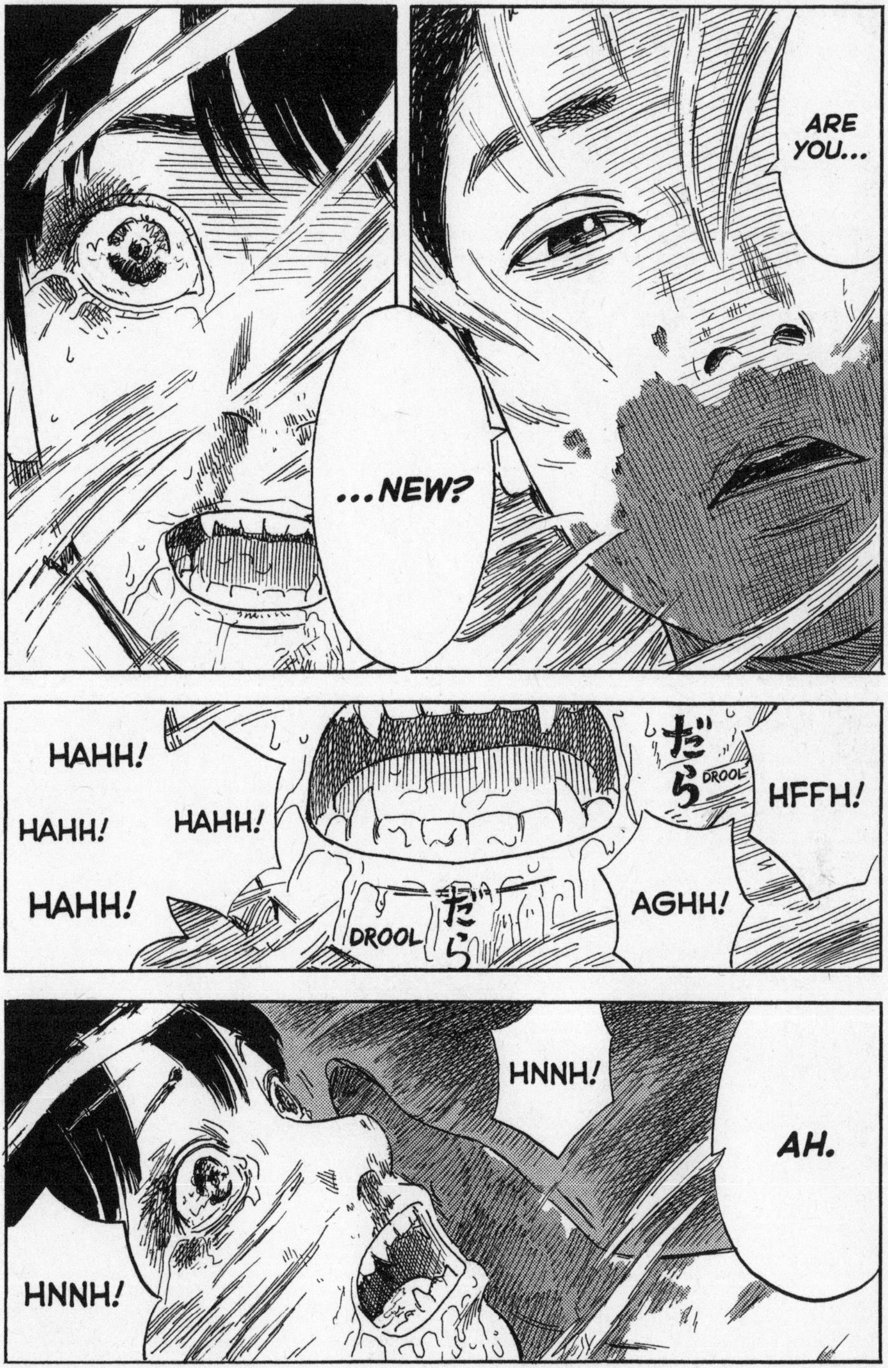
ARE YOU...
...NEW?
だら DROOL
HFFH!
AGHH!
HAHH!
HAHH!
HAHH!
だら DROOL
HAHH!
HNNH!
AH.
HNNH!

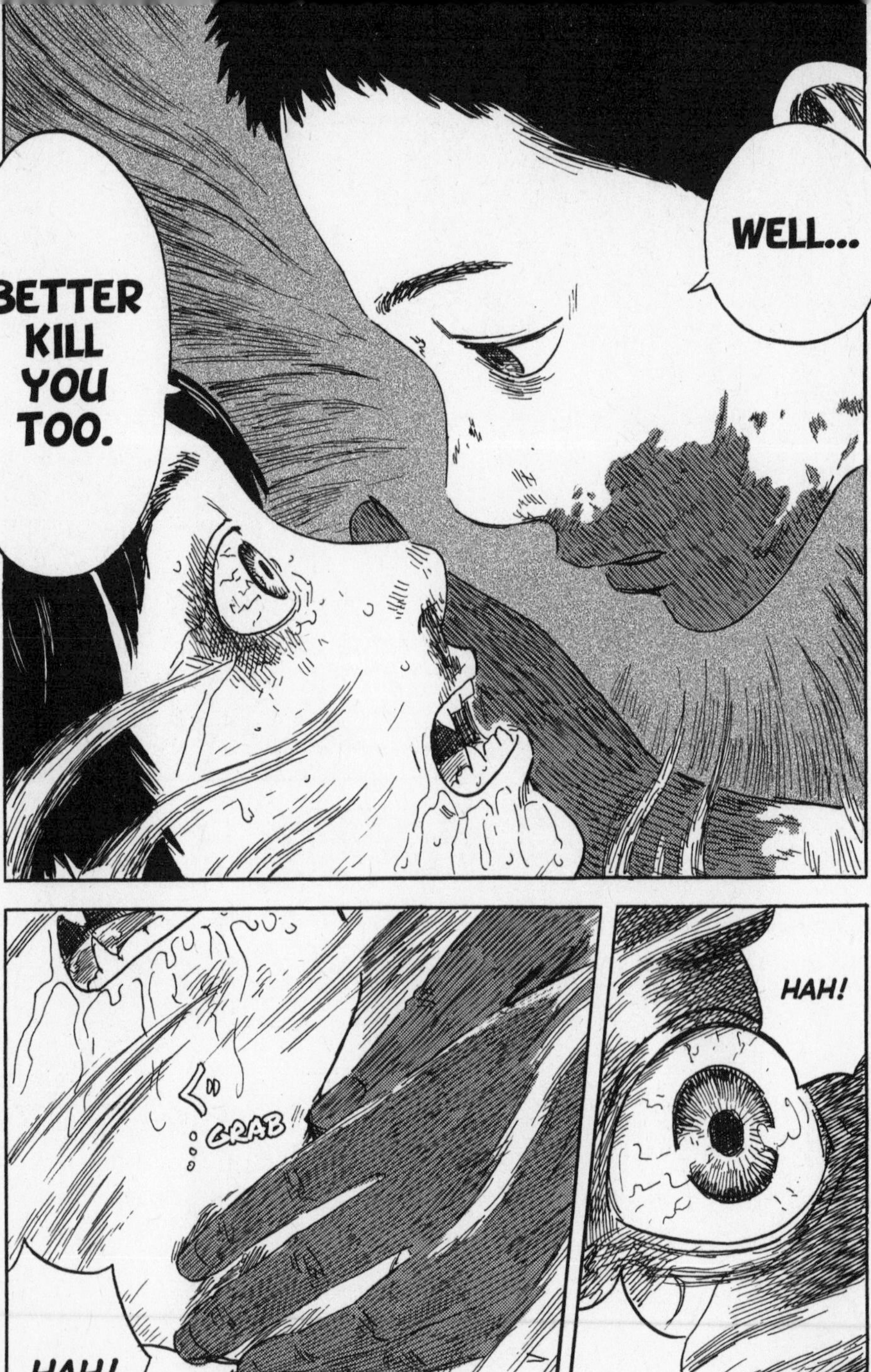
WELL...
BETTER KILL YOU TOO.
HAH!
HAH!
GRAB
HAH!

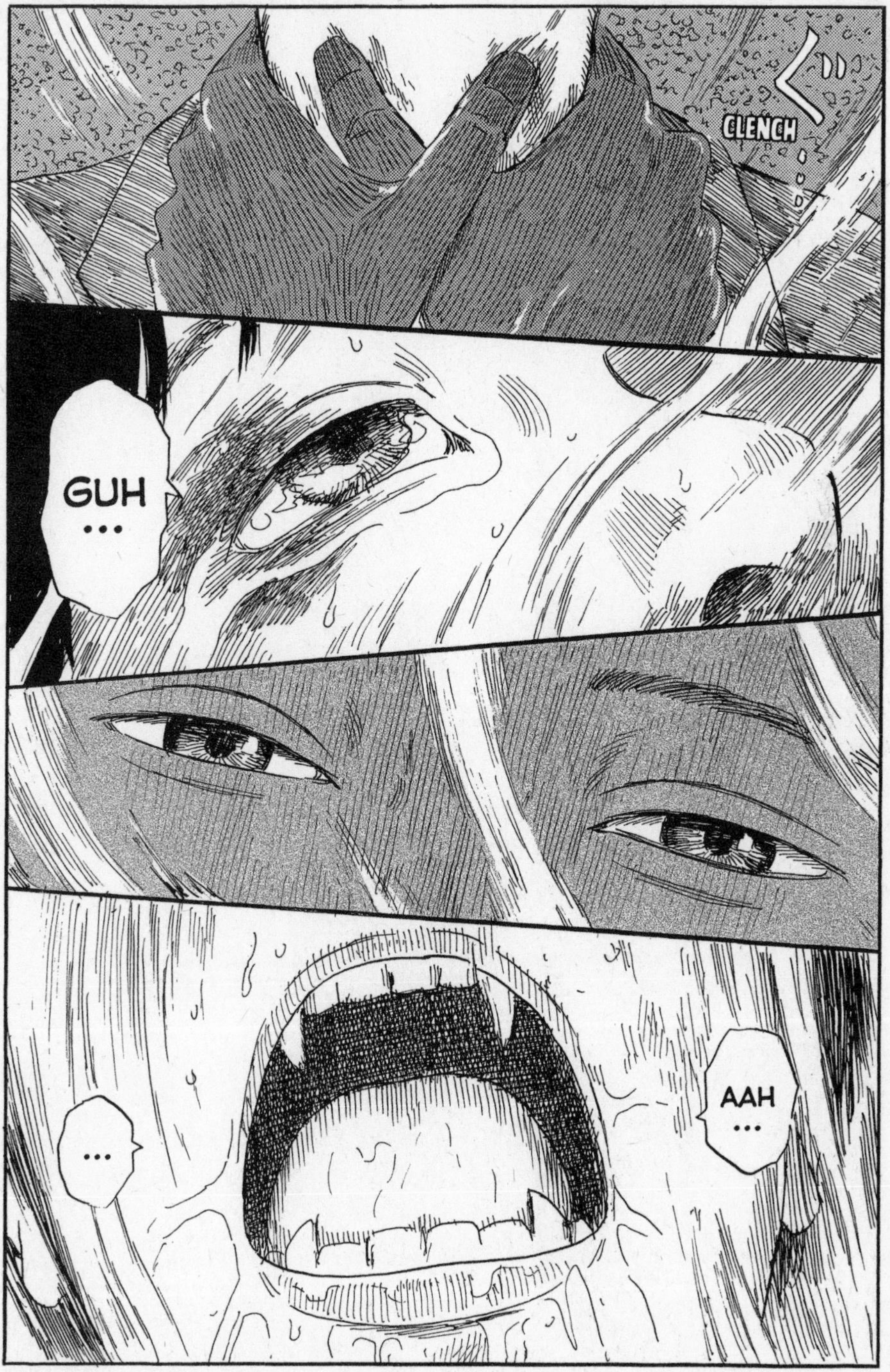

く
CLENCH
GUH ...
AAH ...
...

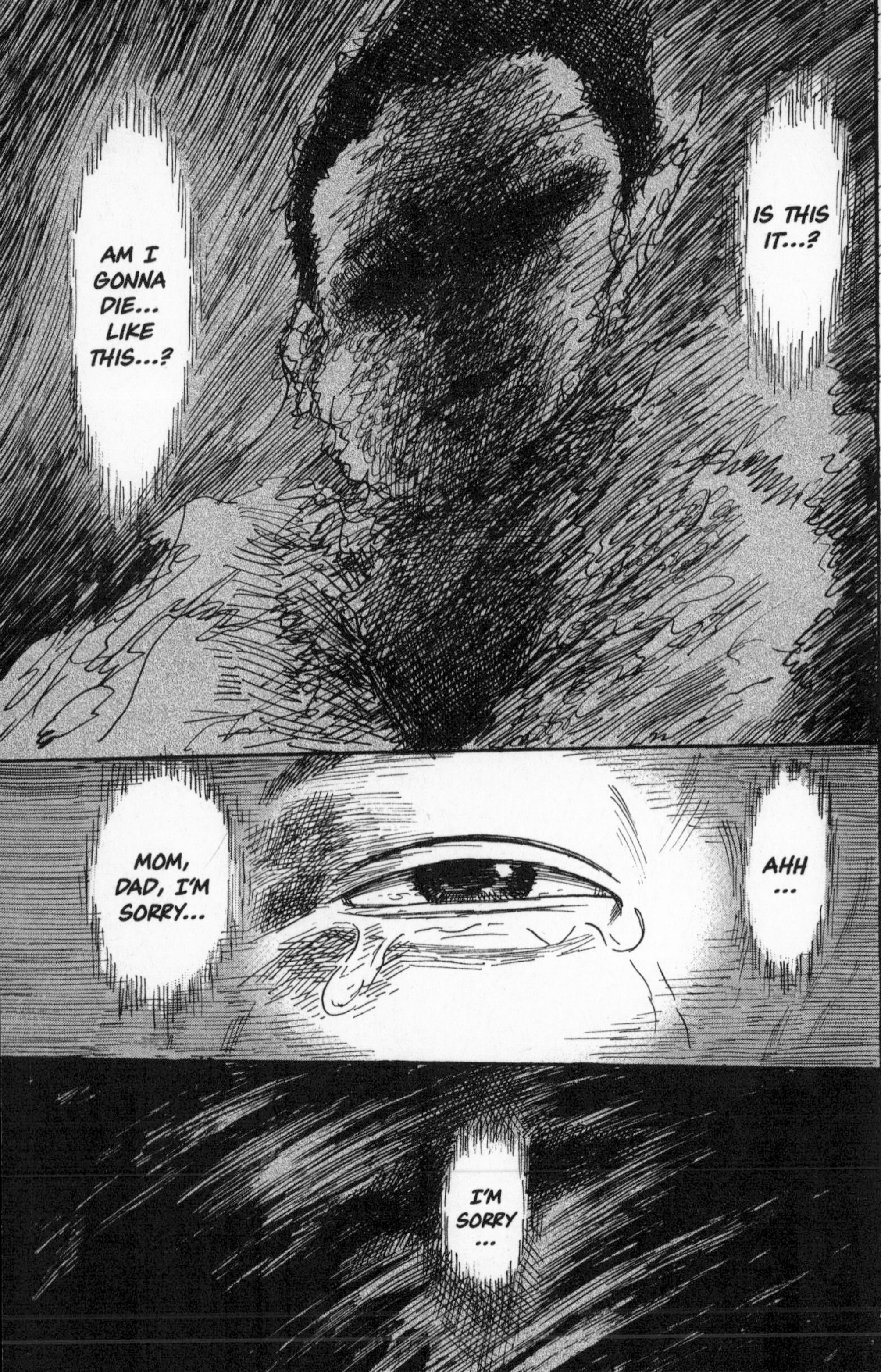

IS THIS IT...?
AM I GONNA DIE... LIKE THIS...?
AHH ...
MOM, DAD, I'M SORRY...
I'M SORRY ...

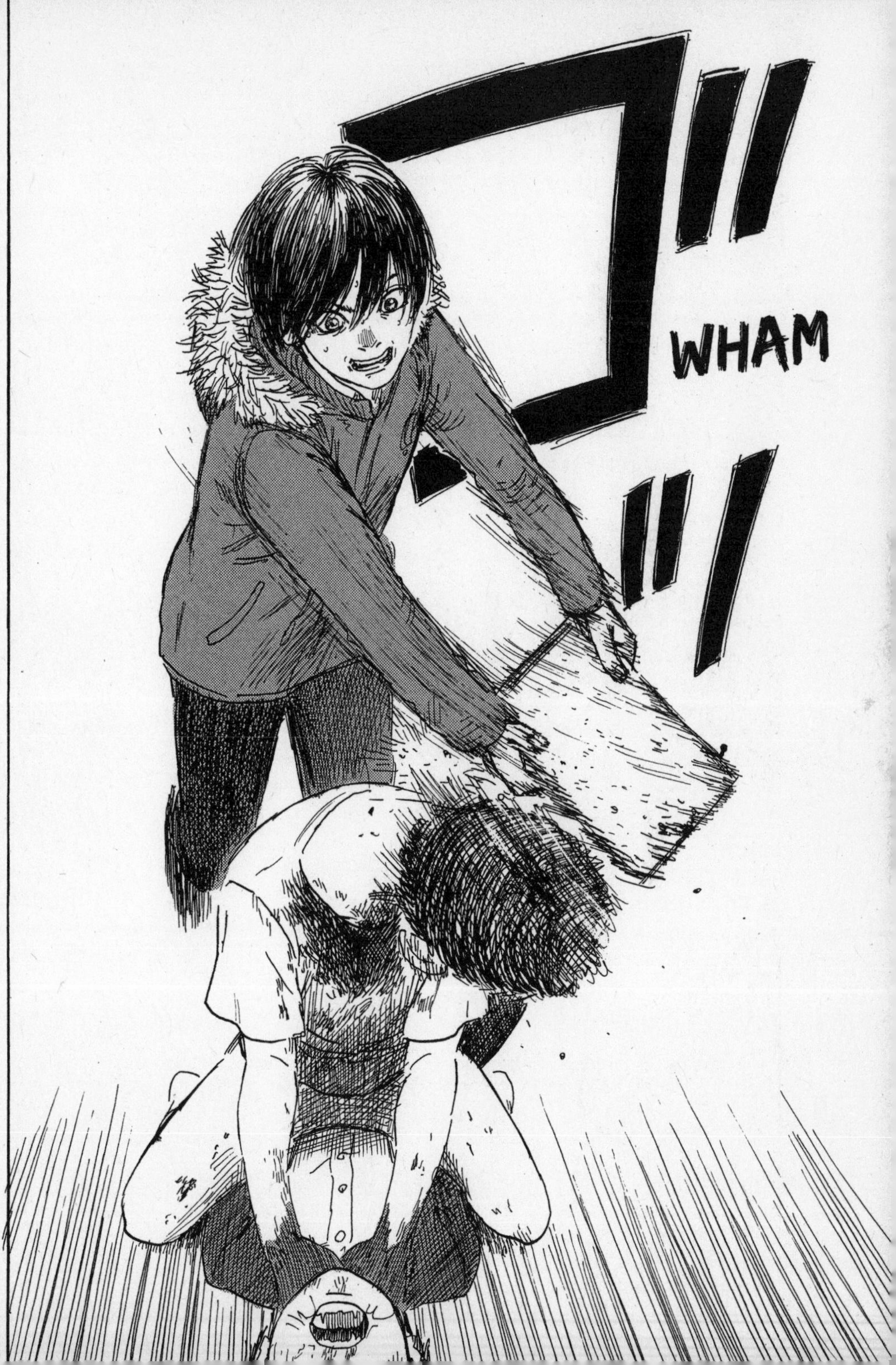
WHAM

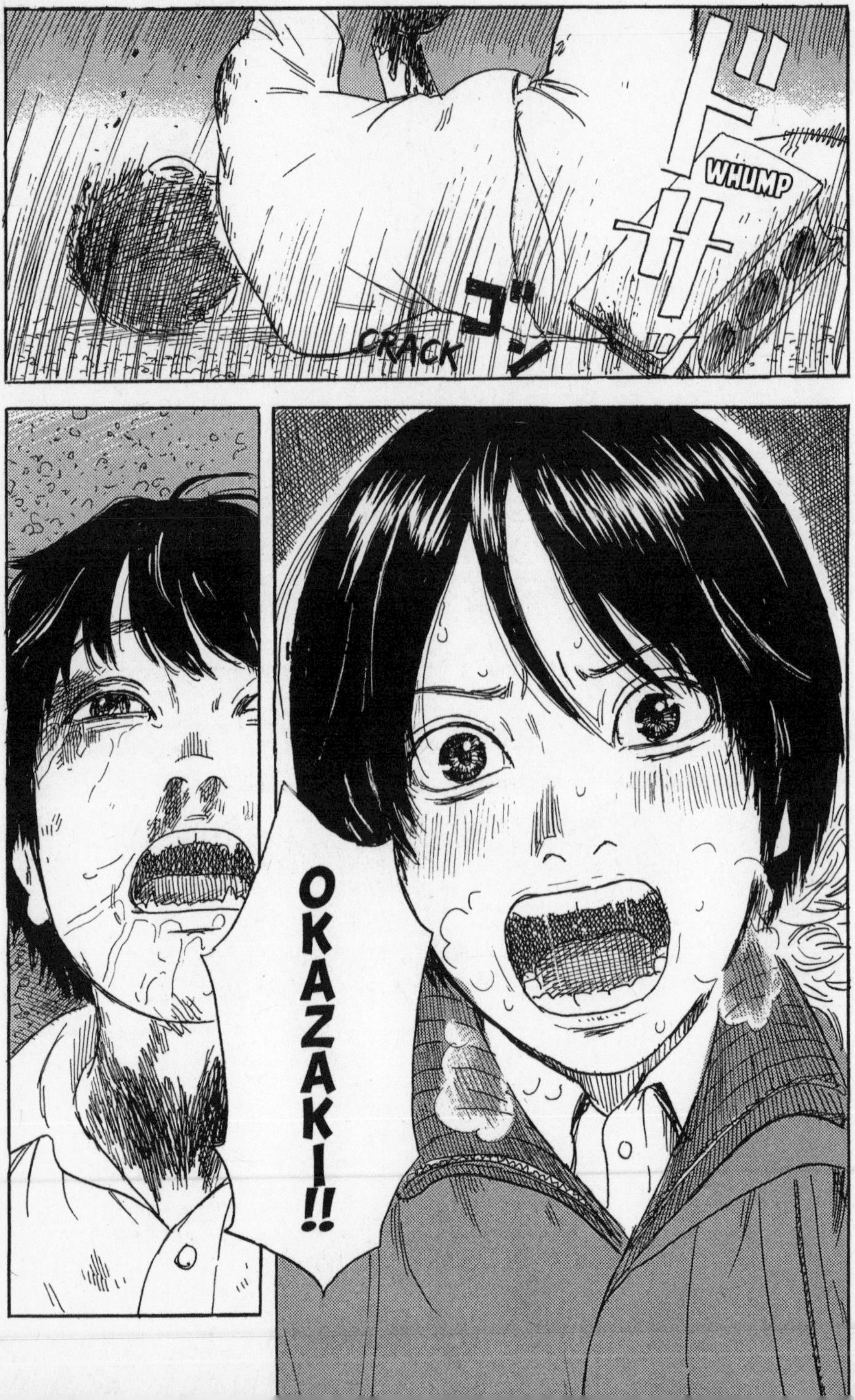
ドサ"
WHUMP
ゴン
CRACK
OKAZAKI!!

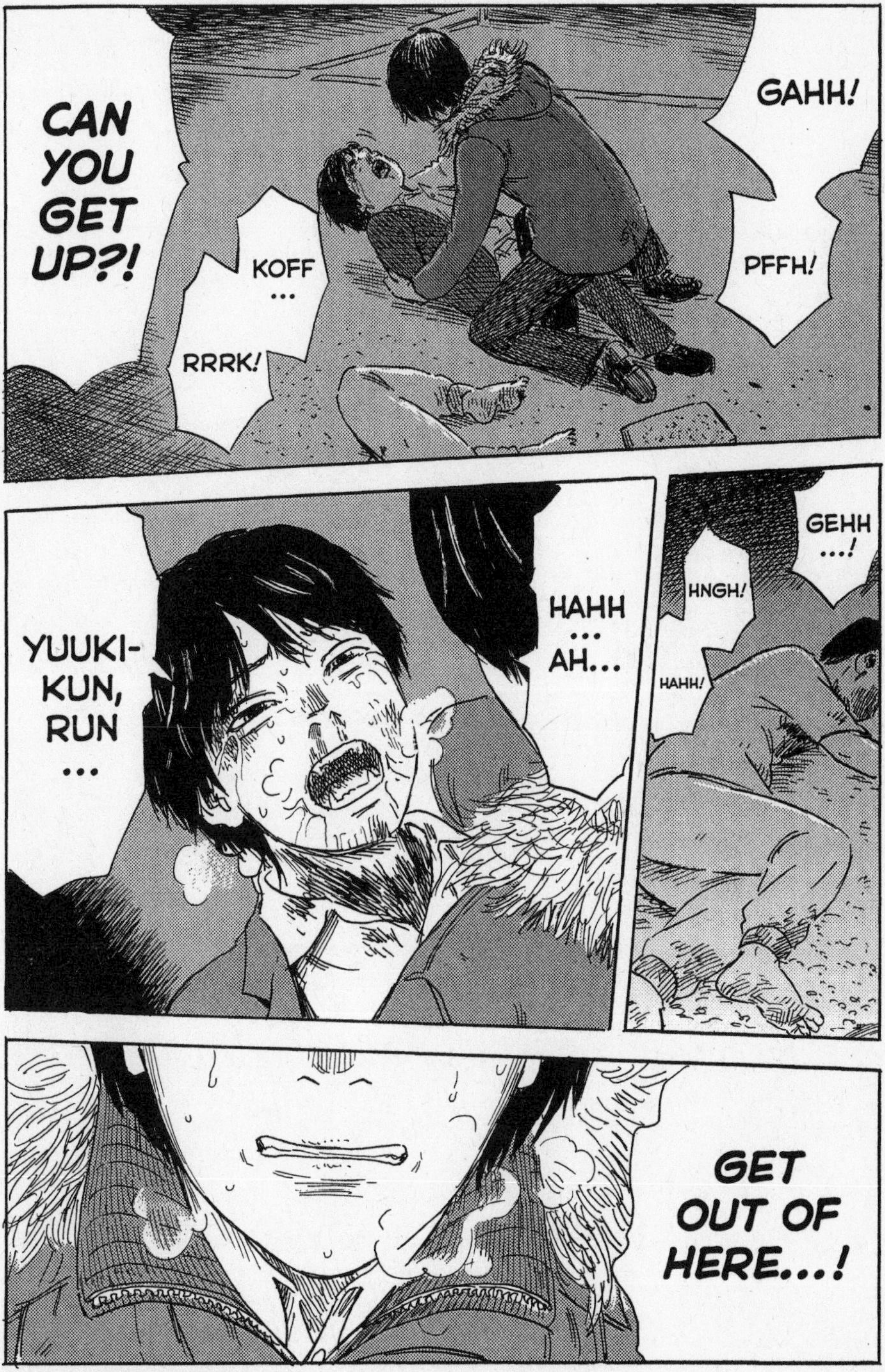
GAHH!
PFFH!
KOFF ...
RRRK!
CAN YOU GET UP?!
GEHH ...!
HNGH!
HAHH!
HAHH ... AH...
YUUKI-KUN, RUN ...
GET OUT OF HERE...!

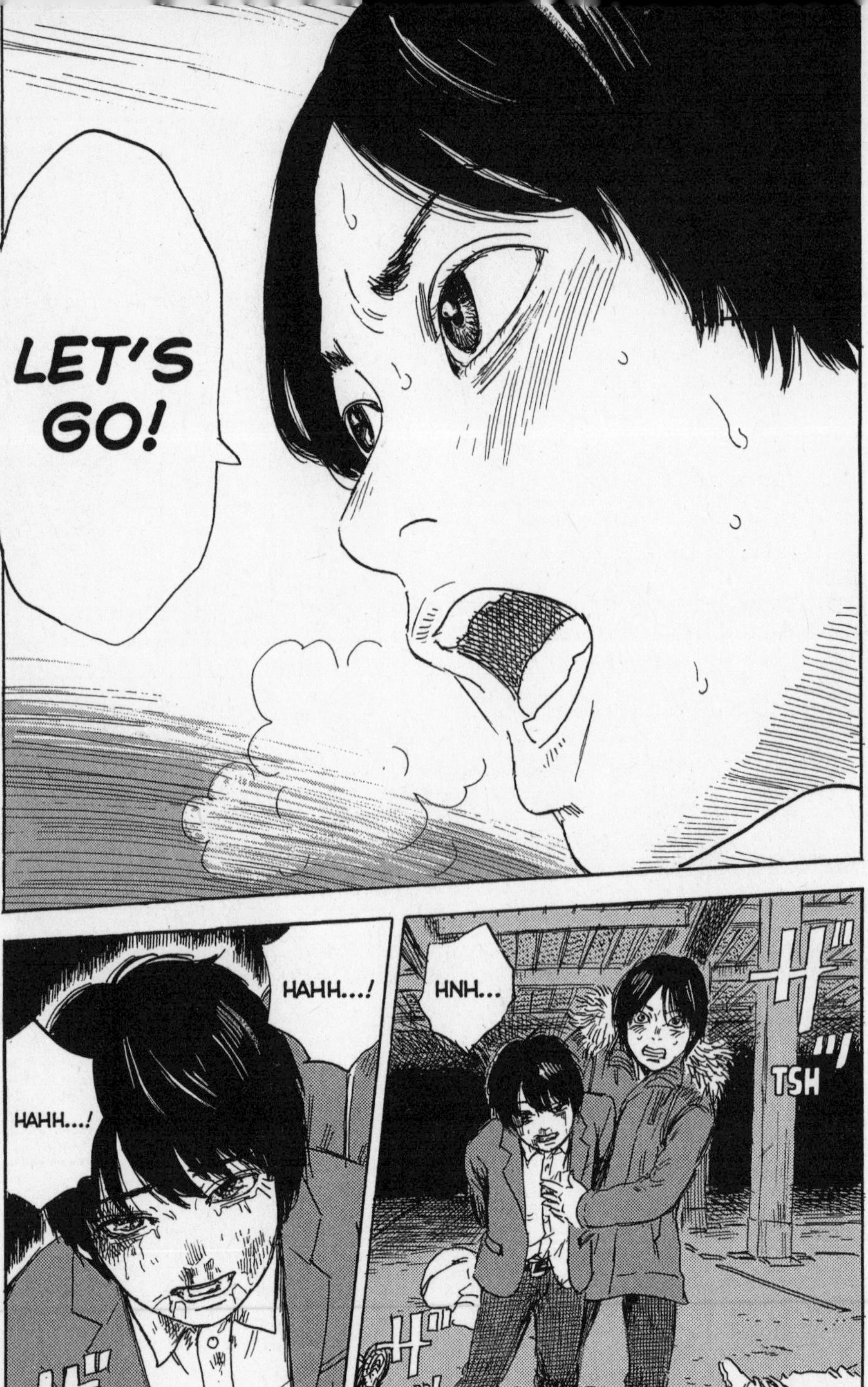
LET'S GO!
HNH...
TSH
TSH
HAHH...!
HAHH...!
TSH

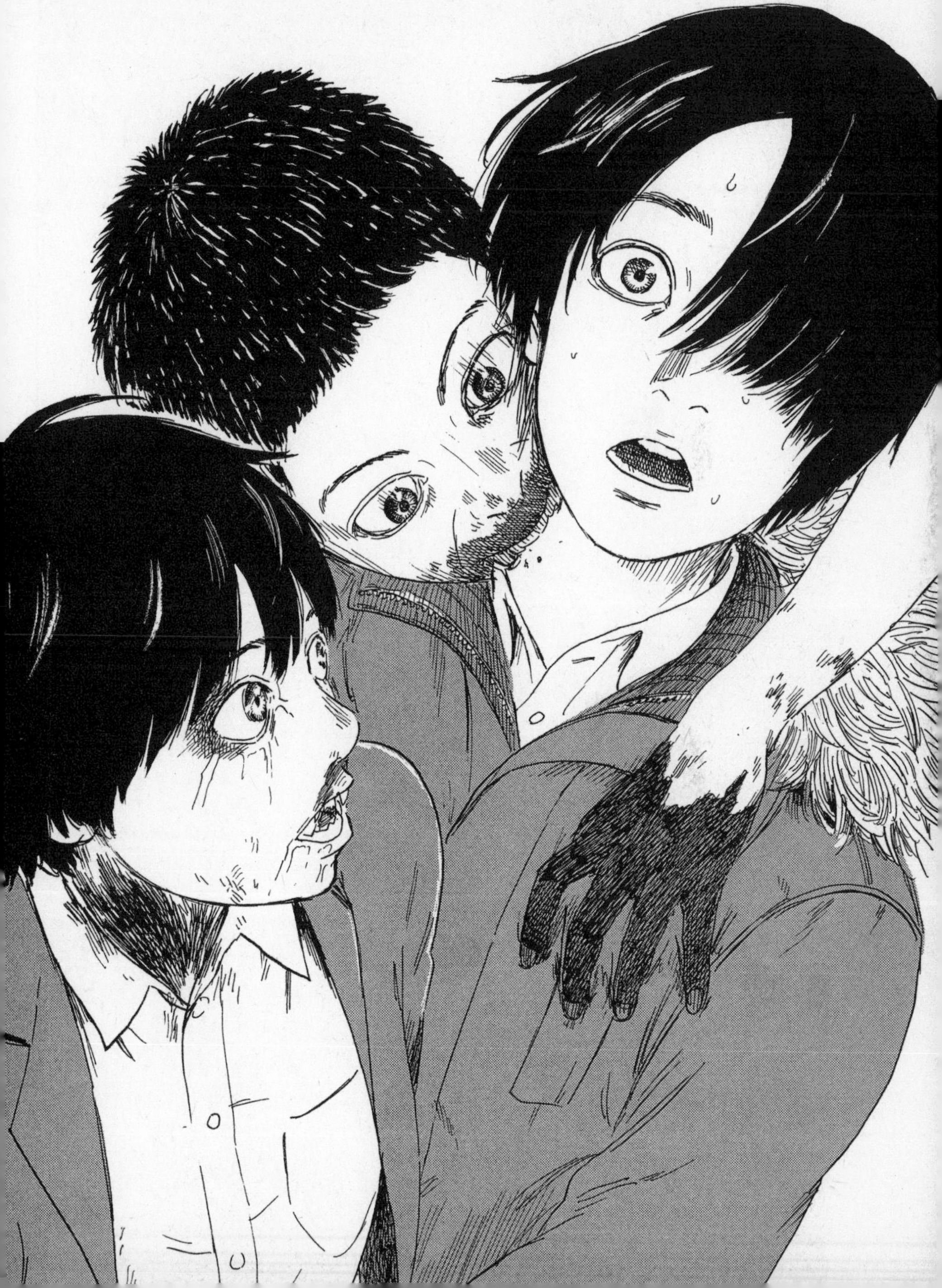

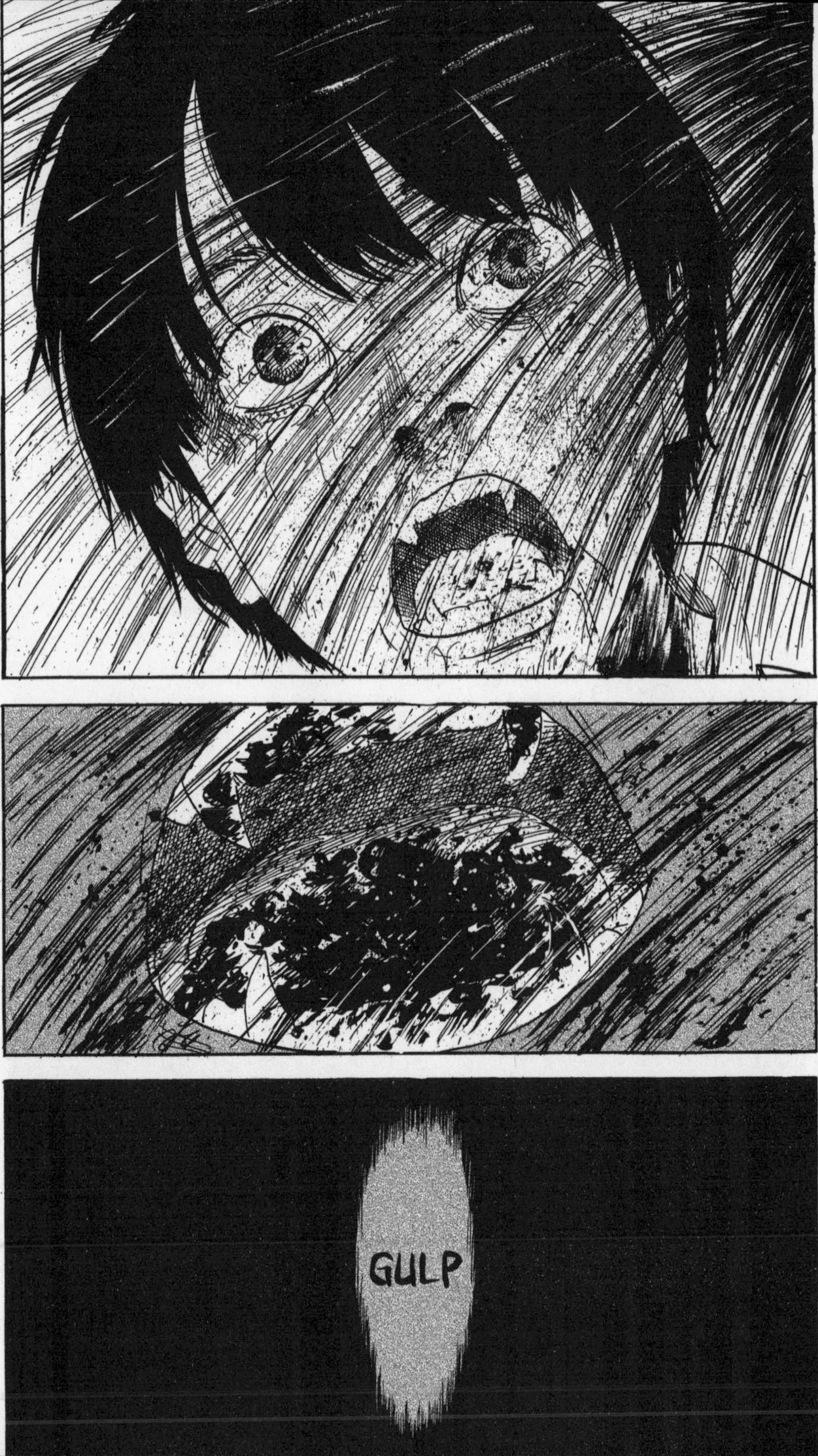
GULP

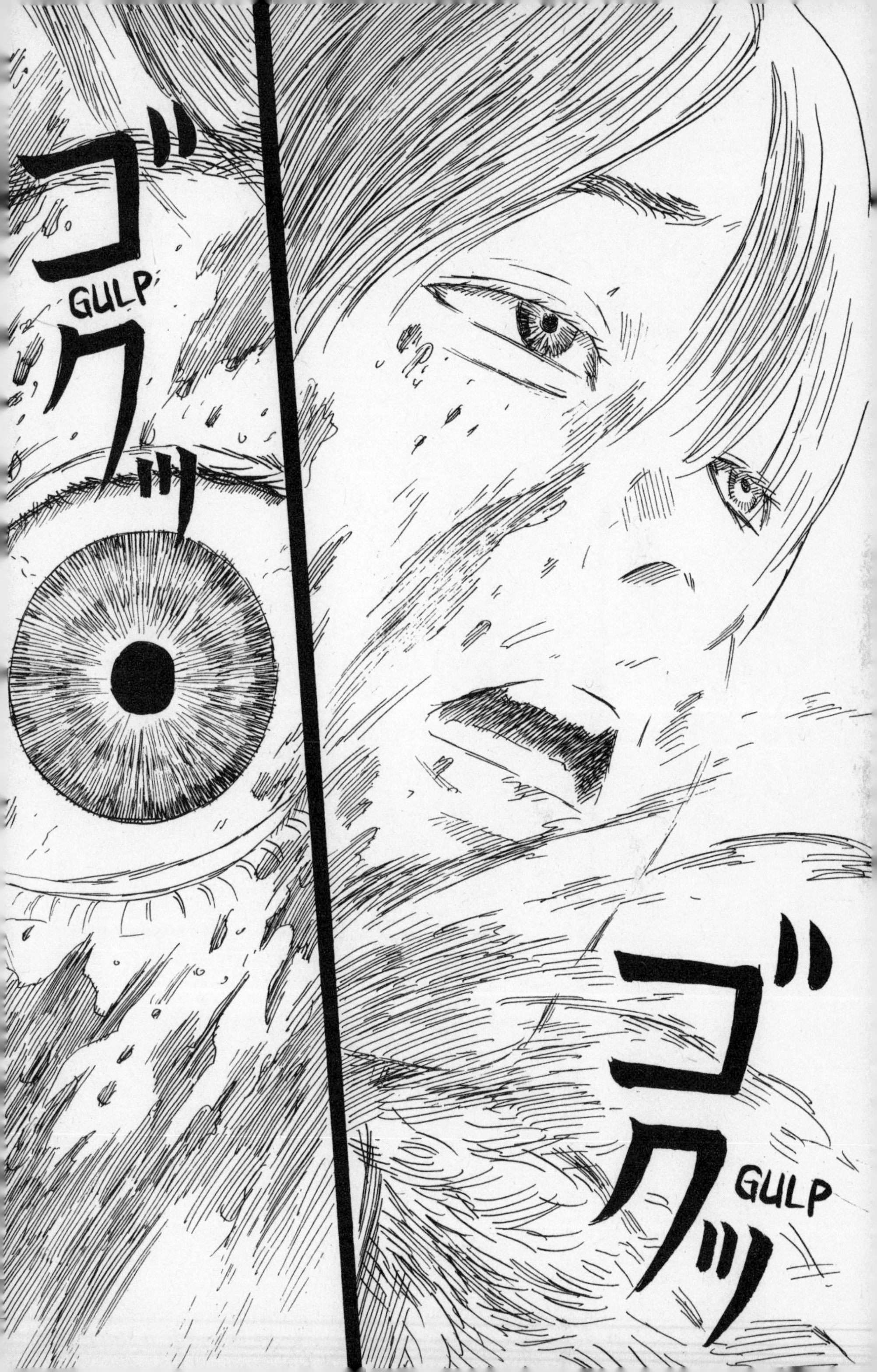
ゴクッ
GULP
ゴクッ
GULP

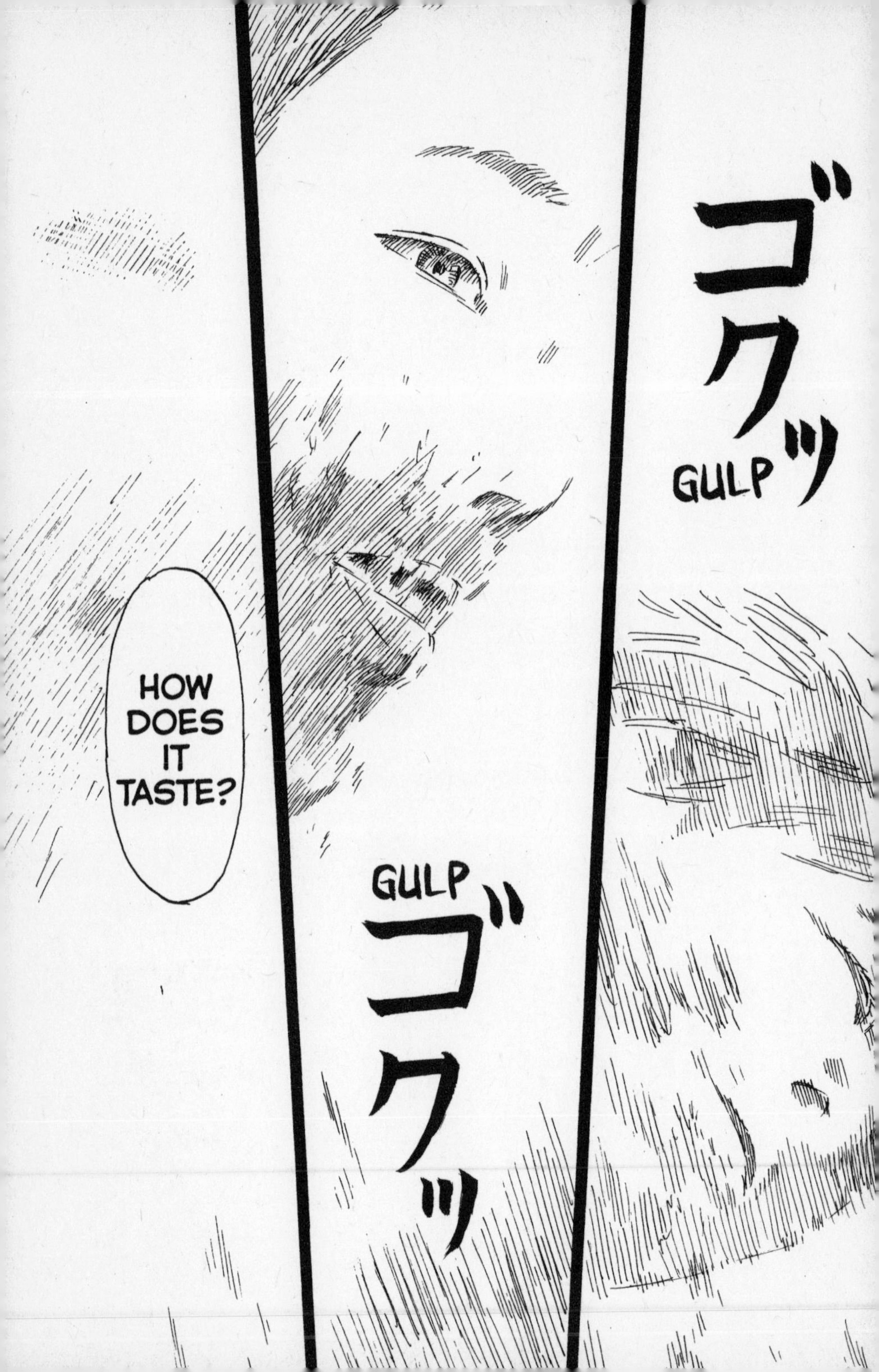
ゴクッ
GULP
GULP
ゴクッ
HOW DOES IT TASTE?

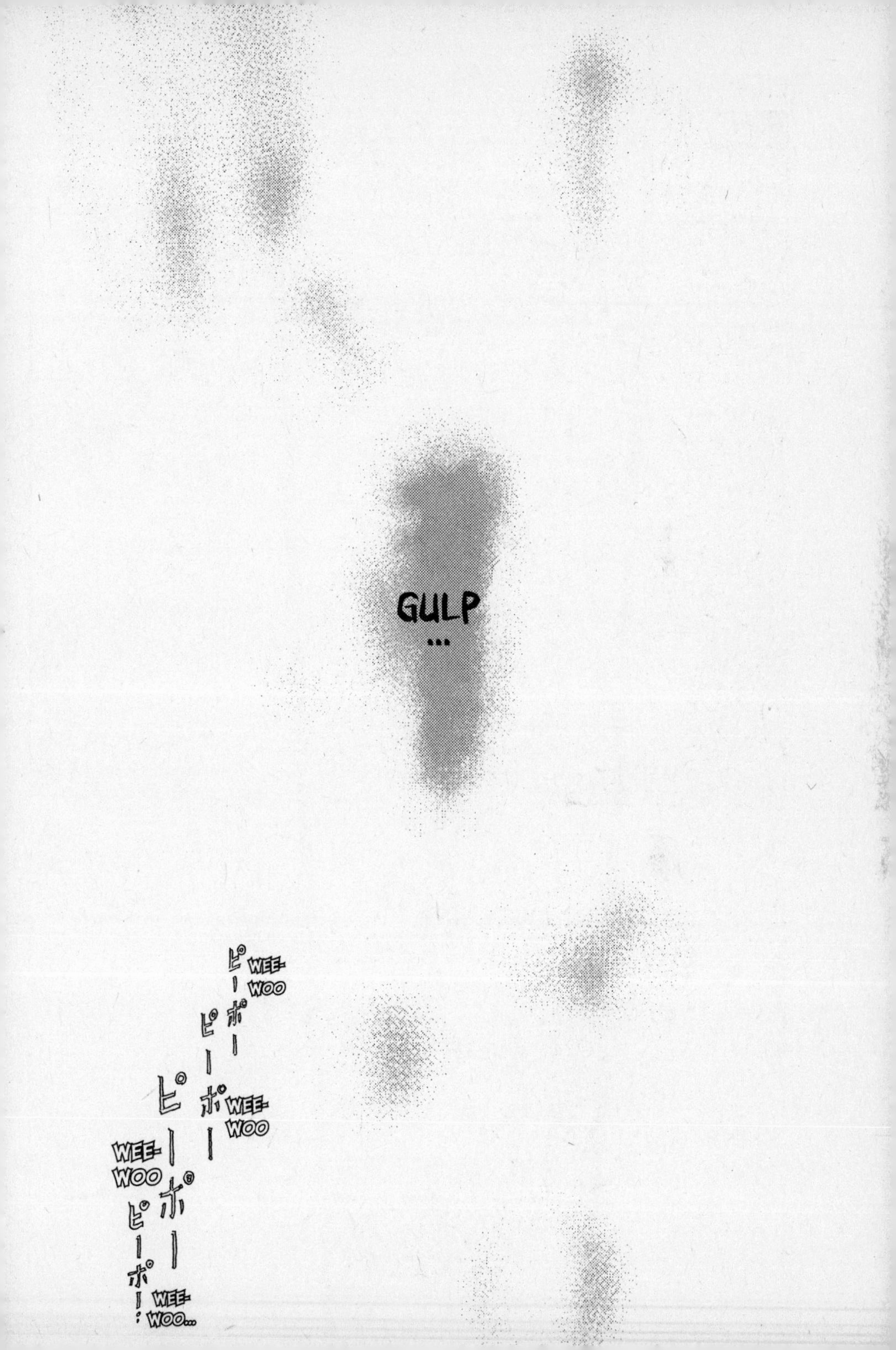
GULP
...
ピーポー
WEE-WOO
ピーポー
WEE-WOO
ピーポー
WEE-WOO
ピーポー！
WEE-WOO...

Chapter 9: Darkness

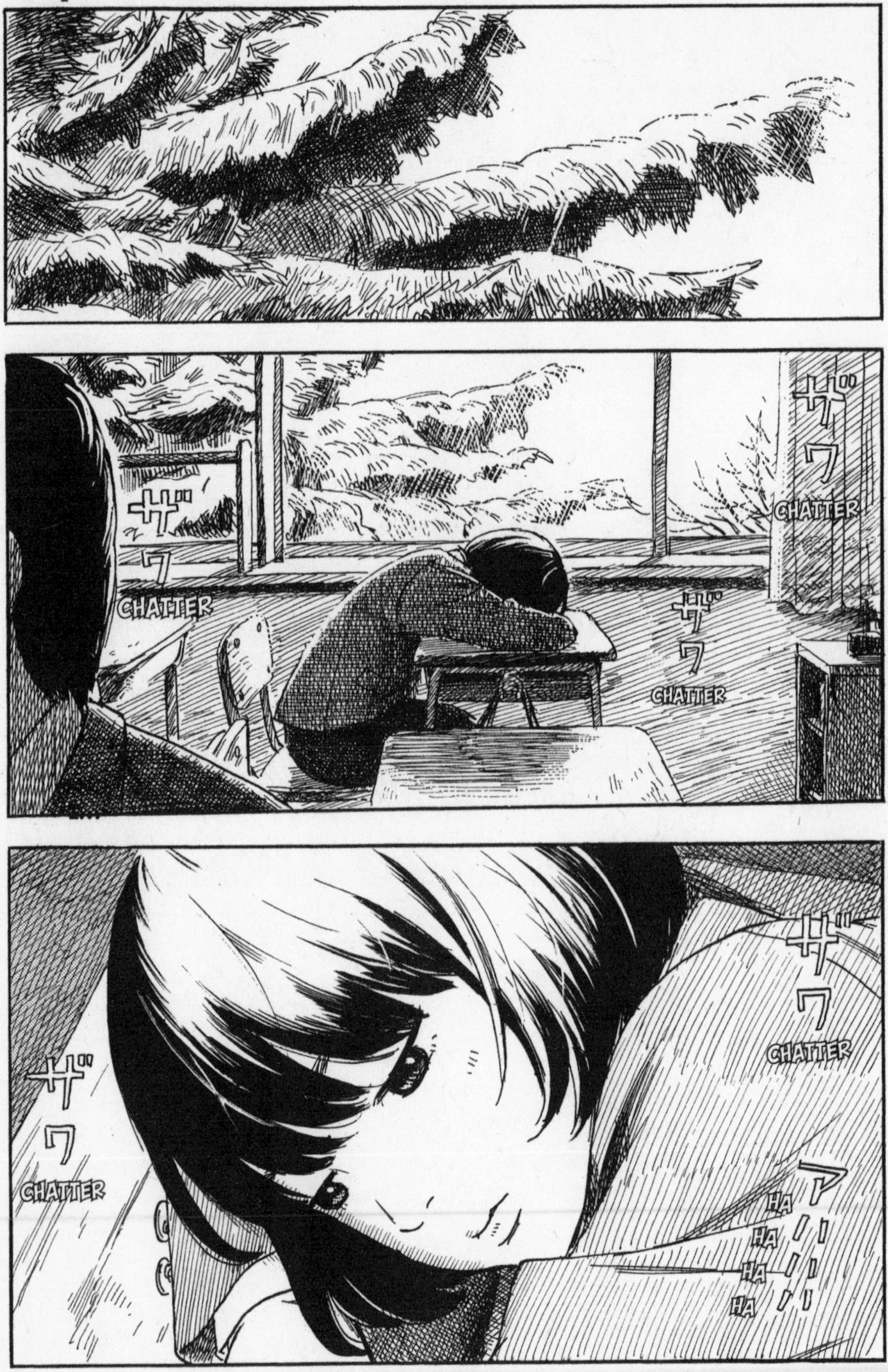
ザワ
CHATTER
ザワ
CHATTER
ザワ
CHATTER
ザワ
CHATTER
アーーー
HA
HA
HA
HA
ザワ
CHATTER

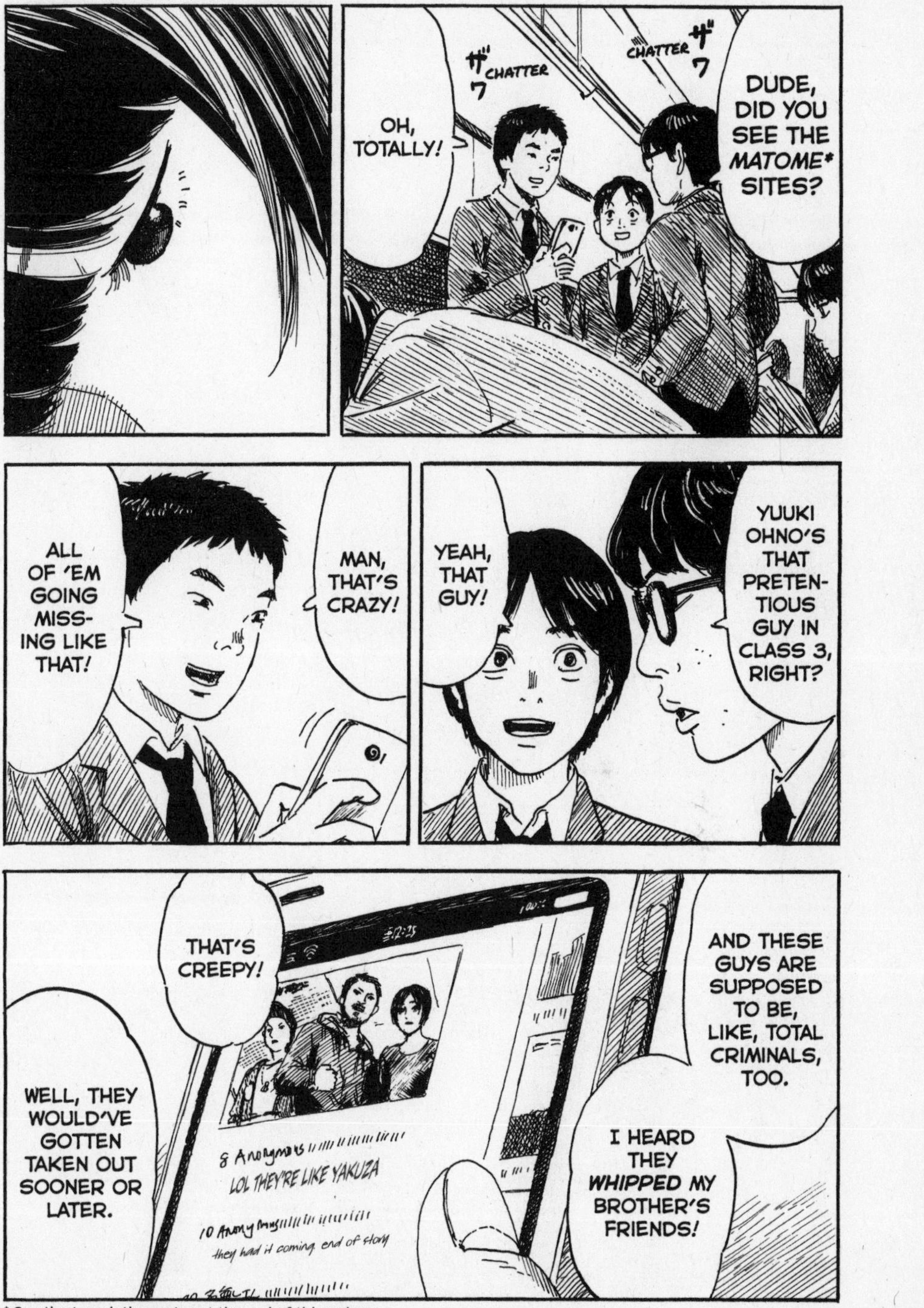
CHATTER
DUDE, DID YOU SEE THE MATOME* SITES?
CHATTER
OH, TOTALLY!
YUUKI OHNO'S THAT PRETEN-TIOUS GUY IN CLASS 3, RIGHT?
YEAH, THAT GUY!
MAN, THAT'S CRAZY!
ALL OF 'EM GOING MISS-ING LIKE THAT!
AND THESE GUYS ARE SUPPOSED TO BE, LIKE, TOTAL CRIMINALS, TOO.
I HEARD THEY WHIPPED MY BROTHER'S FRIENDS!
THAT'S CREEPY!
8 Anonymous
LOL THEY'RE LIKE YAKUZA
10 Anonymous
they had it coming. end of story
WELL, THEY WOULD'VE GOTTEN TAKEN OUT SOONER OR LATER.

* See the translation notes at the end of this volume.

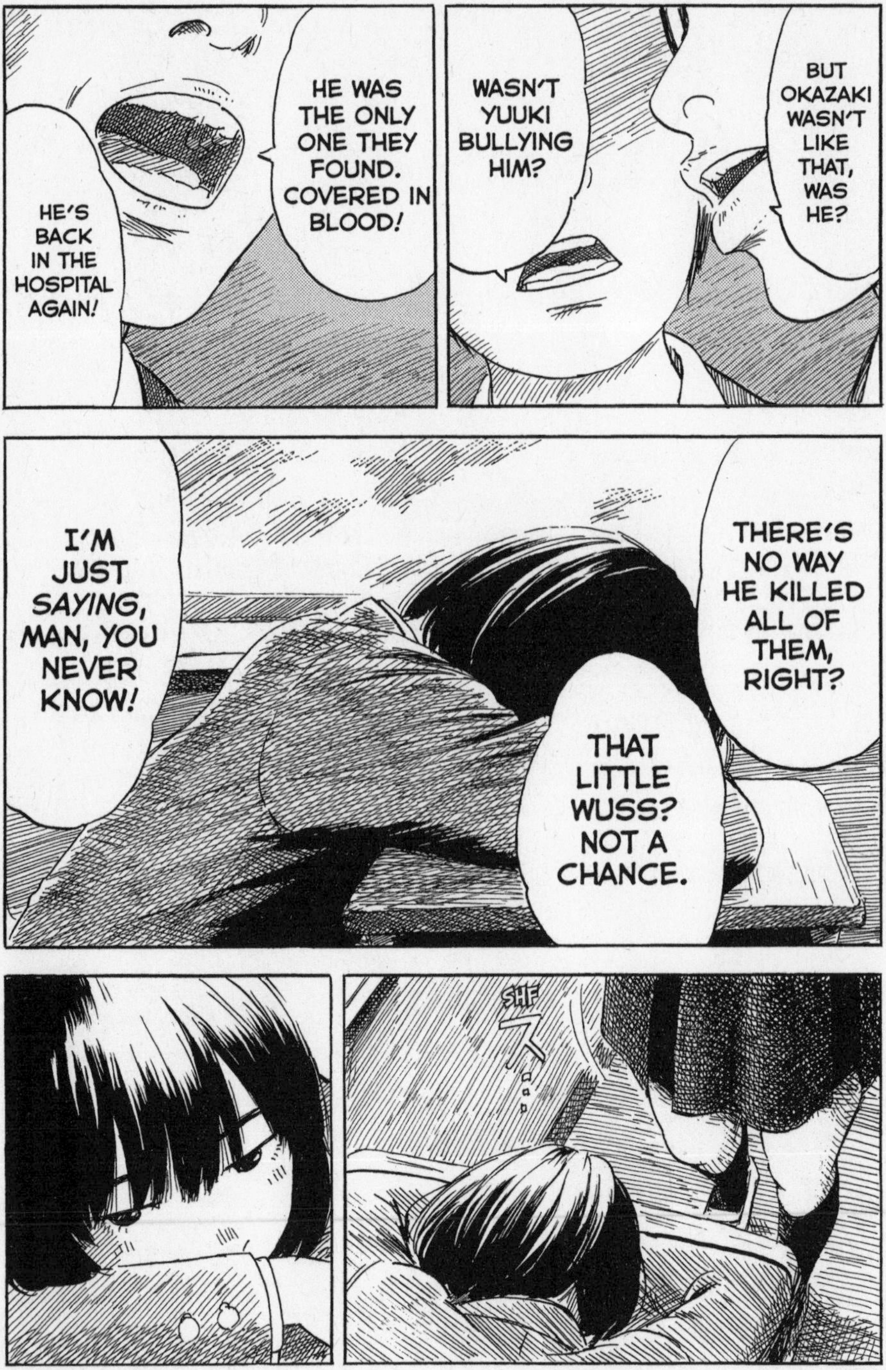
BUT OKAZAKI WASN'T LIKE THAT, WAS HE?
WASN'T YUUKI BULLYING HIM?
HE WAS THE ONLY ONE THEY FOUND. COVERED IN BLOOD!
HE'S BACK IN THE HOSPITAL AGAIN!
THERE'S NO WAY HE KILLED ALL OF THEM, RIGHT?
THAT LITTLE WUSS? NOT A CHANCE.
I'M JUST *SAYING*, MAN, YOU NEVER KNOW!
SHF

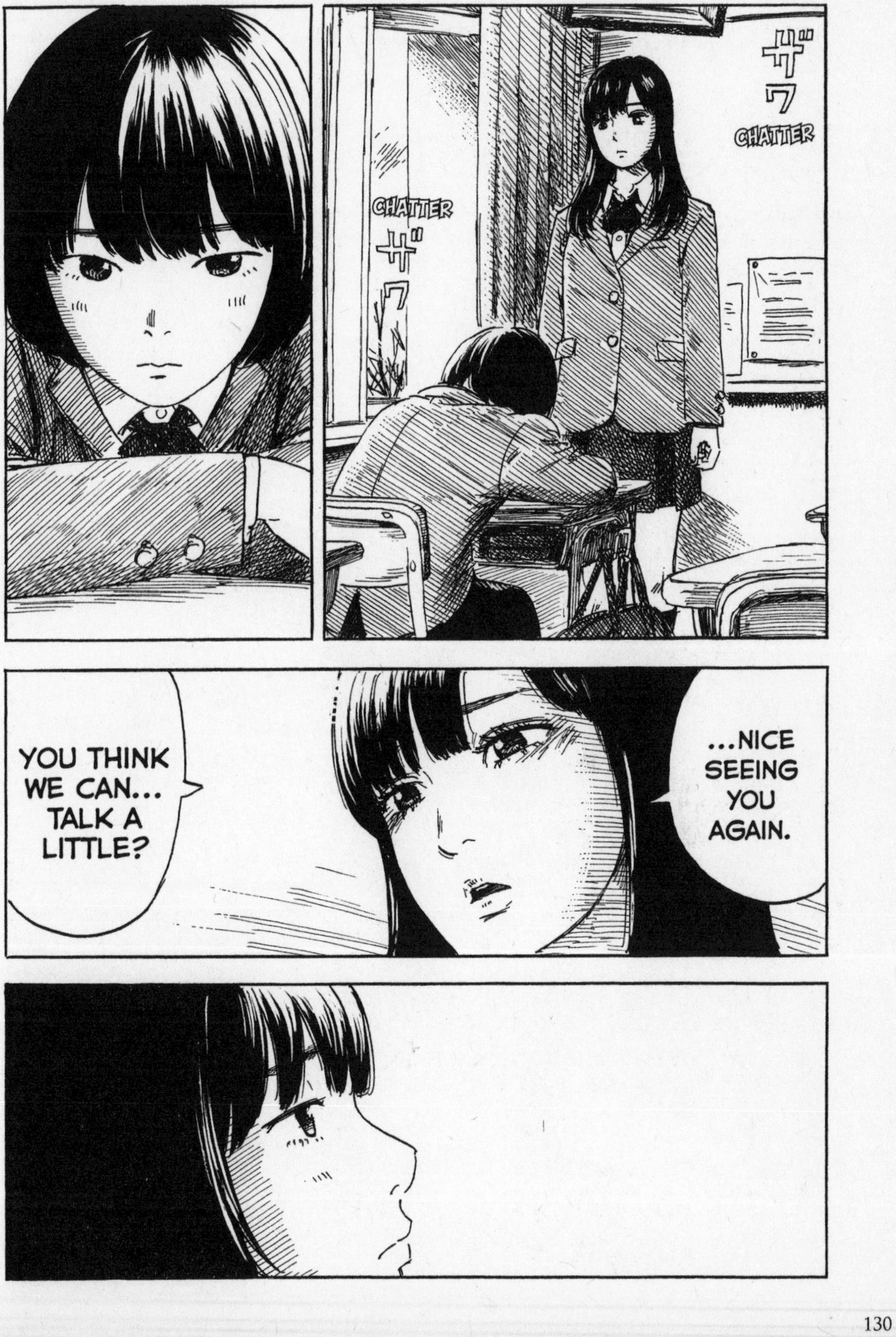
ザワ
CHATTER
CHATTER
ザワ
...NICE SEEING YOU AGAIN.
YOU THINK WE CAN... TALK A LITTLE?

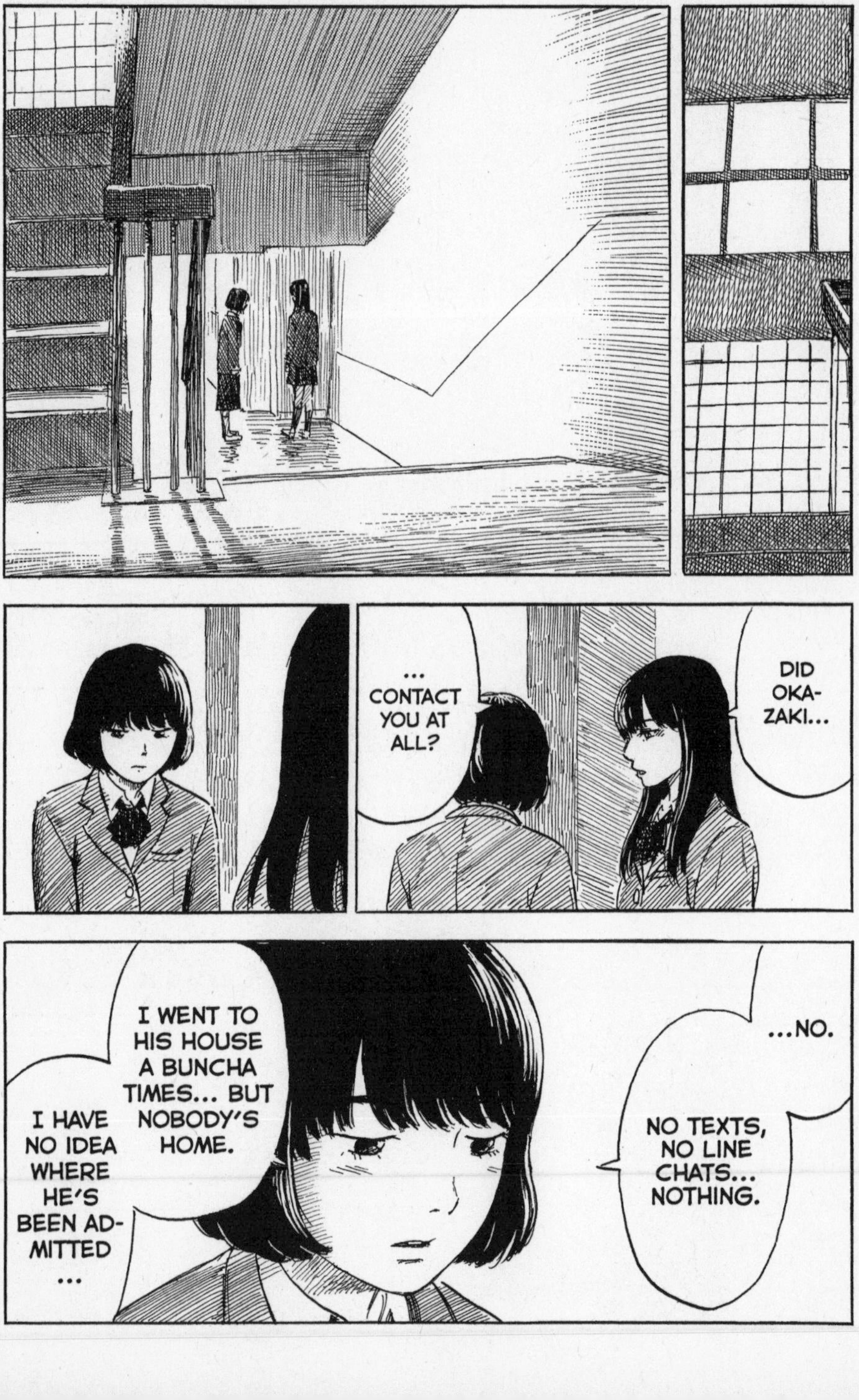
DID OKA-ZAKI...
...CONTACT YOU AT ALL?
...NO.
NO TEXTS, NO LINE CHATS... NOTHING.
I WENT TO HIS HOUSE A BUNCHA TIMES... BUT NOBODY'S HOME.
I HAVE NO IDEA WHERE HE'S BEEN ADMITTED...

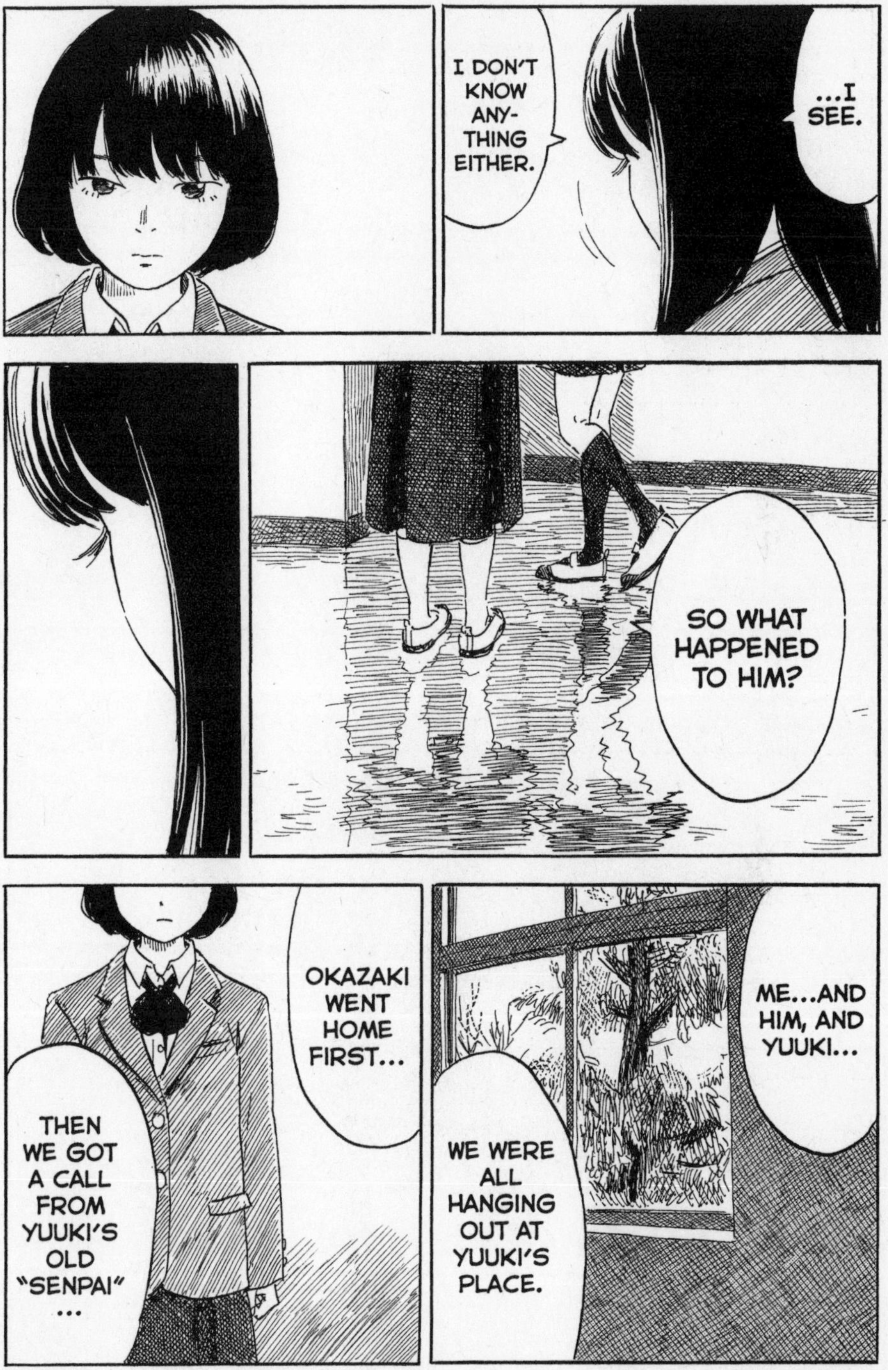
...I SEE.
I DON'T KNOW ANY-THING EITHER.
SO WHAT HAPPENED TO HIM?
ME...AND HIM, AND YUUKI...
WE WERE ALL HANGING OUT AT YUUKI'S PLACE.
OKAZAKI WENT HOME FIRST...
THEN WE GOT A CALL FROM YUUKI'S OLD "SENPAI" ...

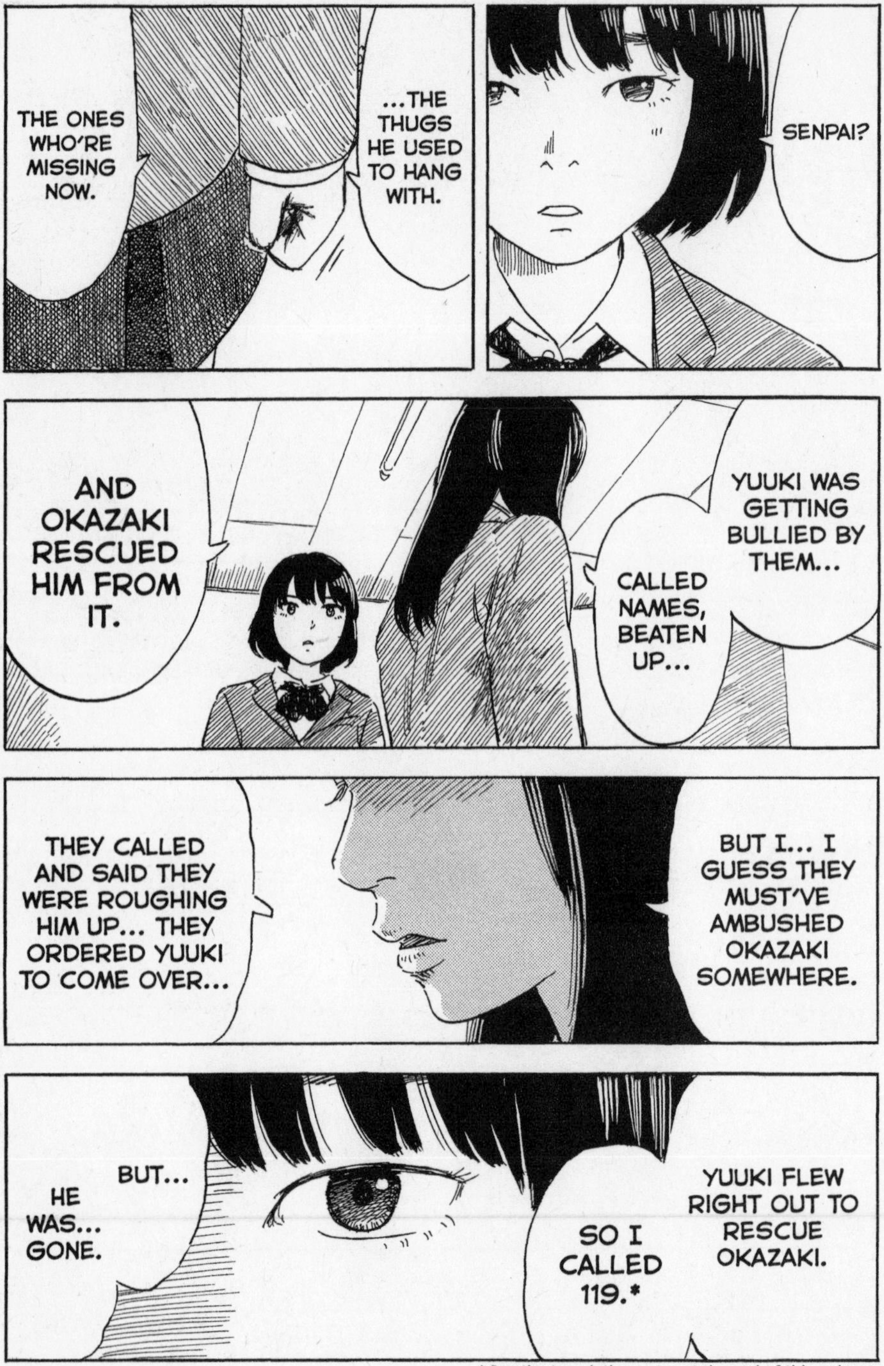
SENPAI?
...THE THUGS HE USED TO HANG WITH.
THE ONES WHO'RE MISSING NOW.
YUUKI WAS GETTING BULLIED BY THEM...
CALLED NAMES, BEATEN UP...
AND OKAZAKI RESCUED HIM FROM IT.
BUT I... I GUESS THEY MUST'VE AMBUSHED OKAZAKI SOMEWHERE.
THEY CALLED AND SAID THEY WERE ROUGHING HIM UP... THEY ORDERED YUUKI TO COME OVER...
YUUKI FLEW RIGHT OUT TO RESCUE OKAZAKI.
SO I CALLED 119.*
BUT...
HE WAS... GONE.

* See the translation notes at the end of this volume.

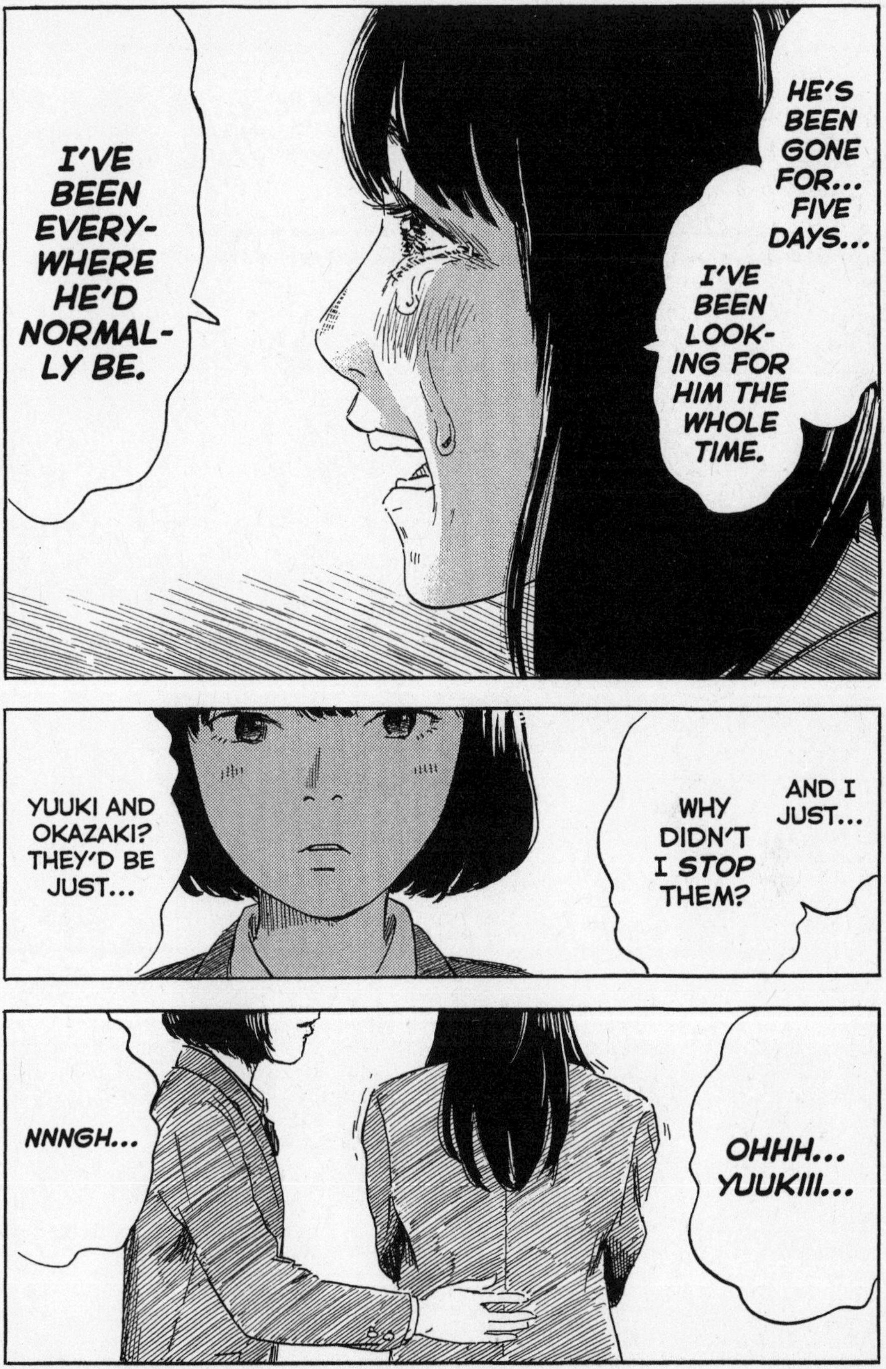
HE'S BEEN GONE FOR... FIVE DAYS...
I'VE BEEN LOOK-ING FOR HIM THE WHOLE TIME.
I'VE BEEN EVERY-WHERE HE'D NORMAL-LY BE.
AND I JUST...
WHY DIDN'T I STOP THEM?
YUUKI AND OKAZAKI? THEY'D BE JUST...
OHHH... YUUKIII...
NNNGH...

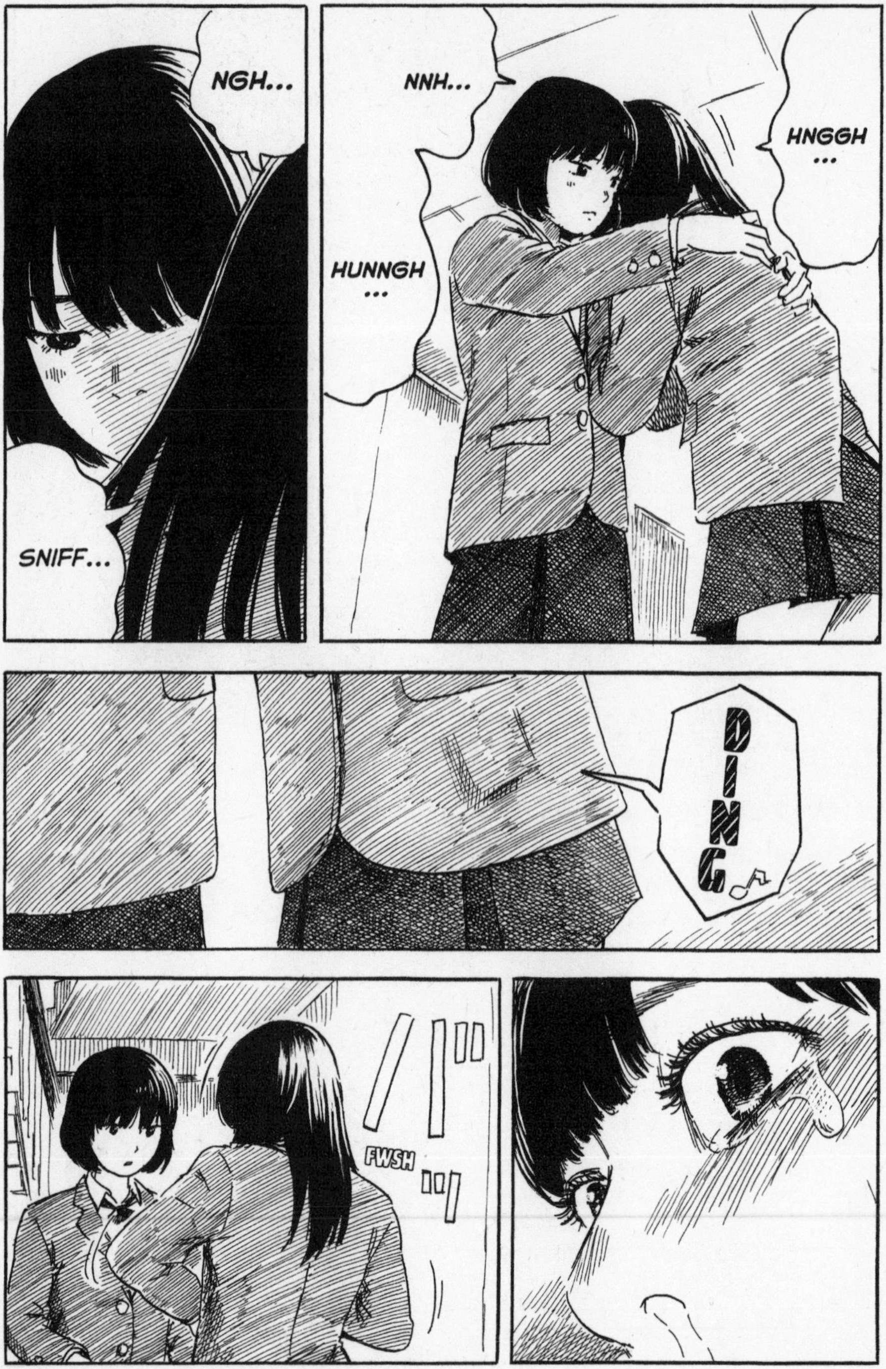
HNGGH...
NNH...
HUNNGH...
NGH...
SNIFF...
DING
FWSH

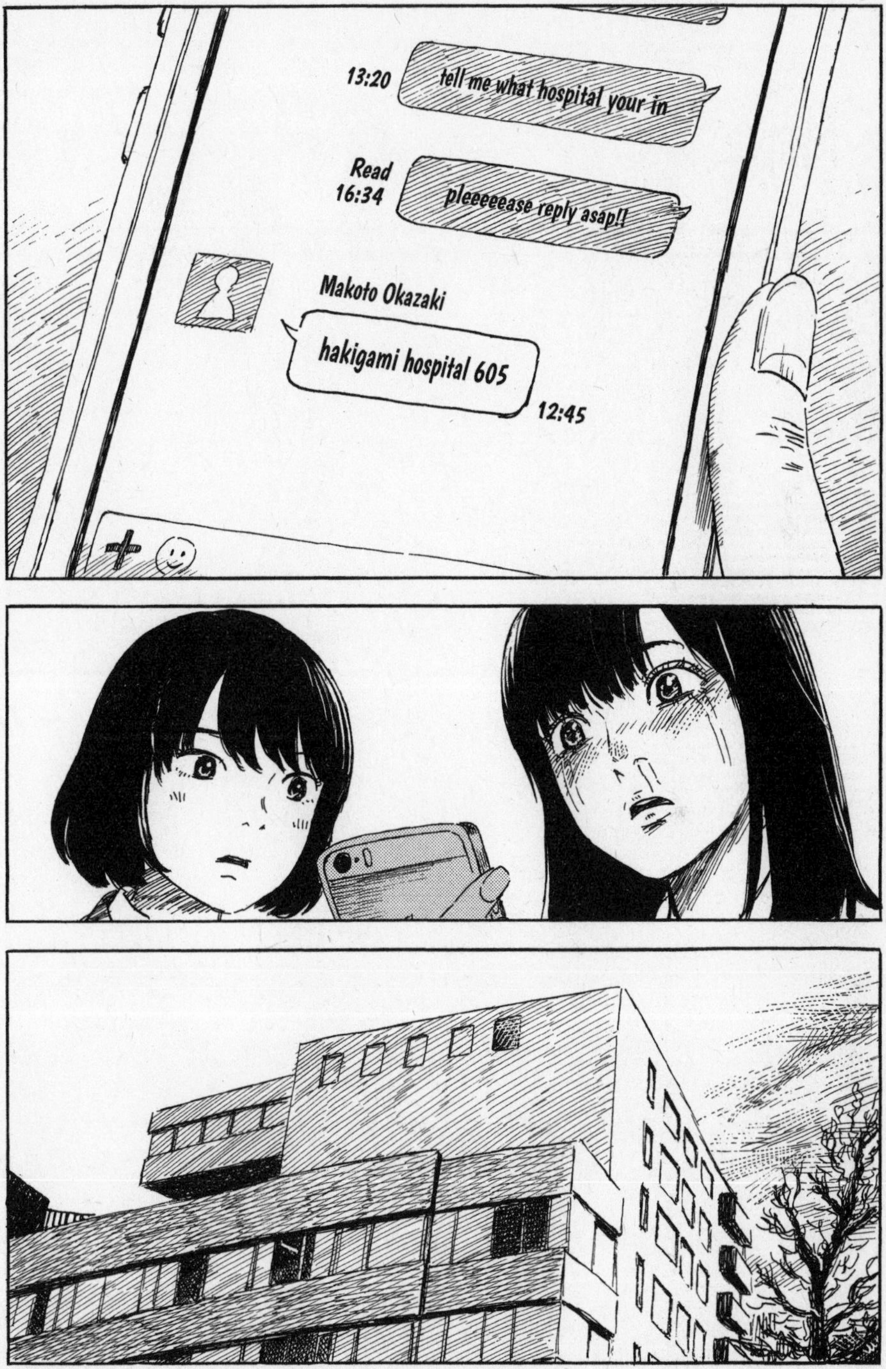
13:20
tell me what hospital your in
Read
16:34
pleeeeease reply asap!!
Makoto Okazaki
hakigami hospital 605
12:45

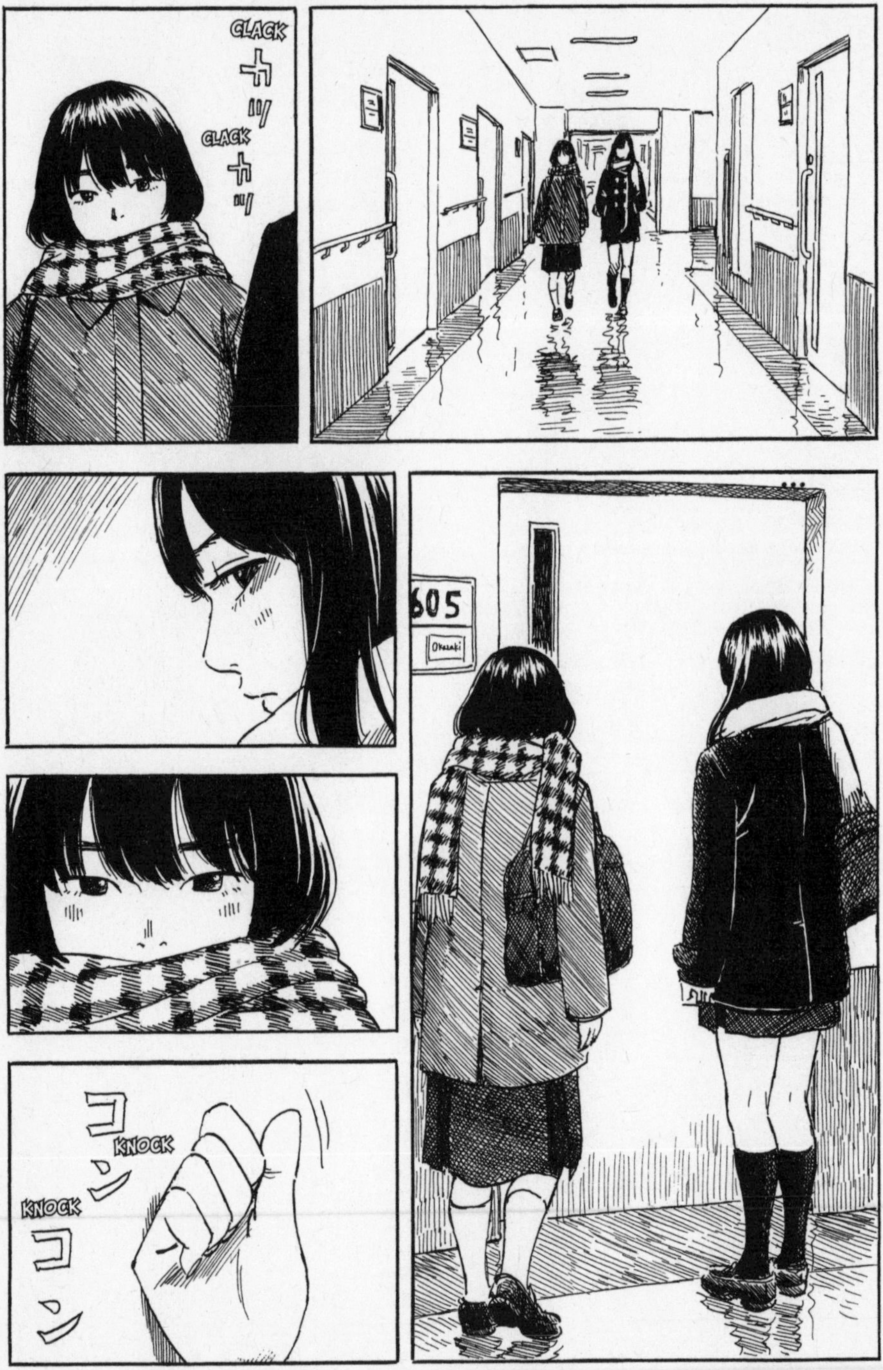
CLACK
カッ
CLACK
カッ
605
Okazaki
コン
KNOCK
KNOCK
コン

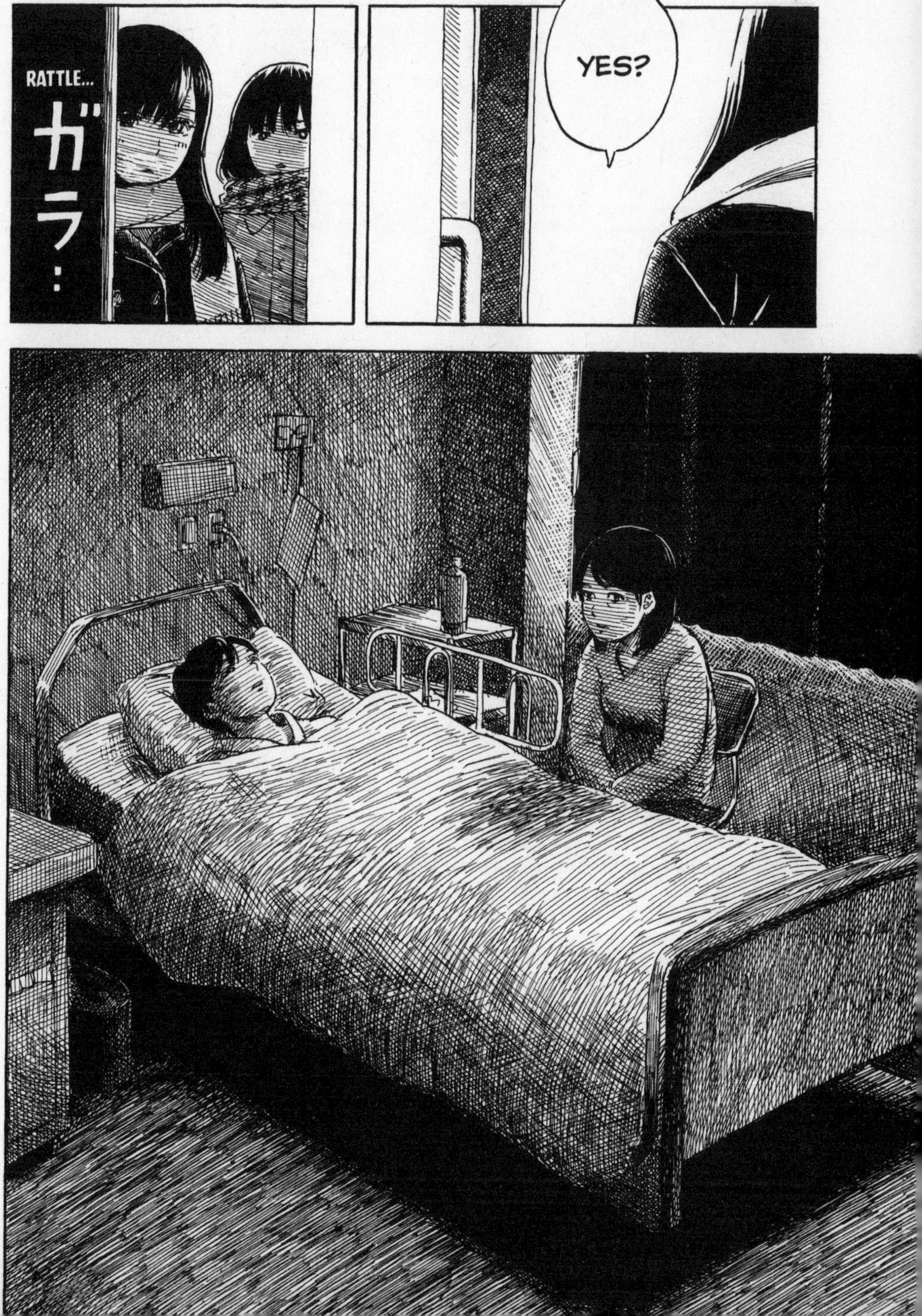
YES?
RATTLE...
ガラ…

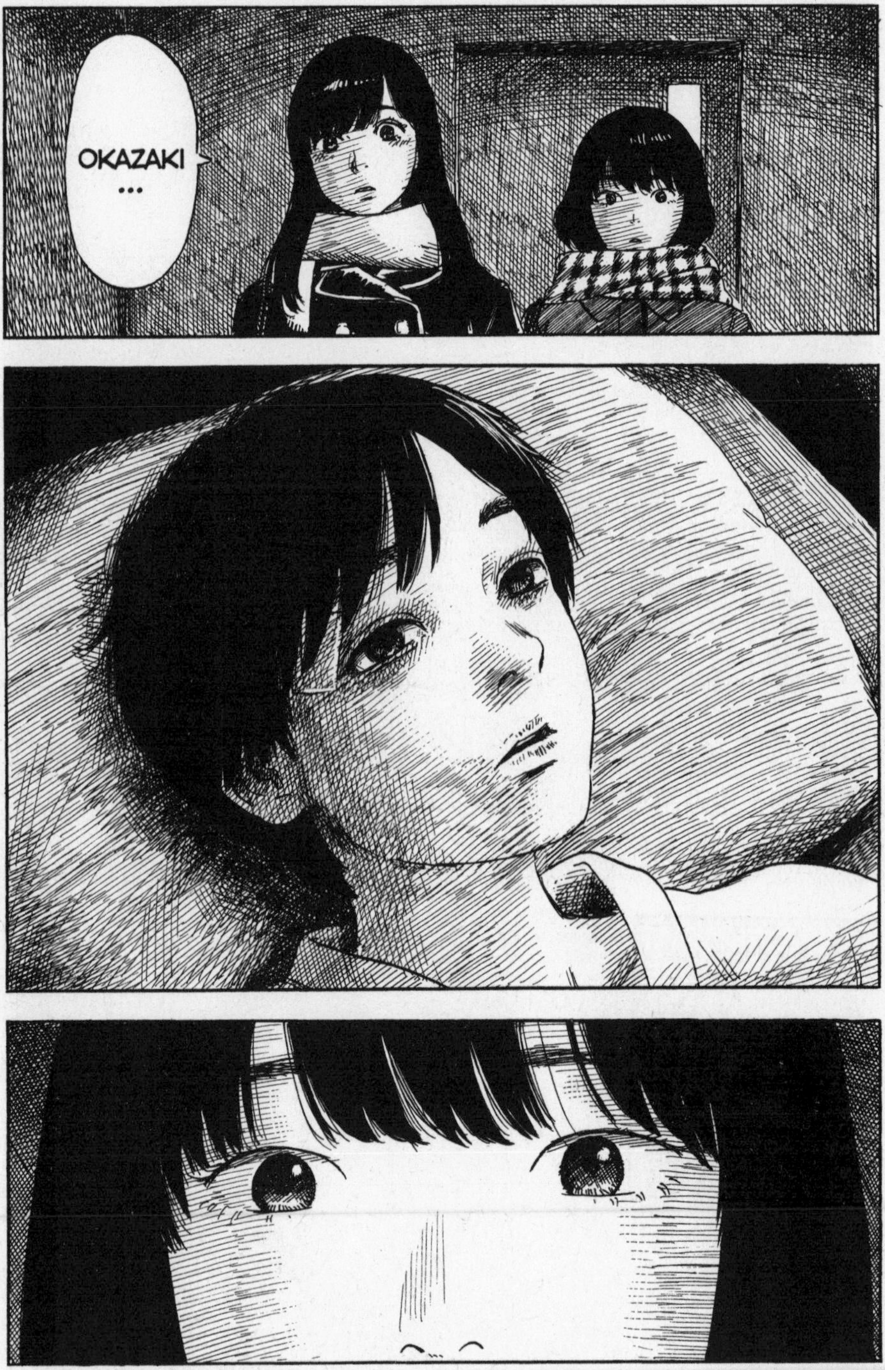
OKAZAKI
...

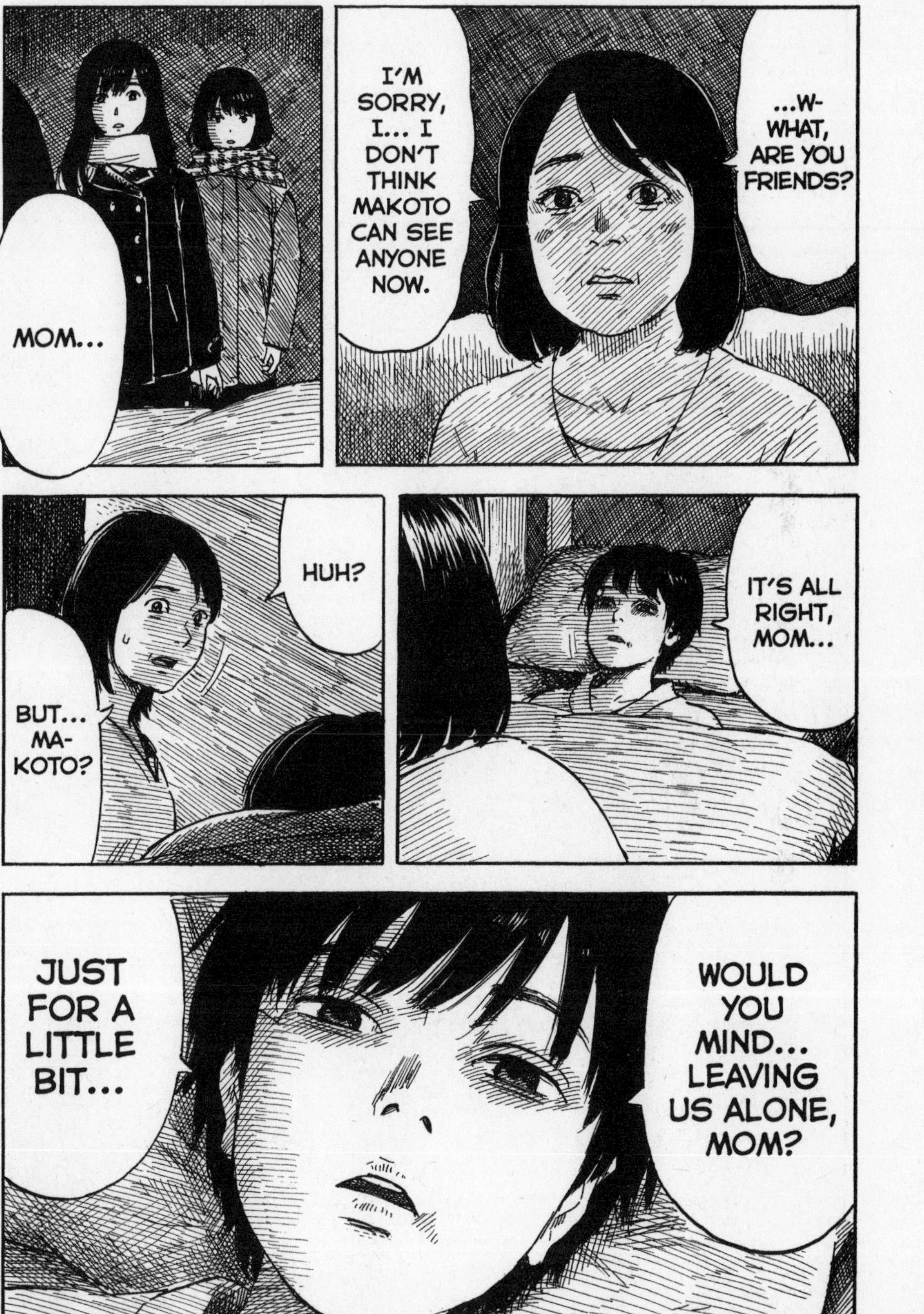
...W- WHAT, ARE YOU FRIENDS?
I'M SORRY, I... I DON'T THINK MAKOTO CAN SEE ANYONE NOW.
MOM...
IT'S ALL RIGHT, MOM...
HUH?
BUT... MA-KOTO?
WOULD YOU MIND... LEAVING US ALONE, MOM?
JUST FOR A LITTLE BIT...

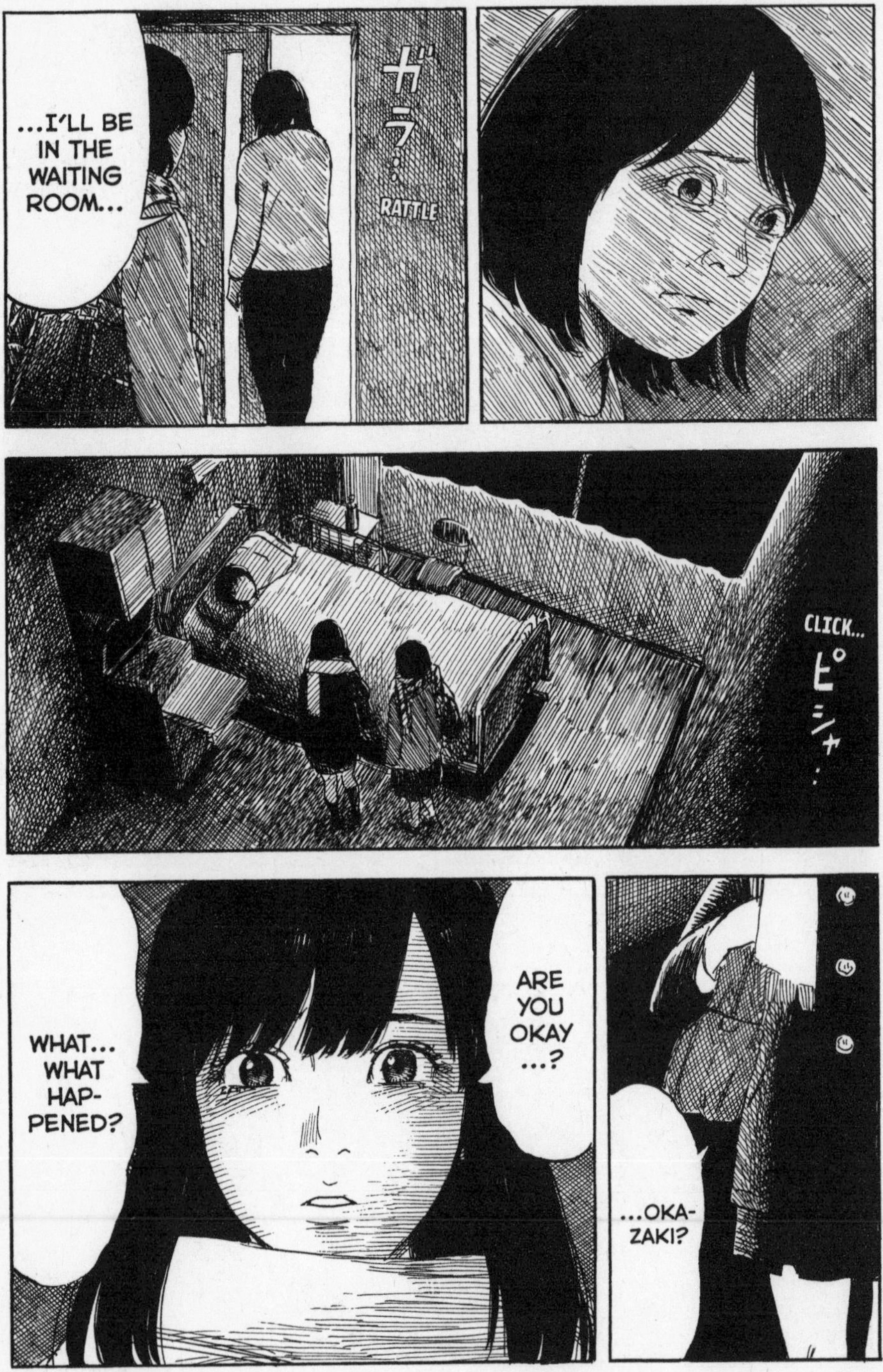

...I'LL BE IN THE WAITING ROOM...
ガラ…
RATTLE
CLICK...
ピシャ…
...OKA-ZAKI?
ARE YOU OKAY ...?
WHAT... WHAT HAP-PENED?

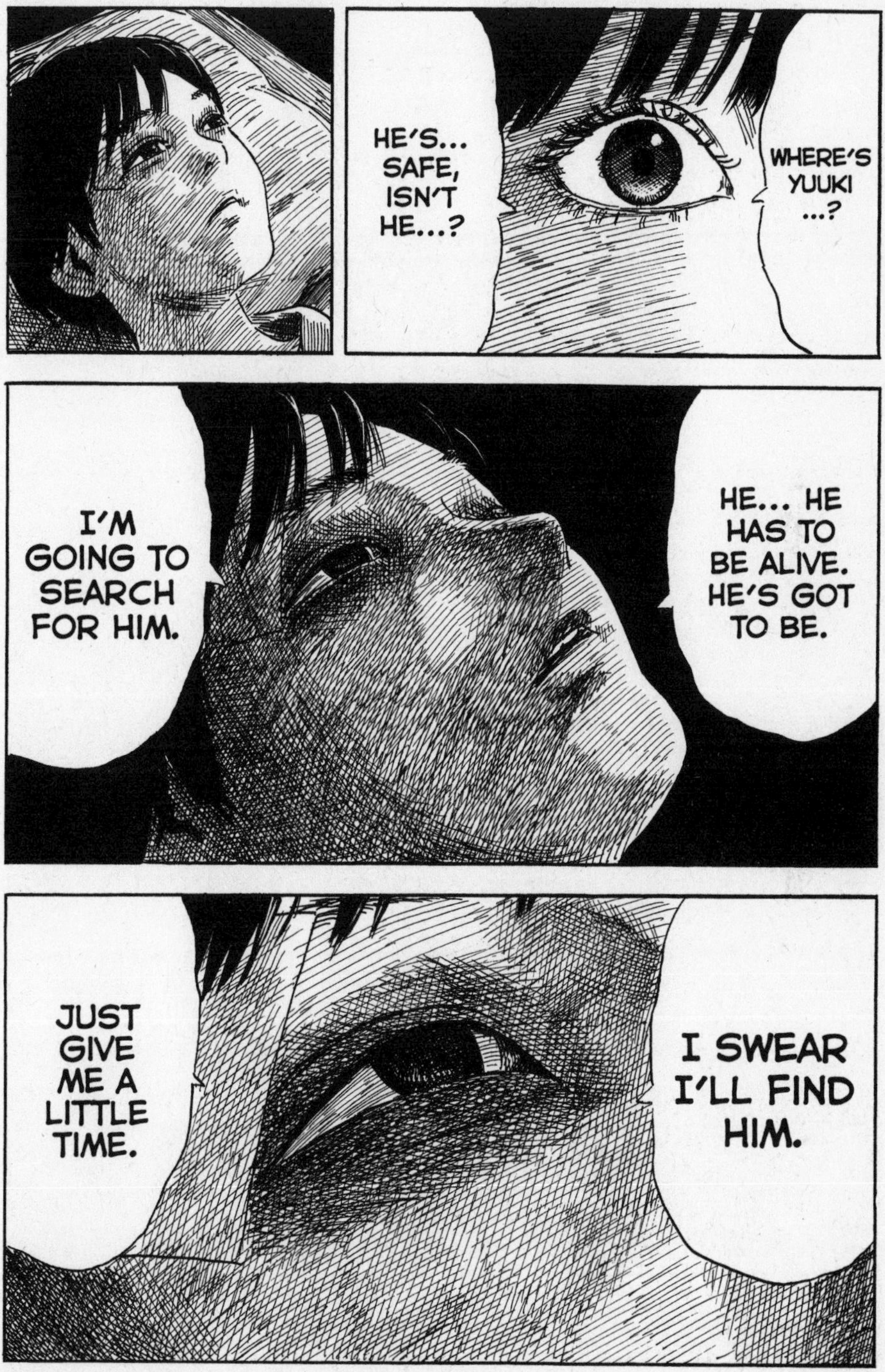
WHERE'S YUUKI ...?
HE'S... SAFE, ISN'T HE...?
HE... HE HAS TO BE ALIVE. HE'S GOT TO BE.
I'M GOING TO SEARCH FOR HIM.
I SWEAR I'LL FIND HIM.
JUST GIVE ME A LITTLE TIME.

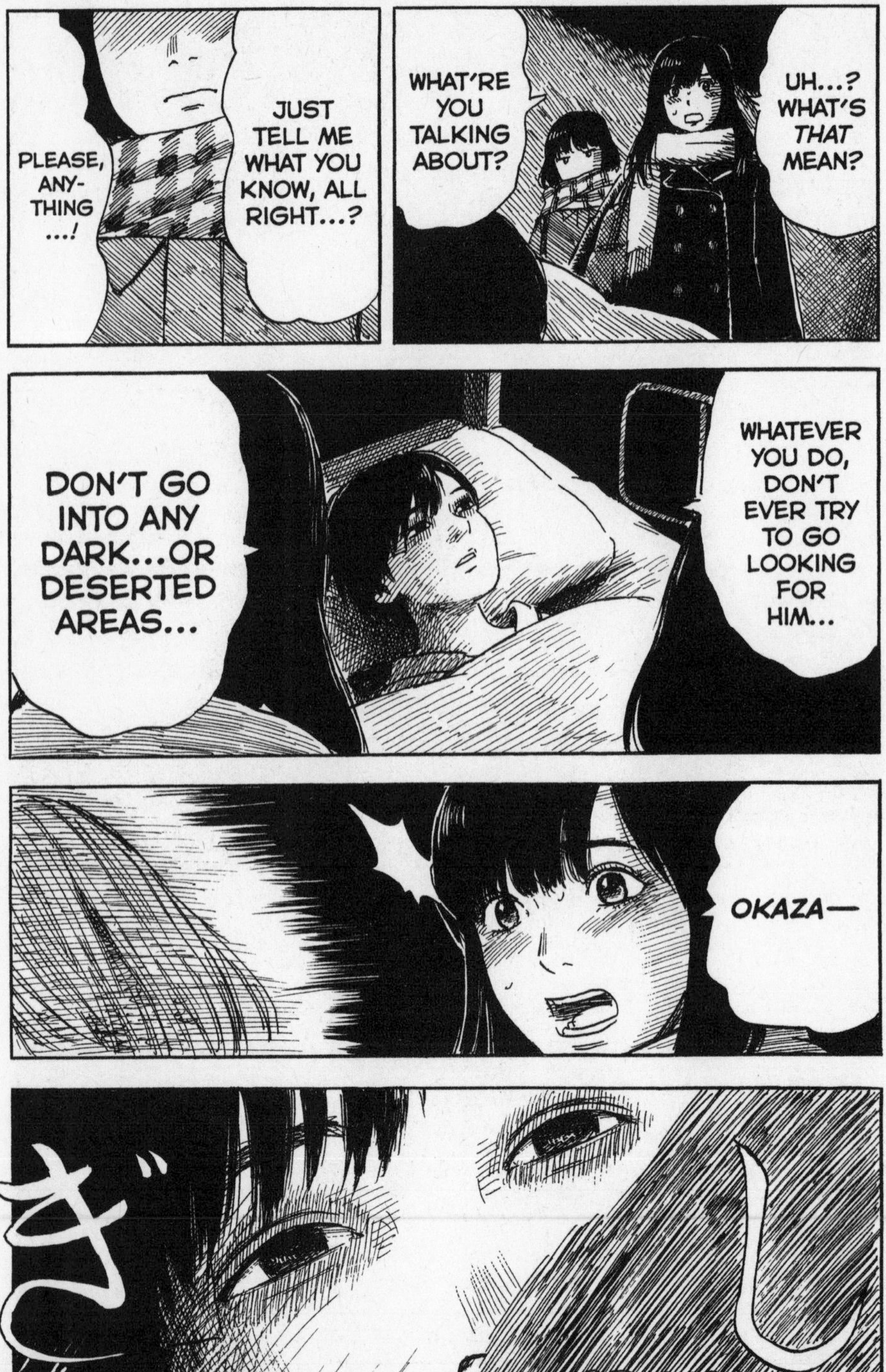
UH...? WHAT'S *THAT* MEAN?
WHAT'RE YOU TALKING ABOUT?
JUST TELL ME WHAT YOU KNOW, ALL RIGHT...?
PLEASE, ANY-THING ...!
WHATEVER YOU DO, DON'T EVER TRY TO GO LOOKING FOR HIM...
DON'T GO INTO ANY DARK...OR DESERTED AREAS...
OKAZA—
ぎし
CREAK

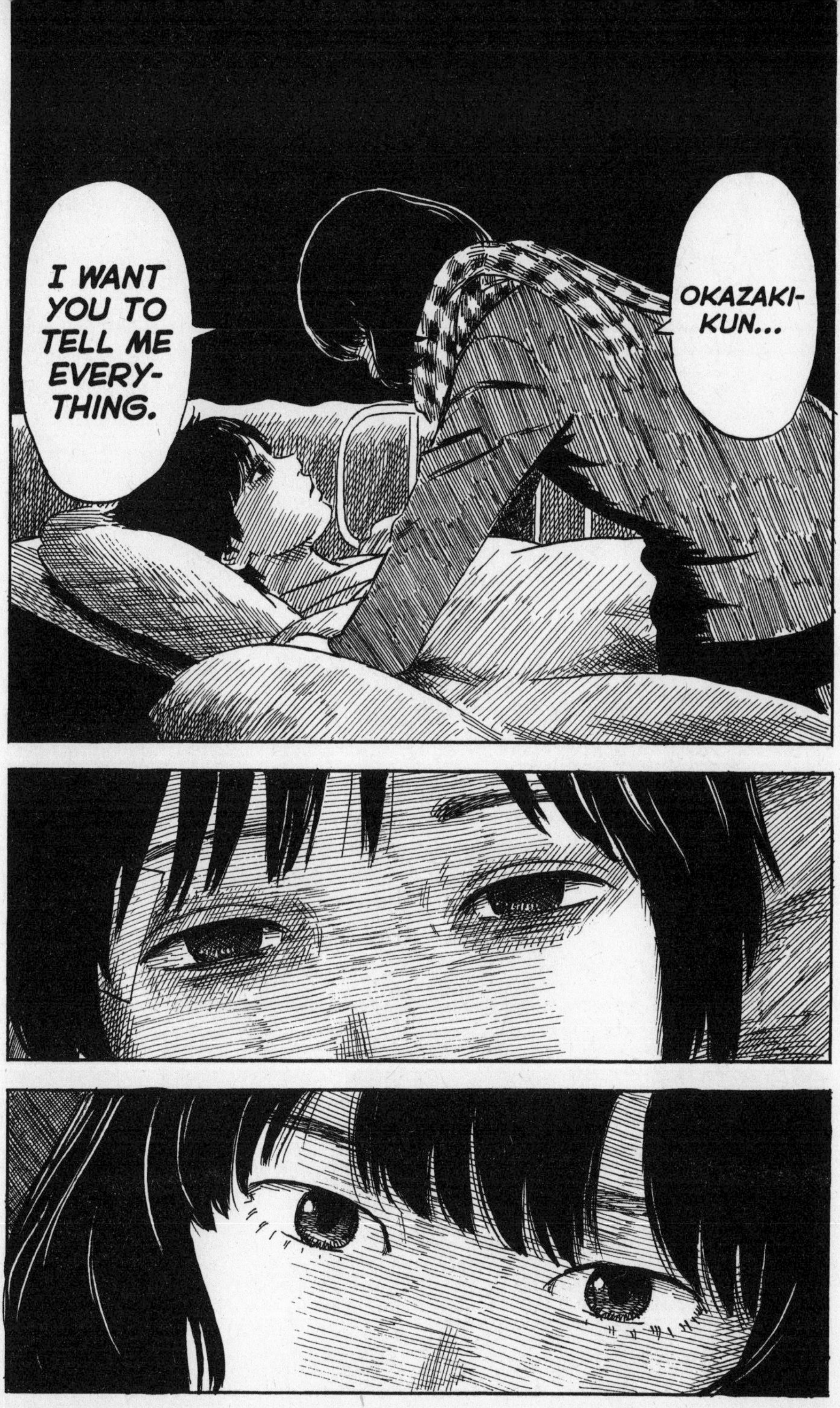
OKAZAKI-KUN...
I WANT YOU TO TELL ME EVERYTHING.

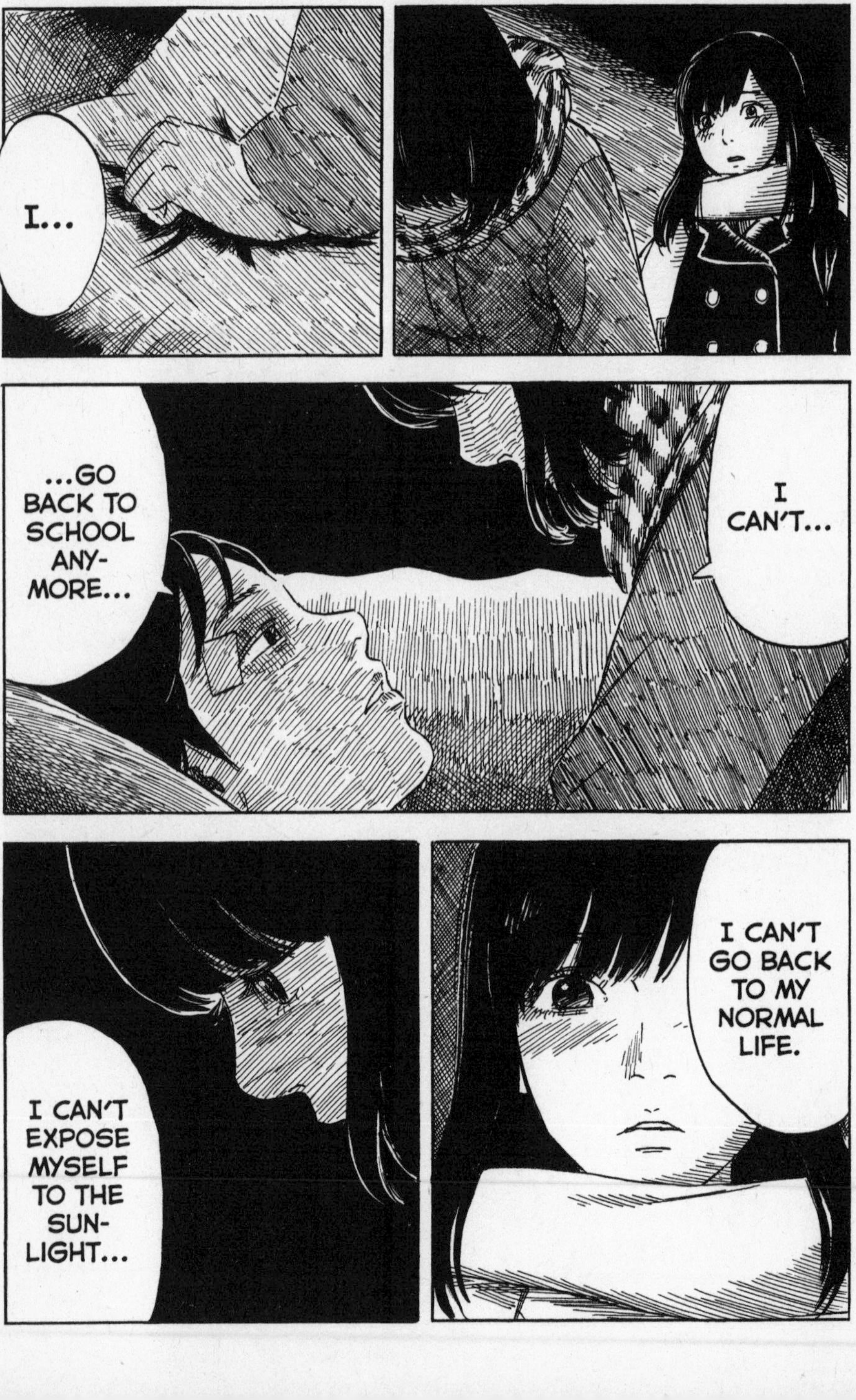
I...
I CAN'T...
...GO BACK TO SCHOOL ANY-MORE...
I CAN'T GO BACK TO MY NORMAL LIFE.
I CAN'T EXPOSE MYSELF TO THE SUN-LIGHT...

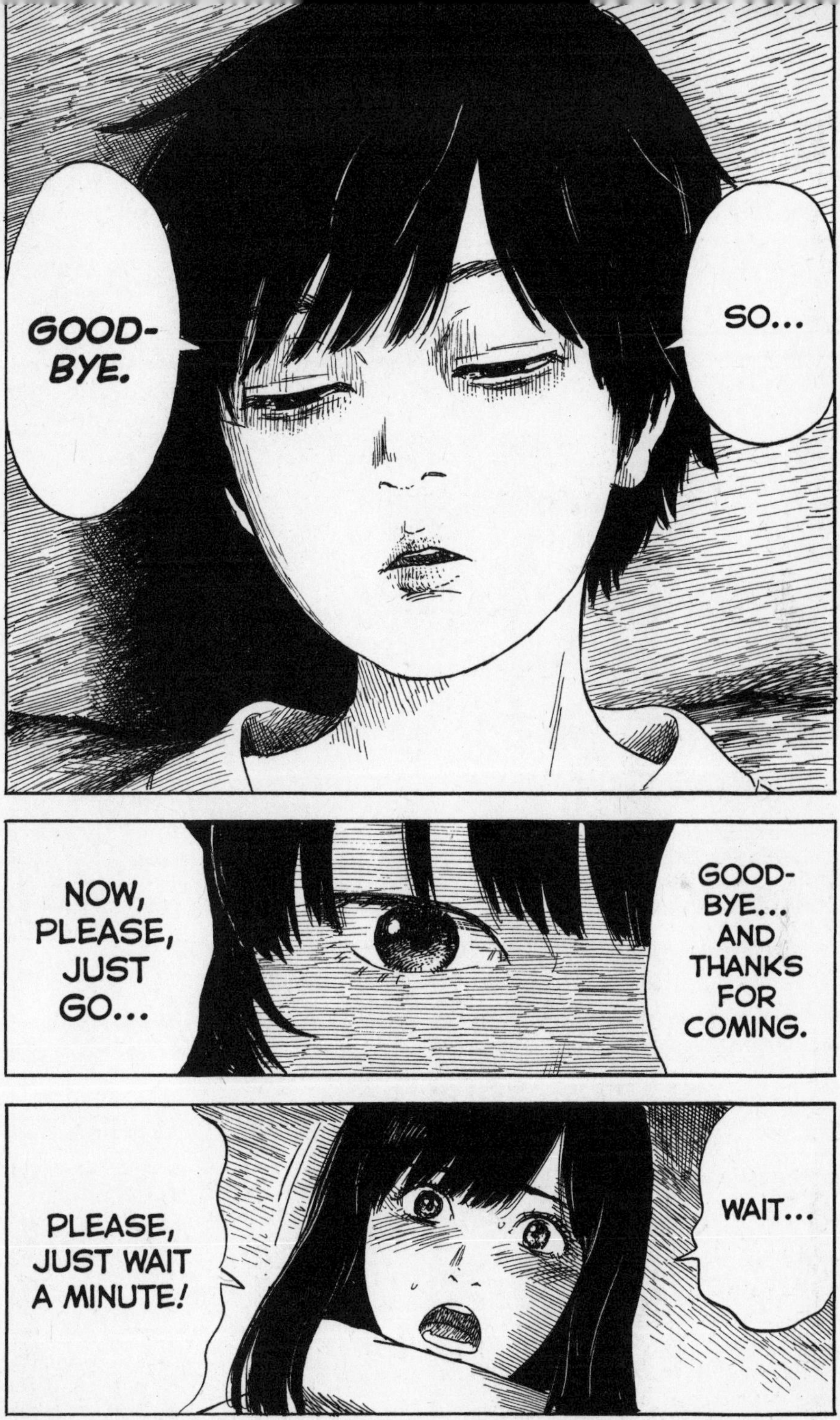
SO...
GOOD-BYE.
GOOD-BYE... AND THANKS FOR COMING.
NOW, PLEASE, JUST GO...
WAIT...
PLEASE, JUST WAIT A MINUTE!

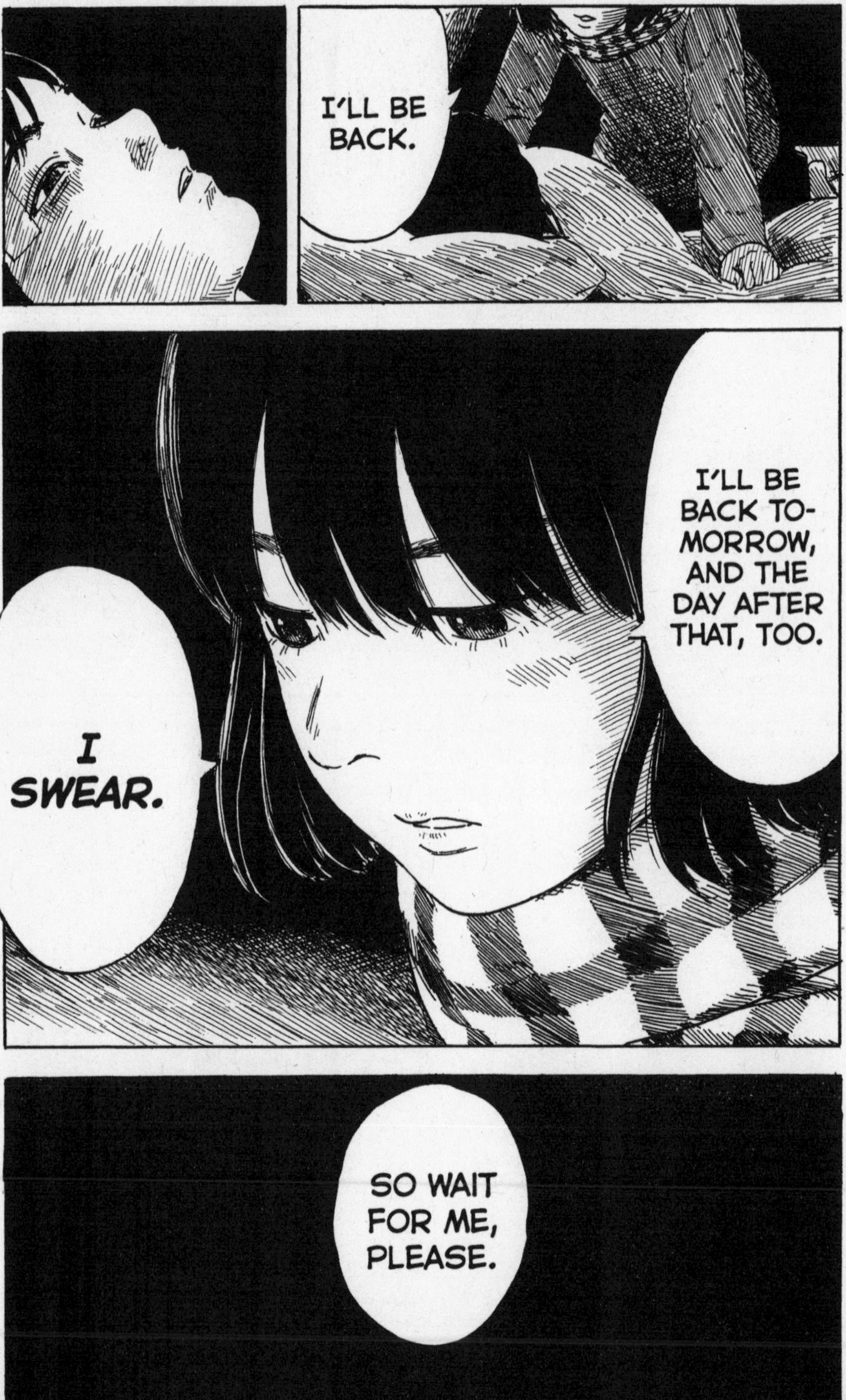
I'LL BE BACK.
I'LL BE BACK TO-MORROW, AND THE DAY AFTER THAT, TOO.
I SWEAR.
SO WAIT FOR ME, PLEASE.

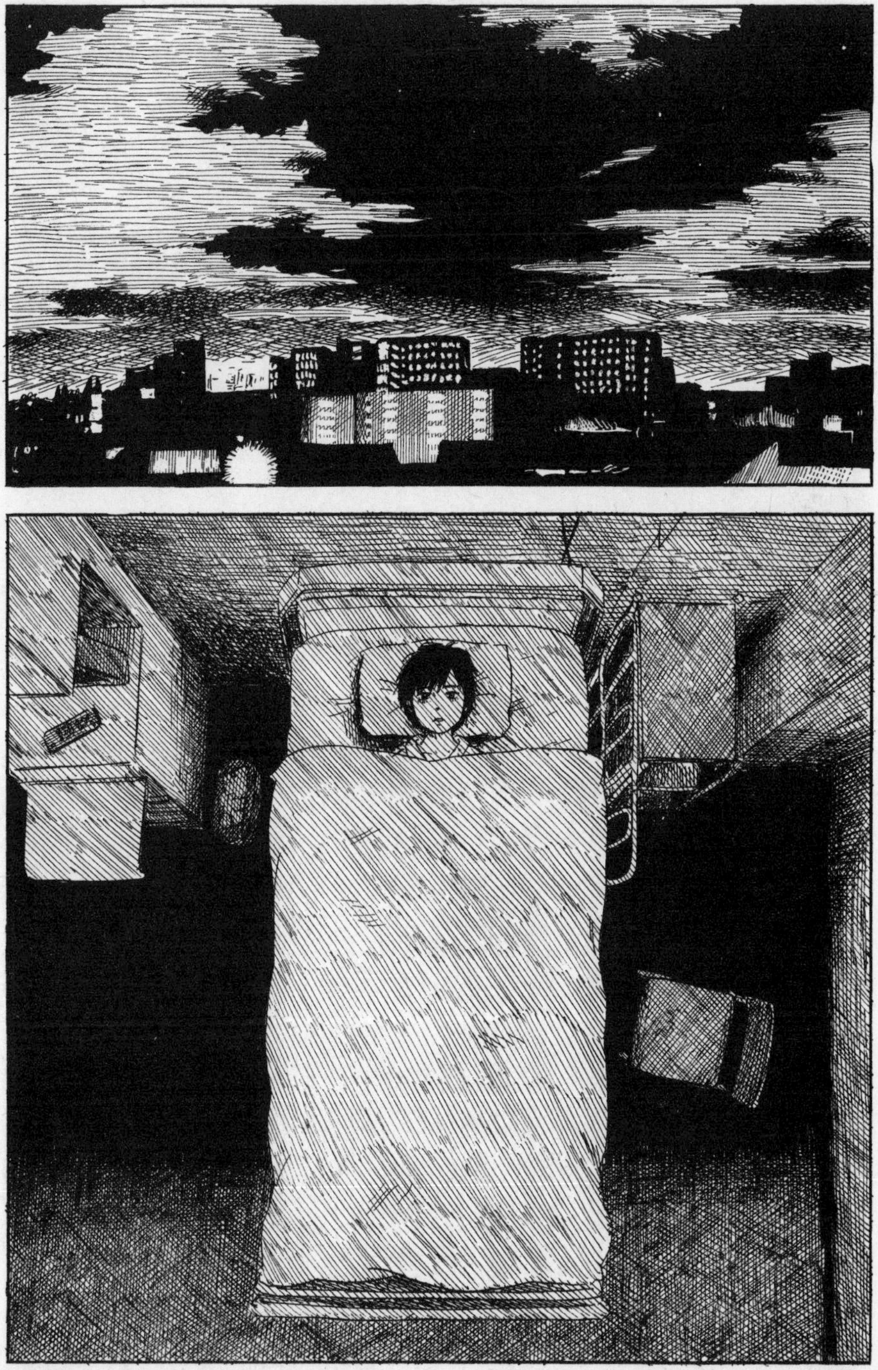

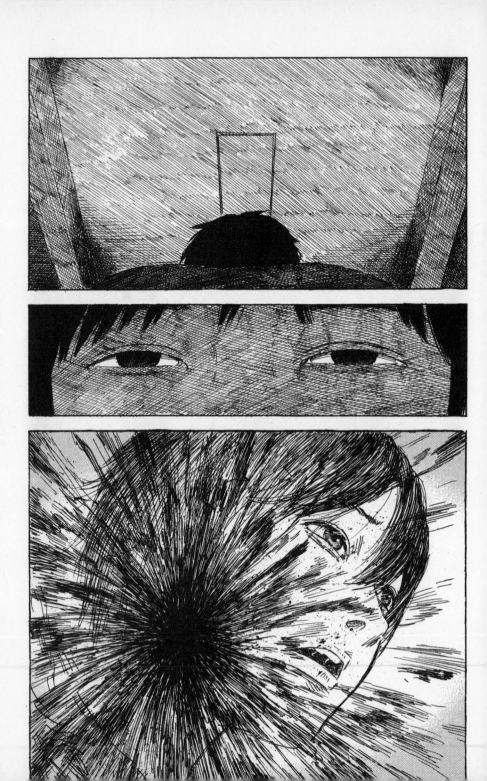

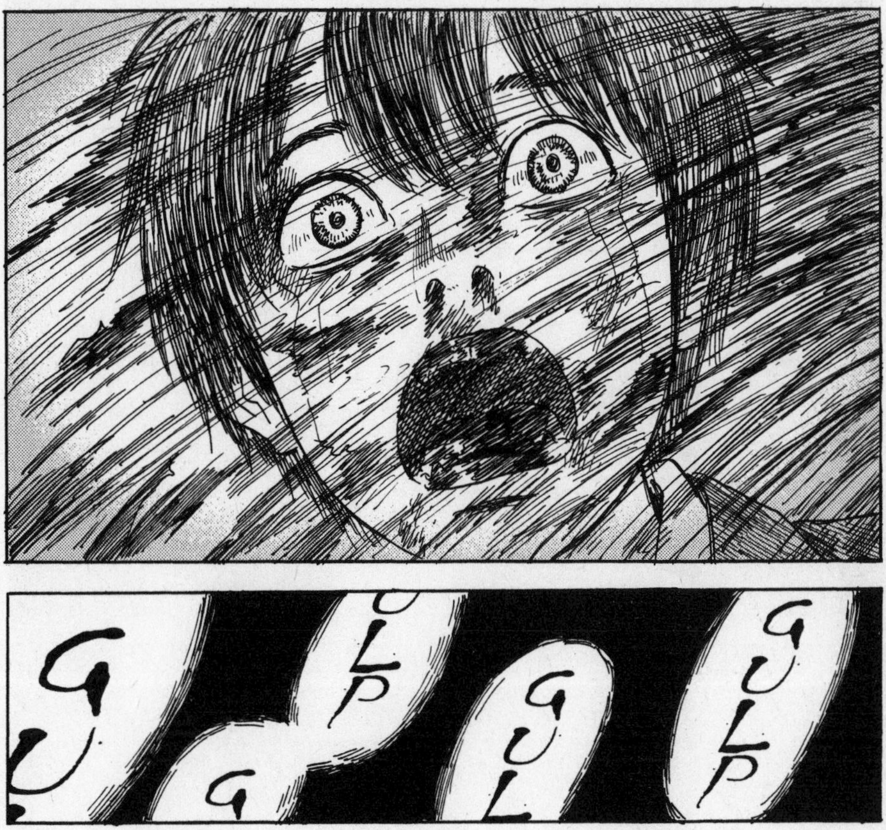
GULP
GUL
LP
G
GU

YUUKI-KUN'S BLOOD...

WAS THE MOST *DELICIOUS* THING...

...I'D EVER TASTED IN MY LIFE.

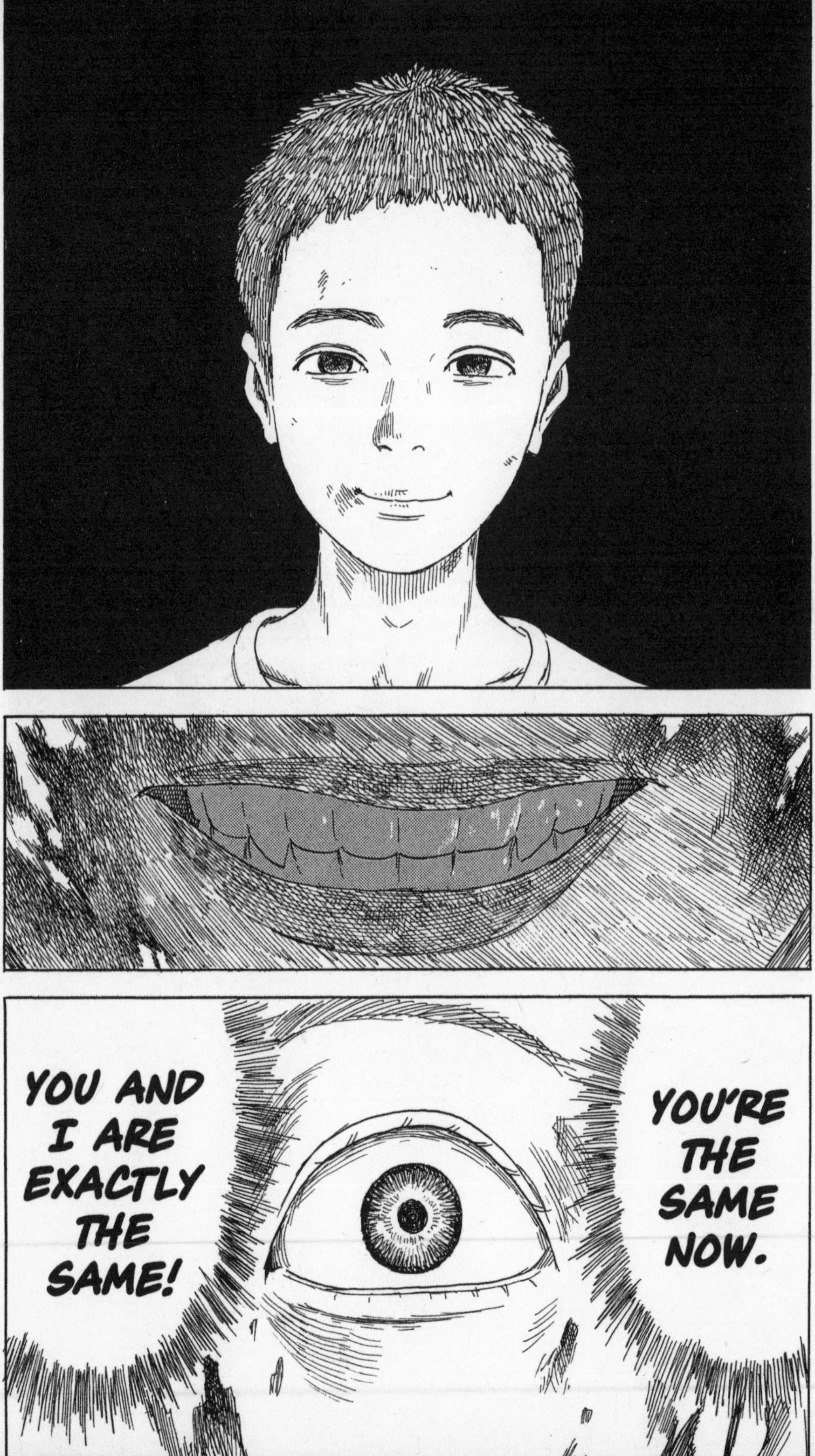
YOU'RE THE SAME NOW.
YOU AND I ARE EXACTLY THE SAME!

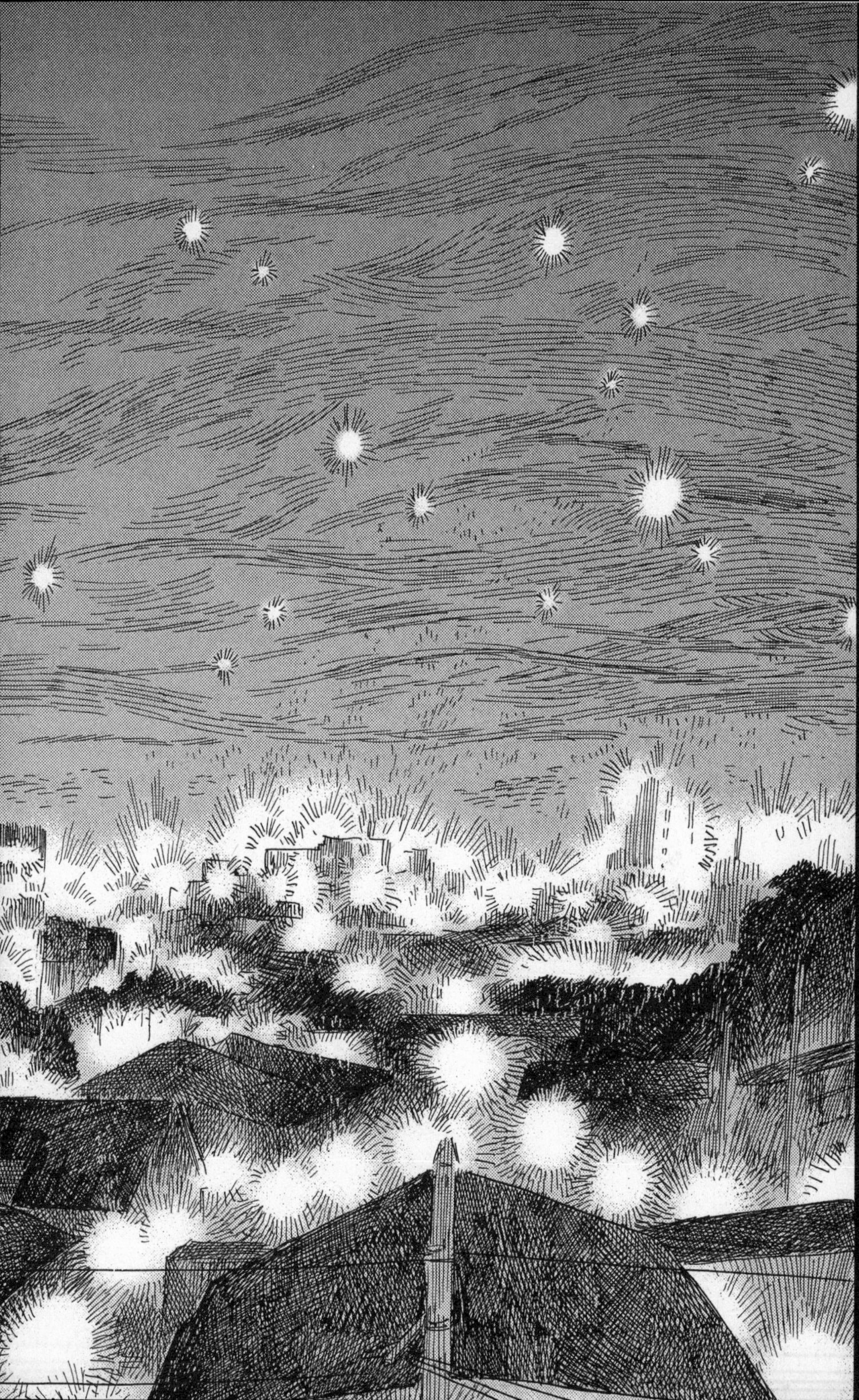

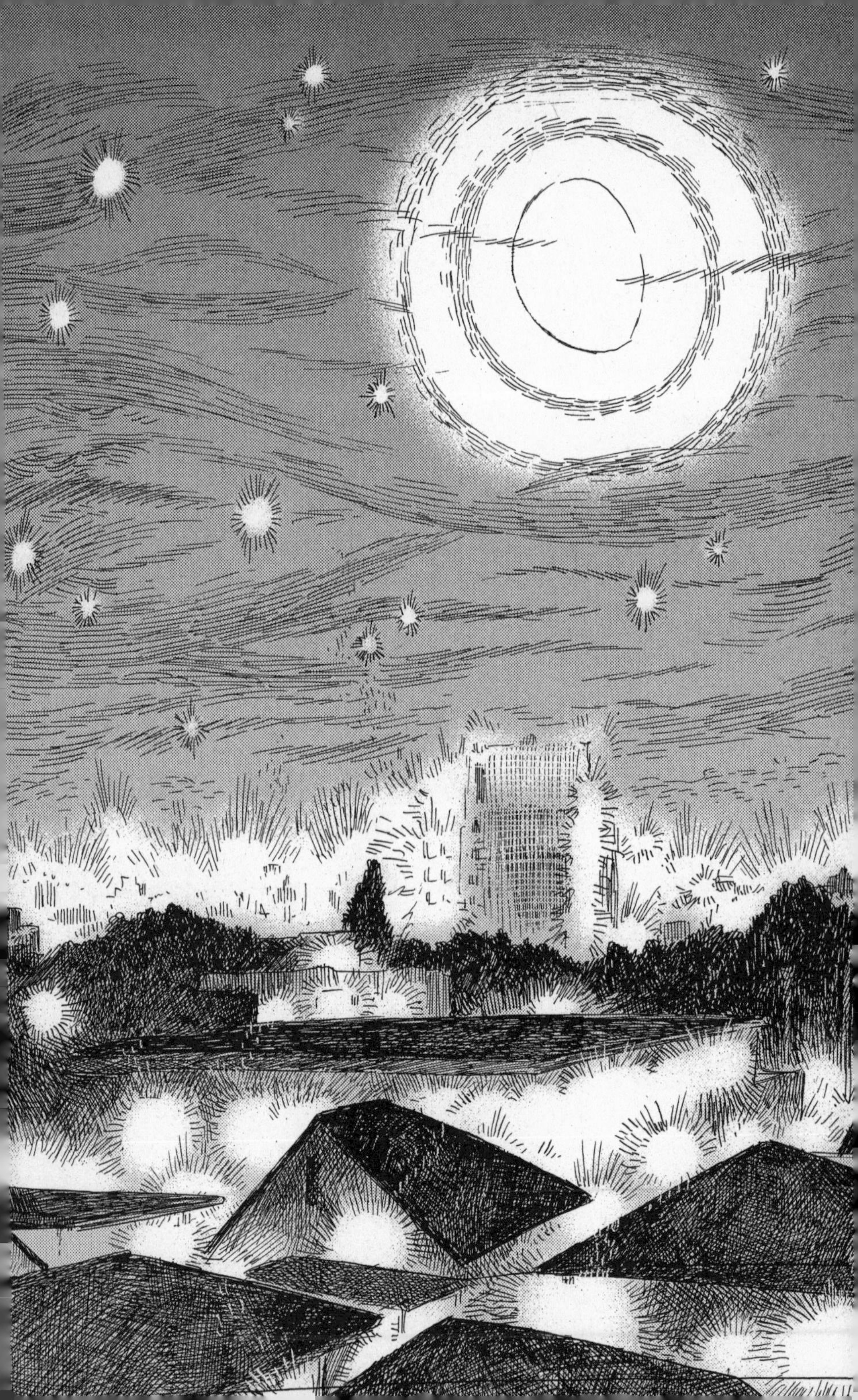

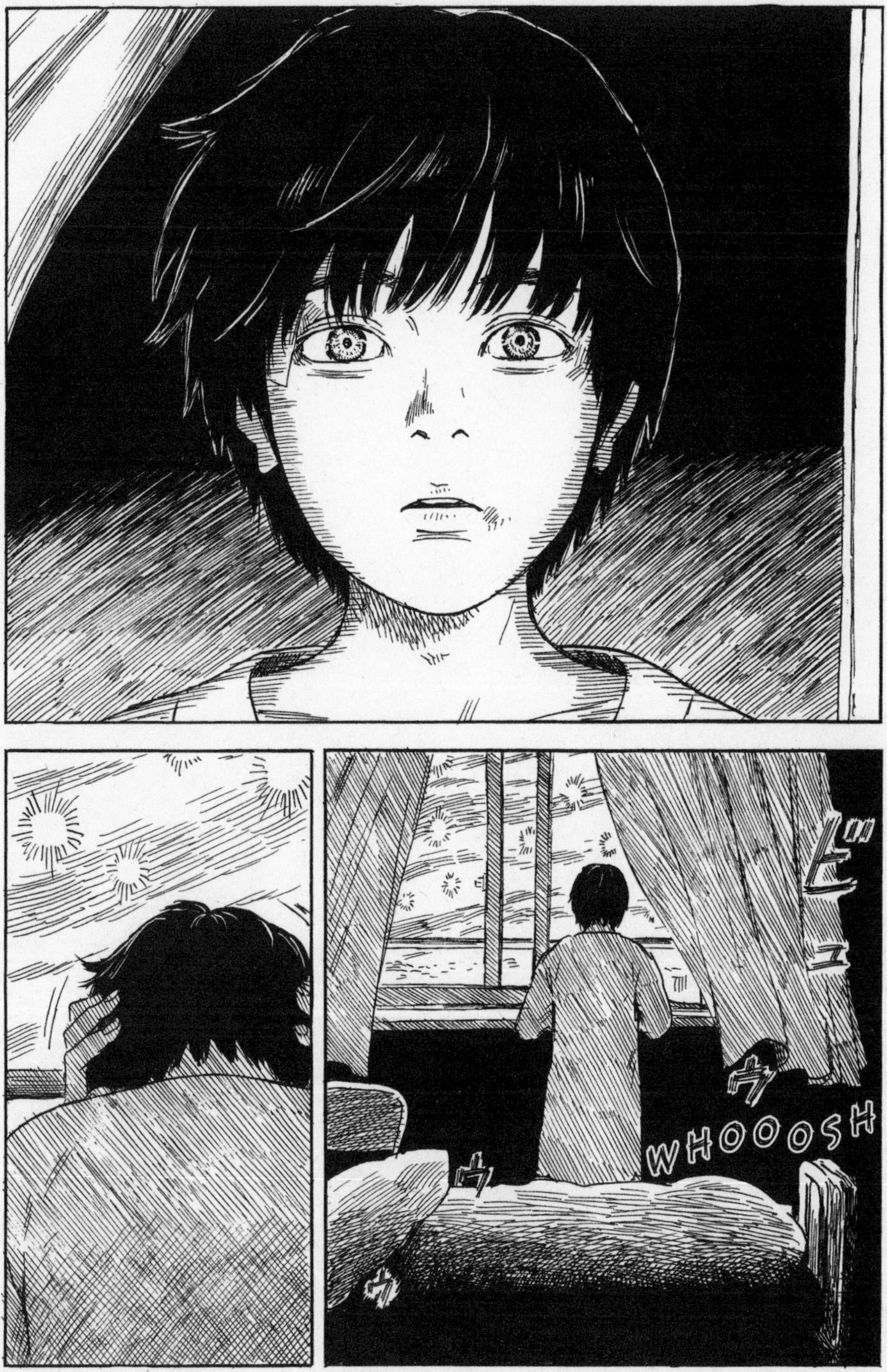
WHOOOSH

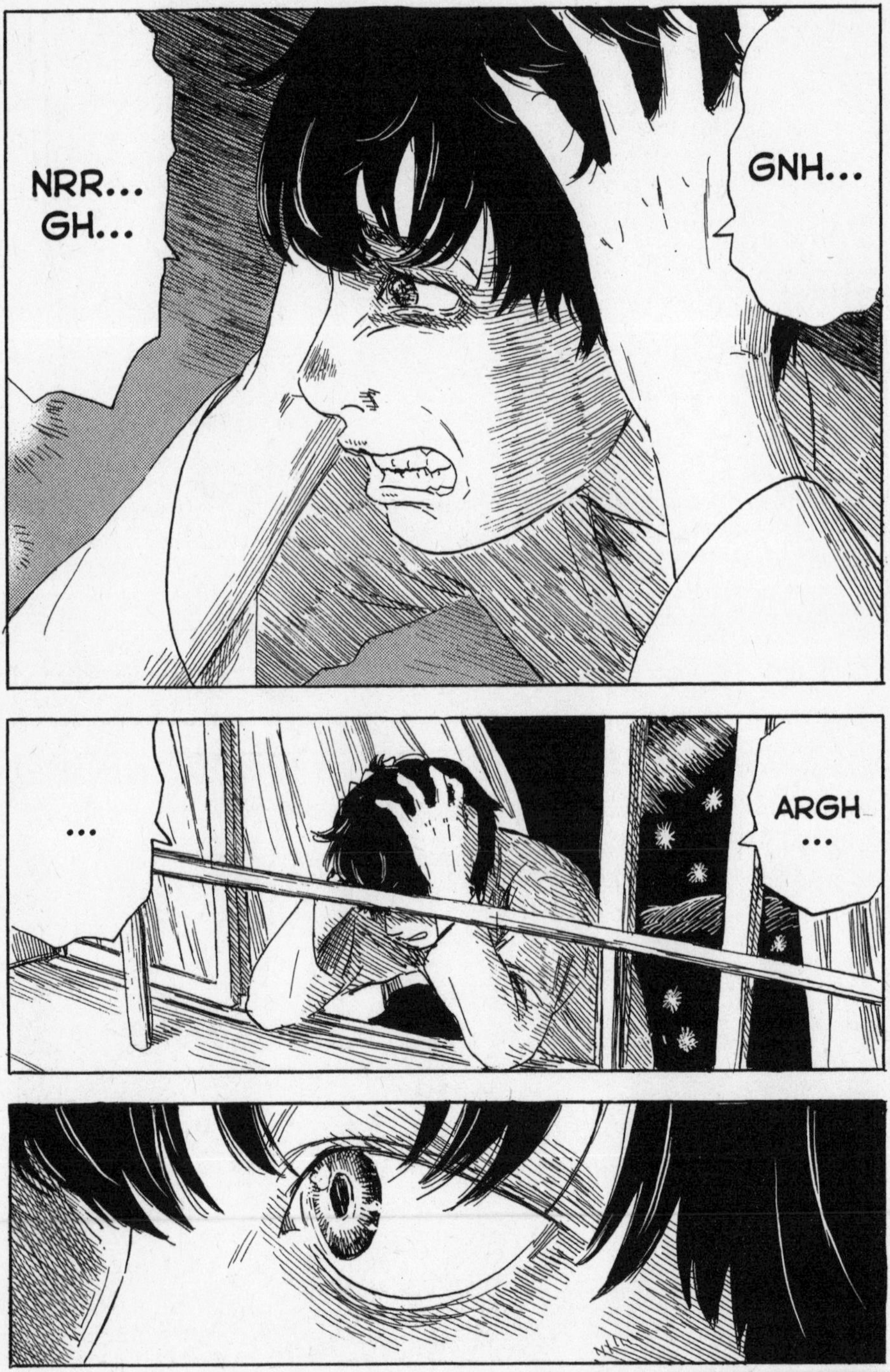
GNH...
NRR... GH...
ARGH ...
...

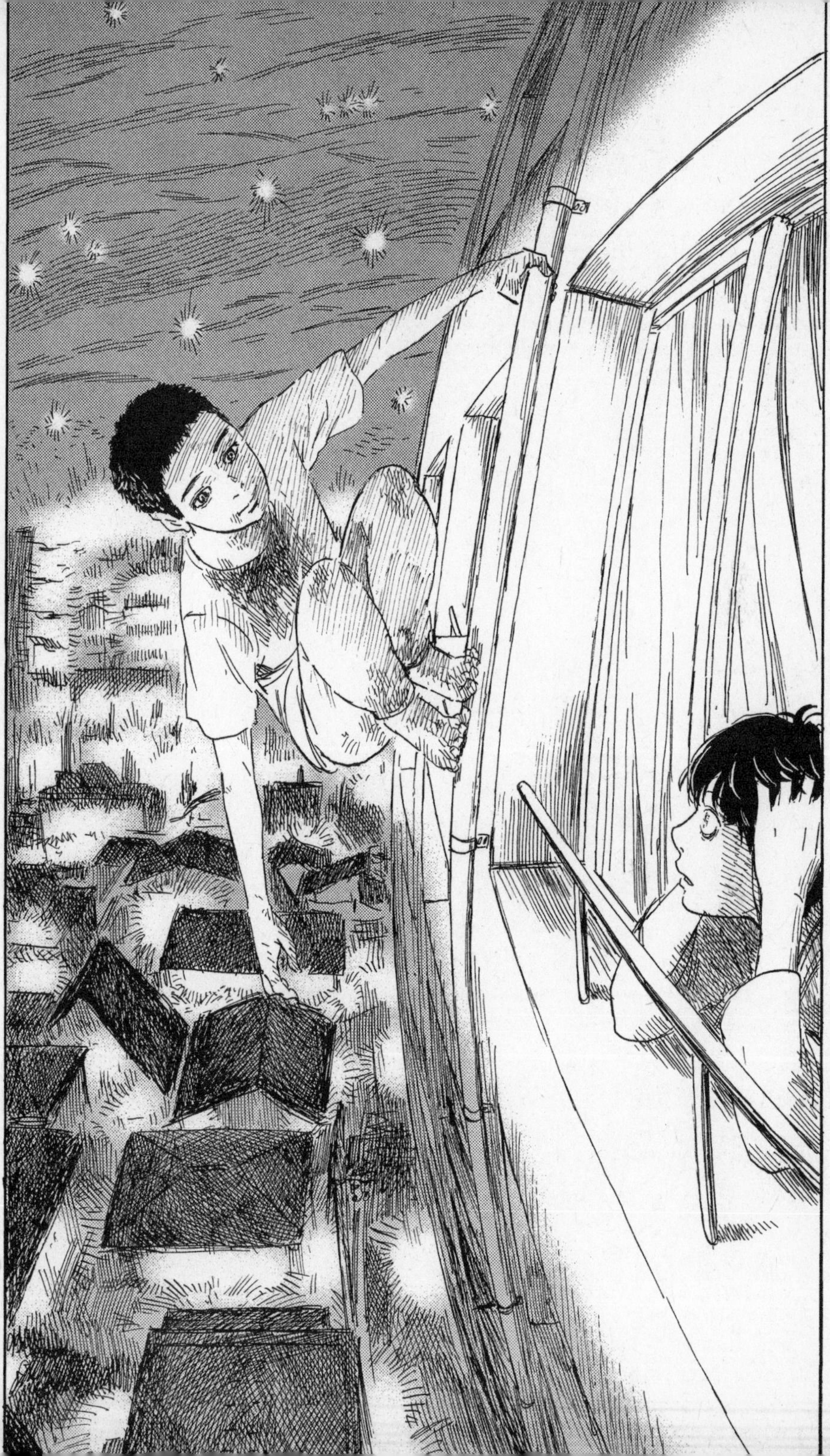

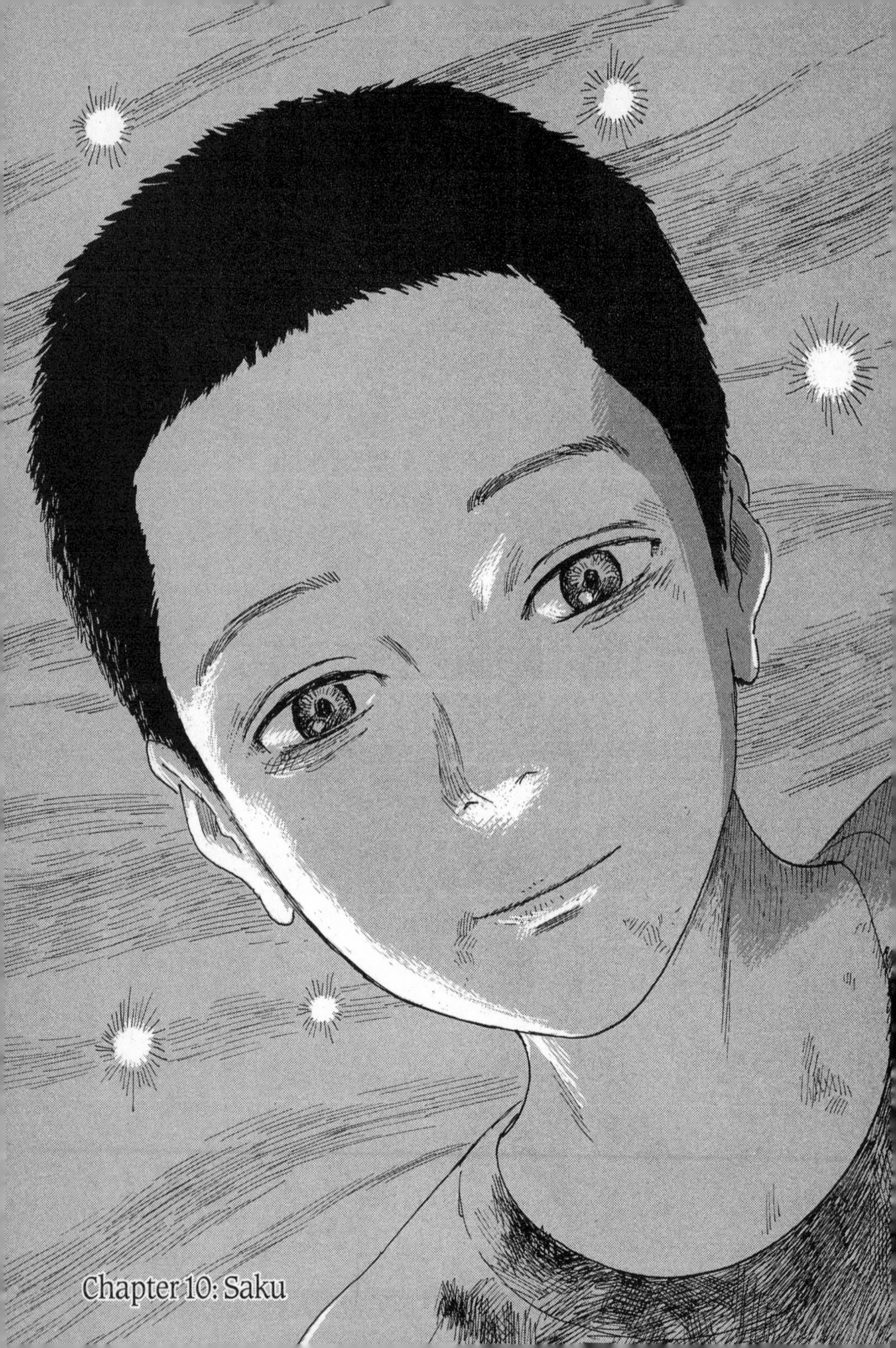

Chapter 10: Saku

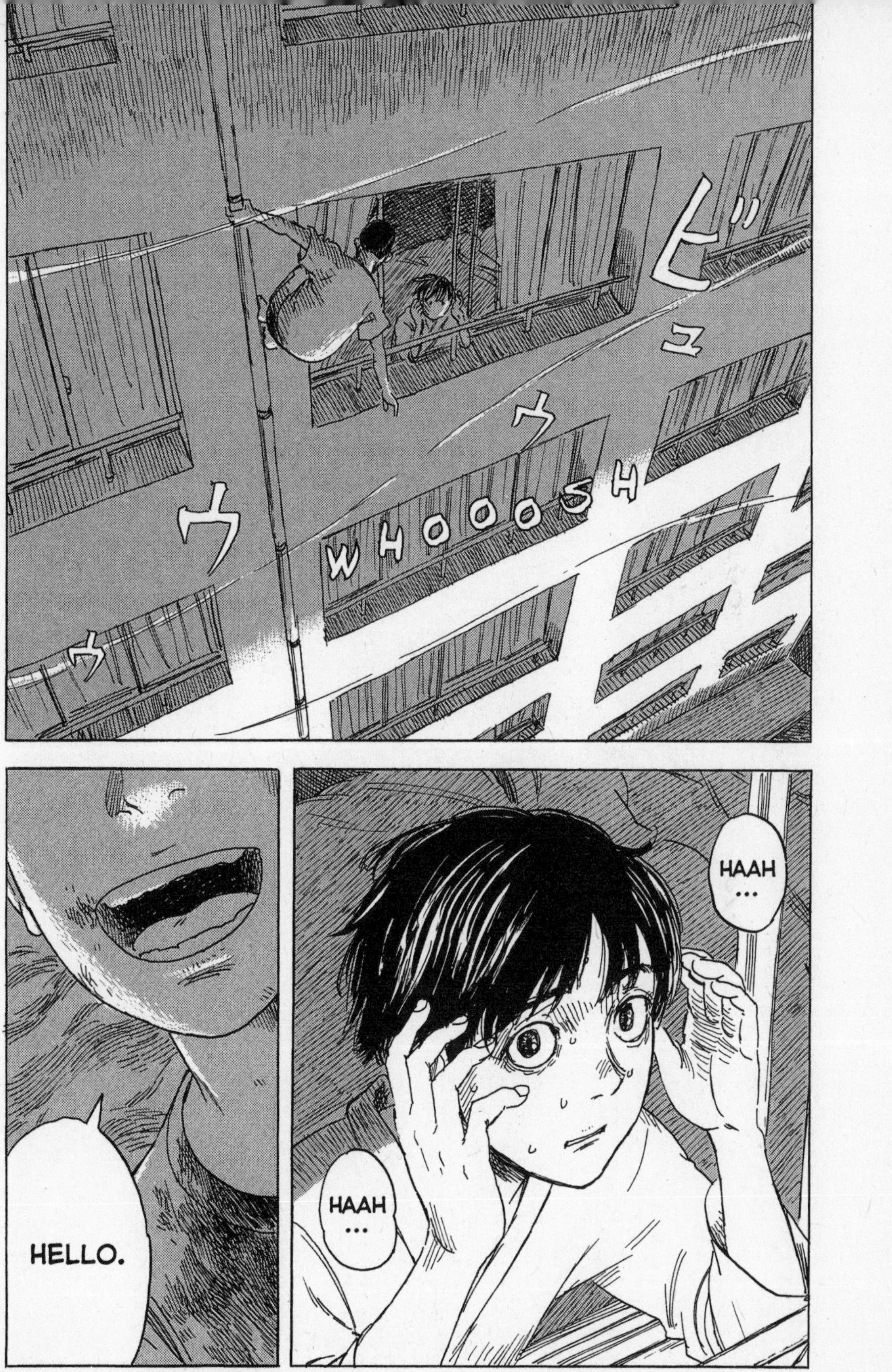

ビッュウウウ
WHOOOSH
HAAH ...
HAAH ...
HELLO.

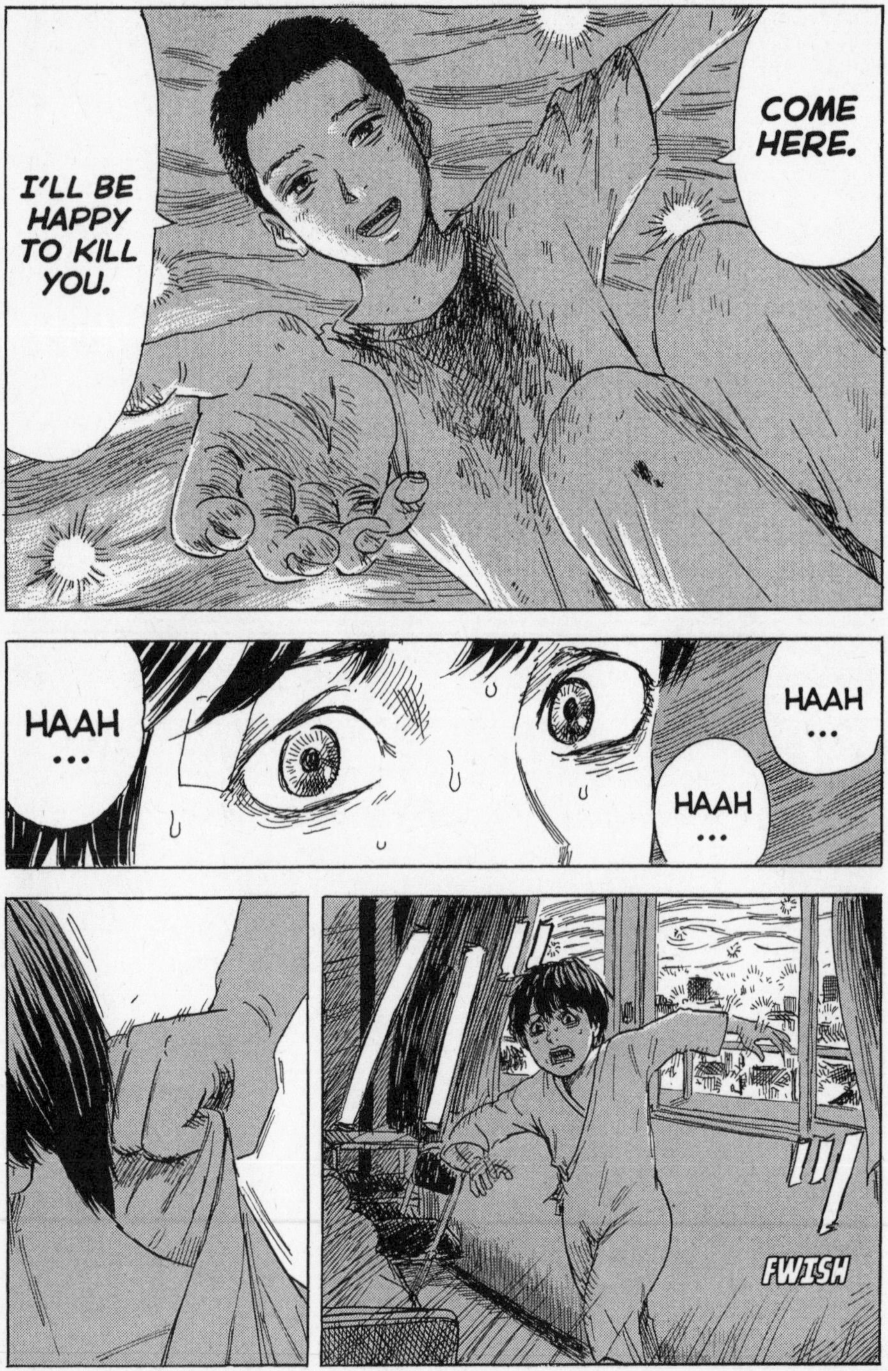
COME HERE.
I'LL BE HAPPY TO KILL YOU.
HAAH ...
HAAH ...
HAAH ...
FWISH

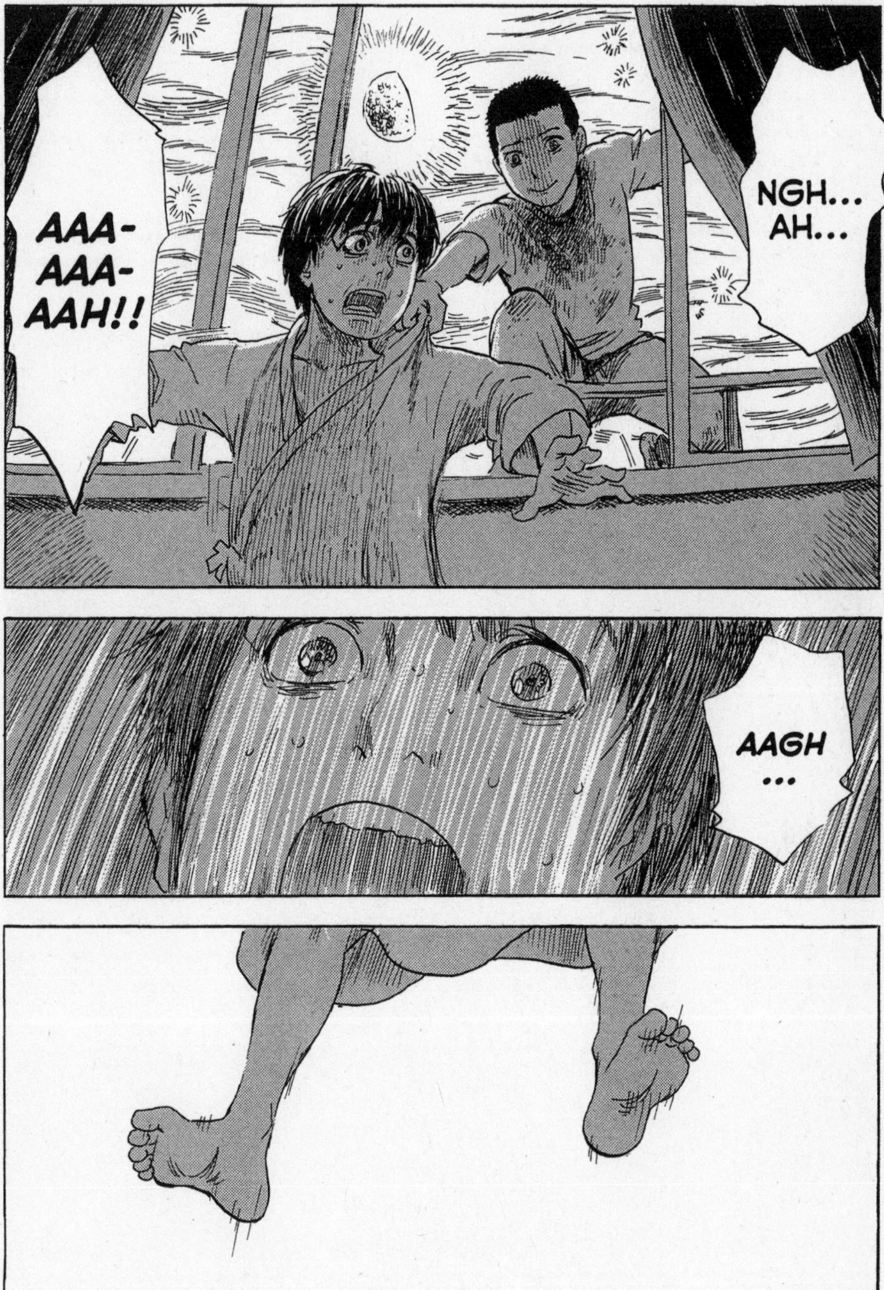
NGH... AH...
AAA-AAA-AAH!!
AAGH ...

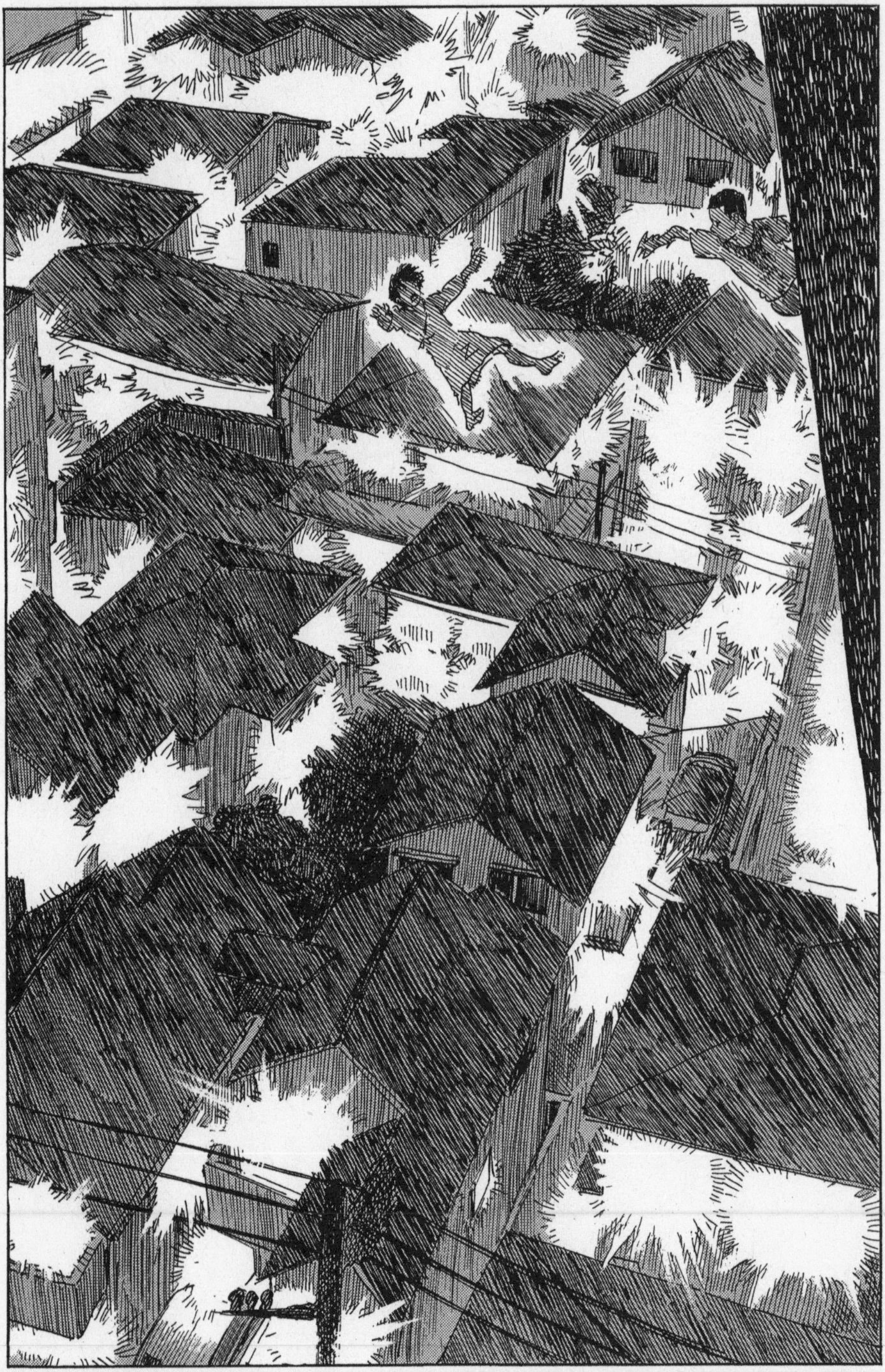

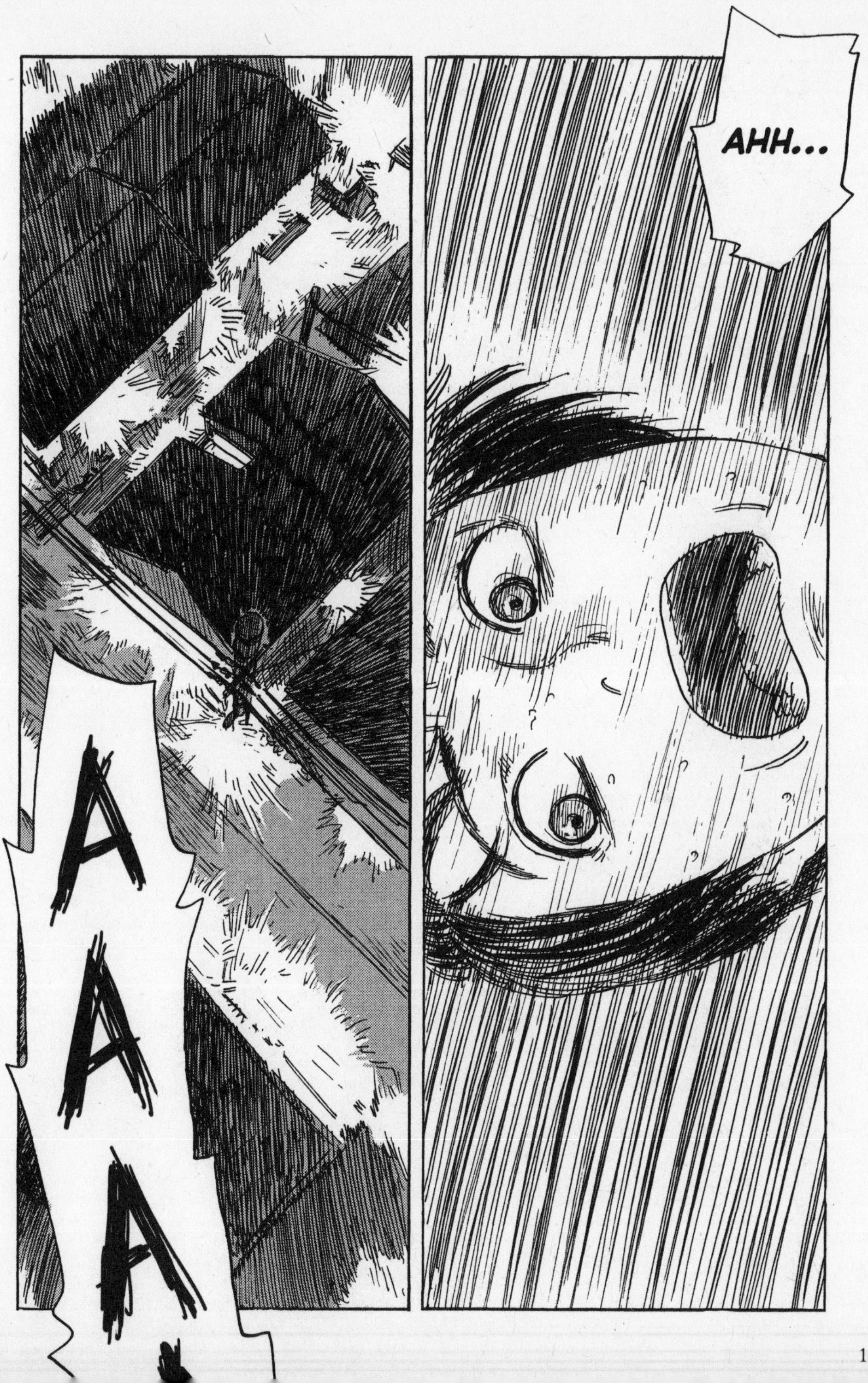
AHH...
AAAA

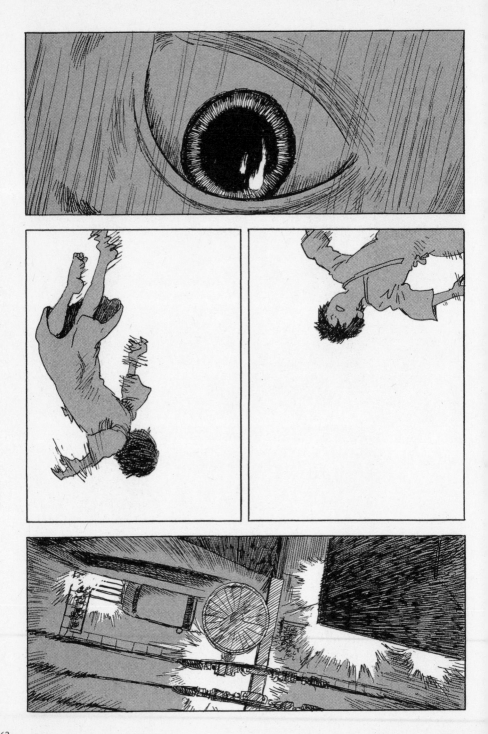

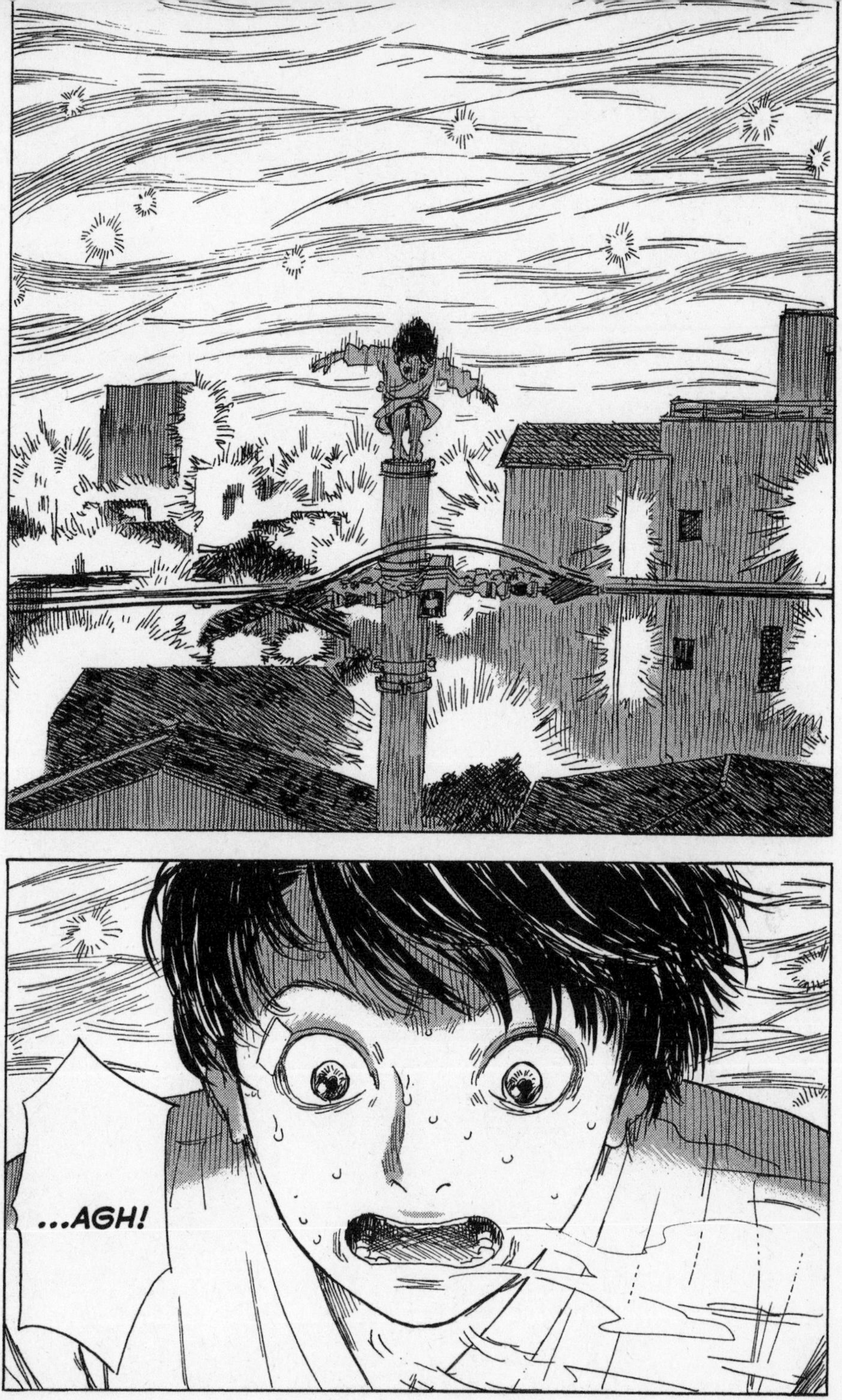
...AGH!

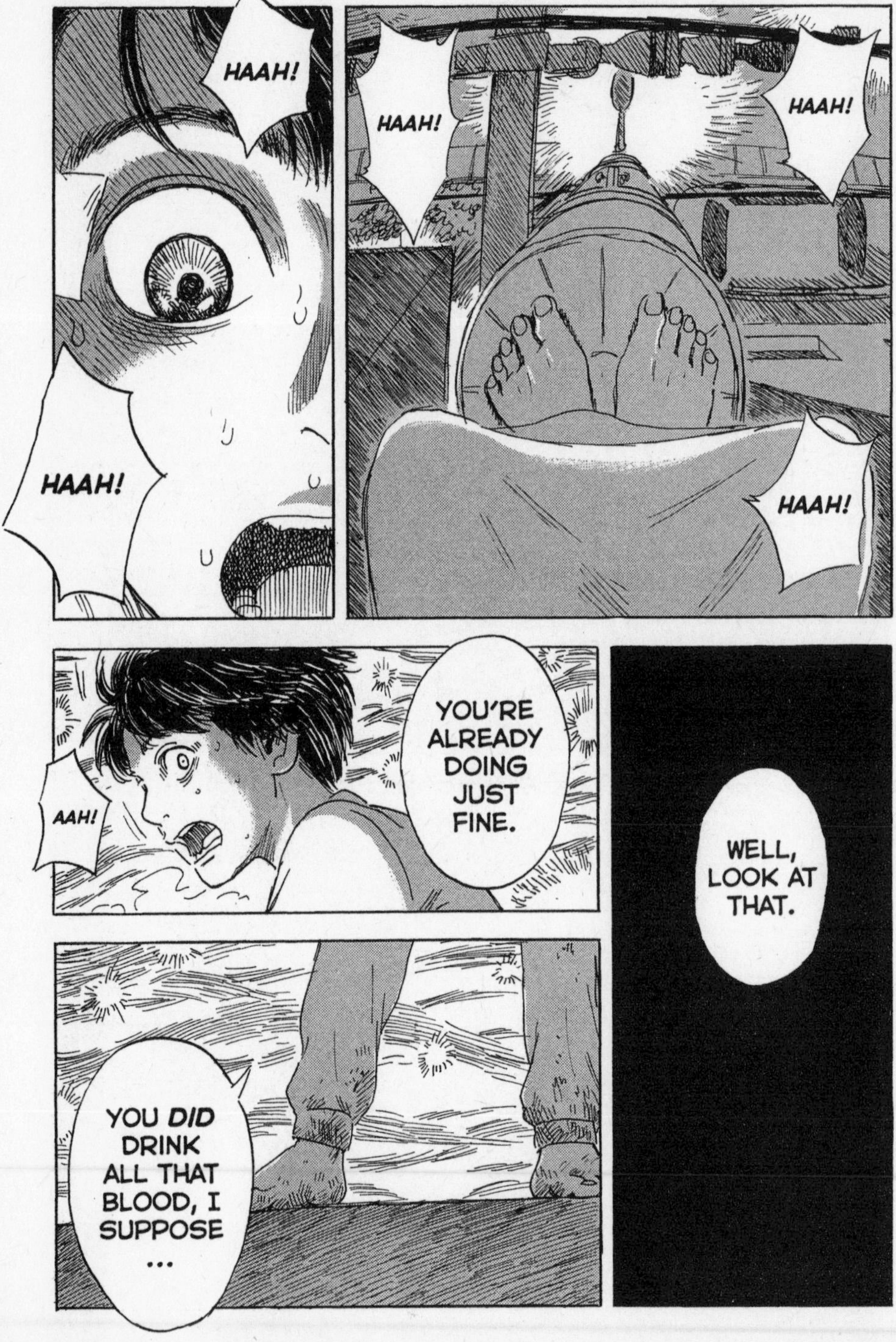
HAAH!
HAAH!
HAAH!
HAAH!
HAAH!
WELL, LOOK AT THAT.
YOU'RE ALREADY DOING JUST FINE.
AAH!
YOU *DID* DRINK ALL THAT BLOOD, I SUPPOSE ...

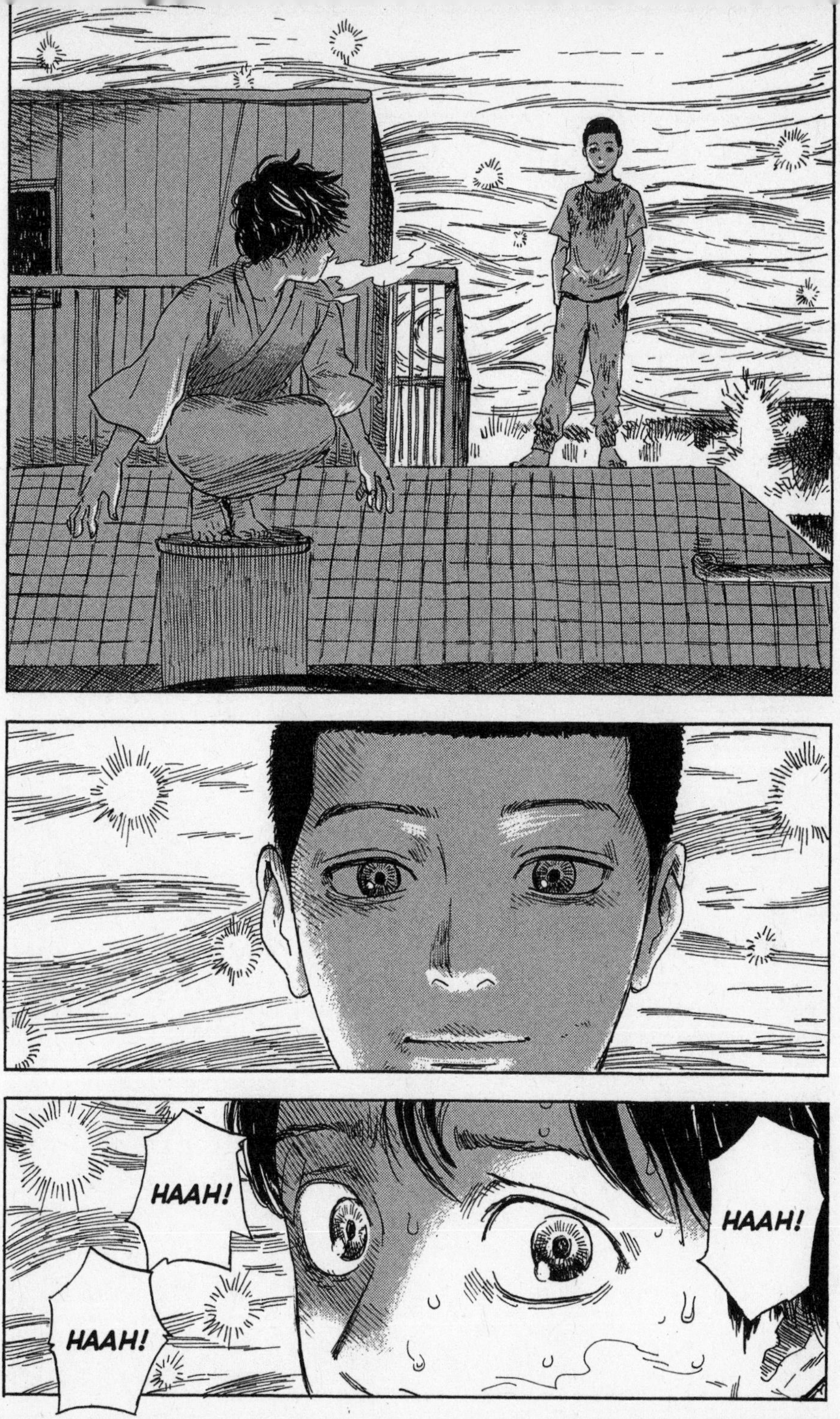
HAAH!
HAAH!
HAAH!

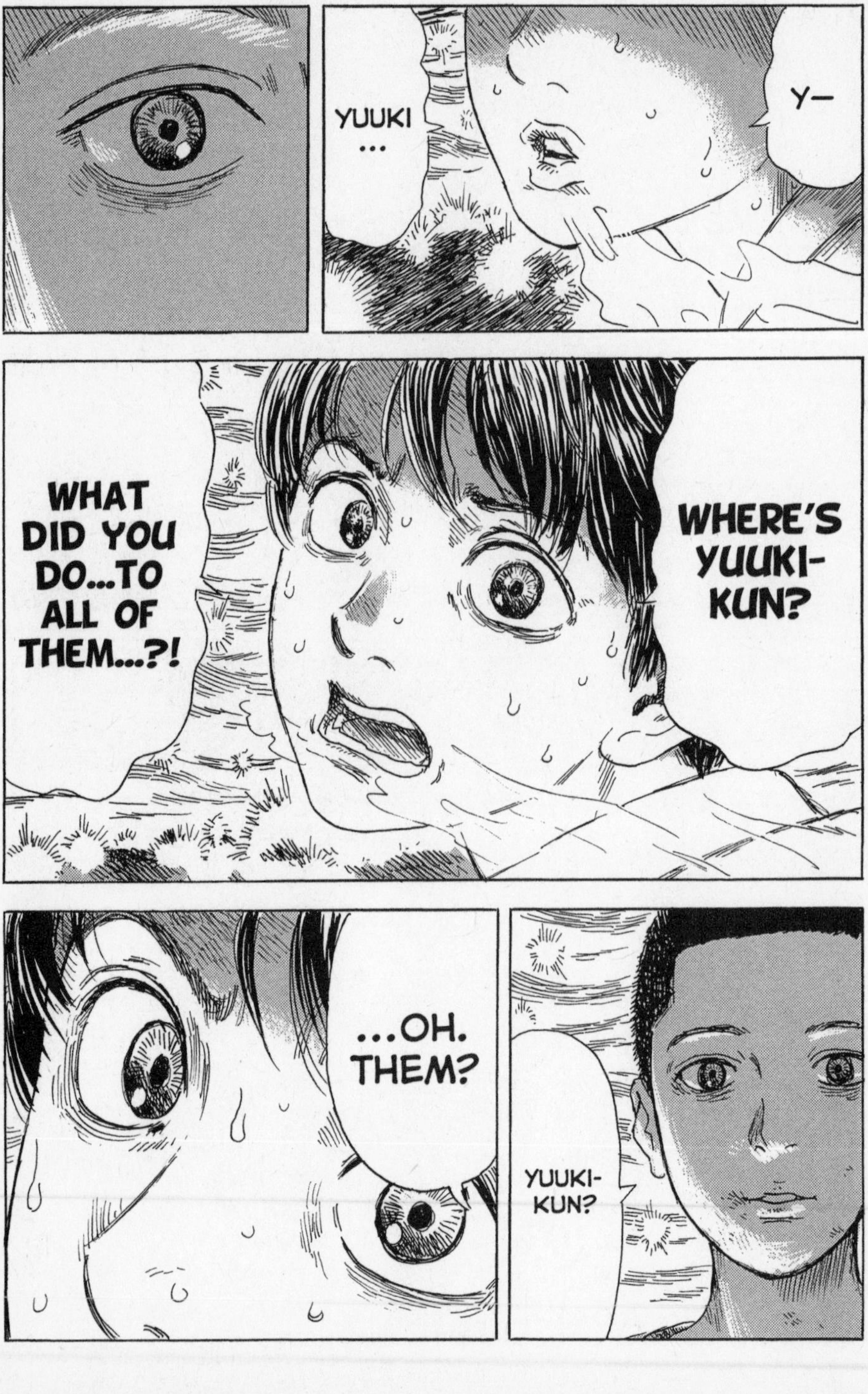
Y—
YUUKI ...
WHERE'S YUUKI-KUN?
WHAT DID YOU DO...TO ALL OF THEM...?!
YUUKI-KUN?
...OH. THEM?

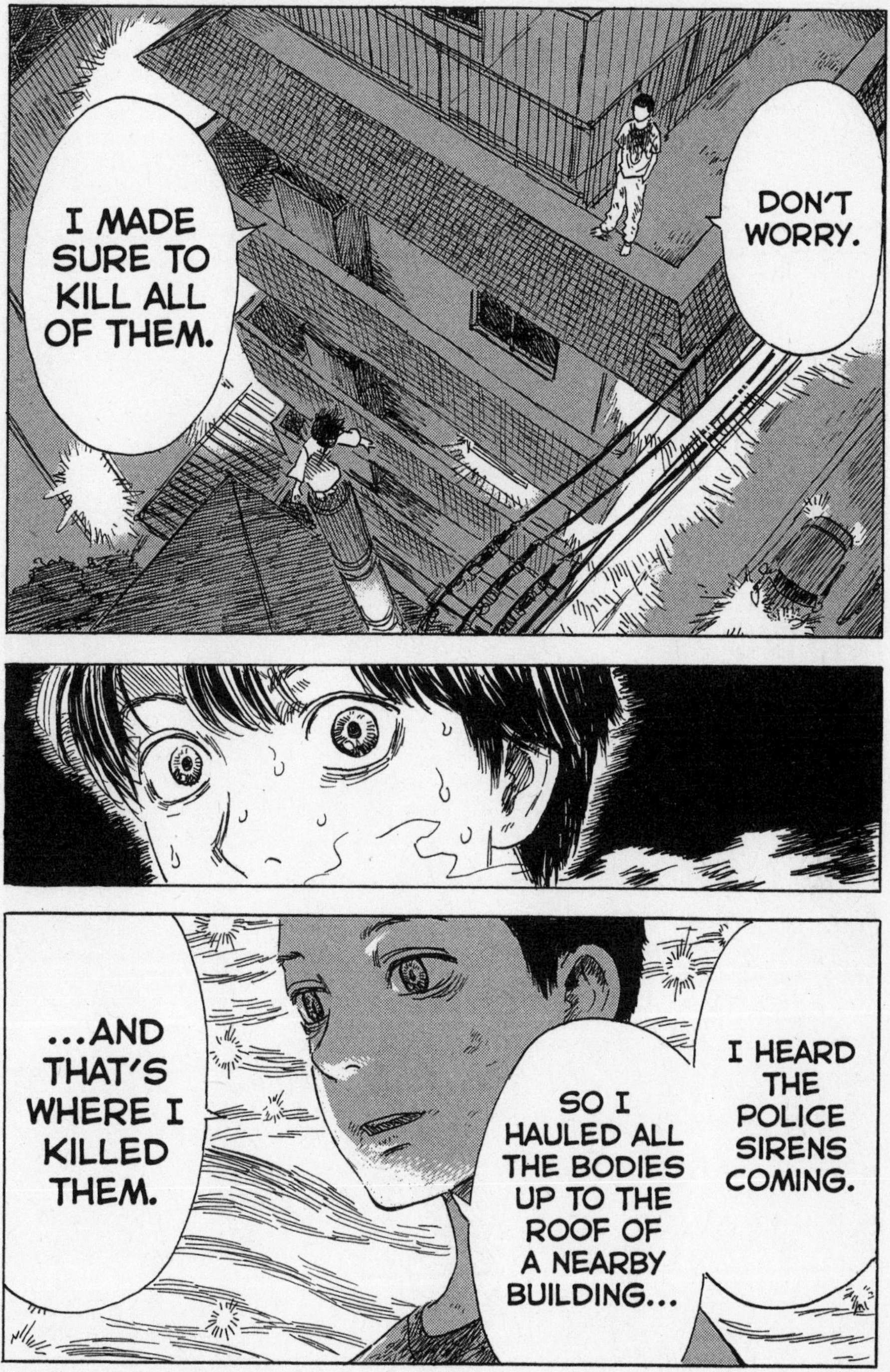
DON'T WORRY.
I MADE SURE TO KILL ALL OF THEM.
I HEARD THE POLICE SIRENS COMING.
SO I HAULED ALL THE BODIES UP TO THE ROOF OF A NEARBY BUILDING...
...AND THAT'S WHERE I KILLED THEM.

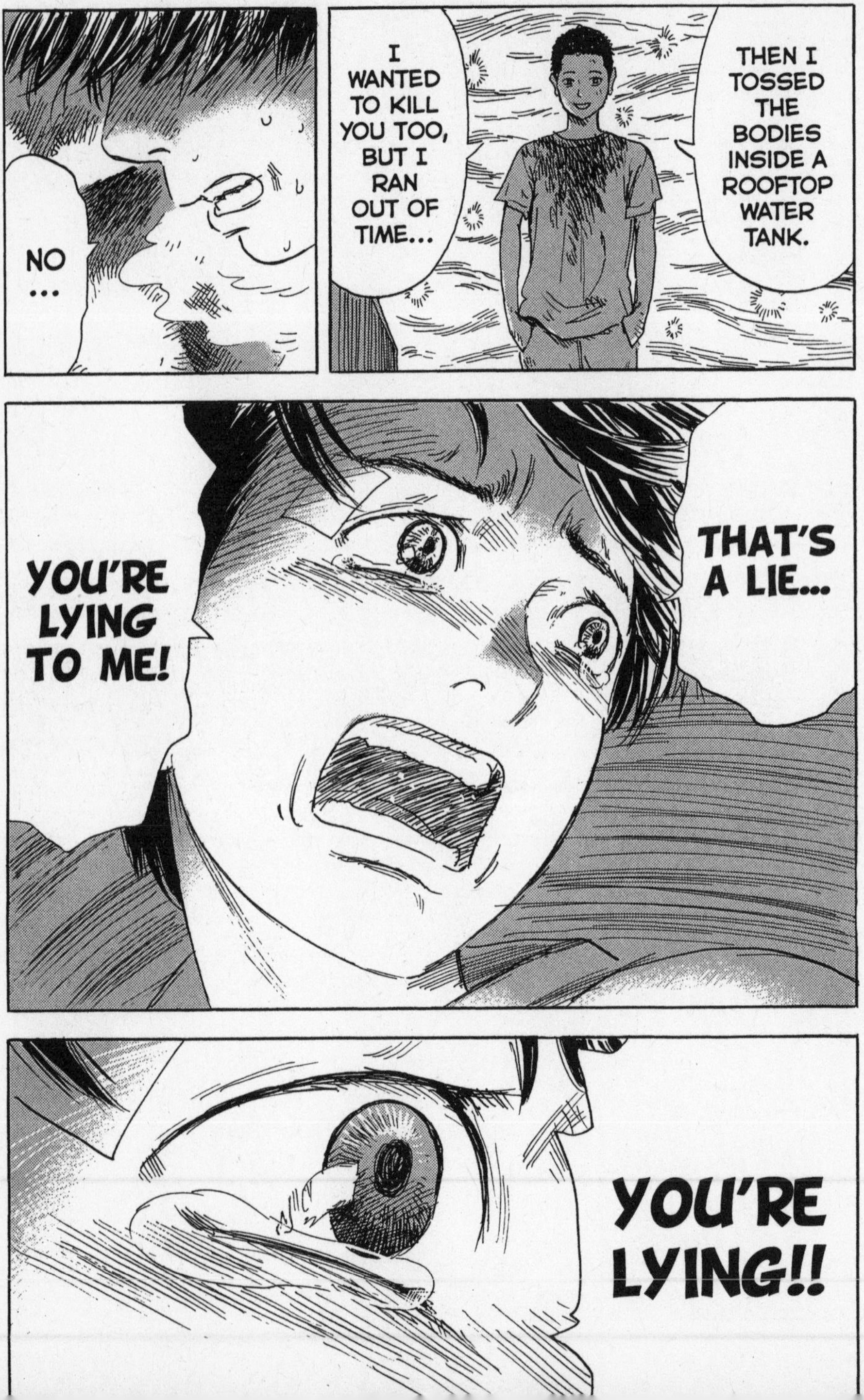
THEN I TOSSED THE BODIES INSIDE A ROOFTOP WATER TANK.
I WANTED TO KILL YOU TOO, BUT I RAN OUT OF TIME...
NO ...
THAT'S A LIE...
YOU'RE LYING TO ME!
YOU'RE LYING!!

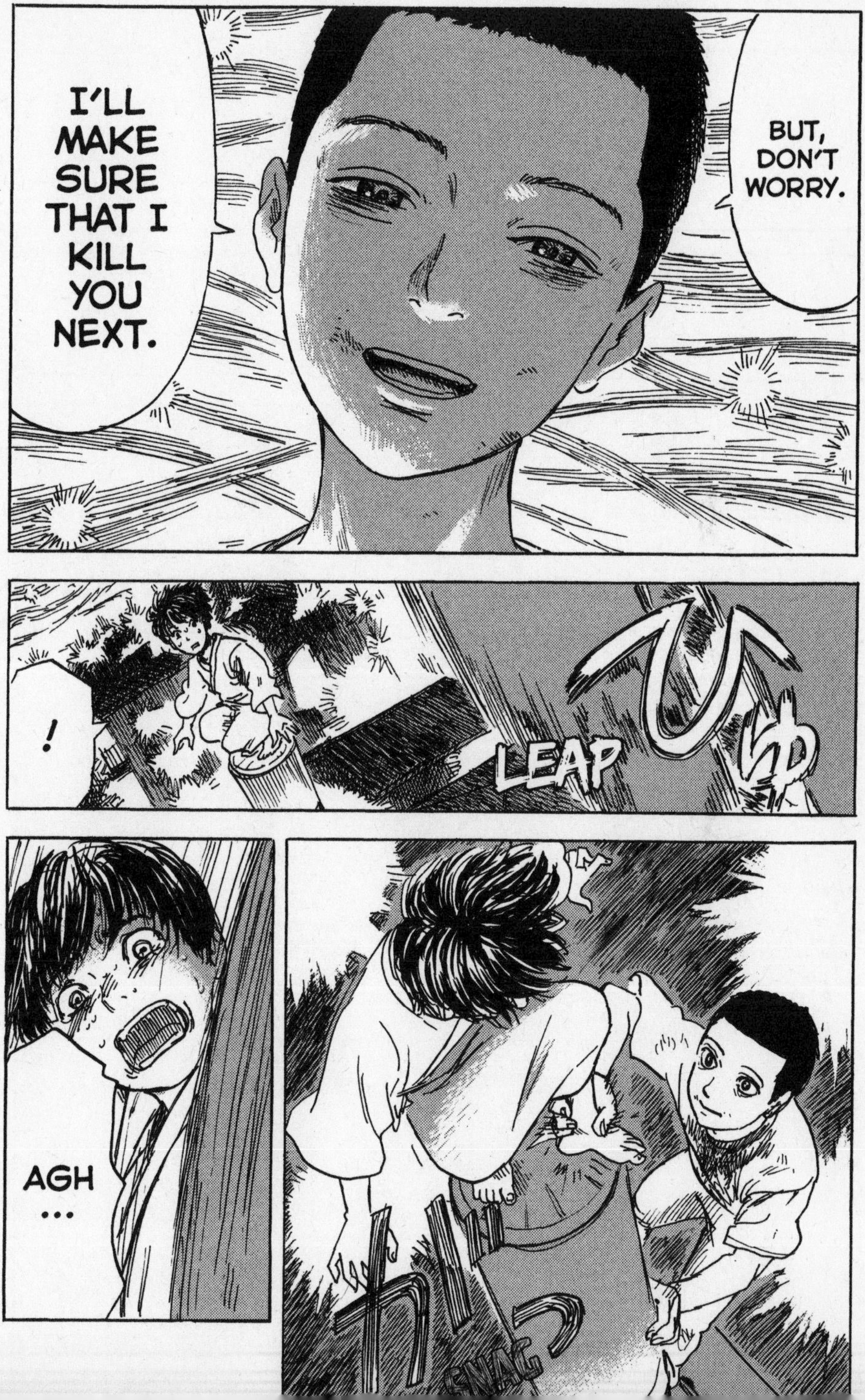
BUT, DON'T WORRY.
I'LL MAKE SURE THAT I KILL YOU NEXT.
LEAP
!
AGH ...

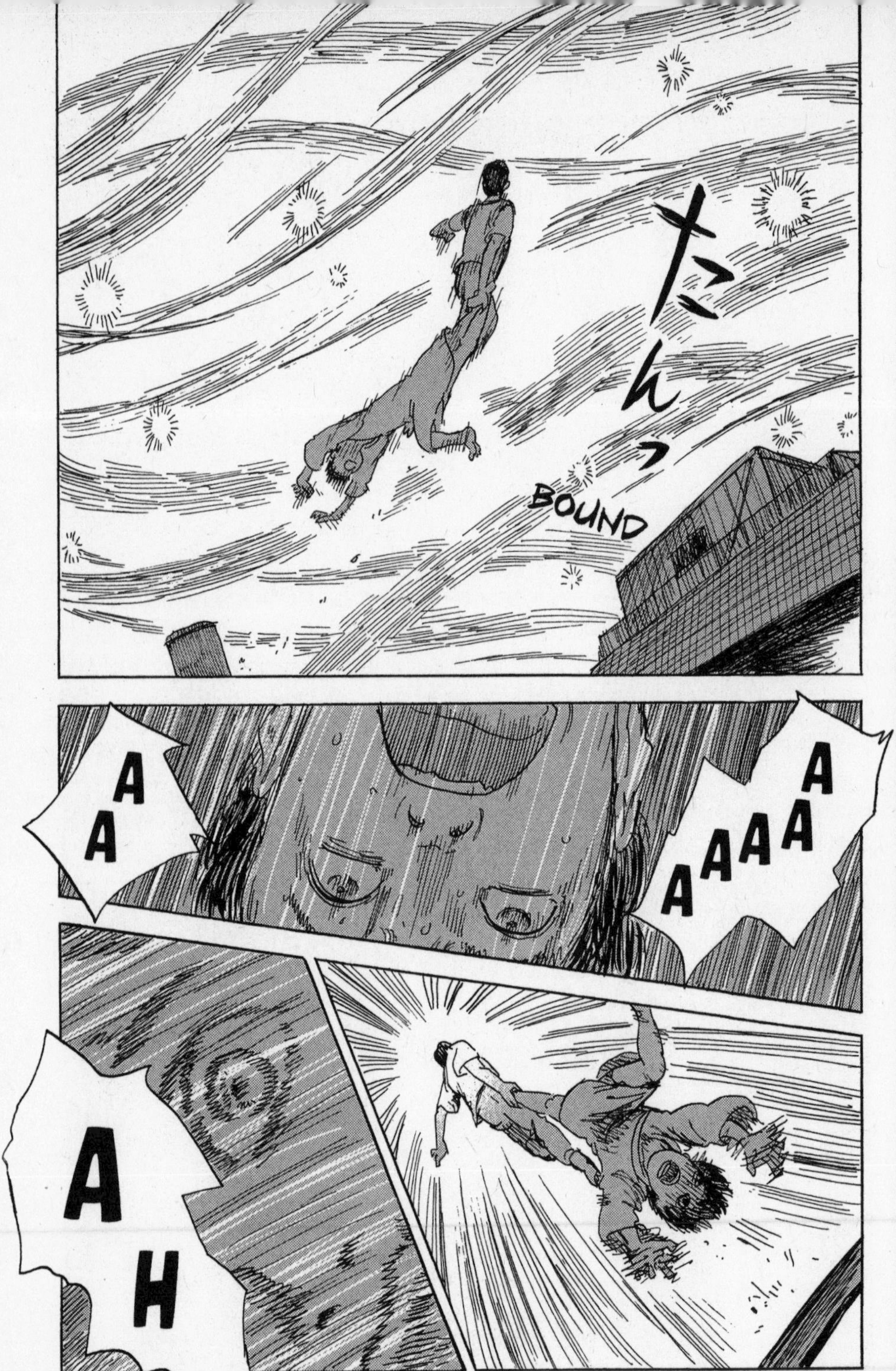
たんっ
BOUND
AAAAAA
AA
AAH

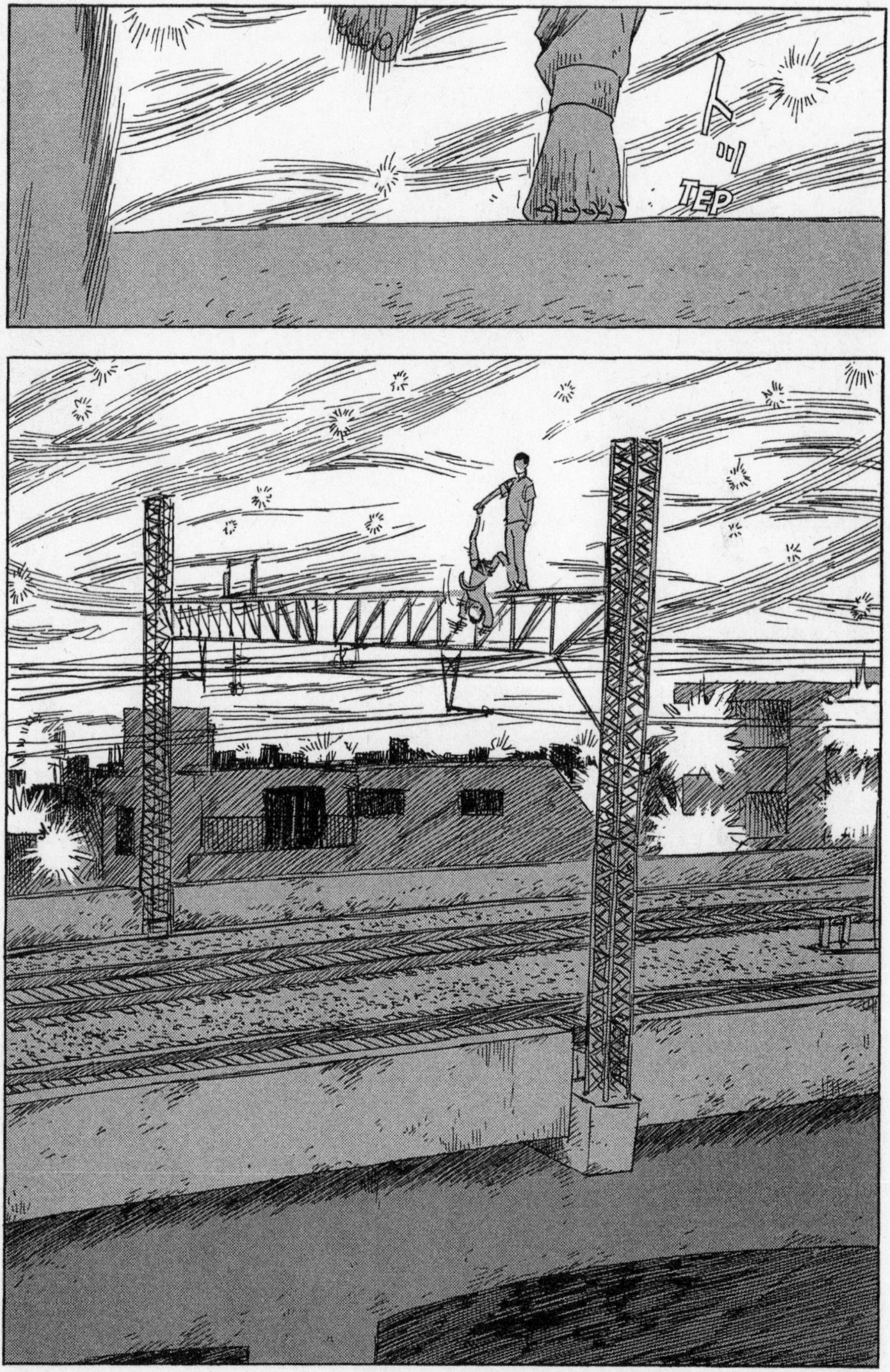
スッ
TEP

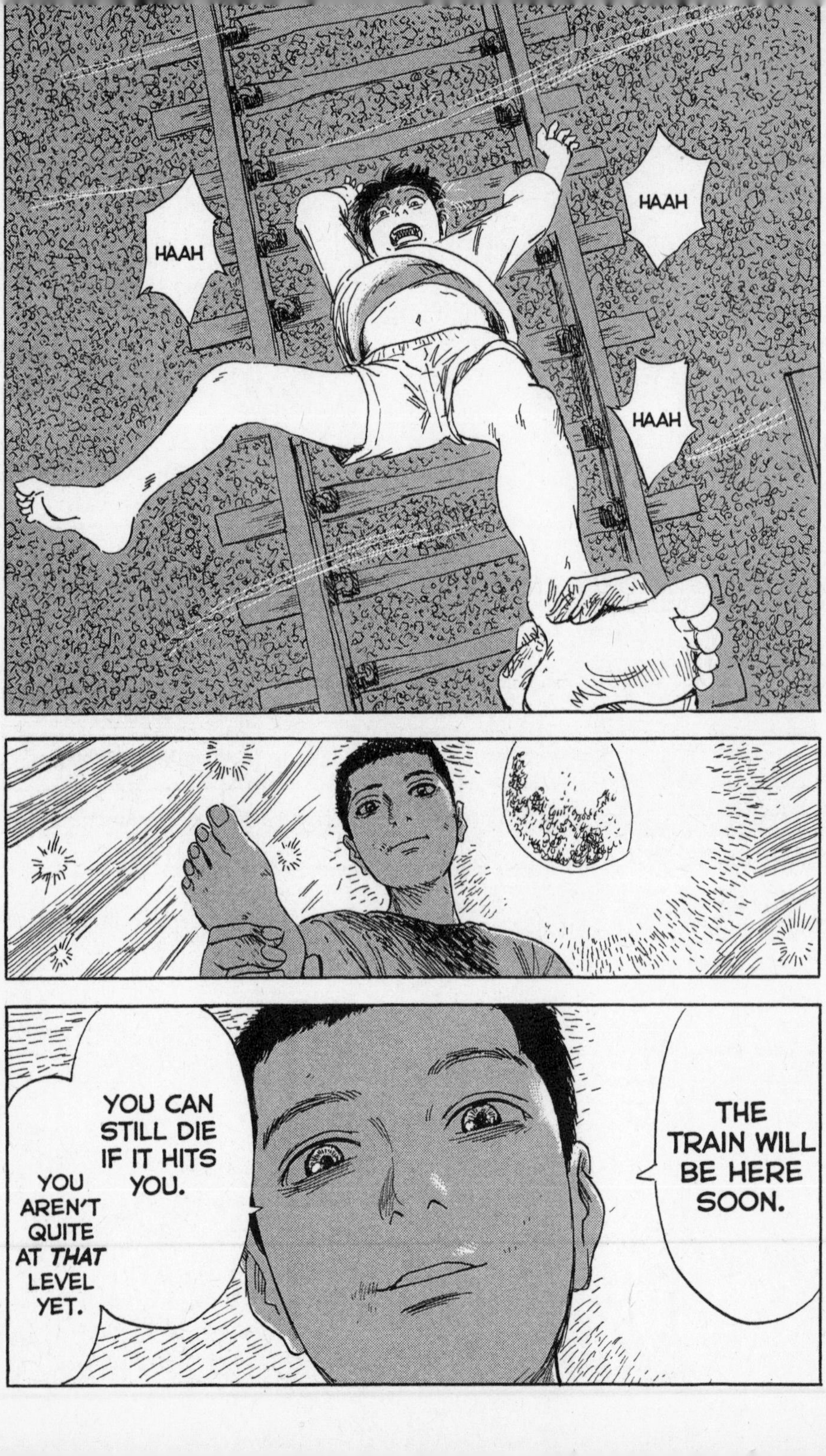
HAAH
HAAH
HAAH
THE TRAIN WILL BE HERE SOON.
YOU CAN STILL DIE IF IT HITS YOU.
YOU AREN'T QUITE AT *THAT* LEVEL YET.

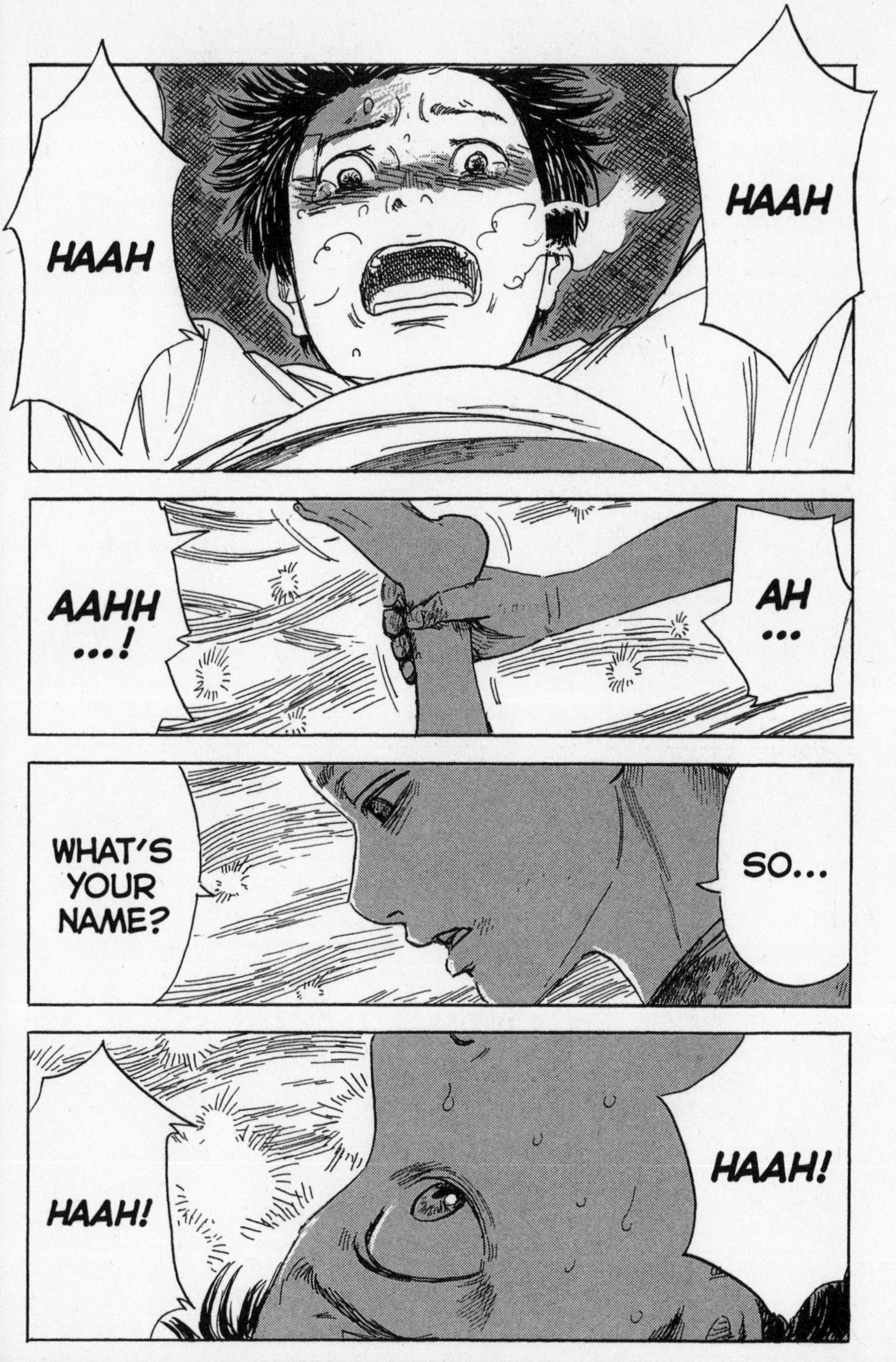
HAAH
HAAH
AH ...
AAHH ...!
SO...
WHAT'S YOUR NAME?
HAAH!
HAAH!

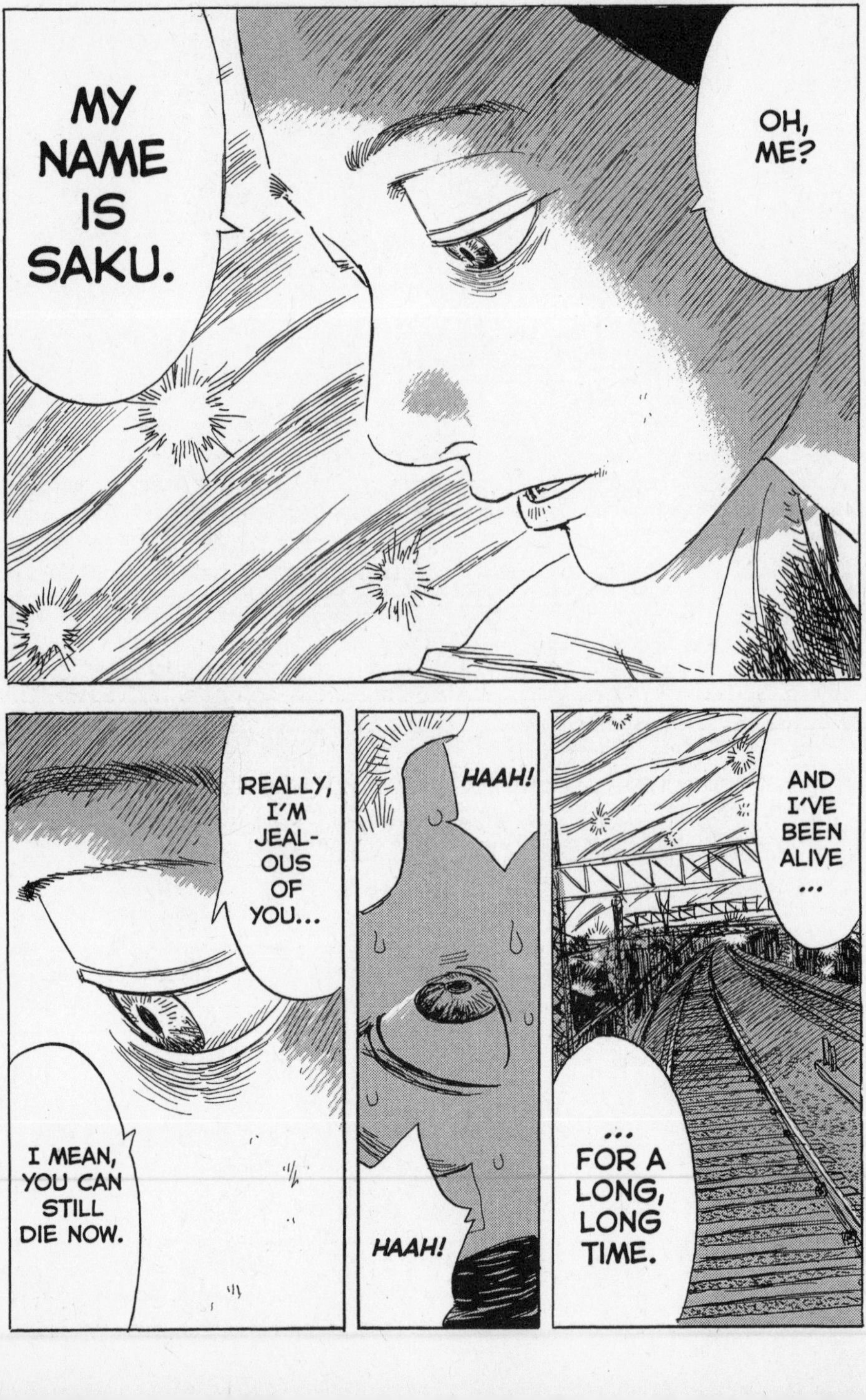
OH, ME?
MY NAME IS SAKU.
AND I'VE BEEN ALIVE ...
... FOR A LONG, LONG TIME.
HAAH!
HAAH!
REALLY, I'M JEAL-OUS OF YOU...
I MEAN, YOU CAN STILL DIE NOW.

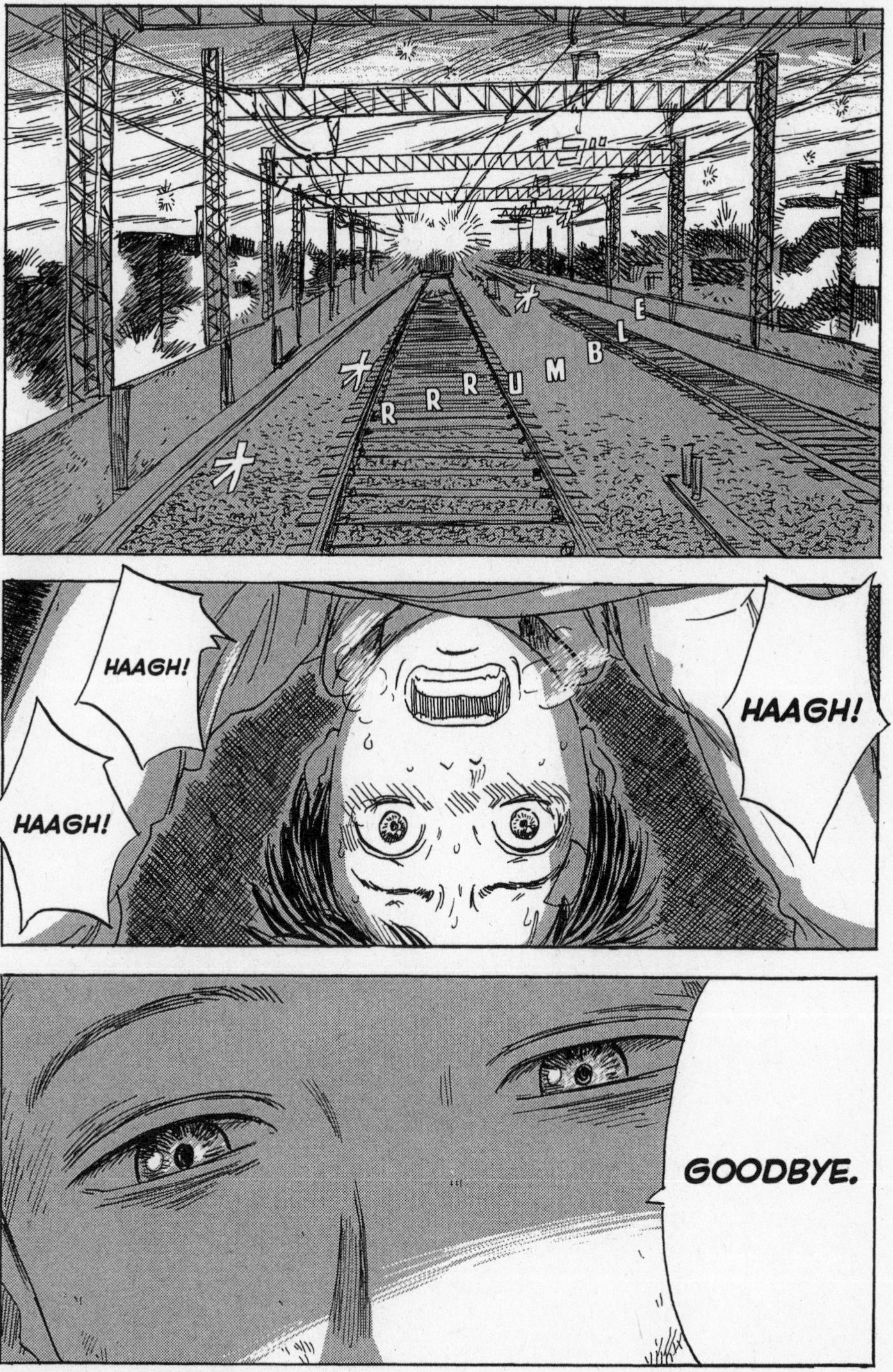
RRRRUMBLE
HAAGH!
HAAGH!
HAAGH!
GOODBYE.

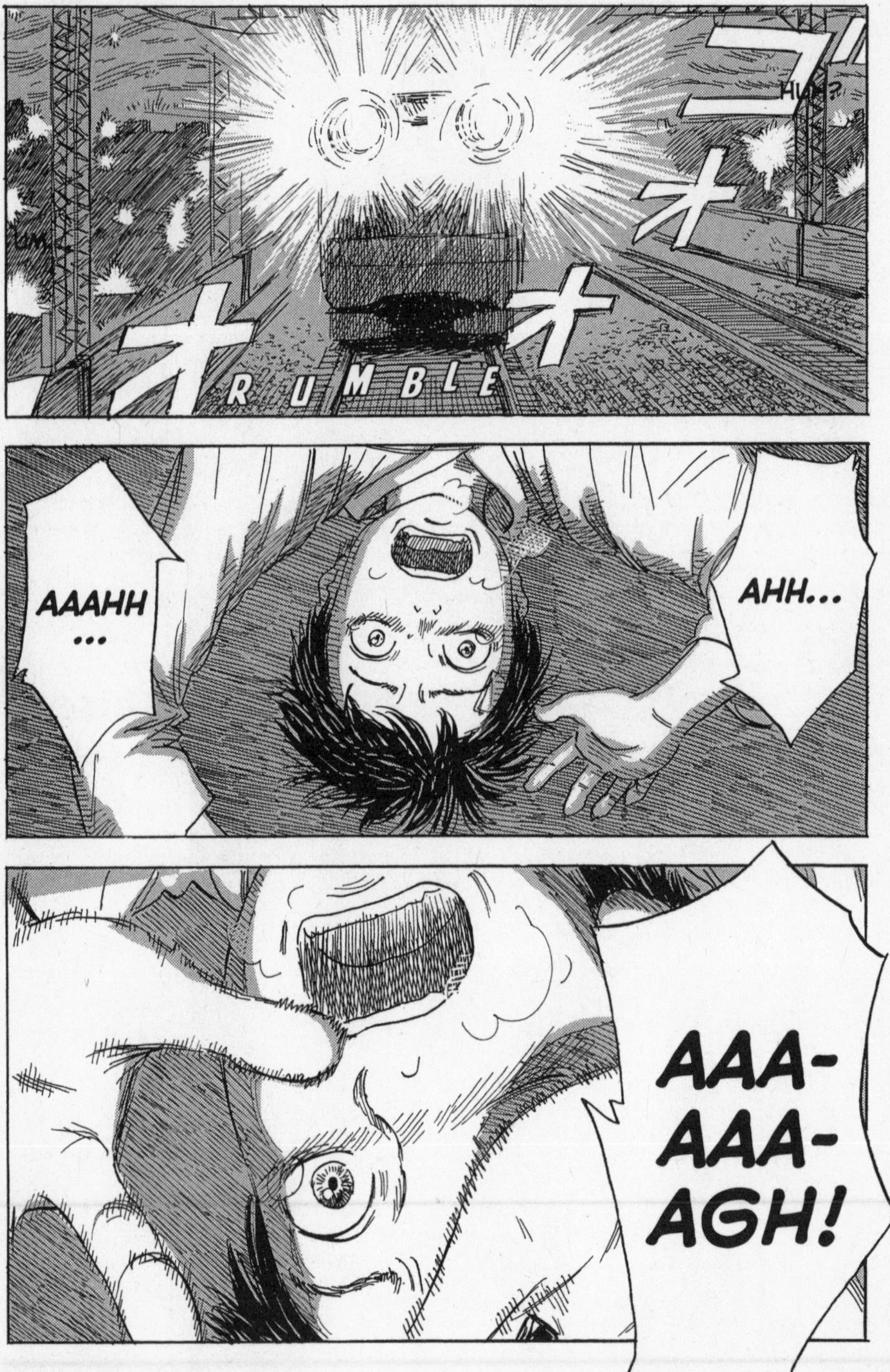

ゴオオオ
HUH?
UM
RUMBLE
AHH...
AAAHH ...
AAA-AAA-AGH!

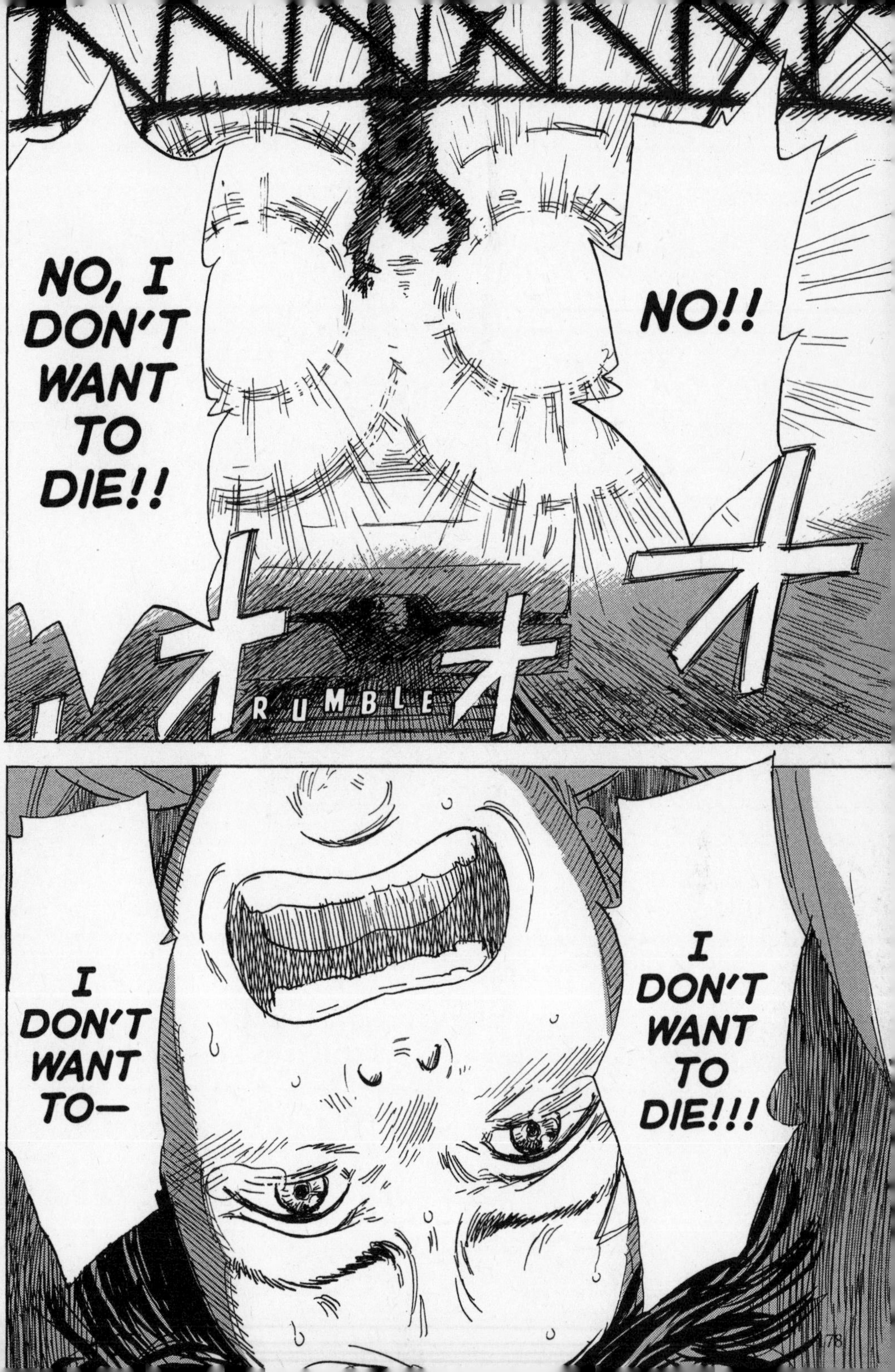
NO!!
NO, I DON'T WANT TO DIE!!
RUMBLE
I DON'T WANT TO DIE!!!
I DON'T WANT TO—

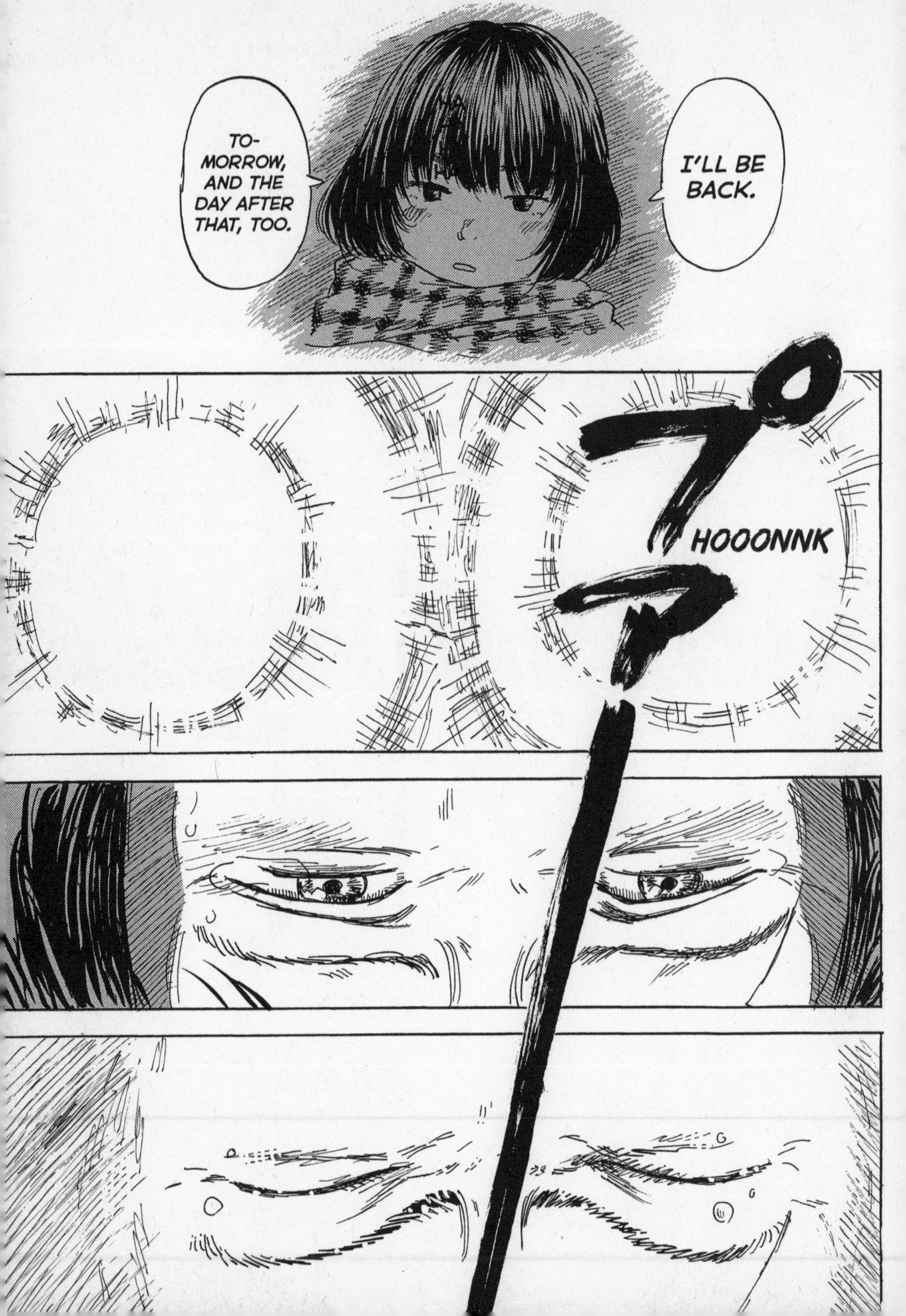
I'LL BE BACK.
TO-MORROW, AND THE DAY AFTER THAT, TOO.
HOOONNK

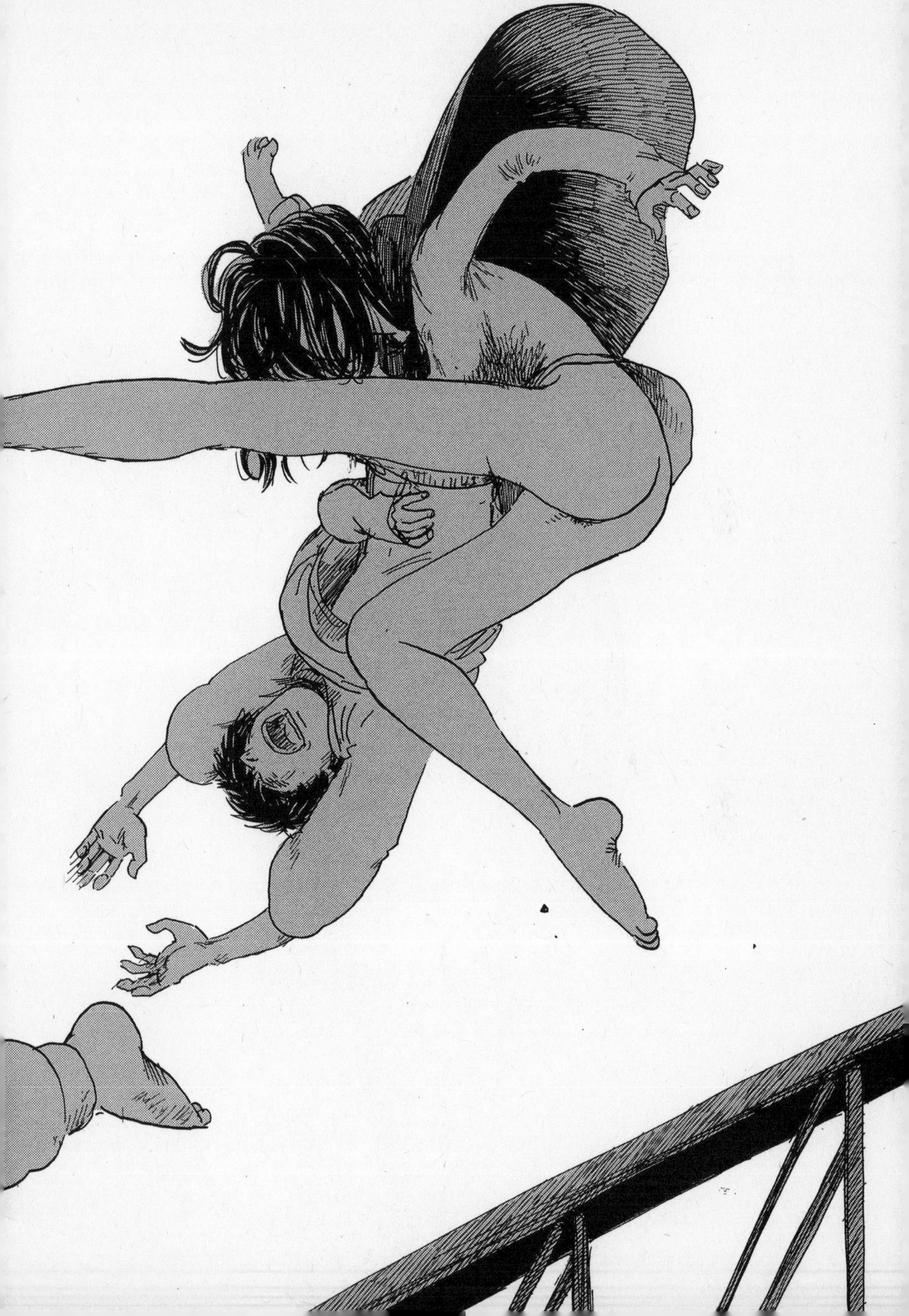

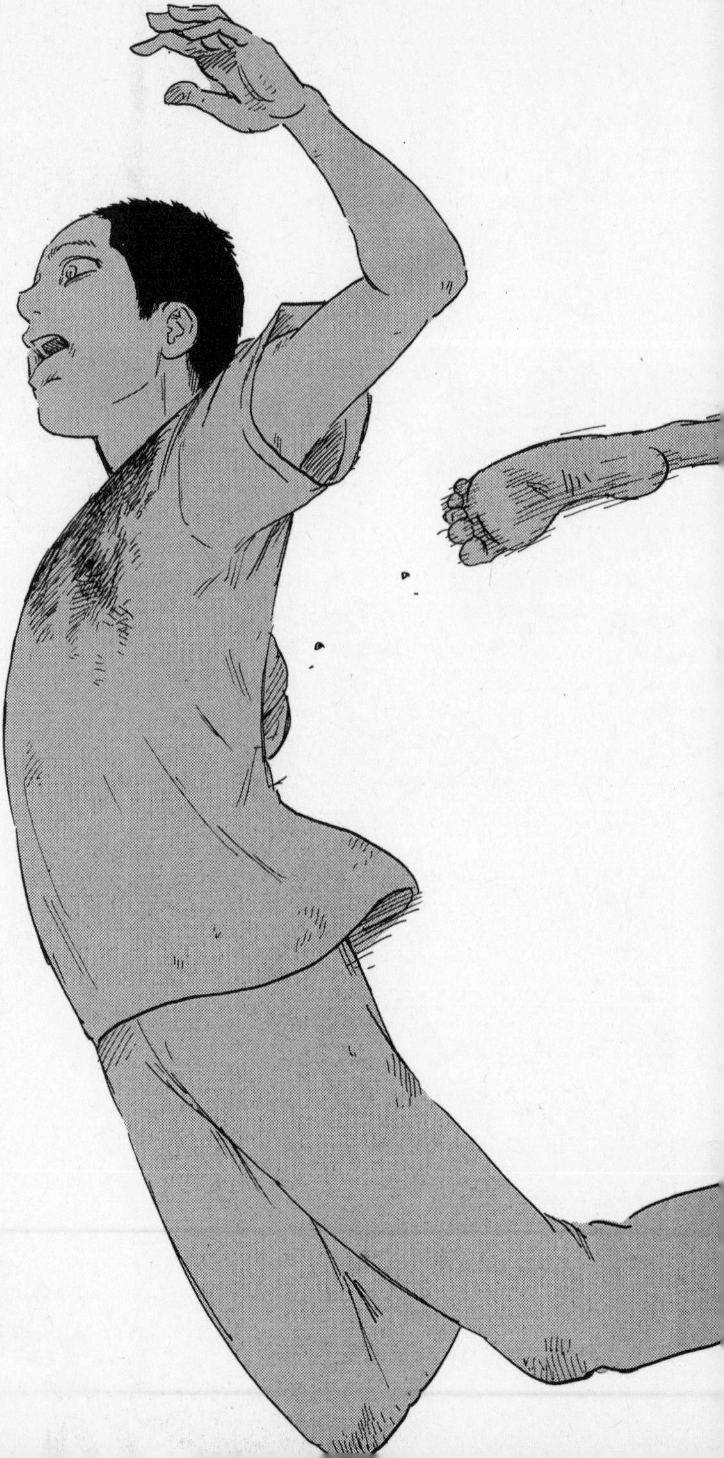

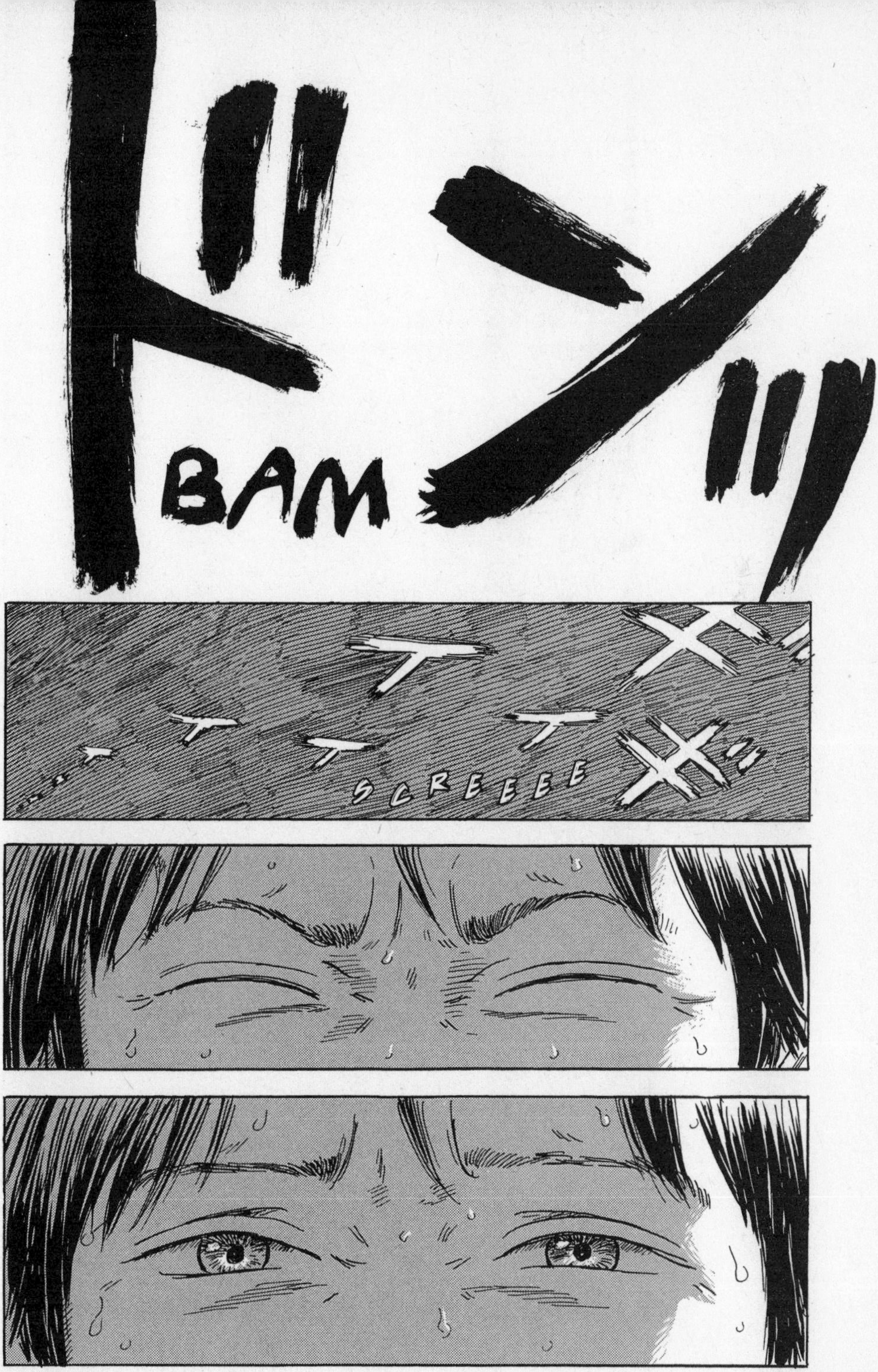
BAM
SCREEEEE

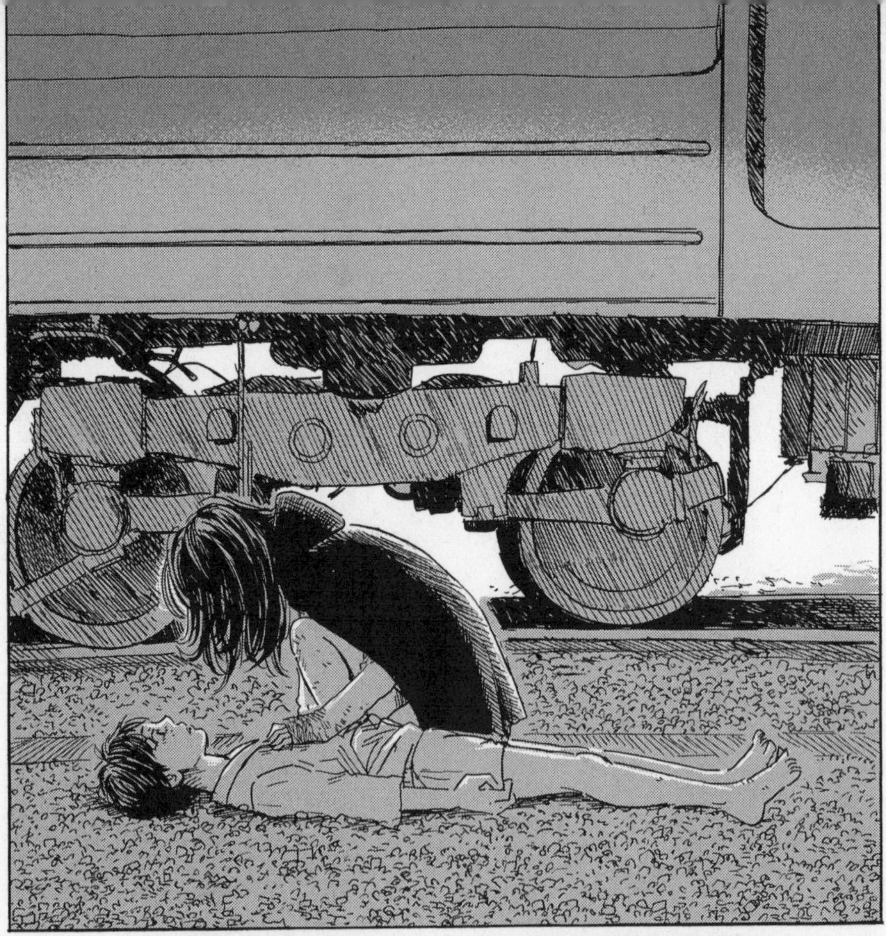
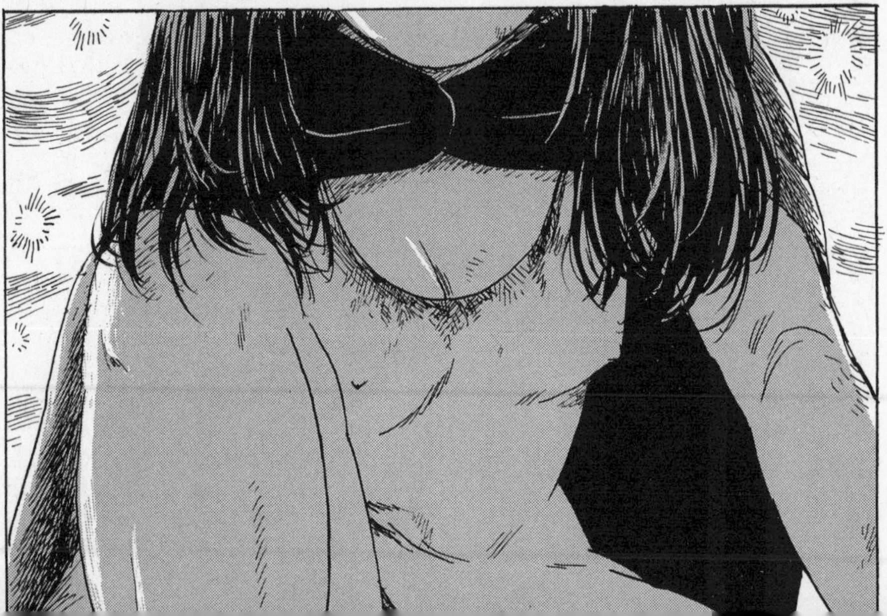

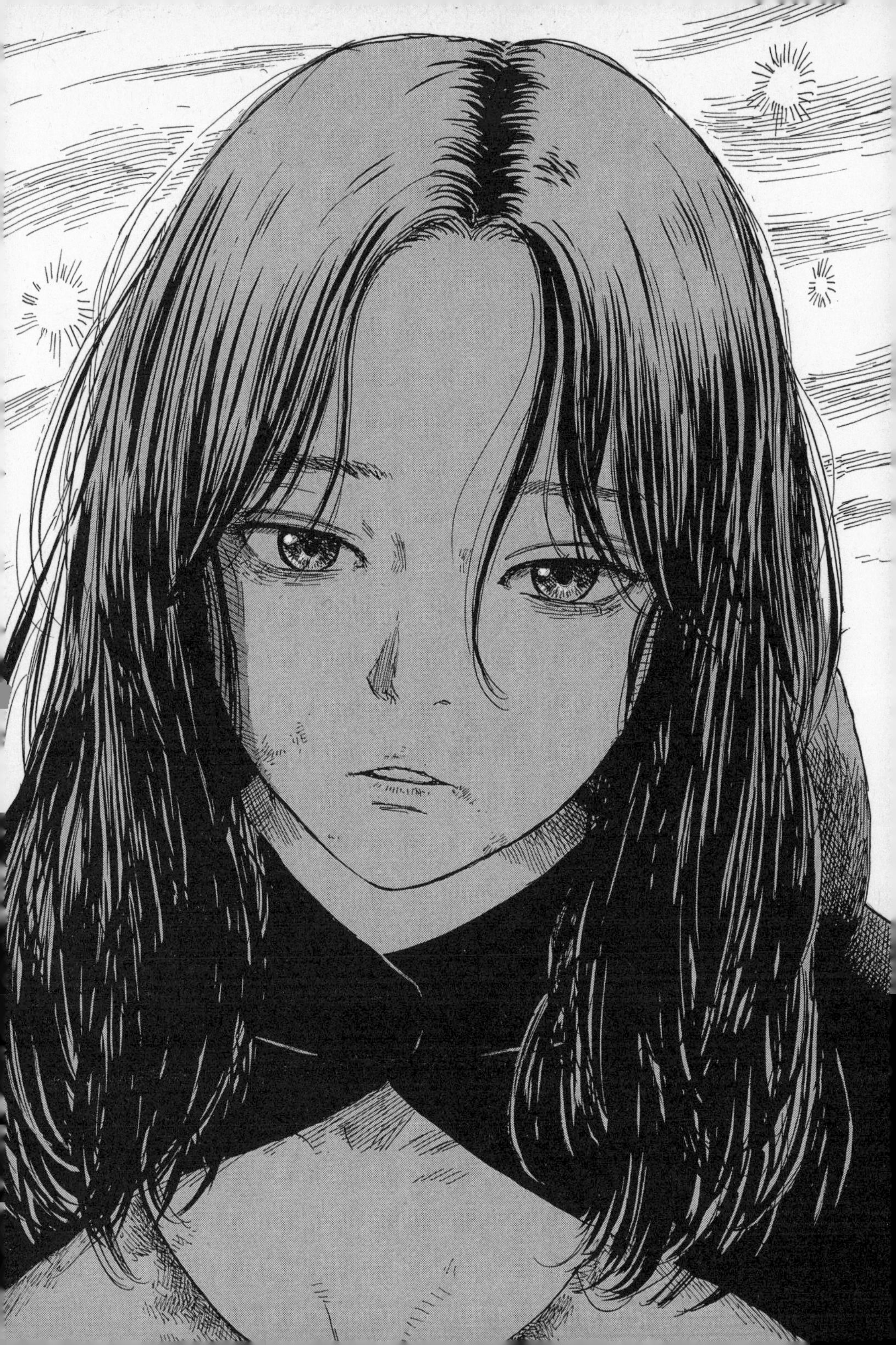

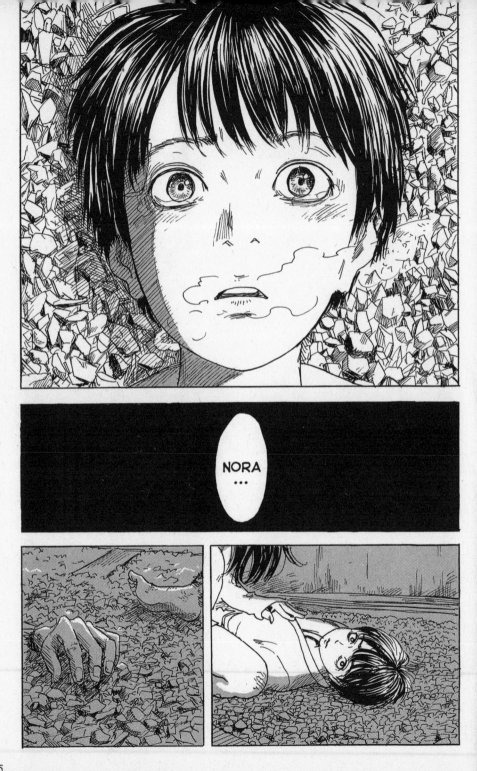

NORA
...

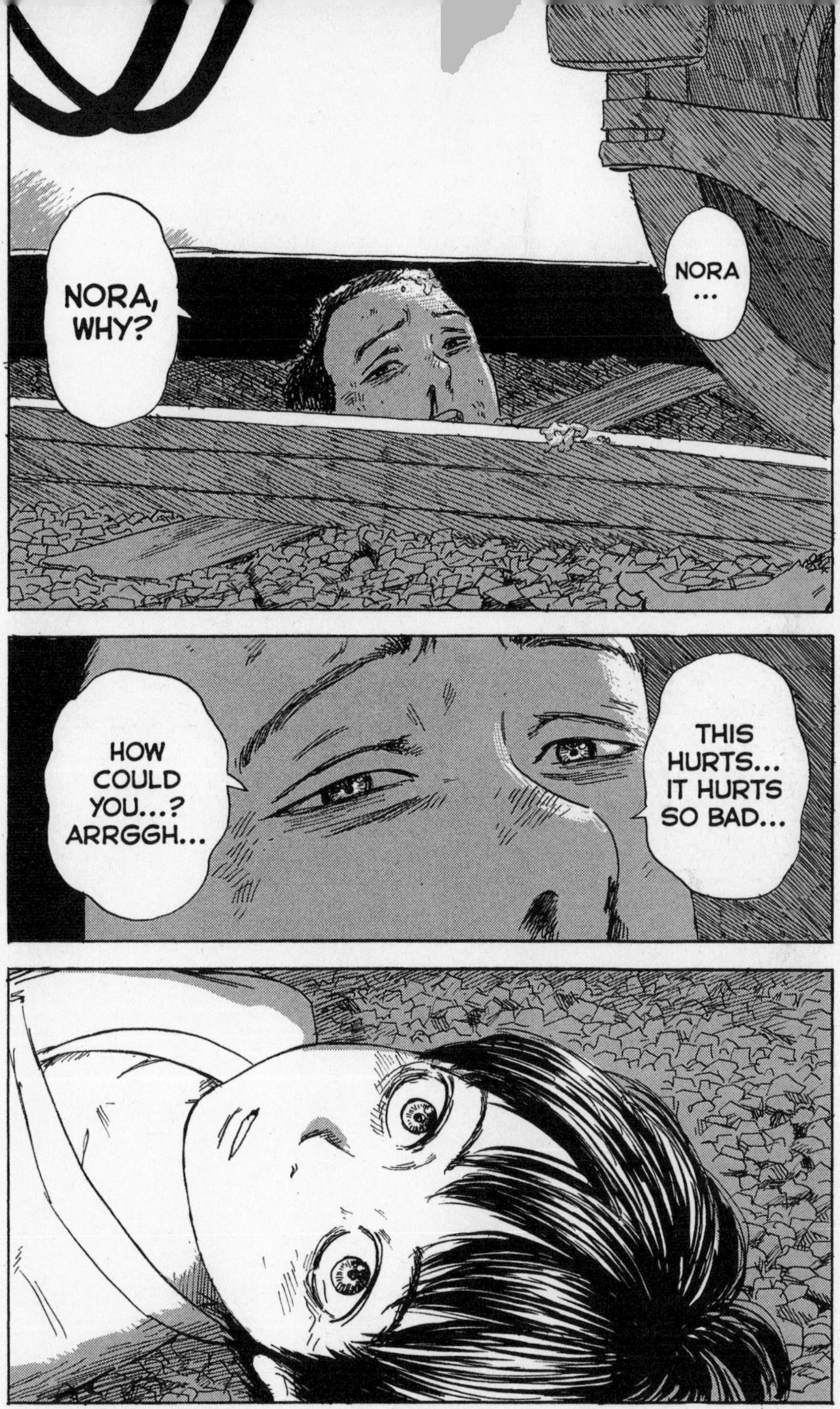
NORA ...
NORA, WHY?
THIS HURTS... IT HURTS SO BAD...
HOW COULD YOU...? ARRGGH...

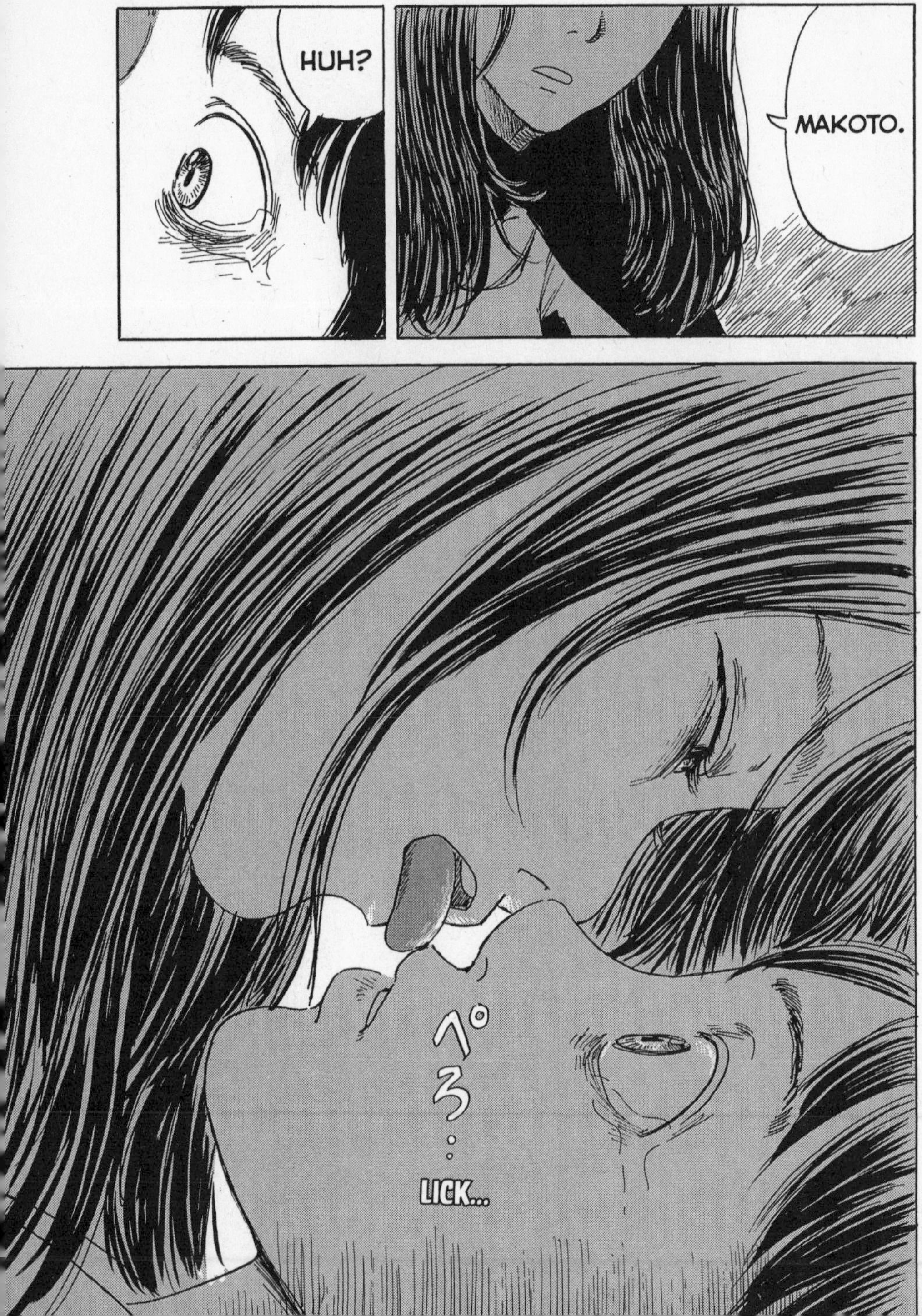
MAKOTO.
HUH?
ぺろ・・
LICK...

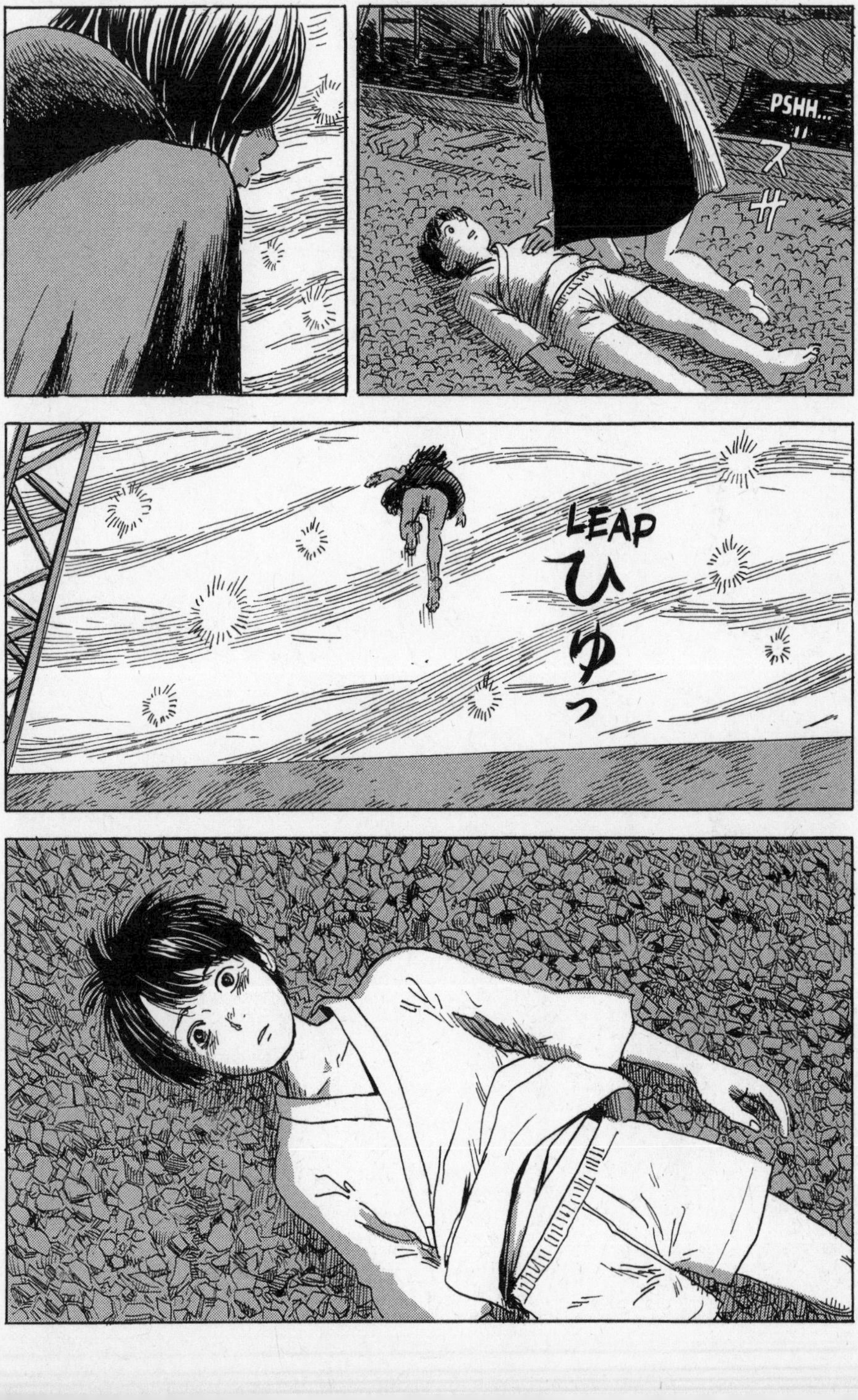
PSHH...
スサ
LEAP
ひゅっ

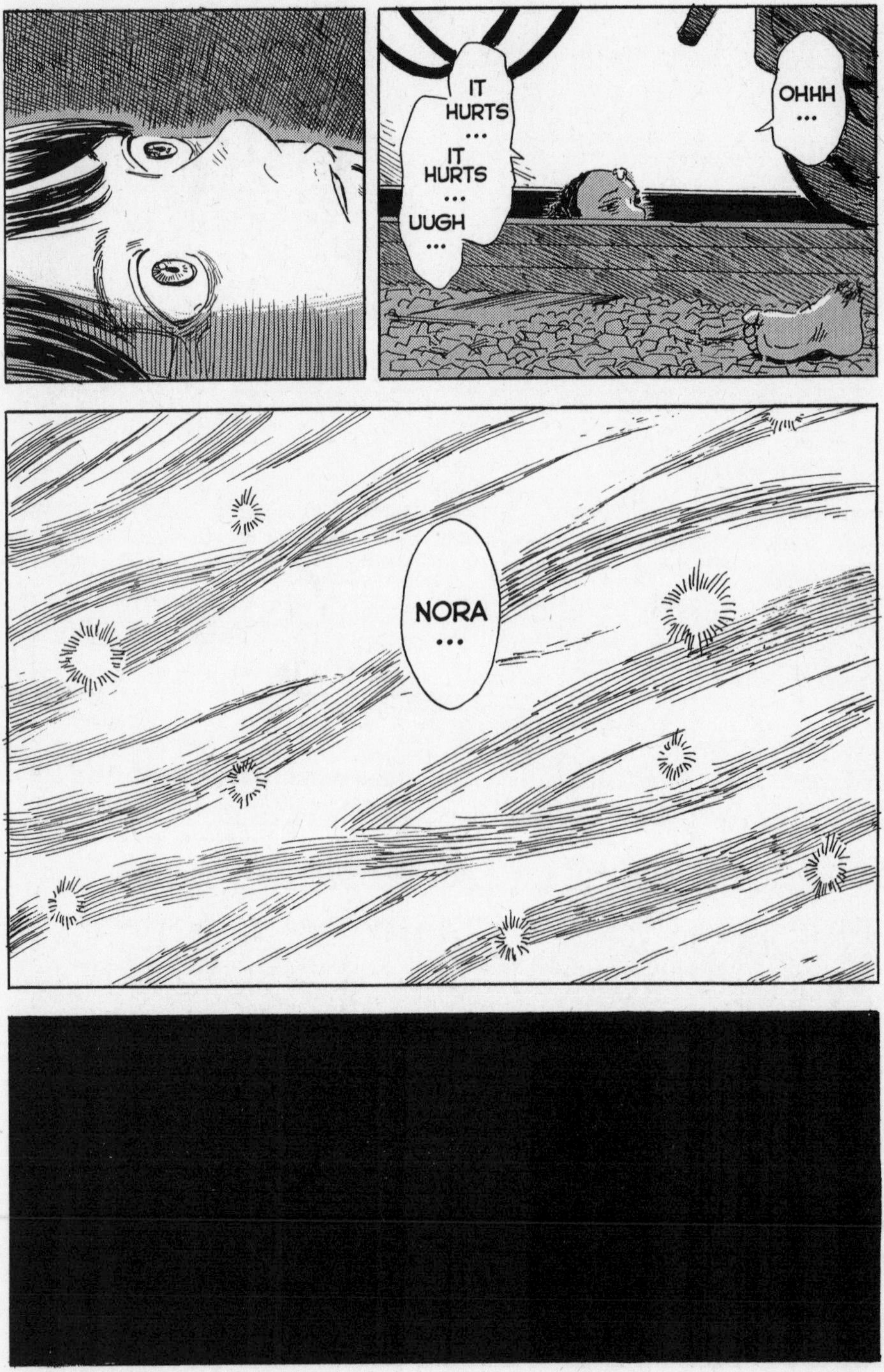
OHHH ...
IT HURTS ... IT HURTS ... UUGH ...
NORA ...

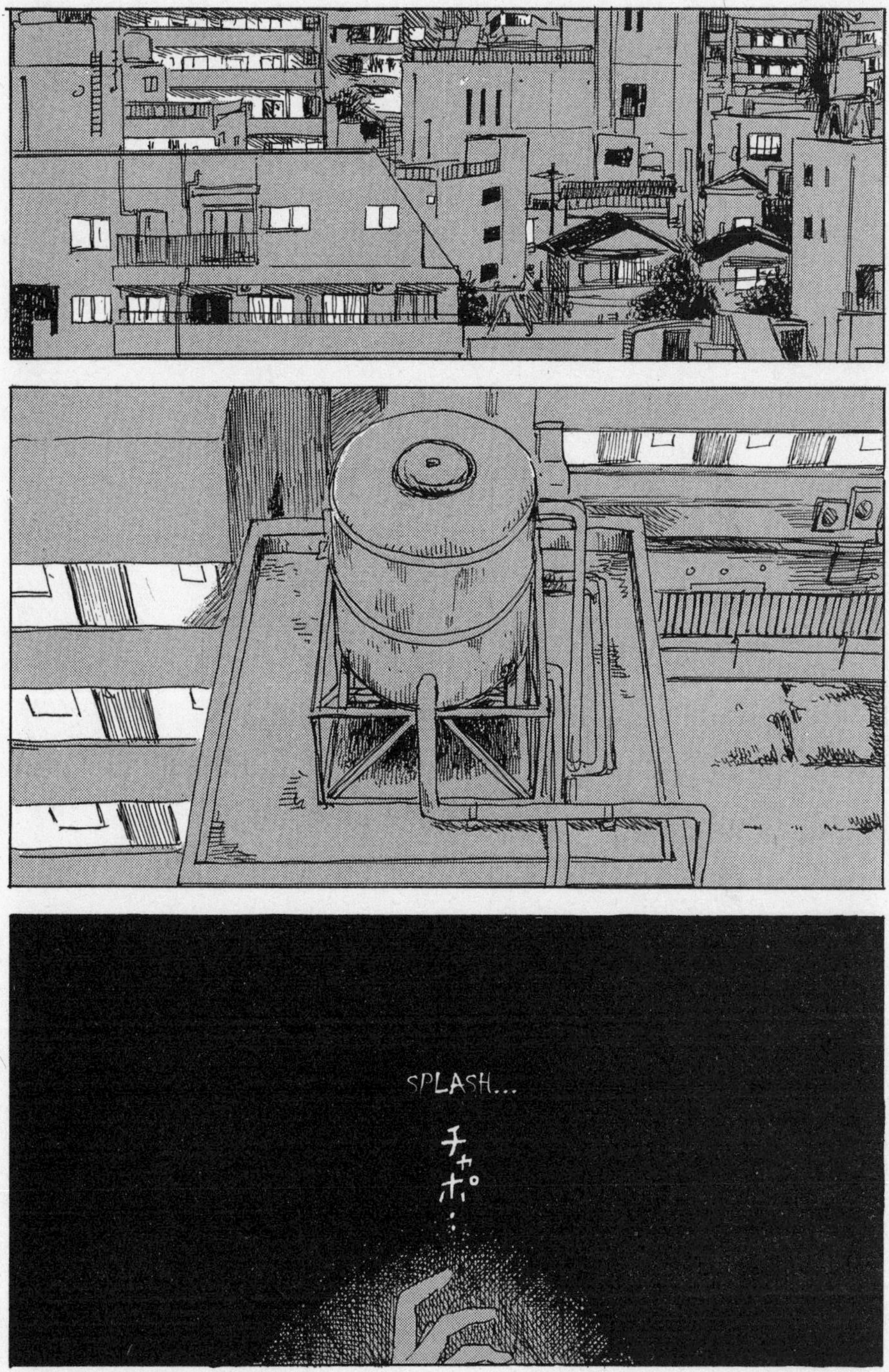
SPLASH...
チャポ…

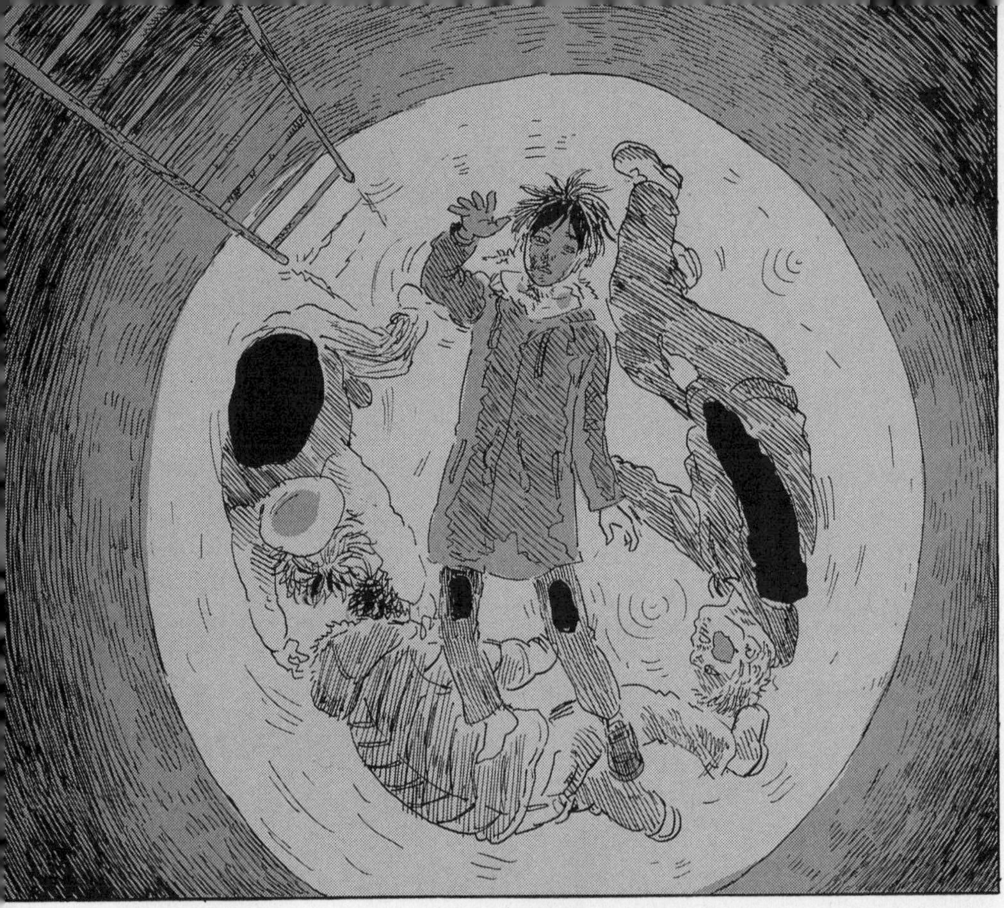
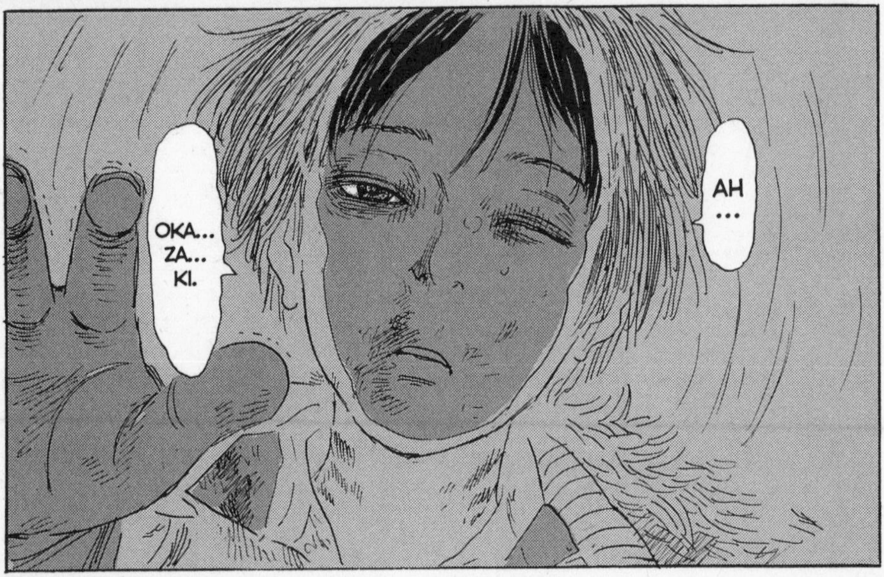
AH ...
OKA... ZA... KI.

CONTINUED IN #3

Translation Notes

Shuzo Oshimi uses minute details in the contemporary Tokyo setting of *Happiness* to convey nuances of both story and character, many of which may be unfamiliar to the native English speaker. Here are brief explanations of some of these details.

Asagaya Station, page 50

Asagaya is a rail station in Suginami ward, located in east-central Tokyo, the facade of which is pictured on page 50. Opened in 1922, it's on the Chuo Main Line—one of the main trunk rail lines in Japan, starting in Tokyo Station and going all the way to the city of Nagoya, almost 250 miles away. Owning a large house within walking distance of Asagaya Station would indicate to the local reader that Yuuki's family is fairly well-off.

Chuhai, page 55

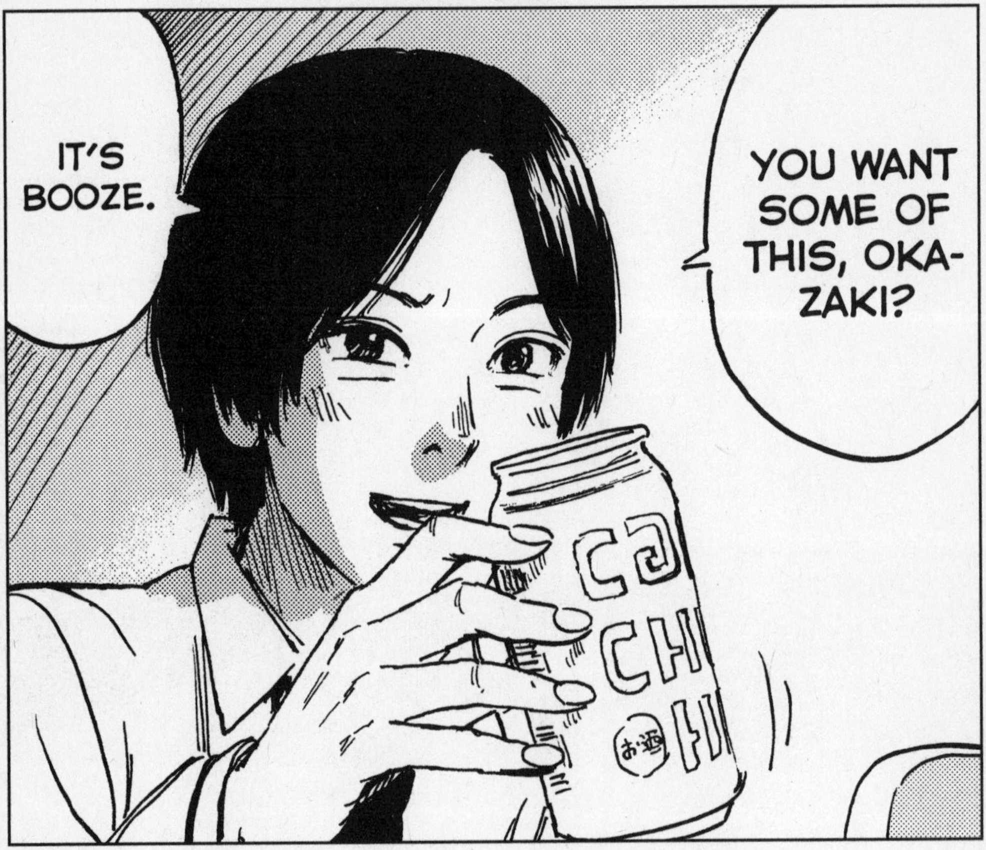
YOU WANT SOME OF THIS, OKA-ZAKI?
IT'S BOOZE.

Chuhai is an alcoholic beverage made by watering down vodka or shochu (a Japanese distilled liquor that may be made from a variety of sources) with carbonated flavored water. A common sight in convenience stores and vending machines, chuhai's sugary flavor and fairly hefty alcohol level (up to 9% by volume) give it a market position similar to malt beverages or wine coolers in the US—favored by college students (or younger) and anyone looking to get drunk quickly. The drinking age in Japan is twenty, making everyone in the room underage by three to four years.

Matome Sites, page 128

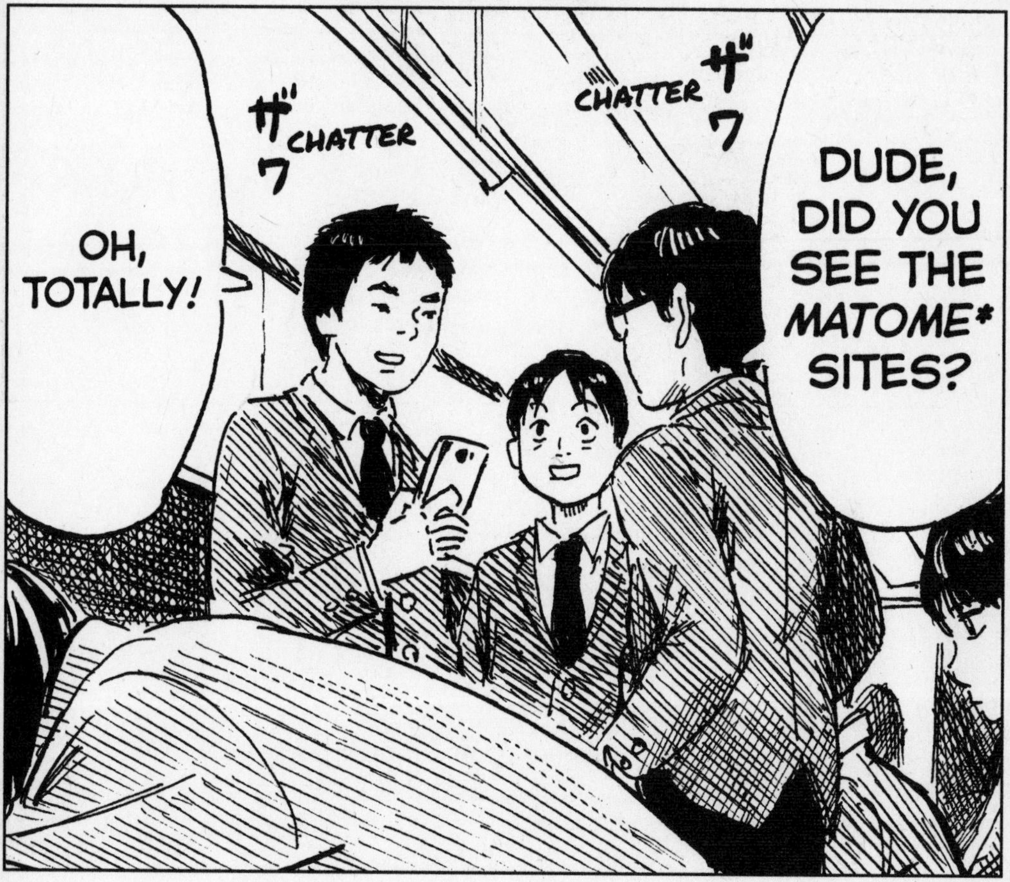
DUDE, DID YOU SEE THE *MATOME** SITES?
ザワ CHATTER
ザワ CHATTER
OH, TOTALLY!

Matome sites (literally, "collection sites") are affiliate websites that collect the best or most interesting threads on Japanese web forums like 2ch (itself a precursor to the infamous 4chan), and gather them in a single convenient spot, a bit like /r/bestof on Reddit. Matome sites are usually administrated by individuals who use the collected content to draw traffic which they sell advertising against, leading to friction with some 2ch users who claim they're unethically profiting from their posts.

Calling 119, page 133

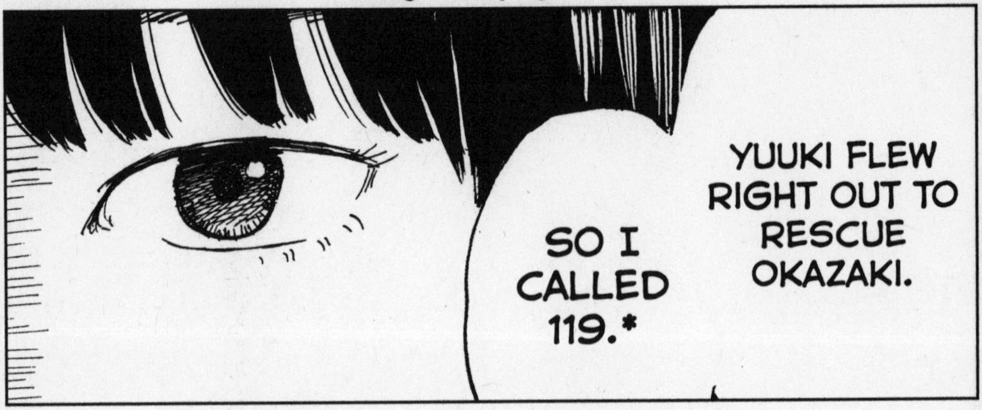
YUUKI FLEW RIGHT OUT TO RESCUE OKAZAKI.
SO I CALLED 119.*

If you ran into trouble in Japan, don't call 911—dial 110 for the police, or 119 for ambulance and fire services. There are English speakers available, too, although you may encounter a delays until the call center tracks down someone who speaks it.

a Silent Voice

"The word heartwarming was made for manga like this."
–Manga Book-shelf

"A harsh and biting social commentary... delivers in its depth of character and emotional strength." -Comics Bulletin

"A very powerful story about being different and the consequences of childhood bullying... Read it." –Anime News Network

Shoya is a bully. When Shoko, a girl who can't hear, enters his elementary school class, she becomes their favorite target, and Shoya and his friends goad each other into devising new tortures for her. But the children's cruelty goes too far. Shoko is forced to leave the school, and Shoya ends up shouldering all the blame. Six years later, the two meet again. Can Shoya make up for his past mistakes, or is it too late?

Available now in print and digitally!

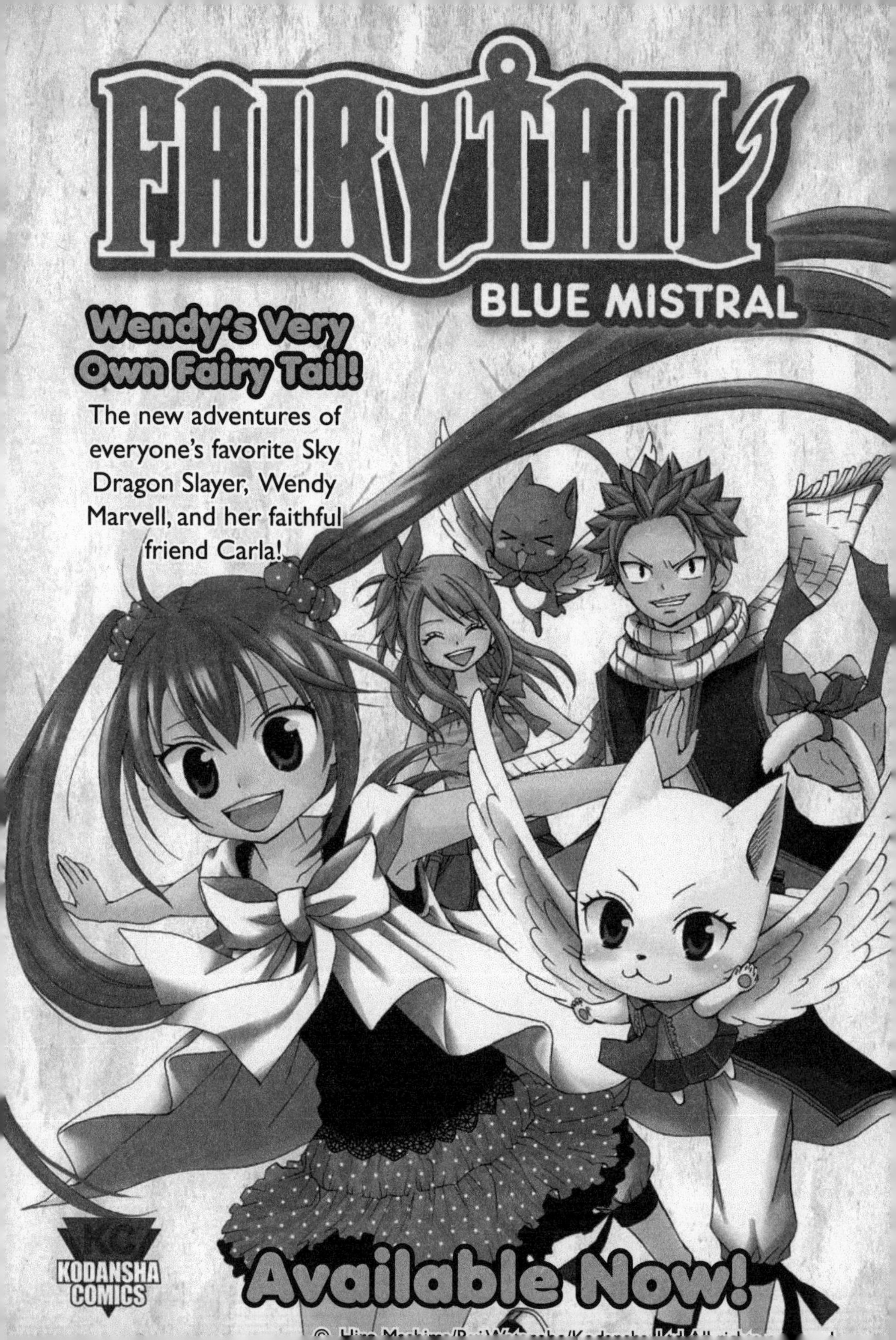
FAIRY TAIL
BLUE MISTRAL
Wendy's Very Own Fairy Tail!
The new adventures of everyone's favorite Sky Dragon Slayer, Wendy Marvell, and her faithful friend Carla!
KC
KODANSHA COMICS
Available Now!

INUYASHIKI

A superhero like none you've ever seen, from the creator of "Gantz"!

Ichiro Inuyashiki is down on his luck. He looks much older than his 58 years, his children despise him, and his wife thinks he's a useless coward. So when he's diagnosed with stomach cancer and given three months to live, it seems the only one who'll miss him is his dog.

Then a blinding light fills the sky, and the old man is killed... only to wake up later in a body he almost recognizes as his own. Can it be that Ichiro Inuyashiki is no longer human?

COMES IN EXTRA-LARGE EDITIONS WITH COLOR PAGES!

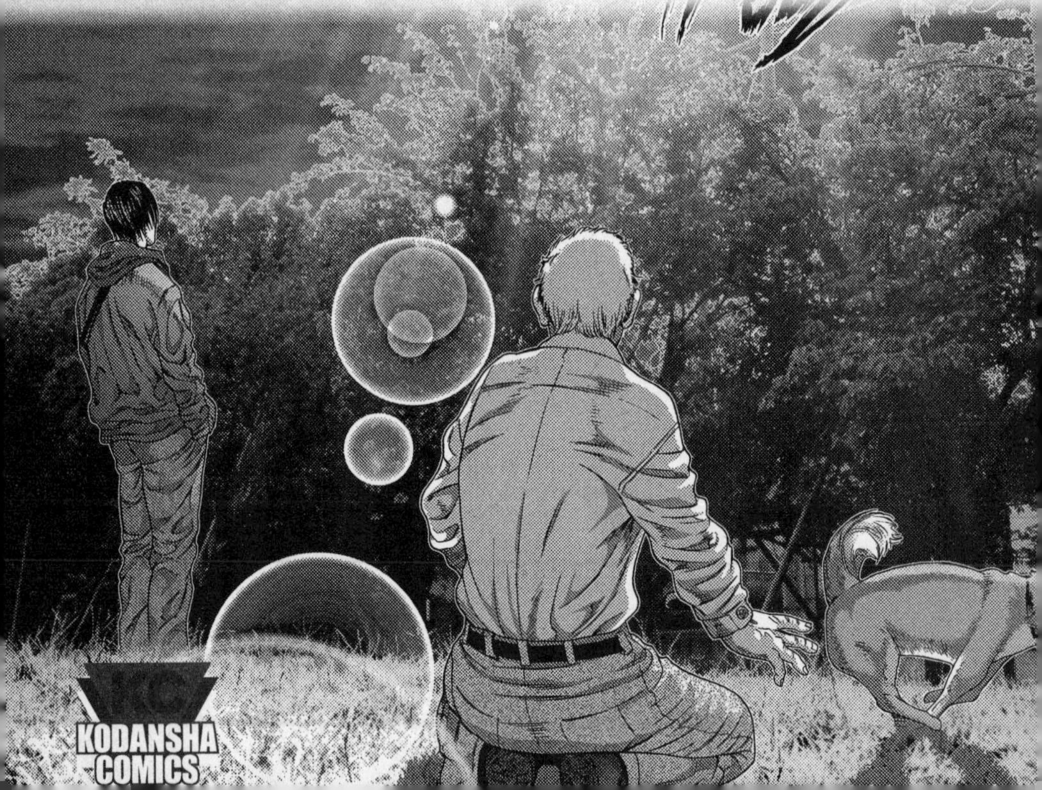
KODANSHA COMICS

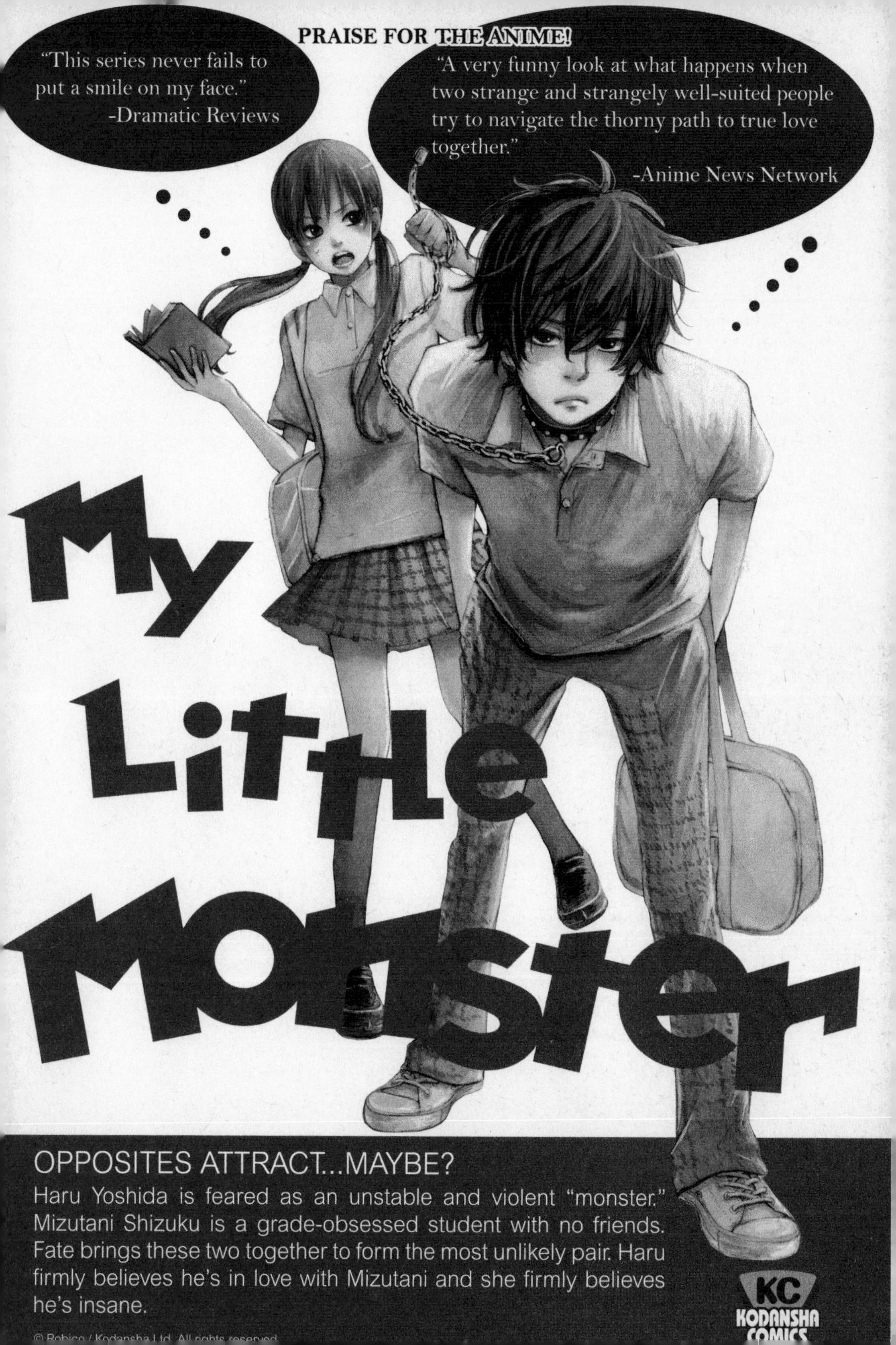
PRAISE FOR THE ANIME!
"This series never fails to put a smile on my face." -Dramatic Reviews
"A very funny look at what happens when two strange and strangely well-suited people try to navigate the thorny path to true love together." -Anime News Network
My Little Monster
OPPOSITES ATTRACT...MAYBE?
Haru Yoshida is feared as an unstable and violent "monster." Mizutani Shizuku is a grade-obsessed student with no friends. Fate brings these two together to form the most unlikely pair. Haru firmly believes he's in love with Mizutani and she firmly believes he's insane.
KC KODANSHA COMICS
© Robico / Kodansha Ltd. All rights reserved.

NO.6

A PERFECT LIFE IN A PERFECT CITY

For Shion, an elite student in the technologically sophisticated city No. 6, life is carefully choreographed. One fateful day, he takes a misstep, sheltering a fugitive his age from a typhoon. Helping this boy throws Shion's life down a path to discovering the appalling secrets behind the "perfection" of No. 6.

KC
KODANSHA
COMICS

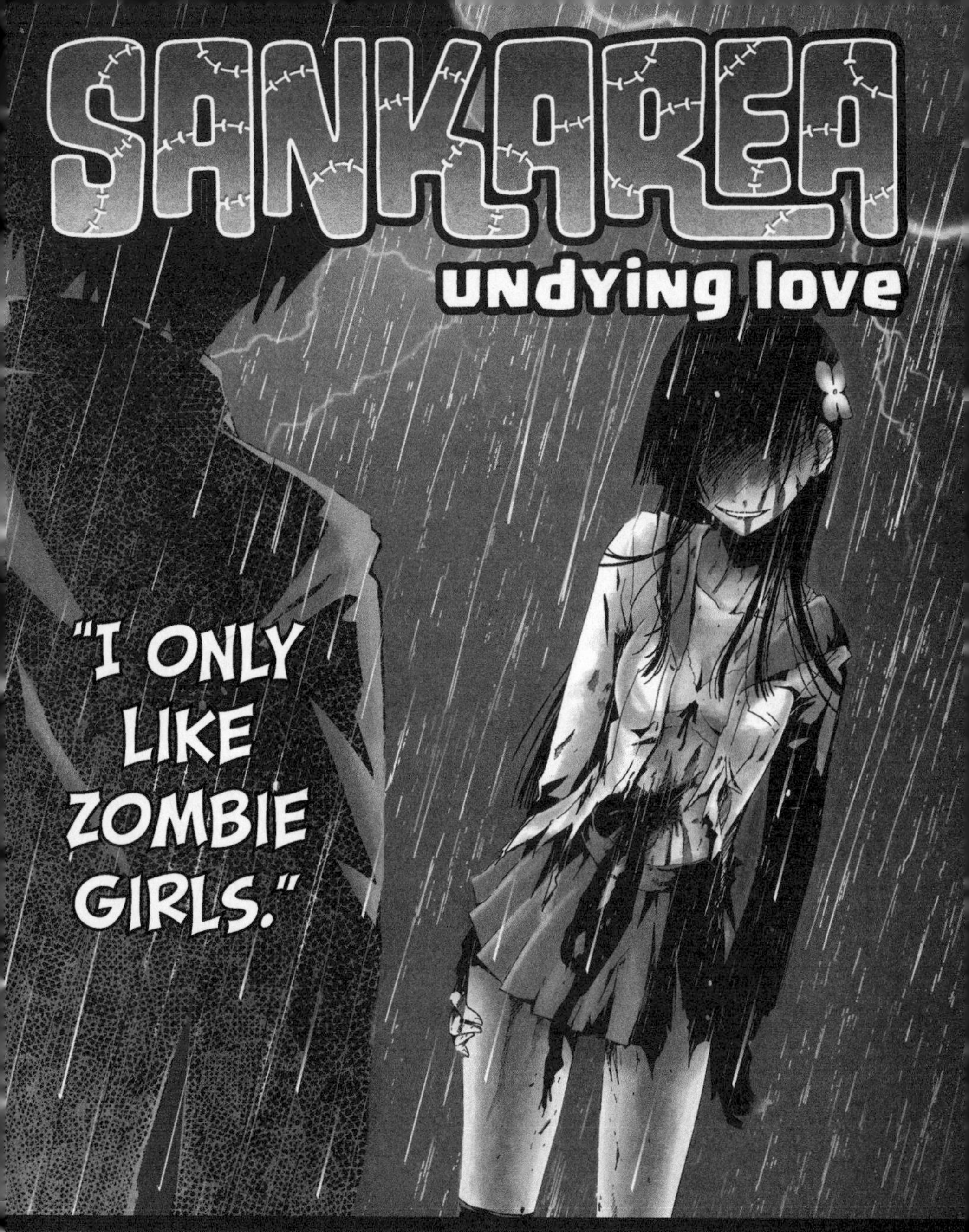
SANKAREA
undying love
"I ONLY LIKE ZOMBIE GIRLS."

Chihiro has an unusual connection to zombie movies. He doesn't feel bad for the survivors – he wants to comfort the undead girls they slaughter! When his pet passes away, he brews a resurrection potion. He's discovered by local heiress Sanka Rea, and she serves as his first test subject!

Say I Love You.

KC KODANSHA COMICS

Mei Tachibana has no friends — and says she doesn't need them!

But everything changes when she accidentally roundhouse kicks the most popular boy in school! However, Yamato Kurosawa isn't angry in the slightest— in fact, he thinks his ordinary life could use an unusual girl like Mei. But winning Mei's trust will be a tough task. How long will she refuse to say, "I love you"?

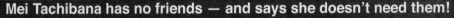

A Kodansha Comics Trade Paperback Original.

Published in the United States by Kodansha Comics, an imprint of Kodansha USA Publishing, LLC, New York.

Publication rights for this English edition arranged through Kodansha Ltd., Tokyo.

First published in Japan in 2015 by Kodansha Ltd., Tokyo, as *Hapinesu* volume 2.

ISBN 978-1-63236-364-0

Printed in the United States of America.

www.kodanshacomics.com

9 8 7 6 5 4 3 2 1

Translator: Kevin Gifford
Lettering: David Yoo
Editing: Paul Starr
Kodansha Comics edition cover design by Phil Balsman

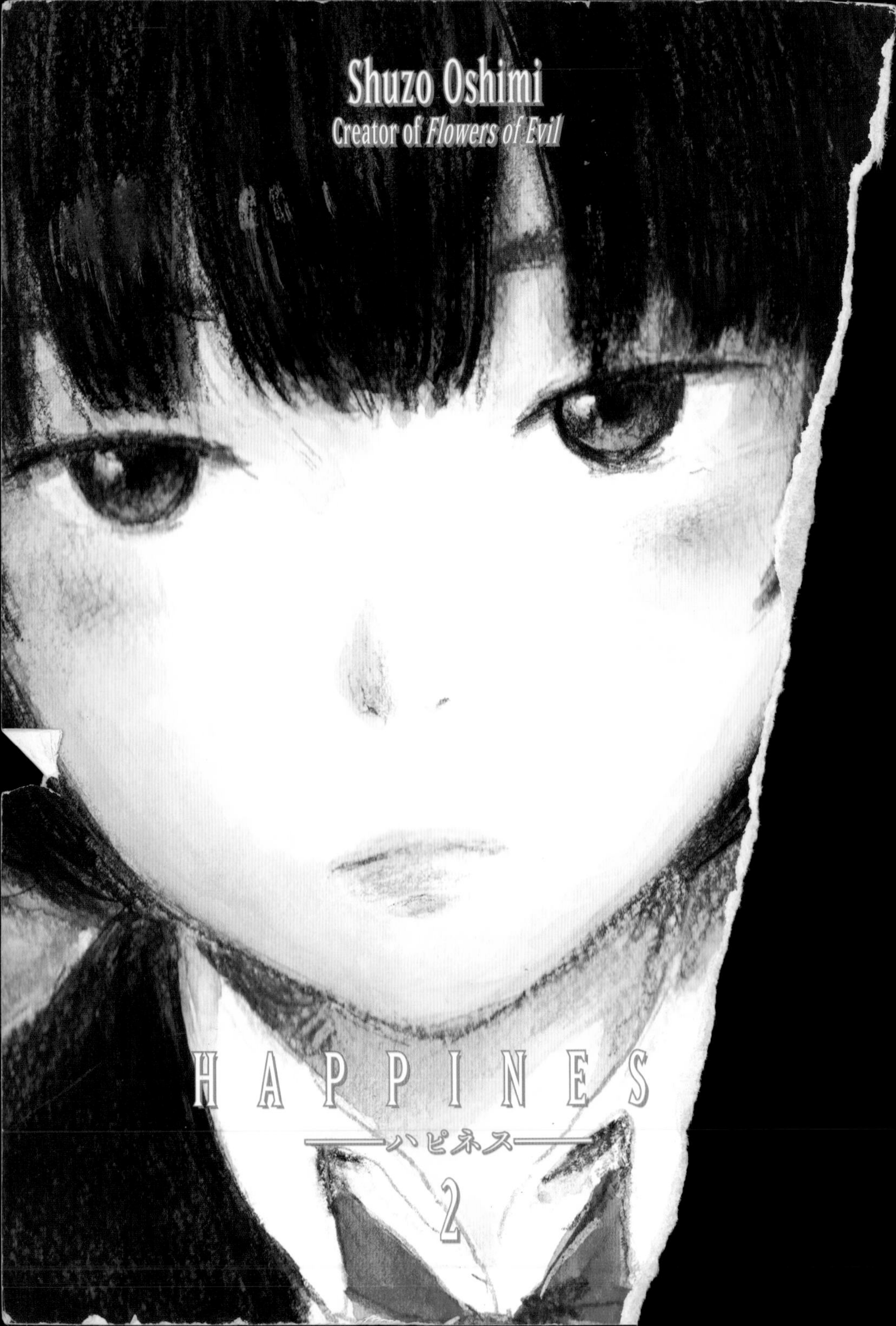
Shuzo Oshimi
Creator of *Flowers of Evil*
HAPPINES
ハピネス
2